2

On the shore dimly seen thro' the mists of the deep,
Where the foes haughty host in dread silence reposes;
What is that which the breeze, o'er the towering steep
As it fitfully blows, half conceals, half discloses;
Now it catches the gleam of the mornings first beam,
In full glory reflected, now shines in the stream_
'Tis the star spangled banner, O! long may it wave,
O'er the land of the free, and the home of the brave.

3

And where is that band who so vauntingly swore,
That the havoc of war and the battles confusion,
A home and a country shall leave us no more,-
Their blood has washed out their foul footsteps pollution!
No refuge could save the hireling and slave,
From the terror of flight, or the gloom of the grave;
And the star spangled banner in triumph doth wave,
O'er the land of the free, and the home of the brave.

4

O thus be it ever when freemen shall stand,
Between their loved home, and the wars desolation;
Blest with victory and peace, may the heaven rescued land,
Praise the Power that hath made and preserved us a nation:
Then conquer we must, when our cause it is just,
And this be our motto_"In God is our trust"_
And the star spangled banner in triumph shall wave,
O'er the land of the free and the home of the brave.

973.52
C

Caffrey, Kate
The Twilight's
last gleaming

16591

The Twilight's Last Gleaming

ALSO BY KATE CAFFREY

Out in the Midday Sun

The Mayflower

The Twilight's Last Gleaming

Britain vs. America 1812–1815

KATE CAFFREY

STEIN AND DAY / *Publishers* / New York

First published in 1977

Designed by David Miller
Printed in the United States of America
Stein and Day/*Publishers*/Scarborough House,
Briarcliff Manor, N.Y. 10510

Endpapers from the original in the Lilly Library, Indiana University

Library of Congress Cataloging in Publication Data

Caffrey, Kate.
The Twilight's Last Gleaming: Britain vs. America
1812-1815

1. United States–History–War of 1812. I. Title.
E354.C3 973.5′2 75-37899
ISBN 0-8128-1920-9

For if the trumpet give an uncertain sound, who shall prepare himself to the battle?

FIRST CORINTHIANS, 14:8

§

Contents

§

Illustrations

§

Foreword

There is a great deal in this book about Orders in Council, Napoleonic decrees, and American embargoes, so perhaps a word of explanation would be helpful.

Orders in Council were measures decided by the British cabinet and subsequently debated in Parliament, designed to assert British trading rights with neutral countries and the powers of ships' captains in the Merchant Marine and the Royal Navy. The Napoleonic decrees were proclamations designed to establish similar rights and powers for the French. The American embargoes were the retaliatory measures whereby the United States government sought to restrain actions taken against her by the warring powers.

All three–orders, decrees, and embargoes–were protective and offensive steps taken to safeguard or admonish to every degree short of actual war. Consequently the period preceding the outbreak of the Anglo-American War of 1812 was filled with debate and negotiation, with the governments of Britain, France, and America each trying to persuade or force the others to modify or withdraw. Their failure led to open conflict.

Say "1812" to most people, and the response will probably be "Tchaikovsky." A few might extend this to "Napoleon's retreat from Moscow," and some Americans might murmur "The Star-Spangled Banner." If one says the whole phrase, "the Anglo-American War of 1812," the reaction, a very rare one, could be: "Oh, wasn't that when the British burnt Washington?" Somebody might help to perpetuate the old untruth that the subsequent repainting of the presidential mansion gave it the name of The White House. Not so; the name was in use before the attack on Washington.

The Anglo-American War of 1812 was obscured throughout by the great conflict in Europe. It was indecisive, scattered, full of mistakes, and basically unsatisfactory. Soldiers and sailors killed in action were 1,877 United States, 3,433 British. The war need never have been fought at all. Yet even so admittedly peculiar a conflict gave something to each side: to America, a new self-awareness and confidence; to Britain, reluctant respect for the former rebel colonies.

Nothing in this book has been invented. Yet I shelter as usual behind Professor A. J. P. Taylor's consoling words: "All sources are suspect." In the many quotations used from more or less contemporary writings, I have tried as far as possible to retain the spelling and punctuation of the originals, because in my opinion this helps enormously in creating the atmosphere of the time.

I am deeply indebted to the following institutions and people for their help, encouragement, and interest: the British Museum, the National Army Museum, the National Maritime Museum, the Imperial War Museum, the National Portrait Gallery; Dr. Stephen Doree and Dr. Michael Martin; Captain John Roe, DSO, OBE, RN; C. D. Black-Hawkins, Esq.; C. J. Brereton, Esq.; L. H. Williams, Esq.; Lady Greene and Mrs. Ilsa Yardley; and, of course, my publishers, British and American.

To hear some people talk today, on both sides of the Atlantic, one would think that the United Kingdom and the United States have never exchanged a cross word since the end of the War of Independence. Well, they have.

KATE CAFFREY

London, 1976.

ONE

§

The World of 1812

It was Jane Austen's England. Men in complicated cravats, high-collared coats tailored by Weston or Stultz, skin-tight breeches, and Hessian boots admirably polished (with, for members of the Dandy set, champagne reputedly mixed into the polish), sugar-loaf hats, and many-caped greatcoats with buttons the size of crown pieces and nosegays as big as cauliflowers ornamenting them, tooled their curricles or high-perch phaetons through the streets or in the park. Ladies with Grecian curls wore slim, high-waisted dresses, gauzy scarves, and filmy shawls, bronze slippers such as little girls wore in dancing class, and hoped to obtain vouchers for Almack's, known unflatteringly as the Marriage Mart. Almack's Assembly Rooms had first been opened in 1770, and were famous for the extreme exclusiveness of their lady patrons when it came to application for tickets to the balls held there, only those of the most assured social standing being admitted. The more dashing ladies attending the balls were said to dampen their petticoats to make them cling revealingly. When the ladies went out of doors, which they never did without a footman or maid in attendance unless they were more excitingly escorted, they put on long coats and poke bonnets trimmed with plumes and tied with satin ribbons, and tucked their hands into muffs, while from their wrists hung the reticule or ridicule, the equivalent of today's bag. These were the ladies of *ton,* or the Upper Ten Thousand; gentlemen who wearied of their gentility could amuse themselves elsewhere with "bits of muslin" or "high flyers" or "lightskirts" from houses of ill fame presided over by Abbesses. The two utterly different sets of ladies never met.

Fashionable gentlemen belonged to various, sometimes overlapping groups. Those who excelled in elegance, polished manners, dancing, and courteous squiring of dames were Pinks of the *Ton* or Tulips of Fashion; those who practised boxing, shooting, and swordplay were Corinthians; those who carried the pursuit of fashion to ridiculous lengths were Macaronis; those who, however well-born, conducted themselves with a brusque disregard for any opinion but their own stood in danger of being labeled Yahoos. Letters of the period were written with long, classically rolling sentences, full of capitals. Snuff-taking was an art, snuff blended for individuals and thenceforth called Lord Tomnoddy's or Lord Somebody Else's Sort was carried in highly elaborate tiny boxes of exquisite workmanship, some devotees even going so far as to help themselves to it with a tiny silver shovel. Matchmaking mammas, eagle-nosed chaperones, watched keenly to make certain no unmarried young girl ruined her prospects by joining in the waltz. Gentlemen asked permission to pay their addresses, meaning that they fully intended to propose marriage. Engagements were announced in the *Gazette,* and, once that fatal step was taken, only the girl's withdrawal could then save the gentleman from his fate, which took some resourceful management if it was the gentleman who wished to withdraw.

In the country, people dined unfashionably early, at six or even earlier; in London, it might daringly be as late as eight. A visit to relatives was expected to last for weeks. If by some unusual chance a lady had to put up at a hotel, she would arrive with her own servants and her own bed linen. In private houses, the signal that bedtime was approaching was the appearance of the tea tray, perhaps at ten o'clock. But a ball, or even a dress party, would go on half the night, and gentlemen visiting gambling houses would, as often as not, walk home to breakfast. Ladies who liked cards played at home, and only the most abandoned would play for real wagers. The male and female worlds were clearly separated, with a narrow strip of neutral territory between them, where the two met: this territory covered all the mixed social functions, and, of course, once safely married, the bedchamber.

A small terrace-house or villa of the period is easy to identify: neat, well-proportioned, faced with white or cream stucco, and ornamented with narrow iron balconies and verandas painted green or black, with a fanlight over the porch. The more devoted lovers of the picturesque elaborated these into a Gothick villa, or Cottage Orné.

England stood on the very brink of its cult for the seaside resort.

The village of Brighthelmstone on the Sussex coast had blossomed into a modish town, with charming houses on the Steyne, and the new Pavilion, built for the Prince Regent, gaslit by David Black, and unkindly described by the celebrated writer Sir Walter Scott as a sort of Chinese stables. Oriental or Egyptian decorations were all the rage. So were the Classic styles, given added impetus by the marbles from the Parthenon brought to England by Lord Elgin.

Sir Walter Scott's were not the only books circulated by Mudie's or Hookham's library. People still read, and enjoyed, the prolific Gothick novels, though it was more than forty years since Horace Walpole had started the vogue with *The Castle of Otranto.* Ladies sighed happily over the romances that had poured out ever since Samuel Richardson had written *Pamela;* both sexes chuckled and gossiped over thinly disguised political-social tales. *Childe Harold* electrified all London in 1812. The bad, the mad, the dangerous-to-know Lord Byron! Not a lady but had read his poems. There were other poets, too, of course–Wordsworth, Coleridge, and Southey, wicked Shelley who outraged every proper feeling with his revolutionary principles, his atheism and vegetarianism, and more orthodox versemakers like Thomas Campbell. That strange fellow, the poet and artist William Blake, who had so startled a visitor by receiving him in his summer-house where both Mr. and Mrs. Blake sat wearing nothing whatsoever, was in his fifty-fifth year. Among the aspiring young unknowns was Thomas Love Peacock, still four years away from bringing out his first novel, *Headlong Hall.* And among the youngest of all were two babies, William Makepeace Thackeray and Charles Dickens. Across the Atlantic, another small boy, a three-year-old, was living in obscure poverty in the wilds of the frontier. His name was Abraham Lincoln.

Reynolds, Gainsborough, and Romney were dead, but Constable was only thirty-six and Turner thirty-seven. Girtin had died in 1802, but John Crome and John Sell Cotman were keeping the English water-color tradition going splendidly, and so was Thomas Rowlandson. Supreme among portrait painters stood Sir Thomas Lawrence. And somewhere in France was a sixteen-year-old boy with the imposing name of Jean Baptiste Camille Corot.

Mozart was dead, but Beethoven was very much alive; so were Weber and the young Schubert. Berlioz was nine, Schumann and Chopin two. Richard Wagner would be born the next year. In England there was no great musician: it was over thirty years since Thomas

Arne had died, but people still sang "Rule Britannia." The national anthem, "God Save the King," first of its kind, was now quite venerable, being over sixty years old; but assembled Britons sang it with relish, especially the second verse, which they proclaimed without the smallest consideration for anyone else's feelings:

> O Lord our God, arise,
> Scatter His enemies,
> And make them fall.
> Confound their Politicks,
> Frustrate their Knavish Tricks;
> On Thee our Hopes we fix:
> God save us all.

Across the Channel, the French were vigorously tramping along dusty white roads to the belligerent words and stirring tune of the twenty-year-old "Marseillaise."

It is a mistake to think that Britain and France were at war without a break from 1793 to 1815. There were breaks. One such came in 1802, when, after nine years of conflict, the Treaty of Amiens called a short halt. The revolutionary madness, as Britain saw it, seemed over: the French appeared ready to settle: Europe wanted an end to the long pattern of battle, march, advance, retreat, and alarm. Thankfully those English people who had been prevented from going abroad for so long crowded the Dover road in their carriages; the two most fashionable hotels in Dover, the City of London and the York, were stuffed full of cheerful, rich travelers.

When they stepped ashore in France they were still cheerful. Decidedly things looked better. Scars of destruction showed in some parts of towns, or around chateaux and religious houses, but titles existed, churches were full again, peasants looked well fed, everywhere stretched well-tilled fields, and the English were treated civilly, sometimes with real warmth. A new road had been cut into Paris through the Norman Barrier, and the beautiful capital itself, full of citizens making quick profits, exercised its perpetual charm. Not only were there restaurants, dance halls, gardens, and shops lavishly filled with alluring commodities, but the people were modish in the classic style that was all the rage. The Louvre was crammed with looted

Italian paintings and sculpture. Everywhere order reigned. Two years before, France had been toppling into a state of collapse; now she was clearly strong, stable, growing visibly prosperous, conciliated, and showing the great signs of all this—new roads, bridges, canals, harbors, and imposing public buildings.

There was a new code of law, embodying two thousand articles that covered every aspect of life; a new education system, clear and thorough; a new hierarchy of promotion, based on talent rather than birth, creating rank without caste. Above all was the army, the pride of France, not a ragged mob of *sansculottes* but a neatly uniformed mass with splendid officers who swanked by in blue and gold. Yet, off duty, privates took snuff with officers and called one another *"citoyen."* To the English, who thought the army a disagreeable necessity and the rank and file of soldiers nothing but scum, this was a surprise.

At the head of the French nation was the man responsible for all this, the leading *citoyen,* the First Consul. He was the principal sight of Paris, indeed of Europe, the small stocky figure in the plain blue coat and plain black hat who worked eighteen hours a day, kept busts of Fox and Nelson on his chimneypiece, and who, already a legend, called himself by his first name only: Napoleon. One young observer, Augustus John Foster, said that it was like a dream to see him riding at the head of his conquering troops who had vanquished Italy and the German states. Charles Lamb wrote to a friend visiting Paris:

> Have you seen a man guillotined: is it as good as a hanging? Are *all* the women painted and the men *all* monkeys? Are you and the First Consul thick?

Nobody was thick with the First Consul. He worked, gave out an endless stream of orders, operated the whole machine. For it was a machine. English visitors realized that France was a military state, run from top to bottom with a clear-cut logical authority that could be switched equally easily to peace or war. Above every door was the word *Liberté,* yet the sentry stationed beneath it said: "No one may pass." Even the most honored traveler, the great Opposition leader Charles James Fox, who had championed the French cause in the Commons, protested at the extremes to which he thought the French had gone. Wordsworth, who had hopefully greeted the dawn of the Revolution, found himself so moved upon his return to England that he wrote, on the very same night:

> Here, on our native soil, we breathe once more.
> The cock that crows, the smoke that curls, that sound
> Of bells,–those boys who in yon meadow-ground
> In white-sleeved shirts are playing,–and the roar
> Of the waves breaking on the chalky shore,
> All, all are English. Oft have I looked round
> With joy in Kent's green vales; but never found
> Myself so satisfied in heart before.
> Europe is yet in bonds; but let that pass,
> Thought for another moment. Thou art free,
> My country!

The coming of peace, or what appeared to be peace, was celebrated by cartoonists showing John Bull reveling with his old, long-absent friends, Old Stout and Prime Hops, Best Wheaten Bread and Excellent Fresh Butter, and Jamaica Rum. After all, thirty-three of the past sixty-three years had been war years. Foreigners from deprived Europe who took refuge in England marveled at the abundance of food, the huge English joints of beef and mutton, fat poultry, salt butter, vats of ale and cider; they observed that, in this unpoliced country, everything was settled with fists. Fistfights were common, but the crowd would intervene if weapons were drawn, putting out armed riot as if they were putting out a fire. Prizefights without gloves and without (apparently) Queensberry rules either, lasting sixty rounds, drew fashionable men, and great pugilists like Belcher, Jackson, and Mendoza were heroes. Cockfighting was widely popular, but a bill to stop bull-baiting was before Parliament. If sports were brutal, it was a brutal age, with tough people and rough justice: public hangings, petty criminals put in the pillory and pelted with garbage, plenty of floggings, enormous quantities of child crime, groups of young men roaming the streets to beat up citizens, an apparently bottomless drug traffic. It was the England described by Mrs. Gaskell in *Sylvia's Lovers,* where Harry Donkin speaks of a typical foray by the hated press-gang, roaming the streets to carry men off by force to man the Royal Navy's ships:

> They shot him through t' side, and dizzied him, and kicked him aside for dead; and fired down t' hatches, and killed one man, and disabled two, and

then t' rest cried for quarter, for life is sweet, even aboard a king's ship; and t' *Aurora* carried 'em off, wounded men, an' able men an' all...

to which Daniel Robson replied that it is worse than in his youth in "th' Ameriky war," and then it was bad enough; and Mrs. Gaskell herself, gentlest of ladies, commented:

Now all this tyranny (for I can use no other word) is marvellous to us; we cannot imagine how it is that a nation submitted to it for so long, even under any warlike enthusiasm, any panic of invasion, any amount of loyal subservience to the governing powers. When we read of the military being called in to assist the civil power in backing up the press-gang, of parties of soldiers patrolling the streets, and sentries with screwed bayonets placed at every door while the press-gang entered and searched each hole and corner of the dwelling; when we hear of churches being surrounded during divine service by troops, while the press-gang stood ready at the door to seize men as they came out from attending public worship, and take these instances as merely types of what was constantly going on in different forms, we do not wonder ... in other places they inspired fear, but here rage and hatred.

London had a population of 864,000, and lived for half the year under a thick pall of smoke. Its streets were fouled by cattle and horses, choked with traffic jams, clamorous with vendors' cries and crowded with jostling groups. Its main streets at night flickered in the fitful light of oil lamps; indoors, the world lived by candlelight, most of it dim and smelly. Even at the top of the heap, manners could lack polish: the members of the House of Commons lounged on the benches, eating oranges and cracking nuts; if the King, safest and best respected in Europe, arrived late at the theater, he was booed, and a perfunctory bow from royalty produced shouts of "lower!" Society, the Upper Ten Thousand, devoted itself to pleasure, to such extent that Wordsworth lamented: "Plain living and high thinking are no more." Both did exist, but it was not always easy to find them.

But a change of mood swept the country. Before 1802 was out, Napoleon seemed once more the monster of Europe. He overplayed his hand in demanding the island of Malta, which Britain flatly refused to give up, at least without a lot more safeguards than existed just then. Napoleon began invasion preparations.

In January 1803 he finally decided not to try for a French empire in the New World, and sold the enormous territory of Louisiana to the United States for eight million francs. With Napoleon now concentrating on what was happening in Europe, international relations rapidly became strained. The poet Thomas Campbell expressed his disapproval of the French by saying that

> the very front and picture of society would grow haggard if that angry little savage, Bonaparte, should obtain his wishes,

and Wordsworth burst out in the *Morning Post* in April that

> We must be free or die, who speak the tongue
> The Shakespeare spake; the faith and morals hold
> Which Milton held.

The morals of Britain in 1803 would no doubt have shocked Milton in many ways; but the faith was clear enough. The British knew little and cared less about the Louisiana Purchase, but they recognized invasion preparations when they saw them. On Wednesday, May 18 war was redeclared against the French. Nelson, who had demonstrated with the Downing Street fire-irons to show the Prime Minister he would oppose the French at all times, exclaimed joyfully: "The Devil stands at the door, the *Victory* shall sail tomorrow!"

England readied herself for invasion, masses of volunteers rushed to join the Fencibles, or Home Guard to use a later term, getting up at four in the morning to drill for two or three hours before going to the countinghouse or the law office and returning for more drill in the evening. Fox became a private in the Chertsey troop, the Lord Chancellor an artillery corporal; the Prime Minister, in a loftier condition, served as Colonel of the Cinque Ports Volunteers. Walter Scott enjoyed slashing at turnips stuck on poles on the Musselburgh sands, in the same way that soldiers today practice bayonet attacks on stuffed figures. Martello towers, so called after the capture of the Martello Bay fort nine years earlier, rose along the Kentish beaches. The old General Cornwallis was heard to say: "When I consider the number of men that we have in arms and that they are all Britons, I cannot be afraid." The sardonic George Canning lightheartedly jibed:

> If blocks can a nation deliver,
> Two places are safe from the French:
> The one is the mouth of the river,
> The other the Treasury Bench!

But most Britons looked for deliverance to the Royal Navy,

peerless among the fleets of the world, commanded by its greatest admiral, the slight, fair, delicate, seasick, indomitable Horatio Nelson.

But Nelson could not have done it without his brother admirals, who, rising to the height of their formidable capacity, sensed as if by telepathy what needed to be done. They were not only capable of altering course at a moment's notice when they spoke a fellow ship at sea, but, what is rarer in the frequently inflexible high command, were willing so to change; and they managed their marvelous craft superbly. They carried out the blockade of the French ports with daring and brilliance, even when appallingly outnumbered: and no one was superior to Admiral the Hon. Sir William Collingwood, a remarkably tough sixty-year-old Northumbrian known affectionately to his men as "Billy-go-tight." He sailed with his dog Bounce, who, he wrote lovingly,

> sleeps by the side of my cot until the time of tacking and then marches off to be out of hearing of the guns, for he is not reconciled to them yet.

One of Collingwood's neatest exploits was at the blockade of Cadiz, where he bottled up six Spanish three-deckers with his three little vessels, described later as "three poor things with a frigate and a bomb." Sixteen French capital ships came over the horizon and tried to hunt him down; he dodged briskly, keeping clear, until they grew tired of the chase and withdrew, whereupon he tranquilly returned to the blockade, signaling in the coolest way to a nonexistent fleet in the empty sea to the west.

This was just one piece of Nelson's grand design, which was to find, and fight, the combined French and Spanish fleets under their valiant but less experienced commander, Villeneuve. It was a two-year job. The French did not, could not, invade Britain; months passed, Napoleon's flat-bottomed boats were smashed in winter gales. The Royal Navy was always ready to pounce. Villeneuve miserably believed that he was up against something too strong for him. In the spring of 1805 he headed for the West Indies, where he hoped it might be possible to gain a breathing space, or even avoid meeting the Royal Navy altogether. Nelson gave chase, commenting that the combined fleets might be "a very pretty fiddle" but that he did not think "either Gravina [the Spanish admiral] or Villeneuve know how to play upon it." He made the 3,200-mile crossing in just over three weeks, at the rate of 135 miles a day. The commander at St. Lucia, Brigadier General

Brereton, misled by a wrong sighting, reported seeing the combined fleets on May 29, but Nelson scoured the Caribbean in vain until a fresh report on June 12 told him that the thirty-two enemy ships were crowding all canvas away to the northeast. Nelson sent the sloop *Curieux* full speed to England with the news. It came in to Plymouth on July 7 and Captain Bettesworth posted at top speed up to London, arriving at the Admiralty at midnight on July 8. Meanwhile Nelson dashed back to Gibraltar, passing Collingwood's blockade on July 18, a fortnight ahead of his adversary. It took him until October to bring the combined fleets to battle: on Monday, October 21 Villeneuve emerged from Cadiz, his battle fleet under full sail spread over five miles of water before it began to close up, the painted ships leading and following two great centerpieces, the French flagship *Bucentaure* and the Spanish *Santissima Trinidad.* The British sailed in battle order, in two lines, weather and lee, aiming straight at the enemy. Villeneuve had never seen anything like it. Nelson and his captains knew exactly what to do: sail as fast as possible for the combined fleet, get to close quarters, and stay there until the job was done. The sight of the two lines of black and yellow checkered hulls coming for him unnerved the French admiral. In two hours it was all over: Napoleon's sea power was smashed forever, England was safe from invasion, at a price. Nelson lay dead in his victorious ship.

In that same year, another ship brought a soldier home from India: it called at St. Helena on the way, and for three weeks in a pleasant irony Napoleon was supreme in Europe while Sir Arthur Wellesley, later Duke of Wellington, was at St. Helena.

Next year a British expeditionary force was proposed to go to Portugal. But these things took time, and it was not until two more years had passed that they were ready. Shortly before setting out, their new commanding officer dined with an official named John Croker who asked him what he was thinking about just then. Sir Arthur Wellesley replied at once:

> Why, to say the truth, I am thinking of the French that I am going to fight. I have not seen them since the campaign in Flanders when they were capital soldiers, and a dozen years of victory under Bonaparte must have made them better still. They have a new system of tactics which has outmanoeuvred and overwhelmed all the armies of Europe. It's enough to make one thoughtful; but no matter . . . I am not afraid of them, as everybody else seems to be.

While he had been waiting, Sir Arthur had been employed by the British government as Chief Secretary for Ireland. Now, in July 1808, he sailed in the cruiser *Crocodile* to fight the battle of Vimeiro. But this short campaign was not enough to crush the French and by October he was back in London, not knowing "whether I am to be hanged drawn and quartered; or roasted alive." It was neither; they sent him back to carry through the business, and for five years he was away. His next sea crossing would be from Calais, and he was to make the journey as the Duke of Wellington, while Napoleon would be in Elba.

War enthusiasm positively rollicked still in England, with lively banners announcing "United and Hearty, Have at Bonapartee," though, with a throwback to the days of threatened invasion, nurses still quieted babies to sleep with the awful warning that if they did not hush them, hush them and not fret them, wicked King Bonaparte would probably come and get them. (And eat them, naturally.)

But alongside the war feeling, England played as hard as ever. The gentlemen of Hampstead and Highgate met the gentlemen of the Marylebone Cricket Club for a five-hundred-guinea match; the Pic-nic Society flourished; Almack's was crowded; people strolled among fairground booths at Smithfield to see the Fireproof Woman washing her hands in boiling oil; or filled Astley's Amphitheatre to admire the equestriennes; or even tooled to the Green Park, or all the way down to Wimbledon Common, to watch a balloon ascension. At night they went to the opera, or to the endless round of balls, dinner parties, routs, drums, and masquerades, sometimes, like young George Jackson, strolling home in his domino at six in the morning and giving "no small amusement to the milkwomen and the butchers and green-grocers going to market." Fashionable ladies bought their favorite number in the lotteries at Richardson's, held card parties and played whist and silver-loo; fashionable gentlemen sat late in the more serious gaming clubs; met to blow a cloud, which is what they called smoking pipes, with a few friends; partnered masked courtesans to Vauxhall Gardens; and took lessons at Jackson's Boxing Saloon or at Manton's Shooting Gallery. There was always so much going on. Whoever had the leisure to think about something as remote, as unimportant, as obscure and far off as the former rebel colony that now called itself the United States of America?

The armies of 1812, in general, presented a colorful sight. Not for almost a century would it be essential for uniforms to melt into the landscape: men did not fight an enemy miles off, as in modern wars, and only long bitter experience of trying to fight opponents who concealed themselves skillfully in the surrounding landscape forced the Europeans to change. Warfare had bands playing and banners flying. And the supreme army of all Europe was, of course, the French.

This was not to be wondered at. The French in battle had carried all before them and their battle honors bore names that still have power to thrill: Marengo, Austerlitz, Jena, Wagram, Friedland, even ill-fated Borodino. They marched in French blue, occasionally in green, always with the tricolor in sashes and cockades; they clanged by to the spine-tingling crash and squeal of the "Marseillaise"; their officers rode past in gorgeous uniforms, encrusted with gold, wearing Napoleonic hats (generals *de division* and Marshals of the Empire) or hats worn like Wellington's (generals *de brigade);* while, in the center, supreme above all others, towered the tall bearskins of the guard, core of the *Grande Armée,* that would waver and break only on the slopes of Waterloo.

A Franco-German-Austrian battlefield was a mass of blue and green, both colors on both sides, which made for confusion in a melée. But when the British appeared, the field glowed bright with scarlet.

No longer, however, did the British Army take the field in the powdered hair and cocked hats that had opposed Washington a generation earlier. Hair powder had been forbidden finally, in 1808, to the undisguised relief of all ranks. The soldiers of Britain now looked, and were, a cross between eighteenth-century troops and those mid-Victorians who charged at Balaclava or relieved Lucknow. Generals wore scarlet coats with narrow turnbacks to the squared-off tapered tails, lapeled to the waist and cross-buttoned, with crimson sashes tied on the left for the infantry, on the right for the rest. Collars, lapels, cuffs, buttonholes, epaulettes, hat and boot tassels all gleamed with gold. White breeches were tucked inside short light boots—"Wellington" boots. The classic black hat was worn fore and aft like Wellington, or sideways like Napoleon, apparently according to the wearer's fancy. Other ranks, with their short red coats, wore, since 1800, the black leather stovepipe shako copied from the Austrians, with a white plume for grenadiers, green for light infantry, and red and white for battalion companies. After 1809 the leather shako was gradually replaced by a lighter one of black felt. The light infantrymen wore bugle-horn badges on epaulettes.

The most finicking details of button spacing and the shape of loops around buttonholes differentiated the regiments. So did the facings and lace. All other ranks had white facings, but officers bloomed like flower gardens with collar trimmings of all colors. Blue facings and gold lace for the Guards, the Royal Scots, the Royal Fusiliers, the Royal Irish and Welsh regiments; black facings and silver lace for the West Kents, purple and silver for the West Essex, pea green and gold for the Dorset regiment. The Inniskillings wore buff and gold, the Cornwalls white and gold, the First Yorkshires red and silver, the North Devonshires dark-green and gold. Orange and silver for Sussex, pale yellow and silver for Cambridgeshire, yellow and silver for the East Norfolks, the Ninth Foot. Of the 104 British regiments, the 100th, otherwise known by the impressive, if lengthy title of His Royal Highness the Prince Regent's County of Dublin Regiment, had dark yellow facings.

Not all the British, however, wore scarlet coats. Two battalions did not. These were the extra-light infantry introduced by Sir John Moore. Before he went on the campaign in which he was killed at Corunna in 1809, he had developed these units on the lines of the German *Jägers* to match, or to try to match, the French *voltigeurs.* Dressed in dark green ("rifle-green"), with scarlet or black facings, they were armed with sword-bayonets and Baker carbines. The rest of the British infantry carried the famous Brown Bess musket, a smooth-bore gun weighing nine pounds and firing a round lead bullet three-quarters of an inch across, one-third heavier than that of the French. It was inaccurate at anything over a hundred yards but could kill at five hundred, and it took twenty motions to reload. The soldier tore open the handmade thick paper cartridge with his teeth, poured some of the powder into the firing-pan, emptied the rest down the muzzle, and rammed the ball, powder, and wad down with a ramrod, an operation that grew harder as the barrel gradually fouled. The flint had to be changed after every thirty shots, and in wet weather it was customary for the pan to misfire. If it fired properly, it let out puffs of dense smoke that quickly befogged a battlefield. In spite of all this, the carefully trained soldiers could keep up an astonishingly steady rate of fire, often firing twice a minute. The Baker carbine had a longer range and was more accurate, but its barrel, with seven grooves, which forced the bullet to move through a quarter turn, was even stiffer to load than the Brown Bess.

The Lowland Scots dressed like the other infantry of the line, but a fresh blaze of color appeared with the Highland regiments, splendid in their tartan kilts and feather bonnets.

Then there was the cavalry. Their tight white breeches were covered by pale gray or brown "overalls," pulled on over the boots and strapped under the instep. Their coats were scarlet, their hats cocked until 1811, after which they adopted the helmet of the French *cuirassier,* crested for the Household Cavalry, maned for the Dragoons. The Hussars copied the superb Hungarian Hussars in bearskin, dolman, and pelisse, and cultivated wide mustaches to complete the effect, a style that was still the height of fashion at Balaclava more than forty years later. The light cavalry (Light Dragoons and Hussars) had curved sabers; the heavy cavalry (Life Guards, Royal Horse Guards, and Dragoon Guards) carried straight swords. In 1811 the sabretache was introduced, a kind of fancily decorated small satchel on long straps fastened to the cavalryman's waistbelt.

In full uniform the private soldier carried a weight of sixty pounds. Officers, who had little direct contact with the men they led, were usually men of fashion: there could be no promotion from the ranks above the rank of ensign because commissions had to be purchased. It took money as well as ability and luck for an officer to rise in his profession; promotion was easier in wartime, when battle casualties left gaps in the ranks, but in peacetime it had to be bought. It was said that the eldest son of a squire became a squire, the second son became a clergyman, and the third became a dragoon. A young officer would buy his own horse, or bring it from the family stables, but all servants came under regimental control, and so did transport animals. Servants had to obey regimental laws as well as their masters' orders, and transport animals could be allocated to their tasks by the regimental commander as well as by their individual owners. Officers' personal baggage went on privately hired baggage animals, and often two brother officers would share one. Of course, officers bought their own uniforms, which were expensive even without the dazzling extra touches they liked to display.

A peacetime battalion, which equaled a regiment, had 8 companies, each consisting of a captain, a lieutenant, an ensign, 2 sergeants, a drummer, and 42 men. That totalled 384. There would be the regimental staff: adjutant, quartermaster, paymaster, surgeon, several orderlies, and a few farriers to attend to the horses. Each such unit was commanded by a lieutenant colonel with a major as second in command. In time of war each battalion was increased to ten bigger companies up to 1,100 full strength, additional battalions were raised for most regiments, and extra regiments were created. They advanced in battle order with the taller grenadiers on the right flank and the light infantry on the left. When making an open attack they formed two lines, one kneeling in front of the other. When facing cavalry they formed the famous British squares, four ranks deep. Reinforcing the infantry was the Corps of Royal Engineers, all of whom were officers, under whose orders came the Royal Sappers and Miners. The field artillery fired guns of six different calibers: their twelve-pounders would carry two miles but were not accurate over one. A great variety of ammunition was used including nails, stones, and bits of scrapiron made up into canisters, nets filled with bullets called grapeshot because they looked like bunches of grapes, and ball shot. Two notable inventions in addition strengthened the artillery: one was the rocket, originally evolved by the Royal Navy, modified for army use in 1808 and further developed by a major general with the surprising name of Sir William Congreve to fire projectiles of six weights from three pounds to twenty-four; it appeared on the battlefields of Leipzig and Waterloo and was not very accurate, though at least it could be depended upon to set fire to buildings. The other was invented by Lieutenant Henry Shrapnel of the Royal Artillery: the cannonball that burst in the air and showered down a cloud of smaller shot, highly effective from the start. It still bears the lieutenant's name.

Many of the artillery companies were made up of volunteers rather than regular soldiers. The oldest of them, distinguished as its name, still survives: The Honourable Artillery Company of London. And there were the Fencibles, recruited to defend Britain or British possessions in time of possible invasion. The New Brunswick Fencibles in Canada did so well and worked with such enthusiasm that they asked to be allowed to serve overseas, and were formed in 1810 into the 104th British Regiment of Foot.

The British Army was recruited by voluntary enlistment. It was true that prisoners could be released from jail provided they would serve, and there were short-term militiamen conscripted by lot to join for four years. One could send up a substitute if one could find him, and a militiaman could transfer to the regular army if he liked. Recruiting officers toured the country, giving out free drinks and telling fantastic tales about the glamour of the service, promising bounty money, making the whole business seem as glamorous as possible. Of course it must be remembered that when daily life is drab and unrelieved, the opportunity of getting away somewhere else, escaping from dull neighbors, nagging wives, squalling brats, tiresome relatives, perhaps harsh employers, is a very real temptation. Life in the army could not be much worse than life at home and, who knew? one could travel, and see foreign parts, in England or abroad, and one might find another wife, who, at least to start with, would be more attractive than the old one. And death in battle was often easier than death in bed in the days before anesthetics, antiseptics, pain-killing drugs, and properly trained doctors.

Not all men left their wives when they joined the army. Wives were allowed to go with a regiment in peacetime, where they made themselves useful nursing, laundering, cooking, and mending. In wartime six wives per company were allowed, as a rule selected by lot; those left behind had, of course, no allowance, so they very often married bigamously to save themselves and their children from starving.

Most enlisted men came from the ranks of laborers throughout Britain, and some entered as young as fourteen, though between eighteen and thirty was the common age span. Britain had always disliked the idea of large standing armies and preferred short-term recruitment, so that, although the inner core of the army joined for life, or for active life, and the aging old soldier begging in the streets was a common sight. The militia of the Napoleonic Wars was engaged, by the Act of 1806, for seven years in the infantry, ten in the cavalry, and twelve in the artillery.

Those who grew lyrical about the heroic qualities of the British soldier knew nothing about him: the greatest British soldier alive, the Duke of Wellington (still Viscount Wellington of Talavera in 1811), did know, and stated in his usual uncompromising style that "none but the worst description of men enter the regular service."

"The English soldiers are fellows who have all enlisted for drink–that is the plain fact–they have all enlisted for drink," he commented, calling them "the mere scum of the earth" and pointing out:

> People talk of their enlisting from their fine military feeling–all stuff–no such thing. Some of our men enlist from having got bastard children–some for minor offences–many more for drink; but you can hardly conceive such a

set brought together, and it really is wonderful that we should have made them the fine fellows they are.

The Duke had his own ideas about clothing, too:

There is no subject of which I understand so little; and abstractedly speaking, I think it indifferent how a soldier is clothed, provided it is in a uniform manner; and that he is forced to keep himself clean and smart, as a soldier ought to be. But there is one thing I deprecate, and that is any imitation of the French in any manner.

Unwittingly he broke his own rule. He wore a plain gray frock coat and a simple black hat in an oilskin cover. The trim, spare figure, with its beaky nose, riding alone to survey the ground, was unmistakable to his own men; and his opposite number did the same. Napoleon's staff gleamed with gold lace, flourished with plumes, displayed showy accouterments, but the Emperor dressed in a plain gray coat, and he too was unmistakable.

The greatest weakness in the British Army was probably its staff officers, perhaps because the Duke was a supreme commander who either did not wish to rely on others or who felt unequal to training the staff. The most useful invention of the period was the new military teakettle, taking the place of the old iron pot which needed a mule to carry it and half a barn door to heat it. The new one was light, compact, and quick to boil over an ordinary small fire.

The British Army was kept in order by the ferocious discipline of the lash. Flogging was commonplace, vigorous, and horrible. It was the standard punishment for serious offenses, robbery with violence, pillage and looting against orders, but also for what later observers would consider minor misdemeanors, such as pressing transport from the local population without permission. It was naturally given for absence without leave. Sentences of up to a thousand lashes were pronounced; and not only were those carried out by relays so that the performers would always be reasonably fresh, but if a man collapsed under the lash before the allotted number was given, the remainder would be laid on as soon as the offender was sufficiently recovered.

Flogging was even more frequently used in the navy, where it was possible for an offender to be "flogged round the fleet"—given a number of lashes at the gangway of every ship. The principal difficulty about the navy, as opposed to the army, was that the captain of a ship was the sole authority in sight most of the time, and it therefore depended on the captain's character what conditions his crew sailed under. Some captains were so deeply detested that they were murdered; some so loved that their crews petitioned them not to transfer their command. Between these extremes came the majority–most of them, like the men, sincerely believing that brutal punishments were needed.

Some boys enlisted in the Royal Navy at incredibly youthful ages: ten, or even seven. The majority of Ordinary Seamen who genuinely joined by choice did so, as a rule, reluctantly, for they knew that their life aboard would be passed in cramped, crowded, stinking conditions, with weevily food, hard work, harsh discipline, no freedom, the hazards of storm and tempest, the bloody prospect of battle in wartime, and a pitiful future of begging their bread in old age, if they ever reached that far. Yet the ship represented a kind of security, and the sea exerted its magic magnetism. The sailor was an exotic creature to the landsman, especially so at a time when most people throughout their lives never stirred more than a few miles from their native village. The sailor told fantastic stories, ran wild on his infrequent leaves, had a string of "wives" in every port, and concentrated on drink and tobacco. In the early nineteenth century he called the tobacco "pigtail" because it was twisted into a curl. A letter exists from a sailor to his brother, dated March 24, 1813, written on board an East Indiaman off Gravesend, in which he asks for some decent tobacco. It is pleasantly misspelled.

> Am quite out of pigtail. Sights of pigtail at Gravesend but unfortinly not fit for a dog to chor. Dear Tom–Captains boy will bring you this and put pigtail in his picket when bort. Best in London at the black boy in 7 diles, where go, acks for best pigtail, pound of pigtail will do, and am short of shirts. Dear Tom–as for shirts ony took 2 whereof 1 is quite wored out, and tuther most, but dont forget the pigtail as I had nere a quid to chor never sins Thursday. . . Not so perticler for the shirt as the present can be washed, but dont forget the pigtail without fail so am your loving brother T.P.

Even before the American War of Independence broke out, the British sailor's jacket was blue and his breeches were white. The blue jacket and the red coat existed side by side. One Robert Hay described a sailor at Plymouth in Nelson's day as follows:

> The jolly tar himself was seen with his white dimity trowsers fringed at the bottom, his fine scarlet waistcoat bound with black ribbon, his dark blue broadcloth jacket studded with pearl buttons, his black silk neckcloth thrown

carelessly about his sunburnt neck. An elegant hat of straw, indicative of his recent return from a foreign station, cocked on one side. A head of hair reaching to his waistband, a smart switch made from the back bone of a shark under one arm, his doxy under the other, a huge chew of tobacco in his cheek, and double stingo recently deposited within his belt by way of fending off care. Thus fitted out, in good sailing trim, as he himself styles it, he strides along with all the importance of an Indian Nabob.

Some sailors wore round hats of leather or tarred canvas; some decorated their straw hats with ribbons and flowers. Gunners in action stripped to the waist and tied black cloths around their heads to keep their hair and sweat out of their eyes. Sometimes they made their own clothes: issued with twelve yards of duck, thread, and needles. With brass nails three or six yards apart driven into the decks as measuring guides, all who could sew, or who thought they could, would blacken sticks in the galley fires and draw out the required shape on the material. A man would give his grog to a friend to do it for him. They often wove their own straw hats from bundles of "sennet" taken on board for the purpose.

About one-quarter of any crew, at most, was volunteer. They had enlisted for much the same reasons as the voluntary soldiers, with the sea as an added attraction. Some were influenced by recruiting posters, early examples of the language of the ad man:

Wanted, in consequence of the great promotion of Warrant Officers since her arrival in Port Royal only three months ago, a few *Able-bodied SEAMEN* who will have every chance to work up and fill the vacancies of *Petty Officers,* and who will be sure of obtaining comfortable livelihoods, by entering upon the SALISBURY early; where they will have *plenty of liberty to go on shore* to enjoy themselves, and whilst on board, as much dancing to a first-rate band every night with the PORT ROYAL LADIES as they can stand to. *And as a further encouragement for good men to enter,* the Commander-in-Chief has authorized me to offer a bounty of one guinea *a head* out of his *own pocket,* upon approved seamen, to drink with his messmates and YOUNG LADIES *to the health of the King*–God bless him!

Or even more this lyrical invitation, dated February 16, 1815 at Halifax, Nova Scotia:

All able-bodied SEAMEN and sturdy LANDSMEN, willing to serve His Majesty, and enrich themselves; are invited forthwith to enter for His

Majesty's ship *Tartarus,* Captain John Pascoe, fitting with all expedition to take more American Indiamen; she will be ready for sea in a few days. Those fond of pumping and hard work had better not apply–the *Tartarus* is as tight as a bottle, sails like a witch, scuds like a Mudian, and lays like a Gannet–has one deck to sleep under and another to dine on–Dry Hammocks, regular meals, and plenty of Grog–the main brace always spliced when it rains or blows hard–A few months more cruising just enough to enable her brave crew to get Yankee Dollars enough to make them marry their sweathearts, buy farms and live snug during the Peace that is now close aboard of us.

The bounty sums listed included ten pounds five shillings for able seamen, two pounds ten for "ordinary," and one pound sixteen for landsmen.

But never enough came forward, and the rest had to be found by the press-gangs. Throughout the eighteenth century (and, in fact, up to 1835 when the term of compulsory naval service was limited to five years) these roamed the waterfronts and taverns, seizing men wherever they could, regardless, often, of a man's age or trade, or of his family circumstances. It took three months to complete the ship's company when HMS *Victory* was commissioned in 1769. Some desperate men in the grip of the press-gang would contrive painful accidents to themselves, such as losing a finger and thumb, in order to gain release. The most notorious period was from 1795 to 1815–the exact time we are looking at–and, if the press-gang could not fill up its complement at home, it turned to foreigners, snatching prisoners of war or even sailors and civilians in the ships and ports of other countries. Nelson calculated that, with the fees demanded by each gang, it cost twenty pounds to press a man, and that during the years immediately before 1803 some 42,000 seamen deserted. Tavern keepers sold drunken men to the press-gang; jealous women in port did the same. Some press-gangs disguised themselves as relatively innocuous army recruiting parties, which always drew onlookers; others boarded merchantmen entering harbor and and carried off two-thirds of their crews. When a ship of the line spoke a merchantman at sea her captain usually seized the opportunity of grabbing a few likely looking merchant sailors. So widespread did this practice become that clever merchant masters hid their best men among the slaves and baggage in the hold if another ship approached.

In 1795 William Pitt brought in the Quota Act, whereby every administrative region in Britain was obliged to raise a number of men for the Royal Navy, in proportion to the size of each region: London had to find more than five thousand; Rutland, the smallest county, was asked for twenty-three. Provincial justices did not wish to court unpopularity by driving the quota to its limit if their people were unwilling, so the Admiralty found before long that each quota contained men out of jail, poachers, pickpockets, tramps, and a motley of assorted ruffians palmed off on them by local authorities who were only too glad to get rid of such nuisances. Naturally these debased, and debasing, characters were resented by the true seamen, whose lives were made harder because of them. That the Royal Navy still contrived to win its battles was an astonishing tribute to the dedicated core of professionals; the pressed men who were of low quality immeasurably increased the misery of other well-meaning but helpless souls caught up in the press and unable to evade it.

Other causes of contention existed in the Royal Navy, one of the sharpest being pay. Sometimes crews went unpaid for years. The relatively minor mutinies of Spithead and The Nore in 1797 arose out of this: the men asked for a rate of a shilling a day, making them equal to the army, and were awarded an increase of four shillings and sixpence a month, raised by another shilling a week in 1806. Not until 1853 was sailors' pay fixed at a rate of just over ten shillings a week, which remained unchanged for the rest of the century. There was, however, always the alluring possibility of prize money, given throughout a crew for the successful capture of an enemy ship, or for a victorious naval engagement: the prize money for each seaman for Trafalgar, for example, was six pounds, nine shillings, and sixpence.

The Royal Navy scored over the army because sailors live where they fight: throughout any one spell of active service the men stayed in the same ship. But in the days before refrigeration and airborne supplies food at sea was infinitely worse than food ashore. Sailors, who in spite of rules and savage punishments would bet on anything, used to tap bits of biscuit on the table and place wagers on which piece would walk away first, and from the time of Columbus to well on in the nineteenth century they preferred to eat in the dark so that they could not see the maggots and weevils in their food. Breakfast in Nelson's day was a mixture of coarse oatmeal, molasses, and water, known as "burgoo," accompanied, sometimes, by a drink called "Scotch coffee," made by boiling burnt bread in water and adding a little sugar. Matters improved in port, where a swarm of small boats selling foodstuffs and other goods crowded to meet any ship of the line. The food boats were named bumboats, often under the command of redoubtable women like Gilbert's Little Buttercup. One of these, Mrs. Cary, met Cornwallis's flagship, the *Ville de Paris,* in 1804 at Portsmouth with the message:

> Mrs Cary presents her respects to Admiral. She is alongside with a Bottle of Gin, a Brown loaf, a pot of Fresh Butter, a Basket of garden stuff and a pint of rich cream. If the Commander-in-Chief will not receive her and Party, she will immediately dash off to some of the young Captains.

For centuries no sailor would drink water while there was wine or beer available. In the eighteenth century beer was a compulsory drink and was allocated at a gallon a day for each man.

The Royal Navy has always cherished its rum, and drank it then in the form of "grog," two parts rum to one part water. This well-loved drink took its name from the man who started the practice of drinking rum aboard: Admiral Vernon, who introduced grog in 1740. The Admiral was known throughout the Navy as "Old Grog" from his distinctive grogram cloak (grogram was a coarse stiff silk fabric, ancestor of the elegant grosgrain). Gradually the practice developed of issuing extra grog before a battle.

When a battle was expected the order was "Clear ship for action." Decks were sluiced with water and sprinkled with sawdust, extra rope and axes placed, tubs of water filled on the gun decks, movables lashed up, the galley fire put out. In the after cockpit, painted red for obvious reasons, the surgeon and his helpers set out their instruments and a special tub for amputated limbs, and prepared their antiseptics: salt water, vinegar, and a small quantity of spirits. The ship's carpenter had bolts of wood covered with oakum and tallow to plug into holes, and pieces of hide to nail over bigger holes. The guns needed ten to fourteen men each to man them, and it took nineteen orders to load the biggest ones. The signal for an engagement at sea was the drums beating for "general quarters," an absolutely unmistakable sound throughout the fleet.

The rather plain, severe shapes of ships at this period, with their rows of gunports symmetrically placed along their wooden sides, and the three tall masts with their towers of swollen canvas when in full sail, quite often appeared in black, though a number of British ships were painted yellow. Nelson had his ships painted in a checked pattern. The British practice in battle was to fire as the ship rolled toward the enemy, so that the cannonballs would smash into his hull; the French fired on the upward roll, in order to break their opponents' masts and rigging. This would mean, if it worked, that the Briton could not close or give chase, but it was highly risky, as the British shot could easily by then have reduced the gun-deck of the Frenchman to a welter of blood and damage. In a vessel mounting 70 guns, 225 men and 10 officers, at minimum, would be clustered on the lower deck during a battle. In wooden ships the worst hazard was fire.

Most officers dressed for battle as plainly as possible, though Nelson came on deck with all his orders glittering and sparkling on his coat; it was that which caused his death, as a Frenchman caught the telltale gleam and was able to aim. But already by that time the naval officer's full dress was evolving into what it has since become: one of the three reputedly most irresistible masculine costumes on earth. (The other two are the cowboy and the full-dress Highlander.) It is certainly fair to say that well before 1812 the Royal Navy was as identified with "navy" blue as the British Army was with the scarlet coat.

England's greatest sailor had the good fortune to be killed at the peak of his career, on the deck of HMS *Victory* in 1805. Good fortune: because the long decline from the heights is often a sad, disillusioning business. Nelson went straight into legend.

The British historian Philip Guedalla pointed out that history always sees Wellington as a level-headed man of forty-six, riding his horse Copenhagen on a wet Sunday in June and saying quietly: "Now, Maitland, now's your time." But in 1812 Waterloo was three years ahead, and he was moving up through Spain. Behind him lay four years of war, two of them with only the British Army to take the full weight of the French empire. For one after another the other countries had gone down. Napoleon had reached the point where, when he and the Czar of Russia met on a barge at Tilsit in 1806, they seemed able to deal out countries like cards between them. Napoleon, who happened to be the same age as his eventual conqueror, was the acknowledged master of Europe from Naples to the Baltic, framing laws, distributing kings wholesale, creating dukes and marshals by handfuls. He had only to snap his fingers and all Europe scuttled to do his bidding. Yet

England hung on. Through all her history England has never failed to feel the danger of one country's becoming the supreme power in Europe, and she kept the long fight going, though the only allies left to her were the mad King of Sweden, too mad, according to Guedalla, to change sides, and, in a small way, Portugal, where the area around Lisbon still permitted British ships to enter. Not until 1940 would one country in Europe again hold the same extent of territory and exercise such far-flung influence; and then, as in 1806, only Britain did not fall into line, and then, as in 1812, the all-conquering leader made the same fatal mistake. He moved eastward to strike at Russia, and into the now unequal fight against him came two very great generals indeed, the two that have never failed the Russians in all their history, Generals January and February.

By 1812, Wellington's army was an experienced, hard-bitten force. It had pushed the French out of Portugal and was now pushing them, by way of Ciudad Rodrigo, Badajoz, Salamanca, and Vitoria, out of Spain. It would finally break what was left of the *Grande Armée* at Waterloo: Napoleon's Old Guard, flower of European troops, which had never been known to break till then. The Emperor had to be beaten: beaten at all costs, however long it took, and other considerations were unimportant beside it. That is why the wranglings with America seemed so often nothing more than an irritating irrelevance to the British throughout that period.

But what works against European professionals on European soil would not work against embattled commando groups scattered over thinly populated wild terrain far from home, whether in South Africa in 1900, in Vietnam in the 1960s and 1970s, or in Ireland at almost any time. It had not worked in America during the War of Independence; and it did not work in the fragmentary, scattered, widely separated engagement that made up the Anglo-American War of 1812.

TWO

§

London

It is necessary, before examining what was happening in America, to look at the English side of the coin, to see what problems faced that country in connection with America, and which men decided which measures to deal with these.

English society, in the opening years of the nineteenth century, had a habit of forcing its eldest sons into public life. In return they entered it with advantages unknown today. Living among leaders from boyhood, they were on easy terms with men of state from the first; preferment was simple and swift if one had ability; opportunities opened wide before them.

There were two main parties, the Whigs and the Tories. Neither has much, if anything at all, in common with the main parties of today. The Tories, just then, stood on clearer ground than did the Whigs, because the Tories had always supported privilege and disliked trade. Throughout the apparently interminable, unchanging eighteenth century the Whigs had supported privilege too, but during its closing years some new disturbing elements were revealing themselves. The Industrial Revolution was beginning to show its unlovely face in green England; distant roars echoed from Paris; colonists stood to arms in America; phrases like The Rights of Man, The Principle of Utility, Liberty–Equality–Fraternity, were heard. Where did the Whigs, under their leader, Charles James Fox, stand? For a century they had rested calmly upon the Glorious Revolution of 1688. Under Robert Walpole they had set up the cabinet system. But they were what would be called today as much a part of the Establishment as were the Tories. What were they to do with these new rising manufacturers, many of whom were Nonconformists, whose money would soon bring them into open challenge? These newcomers were already beginning to demand all kinds of reform–legal, electoral, religious, fiscal. To be sure, events in France acted as a check on all progressive measures and ideas; but these could not be staved off forever. The Napoleonic War could postpone reform, but Napoleon would be beaten one day, and then there would be trouble.

The principal difficulty, which made foreign affairs particularly hard to manage, was that the Whigs when in power could not agree upon a policy, and the Whigs when in opposition could not agree about what to oppose. All agreed about the war with France, including the Tories, in precisely the same way. While Charles James Fox lived, the Whigs could appear united behind a leader, but when he died in 1806 the cement crumbled, and by 1809 they were a mere welter of opinions, squabbling groups, and individuals.

Three groups in the Whig Party more or less stood out: the Grenville faction, which consisted of the powerful Grenville family and their close friends; the Foxite remnant, led by Lord Holland and Lord Grey; and the Mountain, a mixed group of young patricians and clever members of the middle class who had been encouraged to enter Parliament by noblemen with seats to spare. The first group hated change but thought that the great Whig families had the divine right to govern; the second group proclaimed pure Whig belief, clung to Fox's ideas which embodied it, rejected economies, made approving noises about reform but took no action to bring it about; the third group opposed war in general, though with reservations when it came to Napoleon, clamored for reform, and were lively in debate.

Around these clustered and split and lobbied and disputed the rest of the Whigs, all bickering. One small set was nicknamed "The Saints" because it had always opposed the slave trade. One Saint was, of course, the great abolitionist William Wilberforce, who blamed both Britain and America fairly equally for the ill feeling that existed between them. Some Whigs advocated a strong line, though they seemed unwilling to specify in which direction. Some thought that the Whigs should make a kind of coalition with the Tories, always a popular move in wartime. Some thought that they might withdraw from Parliament altogether, at least for a time, until they could return full of brilliant ideas as the saviors of their country. Always among them ambitious individuals intrigued and switched positions and plotted for power. The Whig side of the House was a continual buzz of speculation, comment, gossip, and maneuvering. The happy Tories blandly surveyed this deplorable spectacle and thanked the Fates that they were troubled with no such difficulties.

Collapse into total incoherence was checked by the shock of the French Revolution. Its quick development from clamors for reform, far more overdue in France than in England, to the Reign of Terror, which undermined the foundations of civilization itself, appalled Whig and Tory alike. The more intelligent acknowledged that the world was changing, but then it always had; the important thing was to bring about reform without giving way to violence.

The only signs of a constructive political creed in Parliament came from a most unlikely source: the arrogantly sharp-faced, flamboyantly eloquent Whig George Canning, who remarked shrewdly: "It is the business of the legislature to remedy practical grievances, not to run after theoretical perfection," and who, believing that men were only turning to democracy because they thought it the sole way of achieving reform, proposed instead that the old way should reveal, as he was sure it could, that it could bring about reform equally well. He made one remark that deserves to be written up even now upon the office walls of politicians: "Those who resist improvements as innovations will soon have to accept innovations that are not improvements."

Canning was a follower of William Pitt, and, in his own opinion at least, Pitt's most appropriate successor. He was Foreign Secretary from 1807 to 1809, a significant period in Anglo-American relations. He shifted restlessly among various lines of thought, at one time calling America a perversion of her original idea—"Who would have expected to have seen this favourite child of freedom leagued with the oppressor of the world? In the Republic of America we look for the realisation of our visions of republican virtue in vain"—and at another battling beside his colleague Lord Bathurst in an attempt to modify anti-American moves on the part of the government. He quarreled with opponents and colleagues alike, for the innate streak of arrogance in his nature led him into explosive outbursts. Yet he had a genuine sense of humor, which, almost alone among British ministers of the Crown, has secured him a place forever in anthologies of comic verse for his poems, including the Sapphics of *The Knife-Grinder.**

* See Appendix I

The British government led by William Pitt in the closing years of the eighteenth century had been willing to conciliate, to a moderate extent any way, the rebel republic of the United States. Yet it comes as a shock to the modern reader to find that, despite Britain's contempt and resentment of America, the chief British grievance against the United States was that the republic had resolved to stay neutral while Britain was fighting for her life against Napoleon. Just how Britain thought that America would instantly come to the aid of her old enemy barely a generation after the War of Independence is perhaps an illustration of the theory, widely held in some quarters, that politicians never think, or at any rate never think in one piece. Britain's other grievances against America included the fact that America's neutrality acted as a protection to French trade and property (for, as a neutral, she could go on trading and dealing with anyone); that American ambitions in trade expansion made her try to replace Britain, if she could, in European markets; and that her ships seduced British sailors from their duty to the King.

America, for her part, felt that if conditions aboard American vessels were better than those of the Royal Navy, with better pay, food, accommodation, and treatment, whose fault was that? And she objected that the Royal Navy forcibly took sailors from American ships: if those seized were not British, the Royal Navy assumed that Americans would have to do. In addition, and perhaps the greatest of America's complaints, Britain, intent on depriving the French of vital supplies and maintaining essential British trade with Europe, had set up a blockade system under the euphemistic name of Orders in Council. The result was that the United States sailors lost their freedom through wrongful impressment, the United States merchants lost their shipping contracts, and the United States farmers lost their markets for tobacco, grain, and cotton, the three big staples of American foreign exchange. These were not new sources of friction: all these actions had been going on, more or less, ever since Britain went to war with France in 1793. But, as time went by, emotions heightened between the two countries. Many English people felt contempt for the bastard English upstarts who had set up competition in trade, and rated them as politically incompetent.

Many Americans still felt the revolutionary fervor against the old oppressor, wanted to stress their freedom and victory, and, knowing that Europe persistently undervalued them, were touchily insistent on their value as they saw it.

Any privations that neutrals might suffer left Britain unmoved. "God and nature having put the power of the ocean into our hands, we are fully entitled to exercise that power for our complete security, and so as to ensure us the full enjoyment of the naval prosperity consequent upon it," wrote one Nathaniel Atcheson. The poet Thomas Campbell cheerfully remarked that Britannia needed no bulwarks while she had her matchless navy; the poet Robert Southey proclaimed Britain as freedom's own beloved isle, and the Member of Parliament James Stephen, a lawyer, believed, in common with most of his countrymen, that "England is the bulwark and safeguard of all nations which the ambition of the enemy sought to conquer or destroy." James Stephen was one of "The Saints," indeed the most vociferous. He enjoyed argument, in which he was formidably obstinate, and his main interest was the British West Indies. In 1805 he wrote a pamphlet, mainly anti-American, with the resounding title *War In Disguise, Or, The Frauds of the Neutral Flags.* It stirred up tempers on both sides of the Atlantic. American patriots and British sympathizers criticized it bitterly. In it, Stephen advanced the argument that British restraint in dealing with neutral vessels had allowed ships to sail scornfully past British patrols, while on board these supposedly neutral ships were goods destined for the enemy; thereby Napoleon was supplied with goods and the neutrals supplied with money, all at Britain's expense. Stephen urged stricter measures to stop this trade with France, even if it meant antagonizing loyal British colonials who sent their merchandise in the same ships. The Earl of Selkirk, supporting Stephen's view, considered the Royal Navy "the last stay of the liberties of the world," and, if Napoleon was indeed the tyrant he seemed to all but the French, the Earl and the other gentlemen had a point.

The French were brilliantly predominant over the continent of Europe, and in a position to control most European ports. In December 1805 they had demolished the Austrians and Russians at Austerlitz; in October 1806 they had smashed the Prussians at Jena; in the spring of 1807 they defeated another Russian army at Friedland so that the czar was compelled to make a treaty with Napoleon (this was the famous meeting on a barge in the middle of the river at Tilsit); and in the summer of 1809 the French crushed the Austrians once more at Wagram. Britain stood alone. Charles James Fox lamented: "I cannot but think this country invariably and irretrievably ruined," and formed the opinion that "to be Ministers at a moment when the

Country is failing and all Europe sinking, is a dreadful situation." *The Times* of July 15, 1807 announced: "We have no friend, no support, no ally in the world, but our own courage and heroism."

Most readers of Stephen's pamphlet believed that it had been written and published under British government auspices, and, indeed, this was partially true, for Stephen had shown it in manuscript to government officials who in turn had shown it to Pitt himself. Stephen was then advised to print it privately to avoid having "any stamp of Official Communication upon it." When, shortly after publication, Stephen entered the House of Commons to take a seat kindly provided for him by the government, suspicions of government interest in the pamphlet seemed well founded.

The death of Pitt pushed foreign affairs into the background while his followers struggled among themselves for the succession. He died in January 1806, in a villa he had rented at Putney, and, as he lay dying, the news of the French victory at Austerlitz reached London. At dawn on January 25 Pitt breathed his last words: "Oh, my country! How I leave my country!" He was forty-six, the outstanding member of the House of Commons, former Prime Minister, and Chancellor of the Exchequer, the post he had first held at the age of twenty-three. He had lived long enough to rejoice at the news of Trafalgar and to mourn the death of Nelson. Who was to succeed him? The House seemed crammed with nonentities, apart from a small number of aspiring men all of whom were obnoxious in some way or other to the King. Charles James Fox was the best known of these, and the most heartily disliked by George III. But there was no help for it, there would have to be a coalition. The King sent for Lord Grenville, a man already weary with years of service, and asked him to form a government as best he could. Grenville accepted, placed Fox at the Foreign Office (where he had a staff of fifteen civil servants to help him), Lord Howick (the future Lord Grey) at the Admiralty, and filled up his cabinet posts with such people as Lord Sidmouth and supporters like the conservative Chief Justice Lord Ellenborough. The mediocre quality of the new government was summed up neatly in the name given to it by its supporters, the Ministry of All The Talents.

The bland-faced Henry, Viscount Sidmouth, was one of those who cared little whether tempers were frayed or not. He had earned unpopular opinions among his countrymen for his supposedly conciliatory American views during the opening years of the century, and for refusing to take part in drafting bills which might operate against America. (Indeed in 1812 he refused to join the cabinet until he had been promised that the anti-American Orders in Council were going to be changed.) The Americans who knew of him thought him well-disposed toward them, perhaps because he had not exerted himself to say he was not. Surprisingly, for a man of whom so little is thought that, of seven modern historians writing on the subject of the British government during the period, six do not think him worth mentioning, he could control twenty votes in the House, and was in consequence worth consideration at the time, if not since. The truth seems to be that he neither liked nor feared the United States, and it is hard to avoid the suspicion that he acted as he did out of a mixture of lethargy and a wish to embarrass his political opponents.

One devotee of Pitt, Thomas Courtenay, said in a pamphlet dealing with Anglo-American relations that All The Talents clashed rather than combined. As a result "every measure was a compromise. The result was a total want of principle."

Fox, already ill, had to consider the possibility of peace with France as well as the gathering tension with America. The American minister in London, James Monroe, reported that he expected reason and fair treatment from All The Talents, but it was not easy to hold this opinion when some Englishmen were openly declaring that Britain was all that stood between the United States and the Corsican monster, and that America ought to be grateful to Britain for protecting her from Napoleon, even if it meant a few insults. The Earl of Liverpool remarked that America

> ought to have looked to this Country as the guardian Power to which she was indebted, not only for her comforts, not only for her rank in the scale of civilisation, but for her very existence.

Robert Banks Jenkinson, second Earl of Liverpool, was regarded as probably the likeliest successor to Pitt. A tall man with ruddily fair hair and an implacable expression, he had been brought up by a ferociously anti-American father. The second Earl reacted by approving of Pitt's policy of conciliation and compromise. His inherited ferocity spent itself in opposition to liberal measures at home, in severity toward British dissenters, and (perhaps more reasonably) in proposals to curb the excesses of the Prince Regent's enormously difficult wife, Caroline of Brunswick. Liverpool, appointed Foreign Secretary in 1801, had been partly responsible for the least antagonistic British attitudes toward America since the War of Independence. This viewpoint was modifying by the time of the Anglo-American talks leading to the Treaty of 1806, but the United States government had not realized it, and expected Liverpool to agree to the modifications suggested by them. He did not do so. What had caused him to alter his opinion was what he saw as the pro-French, anti-British, and basically weak policy of Jefferson. By April 4, 1810 he was writing:

> The Situation of Affairs in America appears to us here to be as little likely to lead to any amicable settlement, as they have been at any time for the last 3 or 4 years. It is a Satisfaction, however, to reflect, that the Cause of our Country appears to gain ground in many parts of the United States, and if some material Change does not occur in the System of the Government, the result will probably be, the Separation of the Eastern from the Southern States. This Event, whenever it takes place, (and it will take place at no very distant period) will have the effect at least of securing the British Possessions in North America, from any Danger arriving from Foreign Aggression.

He was fifty years out of his reckoning. But the idea that part of America might secede from the Union was fairly widespread among those Englishmen who corresponded regularly with Americans. This was because most of their correspondents were pro-British New Englanders who opposed their own government, the Republican administration headed by Thomas Jefferson, and who from time to time made noises indicative of a threat to secede.

Many Englishmen believed that the United States was incapable of waging war. Those among them who read *The Times* found their newspaper agreeing with them, as, for example, when it stated that

> The Alps and Apennines of America are the British Navy. If ever that should be removed, a short time will suffice to establish the Head-Quarters of a Duke-Marshal at Washington, and to divide the territory of the Union into military prefectures.

Half the Commons were hostile, in varying degrees, to America; the rest were relatively indifferent. There was no pro-American group in Parliament. A few men, who would today be called intellectuals, spoke or wrote on the American side. The mass of the people of Britain, who lived and worked far from articulate centers, neither knew nor cared about America, many of them having not the faintest idea where it was. If any word of foreign affairs reached them, it had to do with Europe. Of course it is essential to remember that English eyes (among those who knew something of affairs) were looking toward Europe most of the time, and only wrenched their gaze away to glance across the Atlantic when America had been, in their opinion, more annoying than usual.

Another prominent parliamentarian, Lord Wellesley, elder brother of Arthur, future Duke of Wellington, made no secret of the fact that he put the Americans mentally on a level with the Indians he had helped to crush in the Mahratta Campaign in 1799. Richard Wellesley had been regarded through childhood, adolescence, and young manhood as the splendid, promising son, Arthur as the dull, disappointing one. Richard was always headed for a glittering career; Arthur might as well go into the army, it was all his awkwardness was fit for. No wonder Richard grew up ambitious, arrogant, and annoying. He was handsome, too, as a young man, with a careless flamboyance of demeanor and more than the usual Wellesley eye for a pretty woman. He was Governor General of all India while Arthur was still a painstaking Sepoy General, a kind of glorified quartermaster, doggedly counting bullocks and bushels of rice. Yet the Duke had hopelessly outdistanced his dazzling elder by the time he was forty; and Richard was unkindly (and accurately) summed up by the Prince Regent as "a Spanish grandee grafted on an Irish potato."

Henry, Lord Bathurst, President of the Board of Trade in 1807 and Foreign Secretary after Canning in 1809, stuck to his own view, which was that it was important to keep America neutral for economic reasons. He believed that some kind of understanding, however incomplete, between Britain and a prominent trading nation like America had greater advantages than a quarrel which might or might not reduce America's trade with France. He was a follower of Pitt in all other respects, a quiet, capable, and unobtrusive person who appears today to be chiefly remembered because a number of colonial islands, pieces of land, and headlands were named after his father, who had been a prominent Tory statesman.

The parliamentary skill of such men as Canning, Liverpool, and Bathurst constantly threatened the uneasy alliance of All The Talents. Among them Grenville and the ailing Fox strove to hold together some kind of front against their abler opposition. Grenville clung to the ideal of conciliation with America through thick and thin, not wanting any side issue to handicap Britain in her fight against Napoleon. In January 1808 Grenville's colleague Lord Grey, though supporting him, voiced a doubt: although he favored "the utmost limit of reasonable concession," yet from both the language and conduct of Jefferson's administration it appeared unlikely that "reasonable concession" would succeed. Over a year later, in May 1809, Grenville noted to Grey:

> With the friendship of America, we might rest a husbanding and defensive system on the basis of an extensive commerce, and so might still survive the storm. Without such a recourse what hope have we?

The basic pro-American attitude, such as it was, containing a hard core of commercial common sense, was summed up in the House of Commons by Fox's nephew Lord Holland, who said that mutual advantages always arose out of friendly rivalry between the two countries,

> but this reciprocity of interest was most remarkable, as it existed between the United States of America and Great Britain. The republican institutions of America, like those of every government in which a true spirit of freedom prevailed, contained energies which were capable of being called forth to meet any difficult crisis that might occur. Nothing therefore could appear worse policy than to wish to see anything like disunion among the people of the United States. Indeed, the more powerful and the more wealthy they become, the better it would be for this country. As they became more prosperous, the customers for our manufactures would become more numerous, and increase of riches would only give them increased means of consumption.

Two members of the House supported the commercial plea with particular intensity. One was Alexander Baring, who owned a banking house with many American government and trade accounts, and whose wife was American, the daughter of a Federalist senator. The other was Samuel Whitbread, who had married Grey's sister, and whose family owned the celebrated brewing business that still operates under his name. Despite a noble connection through his marriage he was a republican (in the British sense) and at times embarrassed his brother-in-law by his blunt manners and tactlessly positive opinions. Most Englishmen in public life agreed with these two that American trade bringing profits into British pockets was highly desirable, but differed from them in not wishing to see American trade expand in every direction, for this might inflate America into a trade rival.

The Ministry of All The Talents fell from office in March 1807 and that which replaced it was a good deal more talented. It included several future Prime Ministers, one of whom, though a junior lord at the Admiralty, was not yet a member of Parliament: Henry John Temple, third Viscount Palmerston, then aged twenty-three. Not until the following year, after two unsuccessful shots at being elected in Cambridge and Horsham, was he returned for Newport, Isle of Wight, where his election campaign could hardly be called demanding, since "he should never, even for the election, set foot in the place," according to its principal landowner.

Canning was Foreign Secretary: a choice that, as time went by, more and more deeply affronted the United States. Of Canning, William Branch Giles of Virginia, a Republican of so contrary a nature that he opposed everything that had not been suggested by himself, said: "He chooses to act by tricks and contrivances," and called him "the energetic, the sarcastic, the facetious, the joking Mr. Canning." The English peer Lord Malmesbury, who had backed Palmerston for eventual cabinet office from the first although he was so young, said that Canning's quick arguments could carry away his hearers:

> He is unquestionably very clever, very essential to Government; but he is *hardly yet a Statesman,* and his dangerous habit of *quizzing* (which he cannot restrain) would be most unpopular in any department which required pliancy, tact, or conciliatory behaviour.

It was exactly these amiable qualities that were needed in dealing with the touchy business of America; and, though the "quizzing" (that is, teasingly joking) Canning was courteous in face-to-face meetings, he let himself go to a dangerous extent on paper.

The first leader of the new administration was the Duke of Portland but, when he resigned shortly before his death in 1809, the leadership passed, not to Liverpool, but to Spencer Perceval. Perceval had agreed to serve as Chancellor of the Exchequer, a post of the highest eminence today and one often believed to lead more surely than most to the office of premier, but which was less well thought of then. Perceval had taken it reluctantly, as he disliked giving up his more lucrative legal practice (he had an enormous family) and, by an arrangement loudly disputed by the Opposition, he was compensated by something completely new: a lifetime appointment with a salary as chancellor of the Duchy of Lancaster. He does not emerge as an exhilarating character: known to be a sound man of finance and a good debater, obstinate, narrow, opposing all concessions to neutrals and believing that Napoleon's defeat came first before everything, he was summed up by his supporters who promised to "fix this honest little fellow firmly in his seat." It was not an easy business. Quarrels had broken out and flared and died and broken out again between various members (culminating in an actual duel, of which more will be said later, between Canning and Castlereagh with pistols on Putney Common). Perceval offered Palmerston the Exchequer, softening the prospect by offering to "take the principal share of the Treasury business, both in and out of the House." Since Palmerston had made one speech in the Commons and that over a year before, and his Admiralty experience had largely consisted in signing papers, he hesitated; and Perceval offered alternatives. Palmerston, he said, could, if he wished, stay "fagging at the business" as a lord of the Treasury for a few months as a kind of training, or, if he disliked the whole idea of finance, he could become Secretary for War, a post which did not carry cabinet status and which, in today's terms, was roughly equivalent to a very senior Civil Service position. Palmerston, understandably bemused, asked for a couple of days to think it over, and reflected:

> I have always thought it unfortunate for any one, and particularly a young man, to be put above his proper level, as he only rises to fall the lower.

He chose the War Office which, although busy at that time in war with Napoleon, seemed "from what one has heard of the office, better suited to a beginner." He prudently refused a seat in the cabinet. As a result, he became a minister of state at the age of twenty-five, in the last week of October 1809, when crowds in London were celebrating George III's golden Jubilee and Whitehall was brilliant with flaring illuminations.

A word here about the Civil Service of the time might not be out of place. Compare it with that of France. In the first decade of the nineteenth century, the French Civil Service was an ordered hierarchy. France having broken the chains of the eighteenth century with accompanying violence, her whole system could be reshaped swiftly and with matter-of-fact brusqueness. The Emperor oversaw all. In this respect he resembled Winston Churchill, who, as Prime Minister in

1940, allowed no detail to escape his interested eye: even at the height of that incomparable and dramatic summer, the dinginess of a flag seen from his window merited a note for something to be done about it. Napoleon similarly showered his subordinates with orders, notes, awkward questions, and abrupt memoranda. Foreign Affairs, the Interior, War, the Law, all worked unsparingly under that hard eye; clerks by the score sorted, copied, and answered papers; uniformed figures reported to anterooms or climbed stairs to reply to questions; sentries saluted as great officers in blue and gold swaggered by to stiffen to attention in their turn before the short figure dressed in the green and white of his own *Chasseurs.* No pattern of tradition entangled them. Action was forceful and uncluttered.

No one could say this about the War Office in London, where young Lord Palmerston touched his hat to the mounted sentries at the Horse Guards and signed his first official letter on October 30, 1809. Here matters were very different. The place was a kind of maze or labyrinth of overlapping office. There were so many heads. The commander in chief ruled the army personnel; the Royal Navy was not even in the building, but over at the Admiralty. There were two secretaries: the Secretary for War and the Colonies (an intriguing juxtaposition), whose office was in the War Office and who was a member of the cabinet; and the Secretary at War, a quite different personage, who was in charge of the finances for the armed services and who reported direct to Parliament. Yet even he did not enjoy undivided supervision: sections of the forces were administered by other bodies. The artillery came under the protection of the Board of Ordnance, with offices in Palace Yard. The Royal Engineers and Military Artificers were ruled by the Master-General of Ordinance and by the commander in chief's staff corps. The Militia, the Volunteers, and the Fencibles served under the Home Office, while Transport, Supply, and the Commissariat reported to the Treasury. Looked at in this way, it sometimes puzzles the present-day observer to understand how Britain ever managed to conduct a war at all, much less to win one.

One of young Lord Palmerston's duties was to present to the assembled Parliament the army estimates for the following year. When he did this for the first time, toward the end of 1809, he had drawn them up under twenty-one separate headings. In criticizing the estimates, one of the eternal voices of the professional soldier was heard, as one General Tarleton, who had known what it was to fail in America where he had experienced defeat in the War of Independence, commented that "where ever gentlemen could hunt, there could cavalry act," and stated that Waggon Trains were an unnecessary luxury. This flatly contradicted the opinion of Wellington, who had learned in India that "if I had rice and bullocks I had men, and if I had men I knew I could beat the enemy." But just then Wellington was not in the House to express this view: he was in Portugal, waiting on the French Army under Masséna. The British military plans, as always in British history, were set at risk by sudden demands for economy in the wrong place.

During the first twelve years of the nineteenth century, British official opinion moved about between the comparatively moderate extremes of wanting American trade yet not wanting it to grow too big; hoping it would grow big enough to safeguard British interests; protecting British interests at all costs; and, of course, defeating the French, if possible without reaching the point of open conflict with America. This open conflict could break out if American actions became sufficiently hostile. That this would happen appeared unlikely to most Englishmen, who thought the United States utterly incapable of offensive warfare. Market fluctuations caused these attitudes to modify from time to time, but not to any startling extent.

The touchiest trading area was the British West Indies, which imported between four and six million dollars' worth of American goods every year, and was considered so vital to local prosperity that the colonial governors often disregarded Navigation Acts passed in London and aimed at prohibiting or limiting colonial trade with the United States. At the same time America steadily increased the quantity of Spanish and French colonial produce that she bought for re-export to Europe, her cotton exports increased by leaps and bounds and, parallel with this, a glut in sugar and coffee–the key British West Indies commodities–developed, after a sequence of excellent harvests, in the markets of the world. On the other hand, America did not need British trade nearly as much as Britain needed hers: at least 80 percent of American cotton went to Britain, almost half of all her exports, a total of over twenty million dollars' worth in a year, and she imported more than twice that amount in British manufactured goods until 1811, when the American Non-Importation Act cut it by seven-eighths. This further deepened the British trade depression that the long-drawn-out war and its commercial restrictions had already helped to create.

Increasingly, too, the American Merchant Marine was growing, almost doubling between 1802 and 1810. The British Merchant Marine was at this time constricted by the demands of war, which also pushed up the national debt, while the national debt of America declined by half. One of the biggest British grievances, it must be remembered, was that America, under her neutral flag, was regularly supplying the French with goods of which they stood in great need, thereby making the British blockade far less effective. All these facts combined to make Britain more hostile, more resentful, more impatient of the gathering strength of the Republic in the West.

Just as Britain placed the defeat of Napoleon first in importance, so Napoleon placed first the defeat of Britain. In his efforts to constrict British trade he neglected to encourage that of America, although this would have given him considerable help, not only in supplies, but in bringing America to war with Britain earlier. In November 1806 his Berlin Decree * had declared a blockade on Britain, though it was a year since Trafalgar and his navy was simply not in a position to enforce it. The Milan Decree of December 1807 went further, stating that once a neutral ship had been searched at sea by the Royal Navy that ship would no longer be regarded as neutral by him. The principle that the very touch of the Royal Navy was enough to tarnish neutrality in French eyes was equally impossible to enforce. Countries occupied by the French, or as yet not fully involved in Napoleon's sweep,were unwilling to give up their profitable British trade. Ports on the Baltic and the Peninsula allowed British ships in and out; Holland was a nest of smugglers; even French officials could be bribed. The Napoleonic system leaked at one point or another all the time. It is true that British exports to Europe fell from sixteen and a half million pounds in 1805 to five and a half in 1808; but they never stopped.

Despite the comparative weakness of the French Navy, it did manage to seize an estimated total of 468 American merchant ships between 1807 and 1812. At the same time, according to James Monroe, the British were seizing an American ship every two days (of course, temporarily: in time, after an official inquiry, the ships were released),

* See Appendix II

though this average fell off after 1808 as American merchant captains became more cautious. But from 1805 to 1812 the Anglo-American storm might have broken at any moment; and America felt her trade and her government were considered only in terms of how Britain and France could best damage one another and, as the great struggle for Europe went on, that she was more and more treated as a pawn by both sides.

Some Englishmen took the danger lightly, for a time at least. The young minister Augustus John Foster wrote from Washington:

> The two greatest Commercial Nations in the Globe cannot move in the same Spheres without jostling one another a little; where we were aiming blows at the French Marine, we want Elbow room and these good Neutrals wont give it to us, and therefore they get a few side pushes which makes them grumble.

But in Britain there were some who took the matter seriously. It had not come to war yet. That it might do so, the press appeared aware. The *Caledonian Mercury* had stated:

> We should think it a very great misfortune for this country to have to go to war with America at this time; but we should consider it a much greater misfortune, if the Government of this country should tamely permit its rights to be violated, or its flag to be insulted by any Power whatever.

The core of the problem was, of course, the British practice of stopping neutral ships at sea, searching them for British deserters, and removing these, by force if necessary or, all too often, if none could be found, taking off a few foreigners instead as the next best thing. Naturally the neutrals objected forcibly; and America, most frequent sufferer as American ships met those of Britain on the Atlantic more often than did those of any other neutral, most forcibly of all. Canning, as Foreign Secretary, played for a policy of delay, rather surprisingly in view of his mercurial temperament. He appointed a special emissary to travel to Washington where this man might settle, or try to settle, some of the thornier difficulties on the spot. Canning's first choice for the post, Nicholas Vansittart, refused, chiefly because he did not wish to act as a mere spokesman for the government in London, so Canning turned to George Rose. Rose arrived in America just as one particular burst of anti-British fury had given way to a more general grumbling equally divided against Britain and France. He reported to Canning: "The premature fury was too violent to last, the feelings excited are deadened, and it would be difficult to move the Nation to war." Canning, realizing that he had won the breathing space he wanted, turned to the work of designing the Orders in Council that were instrumental in moving both nations to war, though that was the reverse of his intention.

In framing the Orders he had to consider his leader's position. Perceval's argument was the central prop of the British attitude. Napoleon, he said, had chosen to disregard international law, and, since Britain was engaged in a life or death struggle with him, few could blame her if she did the same. If neutral states were caught in the crossfire, they must complain to France, who had started all this. Neutral countries were in a false position, too, for in failing to make Napoleon observe their rights they had left their impartial attitude and had become committed, though in a different way.

A number of English statesmen, led by Lord Sidmouth, thought that this was somewhat unfair reasoning. Bathurst questioned Britain's right to argue on these lines. Their protests were too mild to be heard, especially by those who did not want to hear them, and the Orders in Council passed by the cabinet in November 1807 * banned all trade with France and French allies unless it passed through British ports and paid duty to the British Crown. Instant protests from the American ministers and emissaries in London were loud enough to cause the cabinet to hesitate. Eventually they conceded that all American goods might go to Europe without paying the transit duty in England, except for cotton, the one commodity in which real competition existed between America and the British colonies. Later the cabinet decided to prohibit all cotton shipments to Europe no matter where they came from. By early 1808 the regulations had grown so involved that committees of merchants came repeatedly to the Foreign Office to ask for explanations, but two further concessions tangled them still more bewilderingly: an agreement not to intervene in American trade with islands hostile to Britain; and permission for America to re-export enemy colonial produce through Britain on payment of duty. Everyone in government knew that months must pass before the effect of these Orders could make itself felt, but meanwhile it looked as though action was being taken. Debate about the Orders went on until the early spring of 1808, when Perceval asked the House to approve the

* See Appendix III

cabinet proposals on transit charges. The Opposition rushed to the attack, but the government had a two-thirds majority, and, after an all-night sitting, the Commons passed the amended Orders in Council, which the Lords passed before March was out. Perceval approvingly remarked that the debates had "set those Orders so completely in their right light" that there was now no chance that "the public" might be influenced against them.

What public? Many people neither knew nor cared about regulations governing American trade. There was more awareness in the United States, where (as that wise observer Admiral Alfred Thayer Mahan later wrote) it seemed like the old colonial taxes all over again. Some Republicans shouted that the Orders were tantamount to a declaration of war. The British government hoped, however, that in the end America would come down on the side of profit rather than on that of glory, and place trade conditions higher than international prestige. When the United States later riposted with Jefferson's embargo, fresh talks had to begin in London, and these resulted in a new set of Orders passed in Parliament during the spring of 1809. These new Orders declared a full blockade against France, her colonies, and her satellite powers; opened the Baltic Sea and its ports, especially the German ports, to America; regulated licenses to trade with Europe so that these might operate more efficiently; reduced transit duty charges; and tried to prevent some of the hitherto unfair discrimination against American ships, though it must be remembered that this rested with the British ships' captains on the spot. These Orders superseded the first set, which, as Perceval explained in the House, had not exactly been repealed, but had been so modified by the new Orders that it came to much the same thing.

Lord Auckland, the Opposition spokesman on American affairs, lamented that the majority of his countrymen took little interest in them. "The least regarded and ill understood" subject, he called them. "It is like Whistling in the Winds to talk about great public businesses."

It is true that people, even well-informed people, seemed to find it really hard to grasp that Britain was running a very real risk of war with America. The *Courier* of July 29 said:

Pre-eminently is America advantageous to Great Britain, and Great Britain is scarcely less than *necessary* to America, if the gradual formation of a learned class and of a natural gentry, if the growth of arts and sciences, if a stimulus for agriculture, if commerce and commercial cities that alone supply the stimulus, if union, if safety, if national independence be rightly placed among the necessities of a young and free country. It is British capital, which directly or indirectly, sets half the industry of America in motion: it is the British fleets that give it protection and security.

The failure of the American trade embargo to work saved English face in that concessions could now be made by England without appearing to climb down. Britain hoped that the new Orders in Council, superseding the old ones, would put America in a happier frame of mind. Certainly at first they were well received; some of the American merchants saw them as leading to possible future improvement in relations, and William Pinkney echoed this hope in a letter to President Madison on May 3, 1809: "Our Honour is now safe, and by Management we may probably gain every thing we have in View." The British attaché in Washington, David Montagu Erskine, reported to London that a bill forbidding the employment of foreign sailors in United States ships would soon be laid before Congress. If this were true, and if the bill were passed, it would remove all need for British ships to stop American ships for search at sea. The rumored bill and the merchants' optimism encouraged Canning to believe that America would accept British terms in almost any event, in which belief of course he was quite mistaken. Happily unaware of this he wrote to Erskine saying that Britain would repeal the Orders if the United States agreed to go on admitting British trading vessels to American ports, refuse similar entry to French ships, and allow the Royal Navy to seize any American ships that were carrying on trade with the French. This third point would in fact have permitted England to administer American law, for any English captain could then have determined whether or not a United States vessel was trading with the enemy. Erskine, after one look at Canning's dispatches, knew that America would never agree. Deliberately disobeying instructions, he made no formal presentation of the terms to Madison but, in informal discussions, explored the possibility of some sort of mutual agreement. In the end a loose, unwritten kind of pledge was made that if Britain dropped the Orders, America would keep open or reopen her ports to British ships, and that details could be worked out in full when a special envoy arrived from England for that purpose. Erskine reported guardedly to Canning, writing in a hopeful spirit: "In the mean Time, no injury can be derived, I conceive, from that *conditional Agreement.*"

Erskine's letter was dated April 20, 1809; its contents were received in Portsmouth on May 21 and sent to London by semaphore.

On May 22 Canning sat down angrily to reply. He nearly told Erskine to forget the whole thing, but in the end simply conveyed a reprimand. The cabinet discussed the matter for four hours on May 23, and next day at a levée Canning buttonholed Pinkney to tell him that "they must disavow Mr. Erskine." The British government did so, but announced at the same time that American ships which had sailed for Europe believing that the Orders would have been repealed by the time they got there would be allowed to finish their voyages unmolested, whereupon two hundred English merchants came to a protest meeting and sent a delegation to carry their opinions to the Board of Trade. It was not easy for foreign observers to realize that a diplomat who failed to follow instructions must be rebuked, but the most serious failure on Erskine's part had been that he had not pressed home to the United States government the necessity for America to prohibit trade with France. America could still make trade agreements with Napoleon. She was preparing to do exactly that. In addition, Erskine had cut away much of the ground from under the existing Orders. His "conditional Agreement" had been widely celebrated in America, with cannons and bells and lighted candles in windows. America felt that Britain was ready to make real and sensible concessions at last. But within three months came the news that the British government had disowned Erskine's action. Bitterness naturally redoubled.

The trouble was that the two countries were pursuing contradictory aims. America wanted her full neutral trade restored, especially the lucrative trade with France. Britain wanted a neutral ally, if that term itself is not contradictory, against the French. As an opening move President Madison, recalled from a holiday he was taking at Montpelier in Vermont, consulted his cabinet and, on August 9, issued a statement that seemed to revive part of the embargo, for it restored prohibition of trade with Britain. Canning, once more placing his trust in the tactics of delay, sent out another envoy, a thoroughly indiscreet man named Francis James Jackson. This time the position was reversed. Canning had ordered Erskine to state firm terms, and Erskine had softened and temporized; Canning now ordered Jackson to offer settlement for one particularly thorny example of impressment, and to convey the gist of Britain's ideas through exploratory talks. Jackson rapidly contrived to make himself so unpopular with Madison that the American government requested his recall. He had ignored Canning's orders to preserve, as far as possible, a diplomatic silence on tricky points of discussion, and had allowed himself to be drawn into arguments of the kind that Madison was so skilled in, where Jackson himself kept losing his temper.

When his recall was asked for, Jackson reacted by sending Canning a statement full of self-justification, forty-five pages long: it took his legation secretary fourteen hours to copy it. At the same time Jackson's wife wrote disparagingly home: "Francis being accustomed to treat with the civilised courts of Europe and not with savage democrats, half of them sold to France, has not succeeded in his mission." Before statement or letter reached England, Canning had left the Foreign Office: his rivalry with Castlereagh had split the government once too often, and he remained out of office for thirteen years. His place was taken by the more limited, the more unbending, the far less able Richard, Marquess of Wellesley (who, as we have seen, regarded America as another kind of India), and from that time Anglo-American relations took a turn for the worse.

One thing that helped Britain, had she known it, was the fact that Napoleon's minister in Washington was quite as heartily disliked by Americans as any British minister could possibly be. This was General Louis Turreau, who detested America and made no secret of his feelings. (He enlivened his existence in Washington by beating his wife, once to the accompaniment of the violin played by his Secretary of Legation in order, presumably, to drown the lady's cries.) Eventually Napoleon recalled Turreau, replacing him with the abler Louis Sérurier, who equally detested America but who was far more tactful in concealing this.

Meanwhile, the Royal Navy went on interfering with American shipping, which particularly inflamed American tempers when it was visible from the land, as it quite often was. British cruisers lay in plain sight outside the harbor of New York, stopping every vessel as she sailed by and, since there were many of them, British action often caused the American captains to miss the right wind or tide, thus arriving belatedly at the waiting markets on the other side of the ocean. The British Consul in New York, Thomas Barclay, who had found by painful experience what it was like for his house to be the target of an angry mob, summed up the situation very well:

I am persuaded that more ill will has been excited by a few trifling illegal Captures immediately off the Coast and some Instances of insulting

Behaviour by some of His Majesty's Naval Commanders in the very Harbours and Waters of the United States than by the most rigid Enforcement of the Maritime Rights of Great Britain against the Trade of the United States in other Parts of the World. It may easily be conceived to be highly grating to the Feelings of an independent Nation to perceive that their whole Coast is watched as closely as if it was blockaded, and every Ship coming in or going out of their Harbours examined rigorously in Sight of the Shore by British Squadrons stationed within their waters.

And the anti-American lawyer James Stephen warned against excess zeal on the part of the Royal Navy, saying that its attitude was

sometimes salutary, however rash or irregular–it may overawe Kings or Cabinets–but in this delicate case we have to do with a democratical society–and with a maritime people, too, whose feelings resemble our own.

While the pro-American writer William Cobbett struck a sour note when he grumbled that "the greatest curse of all" was

volumes innumberable written upon the subject. There have been, including both sides, not less than from six to ten able bodied writers, and (what makes the thing more serious) most of them *lawyers,* too. . .

Another source of understandable American grievance was the conduct of the British Admiralty Courts, whose function it was to judge the rights and wrongs of individual ship seizures. The courts placed the burden of proof on the shipowner rather than on the Royal Navy, and costs of hearings dismissed early through lack of proof amounted to as much as two or three thousand dollars. Those carried through could cost five thousand. It was estimated that on any given day between nine and thirteen thousand dollars' worth of American shipping was waiting in English ports for trial by Admiralty Courts, and that the whole process was costing America millions a year. When a ship was seized and held for inquiry, it came under Admiralty jurisdiction, and the court hearings habitually went grinding slowly along. American ships had to be maintained at American expense. This added vast sums to the fines imposed by the courts, and the fines had to be paid before the ships could be freed to ply their trade. To this practice, which was at least legal, if only by British law, was added a flourishing protection racket operated by pirates, who also seized American ships and consented to let them go if their masters would pay several hundred dollars to the pirate captain.

The government in London, on the other hand, argued that at a time when Britain was fighting for her life she could not be expected to allow neutral shipping to sail through loopholes in her law. It was all too possible for American ships to shelter behind the permissions of the re-export trade, which allowed, or appeared to allow, neutral cargoes to be carried duty-free by roundabout routes from the Caribbean to Europe. American ships would load up with American goods in American ports, sail to British colonial ports in the Caribbean, and sail from there to Europe, ostensibly carrying colonial produce but in reality still carrying American produce with which they had set out. This cumbersome practice was known as "re-export." American revenue from it had grown by half as much again during the five years from 1800 to 1805; it must be curtailed. Hearing comments like these, British commanders thought they were free to seize ships making indirect voyages, and a number of clashes took place, causing feeling to rise higher than ever on both sides. It reached the point where the British government actually admitted a mistake, in a memorandum from the King's Advocate (today he would be either the Lord Chancellor or the Attorney General) which the Board of Trade passed to American merchant shipowners:

> Some Vessels were seized which probably would not otherwise have been detained, under a notion that it was illegal for an American ship to convey Colonial Produce from America to Europe; and the misapprehension became so strong, that it was fully believed by many here, and by more in America, that special Instructions to that Effect had been issued by His Majesty's Government, though I believe such a measure never in the slightest Degree entered into its contemplation.

This admission did not, naturally, reduce American anger over impressment: the Boston *Independent Chronicle* stated on May 27, 1811 that

> there is another atrocity incident solely to Great Britain, of the blackest and most savage complexion, which would alone convict her of being beyond all comparison to the *greatest aggressor.* We refer to the barbarous THEFTS OF AMERICAN CITIZENS!

With perhaps one-eighth of the seamen in the Royal Navy being foreigners, and more than three-quarters pressed men, this was a protest unlikely to be heard with much sympathy in England. No one could man the Royal Navy without the press; that had been a fact of life since the time of Queen Anne, a century before. Americans were known to encourage British seamen to desert to American ships. Surely therefore America could not complain if the Royal Navy asked for its own men back? And if those men were so lost to all sense of duty as to hide when the Royal Navy came looking for them, surely it was only fair to take a few Americans rather than return empty-handed? Exchange, after all, was no robbery. What were these wretched ex-colonials complaining about?

The Americans, for their part, saw no reason why, since nearly all their ships sooner or later entered British ports, the British could not wait until then to remove deserters from on board. Also, they resented the fact that naturalization, permitted after five years' residence in America, was simply not recognized by Britain. Some anti-government Americans, to be sure, thought that naturalization gave a man two obligations, to his original homeland and to his new one, while others condemned the practice of giving asylum to those seeking it, on the grounds that the indiscriminate acceptance of foreigners deprived native Americans of jobs (the standard argument against immigration everywhere), and that deserters were scum, anyway. Many English-born men were therefore claimed as citizens of both countries: in 1805 there were some 11,000 naturalized sailors serving in American ships, of whom by far the majority had been born in Britain–9,000 according to Albert Gallatin, American Secretary of the Treasury, who added that some 2,500 were recruited every year. One modern estimate places the figure for English sailors on American ships in 1808 and 1809 at 10,000. In January 1812 James Monroe said that 6,257 American citizens had been impressed into the Royal Navy over the previous ten years.

Now there are lies, damned lies, and statistics, and those figures, supplied to Monroe by American agents in London, are imprecise. They left out 802 cases brought forward the previous year, included 200 not heard in London at all, and also included many twice over because of duplicate copies of records. A reliable total could therefore not be reached. The British themselves acknowledged up to a thousand, a total raised to 1,600 or 1,700 by Castlereagh in 1813, and, after the Anglo-American War, the British released 1,800. Of course this number could not include those who had deserted or died or who had been set free earlier, among them 2,000 released before 1812 as a result of strong representations in London.

The impressment issue has been claimed as the central one that brought Britain and America to blows in 1812. Yet to judge by the admittedly wavering policies of the American government during the decade before that, impressment was not treated as seriously as were the economic questions. Great emphasis was laid upon the expansion of American industry. The State of the Union speeches each year dwelt glowingly upon its progress.

Not all American voices, however, joined harmoniously in this hymn of praise to industrial development: for example, in 1808 the Connecticut *Courant* commented wistfully:

> Who that has seen the happy state of society throughout our villages, can wish it to be exchanged for the dissipated and effeminate manners and habits, which extensive establishments of manufactures never fail to bring in their trains?

—an illustration of the eternal idealistic belief that the city was wicked and the countryside was pure. It may seem exaggerated by the standards of today, yet in 1810 America had 269 cotton mills and 153 iron furnaces, a good number for the time.

But for some people an industrial criterion was not enough. Those with wider minds pointed out that America was still culturally naïve. She still got virtually all her literature and art from Europe, and Noah Webster, who had brought out the first edition of his dictionary in 1806, said: "We shall always be in leading strings till we resort to original writers and original principles instead of taking upon trust what English writers please to give us." He said this to Joel Barlow, author of *Hasty Pudding,* whose epic, or attempted epic poem *Columbiad* appeared in 1807. It received almost unbearably condescending critical treatment in Britain, where the most pro-American, or perhaps rather the least anti-American, of British journals, the Edinburgh *Review,* commented acidly that if Mr. Barlow spent a few years in Britain he might possibly claim a place on a level with the minor English poets, and dismissed American literature with the withering remark that its destruction "would not occasion so much regret as we feel for the loss of a few leaves from an ancient classic." To this day one of the deepest European prejudices against America is that she lacks genuine culture.

An informed and sympathetic observer in high places would have helped here, perhaps. But the new British Foreign Secretary, Richard Wellesley, was not that. He was indeed unlikely to improve Anglo-

American relations at all; so much was clear before he had been many weeks in office. He approached his work as though it were something to pick up for a few minutes when he had nothing more interesting to engage his attention. Throughout the whole winter of 1810–11 only formal circulars came out of the Foreign Office. The recalled emissary to America, Francis Jackson, said that "Wellesley never goes to the Office, and is visible nowhere but in his harem"; and the American William Pinkney said of one of Wellesley's rare notes that it was "the production of an indolent man." Wellesley informed America, on Jackson's recall, that a replacement would be sent, but weeks went by without the smallest sign that he had begun to look for a successor, and America fidgeted uneasily, feeling more and more insulted and affronted by British negligence and contempt.

The war with the French colored every British action. If that had not been in progress, it is reasonably safe to say Britain and America could have composed their differences, which would in any event have been diminished to mere competition for markets and arguments about American Indians. But the French factor, like a chemical, altered the innate quality of every element in the contact of the two countries. America hammered away at the question of Britain's repealing her Orders in Council, which operated against peaceful trading between the two. Britain could not, or believed she could not, repeal them unless America agreed to abandon much of her French trade. When the United States government under Jefferson passed the Embargo Act in December 1807, Canning summed up the British reaction in part when he wrote:

> As it has been more generally represented by the Government of the United States, the Embargo is only to be considered as an innocent municipal Regulation, which affects none but the United States themselves, His Majesty does not conceive that he has the right, or the pretension to make any complaint of it; and He has made none. But in this limit there appears to be not only no Reciprocity but no assignable Relation, between the Repeal of a Measure of voluntary Self-restriction, and the Surrender by His Majesty of his Right of Retaliation against his Enemies. The Strength and Power of Great Britain are not for herself alone, but for the World.

When Lord Grenville protested at what he considered Canning's high-handed attitude toward America, Lord Bathurst remarked woundingly that the Grenville family knew more than most about the dangers of arousing American feelings, an unkind reference to their wide involvement in the War of Independence. Lord Liverpool thought that "America had shewed no disposition to act properly towards us," by which, presumably, he meant behaving with proper deference. The anti-American *Courier* stated:

We cannot allow that necessity calls upon us to depart entirely from our policy towards an enemy, in order that America may be relieved from a burden which she pettishly placed upon her own shoulders.

But it was really so difficult for most Englishmen to think about American affairs when such a lot of other things were going on–not just in the war, either. The subjects engaging popular interest just then were (apart from the war), the perennial Irish troubles, the effects of the King's periodic illnesses (then simply dismissed as fits of insanity, now known to be a disease called porphyry), the raising of prices at the Covent Garden Opera House, and, most titillating of scandals, the selling of army commissions through the delectable Mrs. Mary Anne Clarke, mistress of the commander in chief, Frederick Augustus, Duke of York and Albany, brother of the Prince Regent. The custom of buying commissions meant a whole host of middlemen, dealers, contrivers, each taking his cut. The Duke was in debt, he could allow Mary Anne only a thousand pounds a year and she was in debt to a swarm of tradesmen. What else could she do? What else could he do, when matters of military promotion arranged themselves in that way? Mary Anne was approached, the agreed names were put up to the Duke, he granted the commissions, the tradesmen became pressing, the lists of names lengthened, Mary Anne's husband wrote threatening letters to the Duke, he severed the connnection with Mary Anne . . . and then it all came out. Newspapers, gossip, scandal, a court hearing. Who in London, besides Lord Auckland ("It is like Whistling in the Winds to talk about great public businesses"), could trouble himself about affairs with America? Even as late as March 1811 The *Times* commented plaintively:

There is certainly a great apathy in the public mind, generally, upon the questions now at issue between us and our *quondam* colonies, which it is difficult to arouse, and perhaps useless to attempt.

Even at the War Office there was little sense of urgency. Young

Lord Palmerston was cheerfully cutting his administrative teeth on "arranging the interior details of the office, so as to place it on a respectable footing." He wanted to work out a perennial problem, that of army clothing. Supposedly paid for by a complex system of deductions from the soldiers' already limited pay, the clothing money forming a regimental fund controlled by each colonel, it requires no great knowledge of finance to see that such funds lay wide open to corruption. When young Lord Palmerston actually started making proposals for control of these funds to pass to the Secretary at War and Parliament absentmindedly agreed, enraged senior officers called for paper and ink, registered their protests, including one to the Prince Regent, and debated the question, using up vast energies, for the best part of thirteen years. Between the bouts of this argument, the Secretary at War went on corresponding about medical supplies, pay, returns for forage and bread, bayonets, tunics, and alphabets for soldiers' children.

The Prince Regent was at Brighton in May 1811, where the footmen in the Pavilion served iced champagne punch; people were reading Scott's *Lady of the Lake* and Jane Austen's new novel *Sense and Sensibility;* William and Caroline Lamb were drifting further apart and he was taking more and more interest in the tangle of political opinion, thus starting to equip himself to become, in time, Queen Victoria's "*dear* Lord Melbourne." The rain was falling at Albuera in Spain, where through the battle smoke a British colonel was heard to roar: "Fifty-seventh, die hard!" America was a long way off; and, perhaps, behind the great shadow of the really important war, it would recede still further.

Let us now cross the Atlantic and see what was happening in the American sphere.

THREE

§

Washington

Those who visit the District of Columbia today, whatever their opinion of the government of the moment or of any individual member of it, have to admit that Washington is unquestionably a capital city. The great white blocks of well-proportioned buildings framing The Mall, broken only by the red-brick Victorian Gothic of that most lovable of museums, the Smithsonian, the line of landmarks from the Jefferson Memorial to the Capitol, the radiating avenues, the pretty little White House, all bear unmistakably the stamp of classic authority. The visitor, making the best of the humid climate, feels an overwhelming impression that members of the government, before discussing any bill, ought to take a walk around the center first, and then ask themselves: "Is this measure worthy of this city?" For its concept, like the original ideas that made America a nation, was noble.

The District of Columbia was deliberately set aside to house the capital, one hundred square miles ruled off on a map at the point where two branches of a river meet near the Atlantic coast. It was selected in 1791 to be at the middle of the existing states, halfway between Vermont and Georgia. The land was taken from Virginia and Maryland, though in 1846 Virginia reclaimed its piece. The city was central and national in theory, southern in physical location. The 1791 plan was originally suggested by George Washington himself. He chose the area so that it included Georgetown and Alexandria, sent Andrew Ellicott, who had successfully surveyed the New York and Pennsylvania boundaries, to fix the exact limits, and named Major Pierre L'Enfant to draw up the design for the city.

George Washington's choice of site was not just picked out of the air. The southern states favored the location on the Potomac, though the northern states would have preferred something nearer Philadelphia or even New York, established focal points of trade and finance. Alexander Hamilton, who happened to need a few extra votes for a bill whereby the national government would assume the states' debts, made an arrangement with the Virginia representatives: they would vote for the bill and in return Hamilton would support the Potomac site for the city.

The area at that time was the property of about twenty landowners whose natural first reaction was to suggest a huge increase in the price of the land. George Washington cleverly got past this by asking L'Enfant to do two surveys, one near Georgetown and the other centered on the little village of Carrollsburg, and to leave the landowners in doubt as long as possible about which of the two he would actually choose. He went in person to the area, called together the owners of land in a tract bounded by the Potomac and Anacostia rivers and an approximately southeast line drawn from a point on Rock Creek, and told them that, instead of competing to sell the nation a small district, they should make a common cause of it and allow room for a really imposing federal capital. The landowners agreed, and the Father of his Country got the whole space he wanted for a city with room for expansion, with the understanding that the owners would receive, after survey, whatever land was left over after the streets and future public buildings were laid out. As surveyed, the District included not only Georgetown, Alexandria, and Carrollsburg, but the tiny hamlet of Hamburg and an extra stretch of Maryland territory. The lots were paid for at twenty-five pounds an acre.

L'Enfant, trained as an architect and engineer in Paris, had eagerly volunteered to support the American cause in the War of Independence, and in 1789 had written to George Washington to propose a plan for the capital. He rather endearingly said that such a plan would make his reputation: "a Federal City which is to become the Capital of this vast Empire, on such a scale as to leave room for that aggrandizement and embellishment which the increase of the wealth of the Nation will permit it to pursue to any period however remote." Now he had an area of from three to five thousand acres to play with.

L'Enfant's plan was grandiose. He wanted a grid of streets split and opened up by wide diagonal boulevards with parks at intersections, dignity and splendor of space, an atmosphere of virtuous promise, a mingling of art and nature, room for heroic statuary and pure harmonious public buildings. There were to be squares with fountains and statues, and two main links, two pieces of landscaped ground joined by the wide mall crowned by the Capitol on its little hill, and a tree-lined avenue connecting the Capitol with the "Presidential Palace."

As usual, reality fell short of aspiration. George Washington appointed three commissioners to supervise the actual construction of his city. They began selling lots and, of course, wanted finished plans to show prospective buyers. L'Enfant stalled as long as he could, and ordered the clearing of huge tracts far in excess of the money available. He came to grief when he ordered the house of Daniel Carroll of Duddington pulled down because it stood in the path of his clearance. Carroll was not only a prominent landowner but was the nephew of one of the commissioners. The commissioners promptly put on the pressure, and within a year George Washington reluctantly dismissed L'Enfant, who spent the rest of his life brooding gloomily over his rejection.

But he had set his stamp on the city for all that. Many of the features of his design are those which every traveler instantly identifies with Washington, and ever since his day the city's principal public buildings have been created and placed for looks. The designs were finished by Andrew Ellicott and his assistant, a man of considerable talent often ignored by history, a free Negro named Benjamin Banneker. But in the early stages the development was slow: even as late as Abraham Lincoln's First Inaugural the Capitol still lacked its dome, and the statue of Armed Freedom which crowns it lay forlornly on the ground. The government moved in long before Washington was properly habitable. In 1800, Pennsylvania Avenue was a muddy gash through thickets of alder trees, only one wing of the Capitol was up, there was a single office building near the President's house and that was not fully usable. The mighty showpiece was a string of poor hamlets, primitive and swampy, and the White House itself was unfenced, its rooms still wet with plaster. Abigail Adams, wife of the second President, had to hang up the family washing in the East Room. On her arrival in 1800 she wrote as follows to her daughter:

My Dear Child,

I arrived here on Sunday last, and without meeting any accident worth noticing, except losing ourselves when we left Baltimore, and going eight or nine miles on the Frederick road, by which means we were obliged to go the other eight through woods, where we wandered two hours without finding a guide, or the path. Fortunately, a straggling black came up with us, and we engaged him as a guide, to extricate us out of our difficulty; but woods are all you see, from Baltimore until you reach *the city,* which is only so in name. Here and there is a small cot, without a glass window, interspersed amongst the forests, through which you travel miles without seeing any human being. In the city there are buildings enough, if they were compact and finished, to accommodate Congress and those attached to it; but as they are, and scattered as they are, I see no great comfort for them. The river, which runs up to Alexandria, is in full view of my window, and I see the vessels as they pass and repass. The House is upon a grand and superb scale, requiring about thirty servants to attend and keep the apartments in proper order, and perform the ordinary business of the house and stables; an establishment very well proportioned to the President's salary. The lighting in the apartments, from the kitchen to parlours and chambers, is a tax indeed; and the fires we are obliged to keep (thirteen of them) to secure us from daily agues is another very cheering comfort. To assist us in this great castle, and render less attendance necessary, bells are wholly wanting, not one single one being hung through the whole house, and promises are all you can obtain.

Briesler [the major-domo] entered into a contract with a man to supply him with wood. A small part, a few cords only, has he been able to get. Most of that was expended to dry the walls of the house before we came in, and yesterday the man told him it was impossible for him to procure it to be cut and carted. He has had recourse to coals; but we cannot get grates made and set. We have, indeed, come into a *new country.*

You must keep all this to yourself, and, when asked how I like it, say that I wrote you the situation is beautiful, which is true. The house is made habitable, but there is not a single apartment finished, and all withinside, except the plastering, has been done since Briesler came. We have not the least fence, yard or other convenience, without, and the great unfinished audience-room I make a drying-room of, to hang up the clothes in.

Up stairs there is the oval room, which is designed for the drawing-room, and has the crimson furniture in it. It is a very handsome room now; but, when completed, it will be beautiful. If the twelve years, in which this place has been considered as the future seat of government, had been improved, as they would have been if in New England, very many of the present inconveniences would have been removed. It is a beautiful spot, capable of every improvement, and, the more I view it, the more I am delighted with it.

Affectionately your mother,

A. Adams.

Mrs. Adams could see cattle grazing from her windows, and congressmen made jokes about starting partridge from the steps of the Capitol. Many houses were nothing but shacks. The few stretches of boarded sidewalk ended in mud. Many government men thought the whole thing was a mistake. Secretary of the Treasury Oliver Wolcott wrote: "The people are poor, and, as far as I can judge, they live like fishes, by eating each other." One New Yorker commented acidly: "We only need here houses, cellars, kitchens, scholarly men, amiable women, and a few other such trifles to possess a perfect city."

The north wing of the Capitol was completed in 1807, and Congress had to make shift with that. The roof leaked, and acoustics were so poor in the main chamber that half the speeches were inaudible to most of those present. By then, approximately six thousand people lived in the District of Columbia. The few boardinghouses were hard put to it to squeeze in the thirty-four senators and the hundred and forty congressmen: several of these often had to share a bedroom, and it was common practice to use the boardinghouse dining rooms as extemporized committee rooms.

At this stage in the life of the capital the majority of congressmen did not bring their wives and families with them during the early months of their terms of office, and some fortunate souls managed never to bring them at all. But one by one most of them acquired houses of their own, and then that eternal phenomenon the American political hostess made her appearance in the District of Columbia, where she has been ever since.

It is essential to remember that the city of Washington is one of the very few capitals of the world whose one function is that of government. In America, too, where the frontier is basic to the country's whole philosophy, it has always been desirable to get to know the people next door. In English cities it is possible to live beside the same neighbor for twenty years and never exchange a word; in the United States this has always been out of the question. Consequently in the city of Washington, where everybody was engaged in government business in some way, government gossip was everyday currency from the beginning. Some married congressmen might wistfully hope to lead a bachelor life in the capital; but the President's wife required feminine company, and it might be that the wife of a political rival might exert influence; so, sooner rather than later, the ladies came to Washington, and the peculiar atmosphere of that city began to reveal itself. Where there are ladies there are dinner parties, balls, little circles gathering in drawing rooms to sew and chat, maneuvers to marry off daughters, and, where the whole place lives by politics, every activity has its political tinge. American women have always taken a prominent part in communal life. Moreover, despite the climate, the city has always possessed an innate vitality. The British junior minister, Augustus John Foster, detected a gleam of it:

> I would not, of course, compare the life we led at the American capital with the mode of spending time in any of the great European cities where amusements are so varied and manners are much more refined, but making allowances for its size and strange position I cannot be so severe in describing it as some travelers have been.

One severe observer had been the English writer Tom Moore, who wrote on June 13, 1804:

> How often has it occurred to me that nothing can be more emblematic of the *government* of this country than its *stages,* filled with a motley mixture, all "hail fellow well met," driving through mud and filth, which *bespatters* them as they *raise* it, and risking an *upset* at every step.

At this time the two principal political parties in America were the Federalists and the Republicans. From 1801 the Federalist power had declined until in 1805 they held only one-quarter of the seats in each House of Congress, and never occupied more than one-third before a short-lived run of success during the War of 1812. Their own weakness rather than the achievements of their opponents was responsible for this.

Both parties, to a greater or lesser degree, clung to the principle of isolationism. The wish to detach themselves from the turmoil of Europe had, after all, been cardinal in the aims of the earliest colonists, and by now was virtually a transatlantic habit of thought. Most Federalists were, more or less, pro-British; most Republicans were, more or less, anti-British rather than pro-French; but, as far as active involvement was concerned, the majority felt in their hearts, or seemed to feel, "a plague on both your houses." The Republican orator Estes Howe, speaking on the fourth of July 1808, said:

> May God deliver us from the contagious politics, which have convulsed the old world. We wish not the deadly embrace of Gallic friendship, or the corrupted influence of the British cabinet; for the moment either become

intermingled with our policy, from that moment we may date the defection of our national prosperity and happiness.

The General Republican Committee of the City and County of New York echoed this sentiment in 1809:

The moment we enlist ourselves by sliding even imperceptibly into European politics, intrigue and warfare, we must abandon our peaceful, commercial, and hitherto prosperous system.

And President Thomas Jefferson summed it up when he described Americans as

Kindly separated by nature and a wide ocean from the exterminating havoc of one quarter of the globe; too high-minded to endure the degradations of the others; possessing a chosen country. . .

while the voice of the "plague on both your houses" was heard from Thomas Rodney, who wrote in 1800:

Is the Patriotism of 1776 no more? Is it all converted, into Fish, Wheat, Flour, Rice or Cotton, or into the love of profit and of gold? The nation is surely paralized by these sordid motives, or they would speak a language That would operate like thunder and Lightning over the Land and Sea. Britain is our inviterate adversary–France is not so, but pursues her own interest and ambition. Let us dread neither of them, for notwithstanding Their present appearances of power, They are both vitally sink[g]. While we are Vitally rising in the world.

Occasionally the isolationists condemned American trade, as when the prominent western Congressman George Campbell said in 1806 that it would have been better if "the American flag had never floated on the ocean" to "waft to this country the luxuries and vices of European nations" because the result had been "to excite the jealousies and cupidity of those Powers" and "to court, as it were, their aggressions, and embroil us in their unjust and bloody contests." But most Americans believed in commerce. Trade with Europe, yes; war, no.

It seemed to many Americans that the French Army and the British Navy formed a kind of balance. Jefferson, years later, wrote to George Campbell saying that during his presidency

We were safe from the enterprise of Bonaparte because he had not the fleets of Britain to bring him here, and from those of Britain because she had Bonaparte on her back,

which was very like his summing-up in a letter to one Thomas Lomax on January 11, 1806 in which he depicted, without enough capital letters,

one man bestriding the continent of Europe like a Colossus, and another roaming unbridled on the ocean. but even this is better than that one should rule both elements. our wish ought to be that he who has armies may not have the dominion of the sea, and that he who has dominion of the sea may be one who has no armies. in this way we may be quiet.

Jefferson himself was convinced that Britain was corrupt, untrustworthy, selfish, and tyrannical. On September 10, 1809 he said that the British government was "the most corrupted and corrupting mass of rottenness which ever usurped the name of government." Six months earlier he had written in scathing terms of British integrity: "Her good faith! The faith of a nation of merchants! Of the friend and protectress of Copenhagen! Of the nation who never admitted a chapter of morality into her political code!" But he was equally ready to condemn Napoleon as "the Attila of the age," or "the ruthless destroyer of ten millions of the human race, whose thirst for blood appeared unquenchable, the great oppressor of the rights and liberties of the world." He and his successor, James Madison, both shared a wholehearted dislike of the Emperor of the French.

Since the death of George Washington in 1799, Thomas Jefferson was unquestionably the greatest living American. Some people are inclined to rate him higher than Washington in the list of American presidents, if only on the grounds that he set down the great vision on paper. In 1803 he celebrated his sixtieth birthday, and was adored by the mass of Republican supporters as the finest man alive. Shy with strangers, easygoing and informal in the White House, he had given up going to Congress in person because his appearance might create awe, though this may well have been an excuse. At this time his tall, upright figure had begun to stoop, his hair had turned gray, he was thinner than before, but his freckled face was fiercely alive and his regard piercing and, when in full spate, he was as magnetic as ever. He had never lost his abiding faith in the noble American concept. He was more emotional, more sensitive and impulsive, than the classic father-figure that history has made of him, intensely human and consequently fallible, but among the most endearing and admirable of Americans even yet.

If, as the nineteenth century opened, Jefferson was the great head of the Republican party, his two closest lieutenants were by no means undistinguished. James Madison, the "little withered apple-john" of Washington Irving's description, was respected and admired, if only for his adherence to Jefferson's principles; he served as Secretary of State and, of course, Jefferson's successor at the White House. Albert Gallatin, Secretary of the Treasury, maintained Republican ideals of straightforward simplicity as far as events would let him, and his prudent, scrupulous temperament acted as a good balance to Jefferson's ardent warmth. But Jefferson was the hero. The Reverend John Foster said of him in the fourth of July oration of 1808:

> With the philosopher, the statesman, the patriot Jefferson at the helm, our country assumed an attitude which the angels of God surveyed with approbation, and which excited the rancours of the enemies of Freedom.

During the eight years of his presidency (1800–08), Jefferson hated and dreaded the thought of war involving "the sole repository of the sacred fire of freedom and self-government," which is how he saw his country. He dwelt lovingly upon peace in his vast correspondence, saying that peace had "been our principle, peace is our interest, and peace has saved the world this only plant of free and rational government now existing in it." For that reason: "I consider Europe as a great mad-house, and in the present deranged state of their moral faculties to be pitied and avoided." He thought that "all the bulwarks of morality and right" had been broken in Britain, so that

> It would have been perfect Quixotism in us to have encouraged these Bedlamites, to have undertaken the redress of all wrong against a world avowedly rejecting all regard to right.

But not peace at any price. On February 18, 1808 he said that American love of peace had "begun to produce an opinion in Europe that our government is entirely in Quaker principles," and therefore "this opinion must be corrected when just occasion arises, or we shall become the plunder of all nations." By May 1811 he was calculating from his retirement that the line must be drawn "when peace becomes more losing than war," and on February 12, 1812 he wrote to Charles Pinckney in his characteristic informal style:

We are to have war then? I believe so, and that it is necessary. every hope from time, patience and the love of peace is exhausted, and war or abject submission are the only alternatives left us.

Many Americans thought James Madison simply Jefferson's echo, or, as some Federalists unkindly put it, "the mere hired attorney" of the Father of the Constitution. It is true that Madison was retiring and unassuming in character. He disliked putting himself forward. In January 1806 he produced a long document called *An Examination of the British Doctrine, Which Subjects to Capture a Neutral Trade, Not Open in Time of Peace.* It was the product of several months' work, and Madison had written it in order to summarize his views and to gain the opinion of Congress. But no author's name appeared upon it when it was placed before both Houses, though members quickly realized that Madison had written it. It was a scrupulous, fact-packed analysis of part of Britain's naval policy, wordy and difficult in style but coolly balanced in tone. It contained, however, no proposed countermeasures, which provoked John Randolph to say to the assembled Congress:

After all, what does it contain? A remedy for the evil? No: a formal declaration that we are diseased! Sir, we wanted no ghost to tell us that!

Madison's strengths were a striking competence in dealing with facts and details, shrewdness in advocacy or debate, an apparently bottomless capacity for work despite the migraines that plagued him, good humor, sociability, and kindliness. His defects included inner uncertainty, a habit of looking on the black side when considering future action, unoriginal ideas, and none of those moments of inspired boldness such as Jefferson was capable of and which might set the nation alight. Compactly built, neatly dressed, with his hair tidily powdered, he gave a quiet, precise impression, totally different from that of his rangy, untidy, eagle-eyed, and commanding predecessor.

Madison appears to have been fortunate in his wife, who, judging by her portraits, did not in the least resemble Ginger Rogers (who played her in a heavily over-glamorized film with the misleading title *The Magnificent Doll).* It is modish at present to refer to Dolly Madison as *Dolley,* a curious spelling that irresistibly suggests the word "trolley." She was a plump, dark-haired, good-humored creature, with a decided twinkle in her eyes, a wide mouth curving upward at the corners, a way of primming up her lips while her eyes brimmed with laughter, and a warm, quick, resourceful, good-humored nature. Her first husband, a Quaker lawyer named John Todd, had died, leaving her a son, John Payne Todd, born in 1792. Despite gossip, inseparable from Washington throughout its history (for there are always people who spread rumors about those in power), she was devoted to Madison, seconded him loyally in all he did, took social burdens off his shoulders, and threw open the doors of the White House to everybody. Once she entertained to dinner twenty-four Missouri Indian chiefs with five interpreters. She wore on one occasion a "rose-coloured satin robe trimmed with ermine, her turban fastened by a crescent whence towered white ostrich plumes . . . like the emblem of Navarre"; on another "a crimson cap that almost hides her forehead and reminded one of a crown from its brilliant appearance." She was friendly with everyone. She waved cheerfully to passers-by as she drove through the muddy streets in her carriage, specially built by Fielding of Philadelphia, and drawn by four horses. She chose yellow satin for the upholstery of the sofas in the White House drawing room. When Joel Barlow went to Paris as American Chargé, she asked him to let her know about the latest fashions in "French cloaths," to which Barlow promised that "our girls will write you about Courts and fashions and finery." Mrs. Barlow sent Mrs. Madison such a large parcel of French dresses that the President had to pay a duty of two thousand dollars on them, after which she had her dresses made at home.

The third member of the Republican triumvirate, Albert Gallatin, was the financial expert, frequently consulted by Jefferson and Madison on matters not only of money, but also of foreign affairs. His brother-in-law, Joseph Nicholson, was a member of the House of Representatives until 1807, and Gallatin was able to act informally sometimes between Madison and the House. Among hard-core Republicans he was faintly suspect because his people had come to Pennsylvania from Geneva and he seemed the "foreigner" of the Administration, rather like Dr. Henry Kissinger in the 1960s and 1970s. Gallatin was cooler and more detached than Jefferson, but, although he disagreed from time to time with Jefferson's ideas, he loyally supported his policy throughout. Of course occasional disagreement with the party line was easy in comparison with other Administrations, because the Republicans had big clear majorities in both Houses. The second

President, John Adams, had believed that the President should be above party, and wrote in July 1808, eight years after completing his term of office:

> Wisdom and Justice can never be promoted till the Presidents office instead of being a Doll and a Whistle, Shall be made more independent and more respectable; capable of mediating between two infuriated parties.

But Jefferson felt secure enough to come out boldly as party leader. The more uncertain Madison, who followed him, might well have preferred the attitude Adams advised, but he was so closely identified with Jefferson's ideas in Republican minds that it would have been difficult if not impossible to retreat to the impartial heights.

The Republican party had in its ranks some colorful personalities and some who promised better than they could or would perform. One potential leader died prematurely: the Massachusetts merchant, Jacob Crowninshield. One disgraced himself: the New Englander Barnabas Bidwell, appointed in 1805 as a special Administration spokesman in the House of Representatives. First he proved disappointing in the House and then, in 1810, when Madison was about to appoint him to the Supreme Court, he floundered into a financial scandal. His accounts as County Treasurer were discovered to be disastrously short, and he fled to Canada.

The most flamboyant Republican was John Randolph, owner of the Bizarre plantation at Roanoke, Virginia. It was a suitable name. Randolph was a born actor, furious in debate, switching about between moods of merciless rage and velvet courtesy, of wide-eyed naïveté and crotchety decrepitude, who loathed almost everything, or at least so it seems at times. In 1805 he quarreled with Jefferson, or, at any rate, with his ideas, and from then on the former Republican leader in the House opposed the President with such spleen that Jefferson almost came to believe that Randolph's leaving Congress would give the government a greater sense of security than the repeal of the British Orders in Council. In some ways Randolph occupied a position comparable with that of Enoch Powell in the British Conservative party during the period following his split with Edward Heath, though Randolph was fiery where Powell was cool, but Randolph went further, for he attracted a group of supporters calling themselves the Tertium Quids–the newspapers shortened it to "Quids"–who never missed a chance to embarrass, or to try to embarrass, the Administration. Two of the original Quids were Nathaniel Macon and James

Monroe, who stood by Randolph at first because they thought Jefferson had drifted away from some of the old party principles. But Randolph proved an uneasy partner and from 1808 onward both Monroe and Macon moved back from him toward their former allegiance. From that time the Quids were never a real threat. Randolph, however, continued to excite interest and to provoke positive reactions. On April 26, 1810 Benjamin Rush wrote to John Adams about him in critical terms:

> I have long considered him a mischievous boy with a squirt in his hands, throwing its dirty contents into the eye of everybody that looked at him. A kicking or a horsewhipping would be the best reply that could be made to his vulgar parliamentary insolence. It is only because the body which he insults *is what it is* that he has been so long tolerated.

Some other Republicans stirred uneasily in their places too. One was the rich merchant Samuel Smith of Maryland, who had started in politics as a Federalist and was therefore uneasy about the more extreme Republicans, who, he said, "would carry Democracy to lengths dangerous to civil society." He also mistrusted those "whose good sense, talents, and abilities, produce the present state of things and wish to proceed no further in reform." The Republicans had doubts about him, too, as any political party does for a member who has changed sides. Smith was known to be a man ruled and prompted by self-interest. Another "rebel" Republican was William Branch Giles of Virginia, who has been nicely described as a born enemy of practically everything not first proposed by himself. In a way the "rebels" were more self-motivated than Randolph, whose honest blazing hatreds—for Napoleon, for profit-seekers, for the prospect of war as likely to strengthen the federal government, and for Jefferson and Madison who in his view had betrayed their party—were responsible for his outbursts. There were, of course, many Republicans who chafed under Jefferson's domination, which they now felt free to do since the Federalists were weak and divided. The party was full of lively individuals who had cut their political teeth in opposition and refused to follow a party line without an occasional breakout; but these never formed a rebel group. They were instrumental, however, in making Jefferson's second term (1804–08) a good deal more difficult than his first had been, and his manipulation of Congress more complicated.

Perhaps it was this, in part, that caused Jefferson to act more unpredictably than before. At times he suddenly decided, or seemed suddenly to decide, to leave his Administration to make up its own mind about some measure without any word from him about his hopes and wishes. He did this over the Non-Importation Act of 1806 and over the repeal of the Embargo Act in 1808, on both occasions causing weeks of confusion in the House while members endlessly discussed what it was that the Old Man really wanted them to do. Once he took the law into his own hands in a way he would have ferociously condemned if Napoleon had done it. This was in 1807 when the meetings in London between the Americans Monroe and Pinkney and the English Auckland and Holland drew up a draft treaty formulating certain concessions from both sides, the English showing willingness to relent on impressment and the Americans doing the same on the re-export trade. Jefferson, considering this entirely unsatisfactory, turned it down without a word to the Senate. In fact he did not present the relevant papers to Congress until March 1808, fifteen months after the four men had appended their signatures to the draft in London.

The Federalist party, whose strength lay in New England, was on the side of Britain, which country seemed to its members to possess the model political, social, and cultural structure, and was, after all, "the country of our forefathers, and the country to which we are indebted for all the institutions held dear to free men," as the Federalist Congressman Timothy Pickering put it. Another prominent Federalist, Henry Lee, considered that Britain and America were the only two nations in the world who understood the meaning of liberty. The Maryland Federalist Luther Martin wrote in 1810 that Britain was not "a fancied Eutopia" but

> a Country, which the Creator in his infinite Goodness disconnected from the rest of the World for the abode and the protection of all that is best, most perfect, most virtuous, most dignified, most noble of the human race,–of all that distinguishes Man from the Brute and from the Daemon.

The demon, to many Federalists, was of course Napoleon, referred to, as a rule, in terms quite as violent as those used by the most rabidly involved Englishman: tyrant, monster, anti-Christ, rival of Satan, "at whose perfidy and corruption Lucifer blushes and Hell itself stands astonished." This extremity of view led them to call their opponents pro-French, an opinion which did them a lot of political harm. The Federal Judge Richard Peters, irritated by the excessive language used on both sides, wrote to Pickering on February 4, 1807 in honest exasperation:

I think myself sometimes in a Hospital of Lunaticks, when I hear some of our Politicians eulogizing Bonaparte because he humbles the English; and others worshipping the latter, under an Idea that they will shelter us, and take us under the shadow of their Wings.

But perhaps the central thread of Federalist feeling was summed up by Rufus King, formerly one of the leaders and now rusticating in the country peace of Long Island, who said in 1808: "If England sink, her fall will prove the grave of our liberties."

The Federalist opposition was weak and sadly lacking in leaders: the kind of big leaders who can rally and gather support. John Adams had retired to Quincy; Alexander Hamilton had been shot by Aaron Burr; Rufus King preferred farming on Long Island to the political struggle in Washington. In their places stood an obviously second team: far narrower minded and unthinking men like Senator Timothy Pickering, opinionated and stern, who opposed moderation and who was ready to gamble with the Union itself for party gain (he appeared quite prepared to risk provoking the secession of the New England states). He was abetted by a New Englander with a marvelous name, Barent Gardenier, who had learned his politics in the rough and tumble of New York electioneering. The prejudiced Josiah Quincy wrote of Gardenier that this roughness, together with his wit and "desultory reading," showed up in debate "in an honest, unguarded, inconsiderate manner, very well calculated to inflame the party passions opposed to him, but not to make converts." Randolph, from the other side, commented that Gardenier gave to the House "a strong proof of his candor, whatever it may have been of his discretion." Some greater men had left, or were in the process of leaving, the Federalist camp, notably the future sixth President, John Quincy Adams, and Oliver Wolcott.

The main reason why the Federalists put up such a poor show was that they were, politically speaking, facing the wrong way. They were trying to keep the garrison in, instead of mustering for the attack. They had taken it for granted for so long that Americans would wish to be led by good men of good family, and by men of good will, both of which meant them, that they had scarcely troubled to form a policy. Still less had they tried to equal the Republicans in lining up support. All they seemed able to do was to oppose, in the nursery manner of keeping on shouting "You're a liar"–"So are you." The newspapers did not help much in clarifying ideas, either, for they were either pro-Republican or so extremely Federalist that they did more harm than good, except for a few dignified papers in Federalist areas, like the *Columbian Centinel* of Boston or the Connecticut *Courant,* printed in Hartford. Apart from such publications as these, the Republican press had better quality and wider circulation, though of course there were some vicious Republican newspapers that lowered the tone.

One of these was the Philadelphia *Aurora,* which never lost a chance of baying against Perfidious Albion. When William Pitt died in Putney, the *Aurora,* on March 21, 1806, congratulated America on the death of "this offense to God and to man, the late execrable Prime Minister of England." Its editor, William Duane, wrote on June 18, 1807, eight years to the day before Waterloo, that Napoleon was "the best negotiator we have" as "the avenger of neutral wrongs, and the asserter of neutral rights, independent of the service he renders mankind by curbing the tyranny of Britain." And on another occasion he burst out furiously: "The friendship of Britain–is *damnable,* it is deadly–it is destructive–her *blessings* are *curses."* One Republican spoke, apparently, for many (both then and throughout the course of American history) when he said in Congress in 1811: "Her [Britain's] disposition is unfriendly; her enmity is implacable; she sickens at our prosperity."

Jefferson and his fellow Republicans in government believed that America could maintain her rights and increase her world prestige through trade and economic influence rather than by force of arms. One principle that was central to Republican thinking was the reduction of the national debt, at which they worked so hard that they reduced it by 40 percent between 1801 and 1812. Most of the extra money came from customs revenue, now running at twice the rate it had achieved under the previous (Federalist) government. The special priority given to debt reduction and the obtaining of the bulk of the revenue from trade produced two results, both unfortunate. No federal credit system could be developed while the Treasury was working on reducing the national debt and, for reasons of economy, the American armed forces were cut back to the point where in 1806 there was only one naval frigate on active service. Instead the Republicans, especially Jefferson, pinned their faith on scores of small gunboats, which cost one-thirtieth of the price of proper ships of war. As time went by, a few more warships were built and put into commission, but the cutback had caused a delay that made a considerable difference to America's war readiness.

The regular army, too, had declined in strength during the period from 1802 to 1807 until it numbered only 2,389 enlisted men and 175 officers. With the increasing tension that had built up by 1807, however, Congress ordered eight new regiments to be formed: five of infantry, one of dragoons, one of light artillery, and one of riflemen. They were meant to serve for five years. Recruitment was not easy. For a long time the new regiments were under strength, and this, coupled with the failure to create a proper navy, weakened the words of American fire-eaters. It fitted with Jefferson's principles, though, as expressed at his Second Inaugural in March 1805:

> With nations as with individuals, our interests soundly calculated will ever be found inseparable from our moral duties, and history bears witness to the fact that a just nation is trusted on its word.

It rather depended on the tone of voice in which that word was given. One forthright American named Benjamin Silliman said that Americans had not gone out of their way to make themselves better liked abroad:

> We have monopolized with so little reserve every attribute of freedom, heroism, intelligence and virtue, that we cannot be surprised if other countries, should be somewhat reluctant to concede, what we so indecorously demand.

This of course refers to another American weakness: the naïve longing to be liked which has always lain at the basis of the eternal European complaints about the United States. America has seen Europe as stuffy, hidebound, snobbish, unforthcoming, dedicated to poky inconveniences, flippant, and hopelessly impractical. There is indeed a grain of truth in this. Europe has in turn seen America as brash, boastful, crude, money-mad, the unforgivable upstart colony which had the unfortunate good luck to strike it rich. From the earliest days of American independence to the present day, England has, either secretly or openly, detested that aspect of America that might perhaps be summed up in one notorious example of it as "Errol Flynn capturing Burma singlehanded." In the early nineteenth century it was the same old song. The Edinburgh *Review* of 1812 informed its readers that America was "less popular and less esteemed among us than the base and bigotted Portugeze, or the ferocious and ignorant Russians." The Earl of Sheffield in 1806 criticized America's "spirit of encroachment, that indiscriminate thirst of gain, that sordid jealousy." Even a relatively reasonable and civilized young man like Augustus John Foster expressed something of the same feeling in a letter home from Washington on December 1, 1805:

> They and we are now the Two rivals in what has always given Power wherever it has extended, Commerce, but I trust that still for a long time we shall maintain the immense superiority that we do now. They are next to us in the Race, but in nothing else are they near us. We drove them into being a Nation when they were no more fit for it than the Convicts of Botany Bay, tho I must say that their leader Washington was a great Character, and one or two others whom the Tumult of the Day drove from their Counters, but since that, Interest and speculation seems to have taken fast hold of the whole Country to the Exclusion of every generous Feeling. The Character of a Gentleman is very rare to be found indeed here, but what has surprised me the Character of an Honest Man of Principle is full as rare.

The Americans could express their feelings freely too. Jefferson, who never saw any need to disguise his opinion when moved, as he frequently was, by moral indignation, called the British government "the most corrupt and corrupting mass of rottenness which ever usurped the name of government," and, on December 22, 1807,* pushed the Embargo Act through Congress. This ill-fated action requires a word of explanation.

During the early part of 1806 the British government made a number of well-meaning moves toward a better relationship with the deplorable ex-colonials. They began by recalling the British minister in Washington, one Anthony Merry, who had belied his name by managing to put up the backs of all but the most extreme pro-British Americans he met, and sent out the Lord Chancellor's son, David Erskine, an affable young man (he was thirty) without any previous diplomatic experience. He evidently hoped to make up for this by his

* See Appendix IV

impeccably liberal principles: he caused the old progressive slogan "Trial by Jury" to be painted on the panels of his carriage, adopted an informal manner, questioned no American attitudes, and married an American wife, described as a chunky young woman who liked particularly low-cut dresses. Foster regarded him with some unease:

> I hope they will keep old England firm; these Wretches speculate on our Debasement, and consequent Compliance with all their unreasonable demands.

The government in London also passed a bill regularizing American shipping trade with the British West Indies. It was not passed without a struggle but, after a good deal of wrangling and late sittings, the last one going on until half past two in the morning, the bill, known as the American Intercourse Act, went through in July. Before then, however, an Order in Council dated May 16, 1806 declared a blockade of the northern coast of Europe from the port of Brest to the mouth of the Elbe, but singled out the section from the mouth of the Seine to the port of Ostend as the part wherein the Royal Navy would enforce the blockade. Neutral shipping might go into port along the rest of the coast provided that it carried no French cargo and no contraband, and had not come from nor was going to any French port or a port sympathetic to France. This Order, nicknamed Fox's Blockade, achieved one of its objects, that of showing the British that the government meant business, but failed in the other, which was Fox's idea of placating, if only partially, the Americans, who immediately wanted to know how the Royal Navy was going to patrol such an enormous stretch of coast. Two weeks later there was an unfortunate incident, when HMS *Leander,* cruising in American territorial waters, ordered an American ship to heave to, and, when she did not, fired a warning shot so badly aimed that an American sailor named John Pierce was killed. Uproar followed in New York, where Pierce's body lay in state; street mobs shouted for vengeance and burned a British flag. Jefferson, whose naval forces were not adequate to force an action, made an official protest, said that the three British ships then in the New York area, were to have their supplies stopped, and asked London to see to it that the squadron commander, Captain Henry Whitby, was court-martialed. The British sent a formal apology, which infuriated their own diehards, and ordered Whitby home to face an official investigation.

Meanwhile, ever since January, Congress had been debating a more or less complete ban on importing British goods into the United States. Proposals and counterproposals were discussed, some members urging strong measures to bring Britain quickly to heel, others counseling greater caution. This was one of the issues on which Jefferson chose to remain silent, and Randolph rebuked him:

> It is not for the master and mate, in bad weather, to go below, and leave the management of the ship to the cook and cabin boy.

He added to this on March 5 and 6 with two long, vitriolic speeches, each lasting more than two hours, which, as so often with him, pushed the bulk of his party into the opposite course. The bill finally went through on March 25, banning such items as hempen or flaxen cloth, high-priced woolen goods, glassware, and beer and ale, but not prohibiting the most important imports from Britain such as cotton fabric, cheap wool, or iron and steel. Moreover, the bill was postdated to November 15, to give Britain time to modify her earlier statements, which brought Randolph to his feet again in thunderous wrath:

> Never in the course of my life have I witnessed such a scene of indignity and inefficiency as this measure holds forth to the world. What is it? A milk-and-water Bill, a dose of chicken broth to be taken nine months hence. It is too contemptible to be the object of consideration, or to excite the feeling of the pettiest State in Europe. You cannot do without the next Spring and Fall importations; and you tell your adversary so.

Randolph was right. His contemporary, the independent William Plumer, also opposed the bill, saying that it had "not sufficient energy to operate on the fears" of Britain, though it might hurt her pride. The British government, in the words of Lord Auckland, thought the Non-Importation Act "a foolish and teasing measure," and asked, first, for further postponement, and then, implying that no serious negotiations could go on while the act hung fire, for repeal. Jefferson decided to send a commissioner to join James Monroe in London to seal an agreement with the British concerning impressment, embargoes, and tariffs; the resulting package might induce the Americans to repeal the Non-Importation Act. Jefferson had some difficulty in picking his commissioner. After a lengthy period of speculation and worry while he tried among other things to persuade Rufus King to go, because he wanted if possible a non-Republican, and King refused because he would not be given a free hand, Jefferson chose William Pinkney of Maryland, a distinguished lawyer who had been in London for eight years as a member of Jay's Commission. The choice surprised many, for Pinkney, while leader of the Baltimore bar, had drafted for the Baltimore merchants an immensely able memorandum directed against British maritime practice.

Pinkney, whose law practice in Baltimore brought in the then enormous sum of fifteen thousand dollars a year, and who had ten children, nevertheless accepted. He had no final interview with Jefferson before sailing on May 21, but he carried with him fifteen pages of instructions from Madison in twelve copies, and the crossing of twenty-nine days to Liverpool gave him time to read them. He was described by an admirer, Joseph Story, as having "the air of a man of fashion, of hauteur, of superiority, and something, I hardly know what to call it, of abrupt and crusty precision." Randolph wrote that he hoped Monroe would have had time to arrange "all matters with the Court of London before that federal interloper P. can arrive to share the honour which does not belong to him."

The general feeling of Madison's instructions was that Britain wanted American trade, and that Fox in his wisdom would agree to make terms with the Americans if the American side of the argument was sensibly presented. Pinkney, arriving in London at the end of June, found Monroe easy to get on with but, to his dismay, discovered that his expected opposite number, Fox, had fallen ill. This was indeed his fatal illness and, to replace him in the American negotiations, the cabinet nominated Lord Auckland, who had been the spokesman on American affairs, and young Lord Holland, Fox's nephew, aged thirty-three, who worked together as harmoniously as did their American opposite numbers. Auckland, then over sixty, believed in cooperation, and agreed with Lord Temple who advised him on August 17 that

> it is absolutely necessary that America should be taken off the high horse she has lately mounted but in taking a Lady off her horse care must be taken not to offend her delicacy or shew her legs.

Fox died on September 13 in the middle of the talks, which spread between thirty and forty meetings over the rest of 1806. One talk lasted seven hours, one nearly five, and one actually took place on a Saturday morning in the otherwise deserted Foreign Office. In general the atmosphere was friendly. The question of the West Indies trade was quietly dropped, Britain agreed to an extension of American territorial waters provided that no third party took advantage of it, the Americans agreed to ask for the suspension of the Non-Importation Act, and the British almost agreed to give up impressment on the high seas, while the Americans were willing to let it go on in British ports. This, of course, was by far the thorniest problem. Auckland reported on September 12 that he had

> insisted much on the Difficulty which this notorious Practice would raise in framing any Article for the due security of the essential Interests of the British Navy. Much conversation ensued on the Subject, but without any satisfactory result.

Lord Howick, later Lord Grey, and Fox's successor, sounded a note of caution when he wrote on November 2:

> If the object for which we have hitherto insisted on our rights to impress British Sea Men on the High Seas could be obtained by more gentle means, nobody would be a more strenuous advocate for such a change than I should. But I cannot satisfy myself that any sufficient security could be devised, and I am certain what is proposed would be none.

At first Monroe and Pinkney held out, but, after several more meetings in quick succession, they quite abruptly gave way on the afternoon of November 7. Auckland reported to Grenville the same night.

> We urged strongly that it would be neither friendly nor wise to press us further for a stipulation which might be injurious to a Claim from which we cannot depart, and which is at present exercised so as to afford no reasonable cause of complaint. We proposed to them to suspend or lay aside this part of the Negotiation, by receiving from Us an indefinite but conciliatory statement respecting it; and to proceed forthwith to the other Articles of the Treaty in which we foresee no insuperable difficulty.
>
> In the result the American Commissioners gave way to these suggestions, though with some hesitation and reluctance.

Both pairs in this diplomatic quadrille were rather like soft-centered chocolates: keeping up a firm, smooth outward appearance, while yielding, or at any rate giving way a little, internally. Neither wished to show undue concessions to their respective governments and peoples, both realized that there had to be in practice a certain amount of compromise. All the time they were aware of critical public opinion, fed on rumors, snapping at their heels. The British *Courier* was typical, stating that, if Britain really intended to relax her terms of trade, "in less than three years the carrying trade of this Country will be annihilated.–War, therefore, with America, rather than concession!" The four men then concentrated upon the matter of taxes on trade goods. After a long meeting on December 6 full of "much Debate and Doubt," they agreed on charges of 2 percent on colonial goods and 1 percent on European goods, and, on the morning of December 31, the last day of 1806, the quartet set their signatures and seals to the treaty.

In sharp contrast to the general harmony and friendliness prevailing when the four men were comfortably sitting in an office, protests broke out loudly on both sides of the Atlantic as soon as some sketchy idea of the terms was known. John Allen, Auckland's secretary, exasperated by hostile comment in papers like the *Courier* and the *Morning Post,* wrote his chief a note in which he asked:

> Did you ever see such impudent and barefaced misrepresentations. Concession to America–What concession was made to her except two additional miles of maritime jurisdiction and that so clogged with exceptions as to be merely an empty compliment.

Auckland, who hoped that the treaty would keep America quiet, declared that it did not abandon "any one Claim, or Principle, or right, or Usage, Colonial or Commercial." His hopes were not fulfilled. When the British minister in Washington received the copy of the treaty and carried it immediately to Madison's office, Madison skimmed through it and took it at once to the President, who also read rapidly through its provisions, saw that the impressment question appeared sufficiently vaguely as to allow British sea captains on the spot to act very much as before, or at any rate to fail to deter them from precipitate action, and said that same evening that he was going to reject the treaty on his own responsibility. The anti-British factions quickly grasped the idea that the treaty degraded America, and the *Aurora* trumpeted:

> Will you abandon your rights? Will you abandon your independence? Are you willing to become colonies of Great Britain?

Even the moderates disliked the Monroe-Pinkney Treaty. Rufus King wrote on March 30, 1807 to Gouverneur Morris that Jefferson would be "*absolutely obliged,* if he regards the national honour, to send the Treaty back." Jefferson himself said simply: "Our best course is, to let the negotiations take a friendly nap."

As we have seen, Jefferson sat on the treaty for fifteen months, during which time enough incidents had occurred at sea for the Americans to be perfectly certain that Britain intended to go right on stopping ships and impressing deserters, or indeed anyone else they could catch, on the principle "Better hang wrong fellow than no fellow," or so it seemed to American eyes. During the summer of 1807 Jefferson discussed with his cabinet all aspects of war requirement, including sending his cherished gunboats into action, invading Canada, and stockpiling weapons. The European situation, which looked as though almost the whole Continent was subsiding into a state of truce under the French, led him to expect conflict between Britain and America to break out. On July 28 he sent young Nicholas Biddle to England on the USS *Revenge* with letters to Monroe asking for "assurances respecting the flag of the United States." He had already issued a proclamation closing American waters to British ships of war. On August 1, he retired to Monticello for a breather.

Biddle's dispatches contained an uncompromising demand for "the entire abolition of impressment from vessels under the flag of the United States." Jefferson, who could have whipped up American sentiment to the point of war during the summer, and who had then refrained, came to believe more and more as the year went on that war was sooner or later inescapable, while the tide of American anger was steadily ebbing. On December 14, 1807 the maverick Republican Nicholas Gilman wrote to future Secretary of War William Eustis: "*(in confidence)* the man in the Stone House is of opinion that the Die is Cast." Four days later, on December 18, Jefferson drafted his first notes to set up an embargo, or prohibition of trade, believing that, as Britain had lost a large proportion of her trade with Europe, she could be coerced into stopping impressment, and any other actions that irritated American sensibilities, by such a powerful threat to her remaining channels of commerce. Although it was to be a general embargo, everybody understood well enough that it was aimed at Britain above all. Many Americans had already suggested such a move. Back in July Robert Livingston had proposed

that we may keep what we have at home and daily get more of our seamen and property out of the reach of the piracy of Britain so as to leave, with the debts we owe them, a balance in our hands to compensate the injuries we may receive.

Madison had pointed out to Monroe and Pinkney in May:

It can no longer be unknown to the most sanguine partizan of the Colonial Monopoly that the necessaries of life and cultivation can be furnished from no other source than the United States . . . [which] are one of the Granaries which supply the annual deficit of the British harvests.

But John Quincy Adams reminded his countrymen that nations do not always follow the common-sense path:

The Embargo affects their interests no doubt, but nations which sacrifice men by the hundred thousands and treasure by the hundred millions in War, for *nothing,* or worse than nothing, pay little attention to their real interests.

With a few cautionary voices raised in warning against letting the embargo go on too long, notably that of Gallatin who said bluntly: "I prefer war to permanent embargo," the Senate pushed Jefferson's bill through in one afternoon. The House of Representatives took longer, but after two days of debate they passed it at eleven in the evening of December 21, and at three o'clock next day Jefferson signed it. He should, according to later historians, have felt the chill breath of warning that he might run into difficulties later, for one-fifth of the Republican members had voted against the bill, in spite of clear pressure from the White House.

Republican doubts about the bill caused Federalists to provoke them further by saying that, since the embargo struck at Britain far more forcibly than at France, the French must have exerted backstairs influence, and furious exchanges on the subject reached such a pitch that in March 1808 Congressman Campbell challenged Barent Gardenier to a duel with pistols, and in the subsequent affray Gardenier was seriously wounded. Such a storm of opposition broke across the country, even in Republican strongholds, that Gallatin felt bound to remind Jefferson that this was election year. Indeed when the State elections took place in April and May the Federalists gained seats all over the place, trebling their 1804 vote, doubling their seats in the House of Representatives, and even sending a sizable Federalist minority to the State Legislature of Richmond, Virginia, capital of Jefferson's own state.

Like Prohibition more than a century later, the embargo proved impossible to enforce. Throughout the rest of 1808, smuggling at sea and across the Canadian border grew and grew. In May, nineteen thousand barrels of flour came in to Passamaquoddy Bay; two ships put in at Havana, one to refill her water casks, the other to repair her mast which the captain said had been split by lightning, and both came away with a cargo of sugar. At one time the Port Collector of New Orleans let forty-two ships out of the harbor. In addition, foreign ships, including, of course, those of Britain, could come in and out as they pleased. It was true that some British goods were prohibited but, as we have seen, these were by no means the most vital and, according to the English civil servant Edward Lutwyche, "Every Article is permitted to enter the American ports as usual. The Americans very good naturedly allow us openly to supply their wants, but will not supply ours in return, except by smuggling." Some American merchants found a loophole for themselves, as Jefferson noted on March 13, 1808:

> The H. of R. were surprised into the insertion of an insidious clause permitting any merchant having *property* aboard, on proving it to the executive, to send a ship for it.

By the end of September 594 vessels with a total of 87,000 tons had been given permission to sail, and by the end of the year more than 400 of them had come back laden with cargo.

The Administration tried desperately to stiffen the Embargo Act so that it could be truly enforced. They were prepared to go to extremes: to station an army along the Canadian border; to forbid shiploading without federal permission; to stop and seize ships anywhere, or goods traveling along the roads toward the border or the coast; to ask for proofs of being blown off course or captured; and a string of Acts actually authorizing all this was passed, with many noisy and heartfelt protests, in January 1809. By then it was too late. It was clear that Britain was not suffering much privation from the embargo, that Napoleon minded it not at all, although for the sake of appearances it included all warring nations, that the West Indies had raised their prices but apart from that had not felt the consequences much, and that the only real sufferer was Ireland, whose linen manufacturers relied almost entirely upon American flax. It was the Americans who were under the harrow. Cotton prices fell by half; five hundred ships were tied up in New York and two hundred in Savannah; soup kitchens had to be set up at Salem in Massachusetts; Gallatin found it hard to balance the national budget; American sailors with a nice touch of irony started deserting to British ships; and Senator Nicholas of Virginia was told by his agents in Richmond: "Nothing is now heard of but Bankruptcies which have taken place and more which are apprehended." Finally, the emphasis on the embargo meant that the government neglected military preparations, and the bitterness engendered by this caused arguments between the northern and the southern states, for the majority in the North wanted to be ready, just in case, and the majority in the South wanted to be left without federal interference as far as possible.

There was no way out. Just before Jefferson left office in March 1809 he signed the bill repealing the embargo.

FOUR

§

Canada

"Never did a prisoner, released from his chains, feel such relief as I, on shaking off the shackles of power," wrote Jefferson on leaving office in 1809. But he continued to take a lively interest in affairs of state, none the less. The repeal of the Embargo Act filled him with gloom: he thought it would damage American prestige. "This is the immediate parent of all our present evils, and has reduced us to a low standing in the eyes of the world," he commented on July 16, 1810. Certainly the "present evils" were many and great.

With the furor over the embargo, the rejection of the Monroe-Pinkney Treaty, and the undeniable fact that those Americans who were anti-British made more noise than those who were neutral or anti-French, it was comparatively easy for outsiders to think that the United States was prepared to assist Napoleon to almost any degree short of war. On January 2, 1809 Jefferson had written to Randolph, of all people, "We must save the Union; but we wish to sacrifice as little as possible of the honour of the Nation," meaning that the independence of America must be safeguarded at all costs compatible with the honor of the republic. On January 24 Wilson C. Nicholas expressed the opinion that when the embargo failed "we must resort to the valour and patriotism of our citizens." The Embargo Act was replaced by the Non-Intercourse Act of 1809,* which prohibited trade with both Britain and France, until either or both withdrew its own prohibitions on trade with America. At once a fresh wave of protest broke over the American government. Jefferson, safely retired to

* See Appendix V

Monticello, wondered agonizedly whether matters could go on as they were without the risk of civil war. The new President, James Madison, wavered uneasily between a resolve to toughen the new act and a condition of near resignation to the disagreeable prospect of war with the old adversary across the Atlantic. Many Americans thought, or feared, or in a few cases even hoped, that war would come: if it did come, old scores might be paid off in more than one tempting direction. After all, Britain was still the old adversary, and many Americans would welcome the chance of another crack at her.

To the newspaper readers of the United States a war with Britain might seem to fight for Free Trade and Sailors' Rights (a phrase much bandied about in this period), but to those who thought about military strategy it was obvious that it would have to be fought out principally on land. There were two main reasons for this: First, the American Navy was negligible compared with the British; second, most of those Americans who lived near the western frontier hoped to crush the Indian menace, as they saw it, and conflict with Britain would give them a good chance of doing this. While fighting the British, a few strokes against the Indians would pass unnoticed–or so they hoped. The British were, or seemed to be, guaranteeing the Indians' rights.

The only part of the British empire that the Americans could reach and attack dry-shod was Canada. Consequently it was in Canada that the fighting would take place, or so they thought.

Canada was a different proposition from the United States. As there is no natural geographical barrier between the United States and Canada, and the great regions stretch from north to south across both countries, it seemed logical to many people that political and economic integration of North America as a whole should develop. Canada would thus become the Scotland of America. This theory was strengthened by the fact that the prairies stretched so far that for hundreds of miles it was impossible to be quite sure which side of the border one was on at any given moment. There was also the fact of population. Canada had fewer than half a million; America, by the census of 1810, had seven and a quarter million inhabitants.

But although the north-south pull existed, the east-west pull, though less predominant in the Dominion than in the Union, exerted its own force. It had done so since the sixteenth century, beginning with the Continental Shelf which, stretching east under the Atlantic, created the enormous fishing grounds of the Grand Banks. Long before the first colonists landed, the fishing fleets of Europe well knew the voyage to these fishing grounds, and provided a kind of stepping stone for the colonists on their way.

In Canada, moreover, the pull operated both ways. The Atlantic provinces of Newfoundland, Prince Edward Island, Nova Scotia, and New Brunswick, backed by the forbidding arc of the Appalachians, looked eastward, and never ceased to cherish their European connections. The principal supporters of close empire ties came from this area. The Maritimes supplied not only fish for Britain and the West Indies but also naval bases at Halifax and St. John's. The land was not fertile, but it had one matchless advantage: it commanded the approaches to the great natural entrance to the interior—the St. Lawrence River and the Great Lakes.

The east-west pull was less open and direct in Canada than farther south because of the Canadian Shield, the enormous high plateau of granite-based sphagnum bog and rock spreading in a huge curve from the Arctic to the south of Hudson Bay. Its forbidding bareness and implacable cold accounts for the thin population north of the lakes and for the sharp spiritual difference between east and west Canada. But the Shield contained the finest beaver, and plenty of waterways, so that, while the English were colonizing the eastern seaboard very much in the manner of the first settlers in New England, basing their prosperity on timber and fish, the French, in small bands of adventurers accompanied by bold priests, were slipping up the St. Lawrence and penetrating the Shield in canoes. To them, the great river was the natural frontier of New France.

The early French settlers hoped to establish villages on the French pattern, but because the only roads were waterways they soon realized that farms would have to be allocated in long strips, each with its waterfront.

The St. Lawrence valley is the focus of Canadian history: 60 percent of all Canadians live in the St. Lawrence lowlands. Here the climate is reasonably moderate, the land fertile, with a readymade through route, and protected on the north by the Shield. The Ontario peninsula lay full in the path of the American westward movement, and to this day ninety out of every hundred Canadians live within two hundred miles of the United States border. In the early years of Canadian settlement, however, the French explored the house, while the English, more or less, kept the door.

Eventual clashes were inevitable. The French, who after all were there first, wanted to stay and consolidate and, if possible, to avoid sharing with anyone. After their defeat by Wolfe in 1759 they knew that sharing was inevitable, but at least they could keep clear of the thirteen colonies. The English rejected separatist ideas and, later, republican principles. These two groups, though opposing, were decisive in Canada's remaining separate from the United States after 1776.

Two documents, the Treaty of 1783 and the Canada Act of 1791, set this down on paper. Forty thousand Loyalists moved north during, and at the end of, the American Revolution, most of them from the East Coast. This increase of population caused the old province of Nova Scotia to be divided in 1784 into three: new Nova Scotia, Cape Breton Island (reunited with Nova Scotia thirty-six years later), and New Brunswick, which became the Loyalist province above all others and took the lead in Canadian affairs. From the Maritimes, indeed, has come the vast proportion of Canada's leaders in every field ever since.

Ten thousand Loyalists filtered up into Quebec, most of them traveling by the classic military route of Lake Champlain and the Richelieu River. They immediately demanded their own legislative assembly, and the French Revolution stiffened their will as well as their dislike of the French in general and of all revolutionary movements, which of course included that of the Americans emerging into nationhood under George Washington in the south.

By 1791 British North America was a mixture indeed. There was Newfoundland, a Crown Colony in the gulf. Prince Edward Island, Nova Scotia, and New Brunswick were Royal provinces with single elective assemblies. Cape Breton Island had an appointed government. Upper Canada, west of the Ottawa River, was mainly English, full of angry merchants who saw their economic empire divided politically as the Treaty of 1783 had already divided it physically. This was because Lower Canada was mainly French, its laws based on the Custom of Paris, its Roman Catholic church established, and the English merchants of Montreal felt themselves to be an island beleaguered in the middle of a French province. Then there was Rupert's Land, under a chartered company in the old style; and finally, the Far North West, an illimitable territory claimed by Britain but possessing no local constitution and no defined northern boundary. Actually the entire boundaries of Canada at this time were imprecise.

This welter of assorted pieces of land contained other explosive elements. The great trading centers of Montreal and New York had been in competition from the earliest days of the fur trade. The 1783 treaty had blocked off Canada from the United States, and the two revolutions (American and French) had made the English Canadians more anti-democratic, and the French Canadians more anti-British, than before. The British government in London saw Canada as a bulwark against the dangerous leveling trends of the age. In Lower Canada, power lay in the hands of the "Chateau Clique," an English-speaking group of rich merchants, landowners, and senior clergy. The French-speaking farmers, young lawyers, small merchants, and parish priests began to form an opposition. They were especially incensed by the immigration of nine thousand Vermont farmers who moved into the Eastern Townships of Montreal under the 1791 Land Act freehold option. In retaliation they set up the inflammatory French newspaper *Le Canadien,* with its uncompromising motto: "Our language, our institutions, our laws." At once in sympathetic response the Quebec Nationalist movement started, combining ultraconservative farmers and clerics, legal and professional opportunists, status seekers, the racially conscious, and all who resented "foreign" controllers of economic power.

Between 1783 and 1812 the population of Lower Canada trebled to 330,000. By 1812 Montreal had 30,000 people in it, commanding as it did the great areas of lakes and forests and the steadily growing trade in timber, potash, and foodstuffs. As a center of money and trade, with firm connections with the commerce of Britain, Montreal sent agents to Fort William to settle, in consultation with the traders, referred to there as "winter partners," the next year's policy, and to bring back the furs of the winter's trading. In their turn the winter partners employed French and Indian canoemen and organized trade throughout the West. Symbolic of the wealth and importance of all this was Montreal's elegant Beaver Club which was said to be the center for the real power élite in Canada. In spite of the high cost of trading over such enormous distances, the furriers prospered, and clung ever closer to their English traditions.

Upper Canada had its troubles too. Between 1791 and 1812 its population had increased from fourteen thousand to ninety, most of the new settlers coming from the United States because the push of the frontier crossed the boundary line. They took the oath of loyalty in return for land grants. There was clear favoritism: ordinary Loyalists got two hundred acres each, but ex-officers could have up to five thousand and legislative councillors up to six, while whole townships were handed to promising speculators for development. The power élite of Upper Canada consisted of the friends and hangers-on of the governor, John Graves Simcoe.

Simcoe, an ultra-conservative soldier who detested the republic and relied upon immigration to keep Upper Canada out of the Union, was an imaginative man and a capable organizer who employed the military to build new roads. What he wanted was to set up a colonial version of eighteenth-century England, for he explained that his whole policy was created to support "that just aristocracy which the Canada Bill has provided for," as "a constitutional provision against those turbulent talents which may otherwise with great facility gain a more than aristocratic ascendancy over a people." He went on:

> I should be very happy was there sufficient property and other qualifications in any members of the Legislative Council to see the provision of the Canada Act, in this respect, immediately completed by an hereditary seat derived from a title of honour being vested in their families.

As most Upper Canadians were struggling to clear the land, set up the diminutive capital at York (later Toronto), and simply to survive, the privilege structure could keep going for a time in comparative safety. But as months went by and the population grew, members of the non-élite began to consider the question of the whole social and political situation in Canada afresh and tensions gradually developed.

The relatively stable Maritimes grew more slowly. By 1812 their population was still under 100,000. Fisheries encouraged shipbuilding, timber forests supplied it. The ships, however, still failed to nudge out the New England ships on the old trade routes between North America, England, the West Indies, and West Africa. A surer source of prosperity, especially during the Napoleonic Wars, was the West Indian trade, which exchanged Canadian fish for Caribbean sugar, molasses, and rum.

The internal dissensions were worst in Lower Canada, where the governor from 1807 to 1811, Sir James Craig, spearheaded the movement for English supremacy over the French. He did, in fact, go too far. Agreeing to the demands of merchants to restrain the French party, he dissolved the assembly, cashiered many French-Canadian officers, suppressed *Le Canadien* and put its owners in jail. Riotous elections followed. The number of aggressive French deputies elected increased. Craig, who was appointed at the age of fifty-nine, had a career that encouraged his natural xenophobia: he had fought in the War of Independence under Burgoyne, at the Cape of Good Hope, in India, and in the Mediterranean and was thoroughly tired of foreigners and colonials. He was governor of Lower Canada but also held the resounding titles of captain general and governor in chief of British North America. He seems largely to have left the other governors, or lieutenant governors, to manage as best they could in their respective provinces, but he liked to be kept informed of what was going on, which led to his becoming embroiled in the odd and faintly unsavory incidents concerning one John Henry.

Born in Ireland in or about 1776, Henry emigrated to Boston as a young man. He lived there with, and on, a wealthy uncle whose prosperous industry he did not copy. Indeed he was a rolling stone with delusions of glamour. He tried the army and then resigned his commission, set up as a lawyer despite his lack of legal qualification, then tried to become a judge. In 1808 he applied for an appointment to the Upper Canada bench. The lieutenant governor, Francis Gore, dismissed him brusquely as the adventurer he was, but Henry managed to open up a correspondence with Craig's secretary, Herman Ryland. The letters written by Henry to Ryland from Boston or Vermont spanned a considerable period and were full of indiscreet gossip. The Federalists of New England, he said, were favorably disposed toward Britain, to the point where they might well secede from the Union unless a peaceful settlement with Britain could be achieved. In fact the letters contained no more than common gossip, but Ryland showed them to Craig, who said that he would be interested to see more, preferably with more details, and Henry delightedly began to see himself as a secret agent. He was, of course, unable to supply the greater detail Craig requested, but he went on writing to Ryland until he knew that Craig had forwarded his letters to London, whereupon he went to London in person hoping for reward and recognition. London, however, simply referred the matter back to Quebec, so Henry returned to Boston. On the ship he struck up a friendship with an agent of Napoleon posing as an emigré French count, whose real name was Soubiron but who presented himself as Count Edouard de Crillon with a chateau just inside the Spanish border.

Soubiron, a gambler as well as an agent by profession, utterly deceived Henry. He had seen through Henry at a glance and, posing as the poor exile, offered the deeds of the chateau in exchange for the letters. His persuasive powers worked perfectly. Both men appear to have had an inflated idea of the price that the letters, or rather the copies of them in Henry's possession, would fetch among the Count's influential Washington friends. The sum of two hundred and fifty thousand dollars was mentioned at some point, by which of the two hopeful conspirators is not clear. The actual price obtained by Soubiron, despite the fact that his American acquaintances liked the idea of dealing a double blow at both Britain and the Federalists, was fifty thousand.

At the moment of handing over, everyone was pleased with his part of the bargain. Soubiron had his money; Henry had his chateau; the United States government had the letters. Soubiron in addition knew that he had doublecrossed Henry: there was no chateau, no estate, no Count de Crillon. Henry knew that he had doublecrossed everybody: the letters were not accurate copies but paraphrases with asterisks all through them instead of names. The United States government felt less satisfaction when they discovered this, but at least when the letters were finally made public in March 1812 there could be no doubt that they inflamed anti-British feeling in the capital. What chiefly surprises the modern reader is that all this fuss resulted from letters some of which were by then four years old.

This incident, though it made the name of Sir James Craig notorious in Washington, was to him a trivial enough matter, especially as he was back in England by the time the letters were published. As his term of office went by he became more and more preoccupied with the question of whether Lower Canada would be invaded; he warned the militia "to be on their guard against strangers" and eventually set it on standby readiness "to assemble, on the shortest notice."

He also engaged in exchanging letters with Francis Gore on the subject of Canadian defense. As early as January 3, 1809 he wrote to Gore suggesting that the loyal militia of Lower Canada, plus those regulars not required for the defense of Quebec, might go into Upper Canada to reinforce Gore's troops, granting

> the preservation of Quebec as the object of my first and principal consideration, and that to which all others must be subordinate. It is the only Post, defective as it is in many respects, that can be considered tenable for a

moment . . . affording the only door for the future entry of that force which it might be found expedient, and which the King's Government might be able to send. . . .If the Americans are really determined to attack these Provinces and employ those means which they may so easily command, I fear it would be vain for us to flatter ourselves with the hopes of making any effectual defence of the open country, unless powerfully assisted from home.

Gore replied promptly, on January 5, agreeing that the whole force of Upper Canada could well be used to harry the rearguard of any American invaders moving on Quebec, and admitting that it would not be practical to defend Upper Canada against anything more than "a partial or sudden incursion." This fact, however,

must be carefully concealed from Persons of almost every description in this Colony, for there are few People here that would act with Energy were it not for the purpose of defending the lands which they actually possess.

And on March 16, 1809 the Upper Canada Militia Act stated:

It shall not be lawful to order the militia or any part thereof, to march out of this Province, except for the assistance of the Province of Lower Canada, (when the same shall actually be invaded or in a state of insurrection) or except in pursuit of an enemy who may have invaded this Province, and except also for the destruction of any vessel or vessels built or building, or any depot or magazine, formed or forming, or for the attack of any enemy who may be embodying or marching for the purpose of invading this Province, or for the attack of any fortification now erected, or which may be hereafter erected, to cover the invasion thereof.

Thus provided, Gore believed that he could keep the upper hand on the Great Lakes for a long time.

Needless to say, these internal problems were not all that the Canadian officials had to consider or deal with. Anglo-American relations were rapidly getting worse. One main cause was the flickering trouble along that ancient contention, the Indian frontier.

After 1783 London and Montreal had two continuing interests in the Ohio country: the fur trade, and the British guarantees of Indian tribal rights, this last stemming from the years of patient pre-Revolutionary work by the superintendents of Indian Affairs. The Treaty of 1783 allowed free entry of Canada for commercial purposes, and also pledged the restoration of property and civil rights to dispossessed Loyalists. With all these in mind, Britain held on to various fortified trading posts south of the Great Lakes, although these posts were now technically on American soil. They included Niagara, Detroit, Sandusky, and Michilimackinac, and all had been meeting places with Indian representatives and traders. The treaty had left the Indians out and, now that Americans were pressing farther and farther westward, it seemed unlikely that the United States government would do anything for the Indians, particularly since most frontiersmen believed them to be no more than savages with tomahawks and scalping knives. The Indians had been known to turn against the palefaces even if these were British, and it seemed sensible to the British officials to placate them whenever possible.

This policy, neatly blending humane ideals with prudence and a hard eye for a bargain, thereby allowing the British a considerable advantage, naturally incensed the Americans, but for years there was little that they could do about it, beyond protesting. Scattered and weak forces of militia were unable to do more than make a token show, and the forts gradually decayed while the British soldiers patrolling the great vague frontier averaged less than one man to half a mile. Several sharp clashes between Americans and Indians in 1790 and 1791 forced the Americans to propose fresh boundary lines. This they did in the summer of 1793, by which time Governor Simcoe of Upper Canada had set up a new fort near Detroit on the Miami River, to protect the route to Lake Erie. The Indians demurred at the American proposals, so Major General Wayne, nicknamed "Mad Anthony," whipped up a mixed collection of troops that he called the Legion of the United States, and advanced into Indian territory to teach the redskins a lesson.

As soon as the news of this reached Simcoe, he called out the militia to the defense of Fort Miami, from which point the British troops were able to observe, on the morning of August 20, 1793, Wayne's defeat of the Indians across the river at a place called Fallen Timbers. The fort commander kept his men inside and his gates shut throughout the action, which did nothing to endear the British to the Indians, though some Canadian militia from Detroit did come to their aid. Mad Anthony was not mad enough to disregard his government's wishes, so he left the British alone. One Indian who was present and who lived to fight another day was a tall, alert, sardonic, stern Shawnee, aged twenty-five, named Tecumseh.

In 1794 Britain accepted the terms of Jay's Treaty, drawn up in

London after negotiations between British representatives and the American Chief Justice John Jay, whereby Britain agreed to evacuate the forts on American territory by 1796. In return America guaranteed free commercial entry and promised to act more decisively to settle the Loyalists' claims for compensation. Britain kept her word and abandoned the forts by June 1, 1796, but the Loyalist question was never settled, Canadian traders found themselves increasingly bothered by United States fiscal laws, and the Indians, seeing the frontier moving steadily deeper into their hunting grounds, remained restive, if not positively hostile. Spurts of conflict kept up their firecracker effect along the frontier for years, during which the more belligerent Americans accused the British of supporting "the Indian menace." By 1811 the menace looked real. Tecumseh had built up a confederacy of Indians prepared to make a final stand for their rights, or for what appeared to be their rights. He made his headquarters at the Indian village of Tippecanoe, built on a river some eighty miles south of Lake Michigan, and here acted in a way which has earned for him a reputation as one of the noblest champions of his race. Hardly less impressive, and devotedly seconding Tecumseh in all he did, was his brother Tenskwatawa. Some chroniclers say this was the younger brother; others say that they were twins. The tall, stately, hazel-eyed Tecumseh was the politician of the two: Tenskwatawa, half-blind and, according to some historians, a reformed drunkard, was the religious visionary. He had won this reputation by such prophecies as foretelling an eclipse of the sun, and was known among his people as The Prophet.

The regions in which the "Indian menace" caused the principal alarm were Michigan, Indiana, and Illinois, none of which yet had votes in Congress. By the 1795 Treaty of Greenville the Indians had gone over to the defensive and, although the United States government spoke of them in kindly terms, its members hoped in time to see every Indian moved west of the Mississippi, and the frontiersmen on the spot frequently lost sight of theoretical impulses of benevolence and brotherhood. Many murder cases occurred, and frontier juries were not inclined to convict frontier killers of Indians. Government officials, also, made a practice of cornering isolated chiefs, plying them with high-flown speeches and plenty of whisky, and thus persuading them to sign treaties that gave away huge sections of their (and others') hunting grounds. The governor of the Indiana Territory followed this practice so enthusiastically that in the fourteen years after Greenville the Indians gave up the best part of fifty million acres. British assistance and encouragement to the Indians from Canada helped to stop, or at least to slow down, this process after 1809. After the British left the disputed trading posts in 1796, they set up two new ones just inside Canada's borders: St. Joseph, near Michilimackinac, and Amherstburg, not far from Detroit. The British superintendent of the Northwest Indians, whose headquarters was at Amherstburg, was Matthew Elliott, a Loyalist of Irish birth, who had been a fur trader. His qualifications for the post included the fact that he had married a Shawnee and could speak her language. He was appointed in 1808 and his instructions were to keep the Indians loyal to the British by keeping alive the land grievances and Indian resentment of the "artful and clandestine" way in which the Americans had obtained the hunting grounds, yet at the same time steering the Indians clear of actual war until the last possible moment. It was at this point that Tecumseh and Tenskwatawa entered the picture.

The brothers set about the immense task of trying, as they saw it, to save their people. They wanted to stop the loss of Indian land, keep the Indians apart from the palefaces, weld all the tribes into a confederacy, and reform their habits of drinking and wild behavior as far as they could. In terms of numbers, the confrontation was quite unequal. The Indians in the region bounded by the Ohio River, the Mississippi, and the Great Lakes totaled barely four thousand; in the Ohio valley there were more than twenty-five times that number of white men of fighting age.

At first the brothers made great strides. The Prophet led a religious crusade that actually caused the redskins to refuse the palefaces' whisky, and the tribes drew clear of contact except for strict trading. It was believed that The Prophet's influence extended from Florida to Saskatchewan, and the Americans were more alarmed than ever. The governor of Indiana Territory, William Henry Harrison, at thirty-eight a lively student of military history and a firm believer in unorthodox surprise tactics, determined in 1811 to do something positive about it, regarding the Indians as "the most depraved wretches on earth." He contrived to get from them some three million acres on both banks of the Wabash, bringing the frontier within fifty miles of Tippecanoe, and sending Tecumseh running for help to Elliott at Amherstburg. Canada still wished to keep clear of war, so Elliott put off Tecumseh;

naturally disheartened, Tecumseh traveled south to call upon the friendly alliance of the Creeks. Harrison, knowing that Tecumseh was away from his headquarters, collected a mixed force of 1,100 regular soldiers and militia, marched them up the Wabash valley, and made camp close to Tippecanoe. The Prophet had been forbidden by his brother to get entangled in any fighting, but a few of his young fire-eaters, finding the situation too much for them, sprang into action at dawn on November 8, 1811 (some accounts date it as November 7), and a full-out fight quickly developed. The Prophet was killed in the course of it and, after two hours' combat, Harrison's men beat off the Indians, drove them back into a swamp, and then advanced on the unprotected village and burnt it to the ground.

When Harrison brought his little army back to his little capital (which had the incongruously elegant name of Vincennes), the Americans hailed this bloody affray as a splendid blow against the wicked British, who had been supporting savages against honest pioneers and, of course, as a triumph over the Indians. Tecumseh took 1,800 braves, virtually the remains, or hard core, of his confederacy, to Amherstburg where, with unusual good sense on the British part, the officers of the Indian Department welcomed them into the defense strategy of Upper Canada. There was one other consequence of note: exactly twenty-nine years later the slogan "Tippecanoe and Tyler too" carried William Henry Harrison and his running mate, Tyler, into the White House as the ninth President of the United States.

Many Britons in Canada, including Governor Simcoe, had dreamed for years of setting up a neutral Indian state in the Ohio country and perhaps thereby undoing part of what seemed to them the crippling boundary terms of 1793 (which pushed the Indian frontier farther north), but actual British policy, and actual events, worked in the contrary direction. There were to be many difficulties caused by, and because of, the Indians on both sides of the border for a long time yet.

It is important, in order to get the details clear, to determine precisely what was meant at this period by the term "militia."

From the earliest settlements in Virginia in 1607 and in New England in 1620 every ablebodied male from sixteen to sixty knew that he could be called upon, and that he would be called upon, to serve in the local defense forces. Only Crown officials, ministers of religion, and men in essential jobs (for example, ferrymen, or millers) were exempt.

Later, conscientious objection was permitted on religious grounds to otherwise highly desirable immigrants like Quakers. In time of peace, each settlement simply provided a proportional militia, filled by volunteers and then by drawing lots, to serve as and when required, very much on the lines of Captain Miles Standish's troop in Plymouth, Massachusetts. In time of war, or of emergency, every available man was mustered. It was generally understood that the militia would be in charge of supplies and of building roads, bridges, or forts rather than doing much actual fighting.

Combat was the task of the professionals–the regular army. In 1786 the combined soldiers of foot and artillery regiments in Upper and Lower Canada stood at approximately 2,500, plus 350 Queen's Rangers in Upper Canada. There were some 1,750 in the Maritimes. There was no cavalry, because in the almost roadless and thickly wooded country regiments of horse were thought to be impractical.

It was a small force to defend so vast a region, but the defense planners seemed unperturbed. They were sure that no American attack could succeed while Quebec was fully garrisoned and the Royal Navy remained supreme on the sea. Fighting was impossible in winter, and one fighting season was not long enough for both Quebec and Montreal to fall. If either or both came under attack, a fresh British Army could come up the St. Lawrence in British ships at the beginning of the following spring. As a safeguard, however, additional forts were built at strategic places, notably on the Richelieu River to protect Montreal. The Provincial Marine patrolling the St. Lawrence and Lake Ontario would be reinforced in war by Upper Canada militia specially detached for that purpose, and two special battalions of Royal Canadian Volunteers were to be recruited. Kingston was thought to be a weak point, so Gore stepped up militia exercises there. By the end of 1807 every fourth man had been drafted, had been issued arms, and had started drilling. A charmingly rueful letter dated January 3, 1808 explains that the men were "to keep themselves in Constant readiness, in case Jonathan should attempt an invasion. We are now learning the Exercises," the writer went on composedly, "and are drilled twice a Week by a Sergeant from the Garrison–and are already much improved Considering our Awkwardness."

For years the governors worried about the French almost as much as they worried about the Americans. After all, the French were the ancient enemy; they had attacked, or were intent upon attacking, almost everywhere else: they might easily try to recapture Quebec, with or without American aid. Pro-French propaganda circulated upward from the United States among the French Canadians, to the point where it was widely believed as early as 1794 that the French fleet would arrive in the St. Lawrence at any moment, just as an American invasion force struck north out of Vermont. This at least had the effect of aligning the Catholic clergy more firmly behind the British, for France, in their eyes, was now a godless nation, cutting off the King's head, and worshipping the Goddess of Reason in no less a place than Notre Dame, when they were not quartering soldiers in that hallowed pile. As for the less fiercely Loyalist immigrants from the United States, they gave little trouble. They cared most about settling on the land, and it was a small price to pay for such longed-for security to stick (more or less) to the words of the Oath of Loyalty:

I promise and declare that I will maintain and defend to the utmost of my power the authority of the King in His Parliament as the supreme Legislative of this Province.

Fortunately for Canada, most of them were able to keep up this pledge, in spite of the invasion's proving one of many false alarms. The panic each successive invasion scare produced was credited by the government to "a long disuse of Military Services, rather than to a spirit of discontent or disloyalty." But the numbers of fighting men dwindled perilously for all that. By 1795 the total force of Royal Canadian Volunteers and Queen's Rangers was barely five hundred, a dangerously low figure to supply the garrisons of York and Kingston and to man the forts of Erie, St. Joseph, George, and Malden. Recruiting remained sluggish even after Britain declared war on France on May 16, 1803, so much so that the colonel of the Forty-Ninth Foot wrote to the commander in chief at the beginning of 1806:

Experience has taught me that no regular regiment, however high its claims to discipline, can occupy the frontier posts of Lower and Upper Canada without suffering materially in numbers. It might have been otherwise some years ago; but now that the country, particularly the opposite shore, is chiefly inhabited by the vilest characters, who have an interest in debauching the soldier from his duty, since roads are opened into the interior of the States which facilitate desertion, it is impossible to avoid the contagion. A total change must be effected in the minds and views of those who may be hereafter sent on this duty, before the evil can be surmounted.

The letter stressed the Americans' persistence in trying to persuade troops to desert, especially the youngest men, the ease with which former rebels had become prosperous landowners, and the difficulty of holding regiments together in full *esprit de corps* when "a regiment quartered in Upper Canada is generally divided into eight different parts, several hundred miles asunder, and in this situation it remains at least three years."

Not only were men deserting at an alarming rate, but new recruits were harder to find. Though supposed to keep within the provincial boundaries, recruiting officers went wherever they thought it worth a try. It was a slow business, however, and by January 1805 the strength of the Nova Scotia Fencibles stood at only 312, while two years later the Canadian Fencibles had managed to gather a mere 124, not enough to form a regiment.

The colonel of the Forty-Ninth Foot proposed that, as Quebec was the vital focus of Canadian defense, the strongest body of regulars should be stationed there. He said that the oldest soldiers should garrison the forts, on the grounds that experienced veterans, near, or fairly near, to their pensions, and presumably of long-established good character, would be more capable, and less likely to desert, than raw young troops, let alone that they would almost certainly fight much better. By Christmas Day, 1806, 10 Royal Veteran battalions, 650 men in all, were ready for duty. Other projected recruitments did not work quite so well. In late 1805 the colonel paid an elderly member of the Lower Canada legislature, Thomas Dunn, the compliment of asking him to call out the militia for training and to repair the Quebec defenses; Dunn was somewhat slow off the mark, for he did not levy his 10,000 men, one-fifth of the maximum possible number, until August 1806. The lots were drawn on the Esplanade on Tuesday, Friday, and Sunday, August 25, 28, and 30, in a cheerful, eager manner, according to the Quebec *Mercury* which reported the event in its own style:

The Artillery company, the two flank companies, and Captain Burn's battalion company, who are the strongest and best disciplined of the British have, to a man, formally tendered their services. Sums of money were offered by individuals for prize-tickets, for such the tickets were called which, in balloting, were for service. Some young batchelors procured prize-tickets from the married men, who had drawn for service; but the greater part of the latter insisted on keeping their tickets, notwithstanding that offers of exchange were made to them by other batchelors.

Too much praise cannot be given to the animating language of the field-officers and others, in their speeches, addressed to the different battalions and companies, on the occasion. The whole has been attended with much festivity and hilarity.

We hear that equal cheerfulness and ardour have manifested themselves in the different country parishes.

The colonel, however, kept his feet on the ground:

The men thus selected for service being scattered along an extensive line of four or five hundred miles, unarmed and totally unacquainted with anything military, without officers capable of giving them instructions, considerable time would naturally be required before the necessary degree of order and discipline could be introduced among them.

Francis Gore, who wrung from Quebec a promise of four thousand sets of weapons, told the Secretary of State for War and the Colonies that at present he was not calling up his militia: the Americans, he said, should not be able to see how weak they were. Sir James Craig tried to raise a corps from among the Scottish settlers in Upper Canada, but had to give up the idea because the recruiting officers' keenness was far in excess of the meager results they obtained. Craig did, however, bring up the Canadian Fencibles' strength to a more impressive showing of 411 men, 24 sergeants, and 22 drummers by the end of 1808. He did not find the task easy, for he was struggling more and more, as time went by, against his own failing health, and he wrote repeatedly to London asking for permission to resign. As a natural consequence he grew increasingly despondent, believed that war with America was certain, and rated the Lower Canada war potential lower and lower. Gore had his own doubts about Upper Canada, too, and he wrote to Craig on January 5, 1808, to say that, while he felt pretty sure of the loyalty of those who lived "from Kingston to the Borders of the lower provinces," he could not say that

the Inhabitants about the Seat of this Government, Niagara and Long Point are equally to be relied on. I have also to observe that excepting the

> Inhabitants of Glengarry and those Persons who have served in the American War and their Descendents, which form a considerable body of men, the residue of the Inhabitants of this colony consist chiefly of Persons who have emigrated from the States of America and of consequence, retain those ideas of equality and insubordination much to the prejudice of this government, so prevalent in that country.

Craig's anti-French policy and worsening health finally combined to persuade London to recall him. Craig sailed for England on June 19, 1811, leaving Thomas Dunn to hold the breach until the lieutenant governor of Nova Scotia could arrive to take over Craig's office. This was a talented, chubby-faced, French-speaking ex-New Yorker of Swiss descent, forty-four years old: Sir George Prevost.

The most reliable defense of Canada was believed to be the Royal Navy. It had a base at Halifax and bases in Newfoundland and the West Indies but, because of the European situation, its principal ships were needed in European waters to protect British sealanes against the French and Spanish fleets and, in time, to attack these. As a result none of the first-rate ships of the line, carrying at least ninety guns, could be released for the New World. All that could were third-rate and fourth-rate ships, many of them with only fifty guns, and a few single-decker frigates with as few as thirty-eight, or even twenty-four. There were sloops and brigs with ten to twenty guns under the command of captains who were in fact often still only at the rank of lieutenant. While Canada could assume that the United States had no navy at all, this force appeared, and probably was, adequate. But after 1798 the United States felt impelled to do something about the increasing threat from France. Jay's Treaty seemed to have produced better Anglo-American relations, at least to French eyes and, if the French could not go on playing off America against Britain, they must, or thought they must, sharpen their attacks on American merchant ships. When the French temporarily severed diplomatic relations with America, the United States Navy Department came into being on May 3, 1798. During the next three years the few United States vessels that existed fought one or two isolated engagements and then cut their teeth as a naval force in forays against the Barbary pirates. But the rise of Napoleon enabled diplomatic relations, of a sort, to be resumed, though it was noticeable to the French that the American attitude fluctuated with every French or British victory in Europe, so much so that General Turreau while French envoy in Washington commented sourly that "their System with regard to foreign countries is to have none."

But there was another reason why the American Navy would soon have become a necessity anyway. With the British likely to stop any ship at sea, whether to search it for contraband or for deserters, the French countered by confiscating British goods carried in neutral ships and then, by The Milan Decree, made the declaration, highly convenient to France, that all vessels so stopped and searched by the Royal Navy would cease to be regarded as neutral. Pressed thus on both sides, the Americans hastened to develop their own naval power.

That this was a prudent course for America to follow was proved in the spring of 1807, for otherwise the results might have been much worse. A squadron of British ships was watching for possible French vessels in Chesapeake Bay when a number of sailors contrived to slip ashore. Some of them merely demanded asylum from the local authority, but others enlisted on board American ships. One of these, a short, swarthy-complexioned man who had been a tailor in his native London, and who was named Jenkin Ratford, enlisted on board the USS *Chesapeake,* and, in celebration of this happy event, shouted insults at British officers in the streets and on the quays of Norfolk, Virginia. This could not be ignored, and the British formally requested the return of the deserters. The Americans refused, and the question was referred to the British commander on the American station, Vice-Admiral Sir George Cranfield Berkeley, MP, at that point stationed in Halifax, Nova Scotia.

Berkeley had been appointed to this post with misgivings as to his capabilities on the part of the government in London, but he was valuable because he voted the right way in the Commons whenever his sea duties allowed him to be present and, what was more, his MP brother voted the right way, too, and led others with him. Accordingly, Berkeley arrived in Halifax to take up his new command in early 1806, and at once began to write down a lengthy sequence of complaints and criticisms against not only the Americans, and Jefferson in particular, but also the Admiralty. Ignoring the usual diplomatic channels, he sent these letters directly to Grenville. He expressed the opinion that America would back down if Britain stood firm, and the first *Chesapeake* report did nothing to change that opinion. He issued an order that "required and directed" his officers in case of meeting with the American frigate the *Chesapeake* at Sea, and without the limits of the United States to shew to the Captain of her this order; and to require to search his Ship for the deserters.

He handed the order to Captain Salisbury P. Humphreys and sent him, in his own flagship, HMS *Leopard,* to carry it to Norfolk, where the *Chesapeake* and other United States ships were in harbor at the time. Humphreys arrived off the Virginia port on June 21.

Next day the *Chesapeake* put to sea, bound for the Mediterranean. As soon as she passed the three-mile limit, the *Leopard* hailed her. *Chesapeake* obediently hove to, and Lieutenant John Meade went on board to hand Commodore Barron a copy of Berkeley's order, together with a note from Humphreys saying that he hoped the matter could be peaceably settled. Barron read both order and note in some bewilderment. The discussion in the commodore's cabin got nowhere, and Meade reported back to Humphreys, who harangued Barron for a while through the hailing trumpet and then, apparently losing patience, fired a shot across the bow of the *Chesapeake.* What happened next was reported by Humphreys later: "Conceiving that my Orders would not admit of deviation, I lament to state, that, I felt under the necessity of enforcing them, by firing into the United States Ship." The *Leopard* opened fire with some of her fifty guns, in ten minutes killing three and wounding eighteen men on the *Chesapeake,* at which point Barron struck his colors. A second boarding party crossed over, lined up the American crew, and removed four men, including Ratford, who was forcibly dragged out of hiding.

The measure of the uproar produced by this unfortunate and highly undiplomatic incident is shown by the panicky behavior of the British government. In an uncharacteristic flurry it entirely disowned the action of the *Leopard,* promised compensation to the wounded and to the next of kin of the dead, undertook to repatriate the four arrested men, and loudly stated that it had never believed itself free to search warships. For good measure, it recalled Berkeley to England.

But London was a long way from the storm center. Humphreys had indeed arrested only four men of the many deserters known to be on the *Chesapeake,* and may be said to have acted with moderation, but it was not as simple as that. Two of the deserters were Negroes, who had originally been enlisted in the United States Navy, had deserted from that in 1806 , and had now reneged again. The third man was also an American. The wretched Ratford was taken back under arrest to Halifax, where he was hanged. Humphreys, because of his restraint in arresting only four, was placed on half pay. Presumably had he arrested none his pay would have been stopped altogether. The Americans cut off supplies to the Royal Navy at Norfolk (it was naval practice to revictual at every port that would agree to supplying the ships), the British responded by interfering ever more frequently with American shipping, and the American press clamored for satisfaction. One leading example was that of the *Enquirer* of Richmond, Virginia, whose editor, Thomas Ritchie, curtailed his honeymoon to rush back and write scorching editorials.

The row spread rapidly. Militia patrolled the coasts to prevent supplies being smuggled to the British, and when one British crew put a boat ashore to look for provisions they were captured by a young lance-corporal aged twenty called Winfield Scott. In New York, Consul Barclay's house had to be put under police protection, and a street mob collected at the harbor, smashed up guns on a British ship, cut its rigging, and carried off the sails and the rudder. Crowded public meetings shouted for war, including one gathering of two thousand angry people in Federalist Boston. Many Americans expected war to break out at once. William Wirt wrote to Peachey R. Gilmer on July 18, 1807:

> The probability of war is very strong: because it is scarcely presumable that British arrogance and injustice will give us that satisfaction which alone will appease the spirit of this nation—and between the alternatives of war and dishonorable surrender, our countrymen will not long hesitate.

Some British in their turn were infuriated by the American action. Berkeley himself thought that a sharp British attack on New York would put the rebel colonists where they belonged. One English commentator, Anthony Steel, described the *Chesapeake* scathingly as "a kind of fly-paper for picking up deserters and other wandering British seamen." But the flames soon began to die down. By September the French minister wrote disparagingly about the "fear and servile deference" shown by America to Britain.

The furor roused by the *Chesapeake* affair prompted Canada to call out the militia, though the achievement of this was often amazingly slow. Thomas Dunn in Quebec managed to do it more than a year after the incident. This exasperated the man who had invited him to take on the job, the colonel of the Forty-Ninth Foot, who was not only acting commander of the forces at the time, but also one of the most remarkable soldiers every produced in Canada: Isaac Brock.

Born in Guernsey in the Channel Islands on October 6, 1769, the youngest of eight brothers in an acutely military family, Brock had joined the army at the age of fifteen. By twenty-eight he was lieutenant colonel of the Forty-Ninth, leading it in the Low Countries, where the regiment distinguished itself in action at Egmont-op-Zee in 1799, and two years later at Copenhagen, where the army's part was overshadowed by that of the Royal Navy. In 1802 Brock took the Forty-Ninth to Canada, where they garrisoned Montreal, York, Fort George, and Quebec. Brock showed energy and a capacity for provoking and dealing with trouble, at one time putting down a mutiny by shooting its ringleaders and at another rowing all night across part of Lake Ontario in pursuit of some deserters, whom he caught and brought back, earning a reprimand for taking the law into his own hands, instead of correctly referring the matter to his superior officer. He was severe with defaulters and suspicious of possible treachery, but humane and kindly toward all other soldiers, an alert, positive, lively bachelor with a strong will and a liking for bold action. In a letter to one of his brothers he expressed this last point:

> I must see service, or I may as well, and indeed much better, quit the army at once, for no one advantage can I reasonably look to hereafter if I remain buried in this inactive, remote corner, without the slightest mention being made of me.

But this mood of despondency did not last. Brock was promoted to Major General in 1810, and on October 9, 1811 to Administrator of the Forces as a replacement to Francis Gore. Gore announced that he had to return to England to attend to private business, so Brock was duly promoted to cover Gore's absence. This was to last longer than anyone expected: Gore remained in England until the time of Waterloo, by which time the Anglo-American War was over. Brock's change of mood is reflected in a letter to the commander in chief in 1811:

> Being now placed in a high ostensible situation, and the state of public affairs with the American government indicating a strong presumption of an approaching rupture between the two countries, I beg leave to be allowed to remain in my present command.

He was too valuable to lose. His three years of garrison duty had made him familiar with the great spaces of his territory, so thinly defended. He speculated about how many ferryboats could carry how many invading troops; he wondered about the Indians who, as he noted after Tippecanoe, "are eager to avenge their injuries." He saw the French-Canadian fur traders and trappers and wondered whether they would declare for self-interest or go over to the enemy. He worried about the French. He worked hard at the defenses of Quebec. By the end of 1811 there were eight cannon of thirty-six pound caliber mounted on the Citadel; a battery of twenty-four pounders overlooking the St. Lawrence; bastions guarding the heights; guns positioned on Mountain Street; and cannon at the gates, the heaviest at Lower Town, Palace, and Hope Gates. He was sure that the Americans, who after all outnumbered the Canadians by more than thirty-five to one, could all too easily invade his province and strike at Quebec. Optimistic comments south of the border seemed in part to justify this opinion. Henry Clay declared: "I trust I shall not be presumptuous when I state that I verily believe that the militia of Kentucky are on their own competent to place Montreal and Upper Canada at your feet." And the great Thomas Jefferson himself, in a letter to the Philadelphia publisher William Duane, remarked that "an advance to Quebec would be a mere matter of marching."

Brock longed to press his defensive actions further. He fretted over the isolated little settlements that, it seemed to him, could so effortlessly be scooped up by an enemy on the attack. Those closest to the border naturally worried him the most, particularly Amherstburg. This tiny place, consisting of about one hundred little houses, a warehouse or two, and a handful of berths for boats, was within easy striking distance of Detroit. Detroit was hardly bigger or better protected than Amherstburg, but Brock, surveying the position with the eye of an experienced garrison commander, expected the Americans to strengthen it at any time, and wanted to capture it before that could happen. He wrote:

> Unless Detroit be in our hands at the commencement of hostilities, not only the district of Amherstburg, but most probably the whole country as far as Kingston, must be evacuated.

Sir George Prevost urged caution, tact, and prudence:

> Whatever temptations may offer to induce you to depart from a system strictly defensive, I must pointedly request that under the existing

circumstances of our relationship with the Government of the United States, you must not allow them to lead you into any measure bearing on the character of offence.

If he could not take positive offensive action, Brock could at least express his ideas on defense to Prevost. In December 1811 he sent Prevost a letter saying that, while the frontier guards were patently weak, few people expected them to make any sort of stand against attack, but "the late increase of ammunition and every species of stores, the substitution of a strong regiment, and the appointment of a military person to administer the government, have tended to infuse other sentiments among the most reflecting part of the community." The strong regiment was the Forty-First and, of course, the military person was himself. "But," he went on, "before we can expect an active co-operation on the part of the Indians, the reduction of Detroit and Michilimackinac must convince our people . . . that we are earnestly engaged in the war." He still refused to give up the hope of annexing Detroit. He reinforced these points by urging increases in the Provincial Marine on Lake Ontario and on Lake Erie as well, to deter a possible American infiltration along the Niagara River.

Prevost's comparatively cautious, urbane, and pacific temperament led him to hold Brock back, but so did his orders from the Prince Regent, which absolutely forbade him to attack and said he was not even to fight except in dire emergency. His reply to Brock was typical: he agreed that it would be a good thing to capture Detroit and Michilimackinac by a swift surprise stroke, but just now the Americans seemed divided about the questions of war and peace and it would be foolish to offend them if offense could be avoided.

He did agree with Brock that Quebec was the key, and that "every other Military operation ought to become subservient" to the safety of that city.

Defective as Quebec is, it is the only post that can be considered as tenable for a moment, the preservation of it being of the utmost consequences to the Canadas, as the door of Entry for that Force the King's Government might find it expedient to send for the recovery of both, or either of these Provinces, altho the pressure of the moment in the present Extended range of Warfare, might not allow the sending of that force which would defend both, therefore considering Quebec in this view, its importance can at once be appreciated.

If the Americans are determined to attack Canada, it would be in vain the

General should flatter himself with the hopes of making an effectual defence of the open Country, unless powerfully assisted from Home:—All predatory or ill concerted attacks undertaken presumptuously without sufficient means can be resisted and repulsed:—Still this must be done with caution, that the resources, for a future exertion, the defence of Quebec, may be unexhausted.

The province of New Brunswick and the peninsula of Nova Scotia present so many vulnerable points to an invading army, that it is difficult to establish any precise Plan for the defence of either, and consequently much must depend upon Contingencies in the event of invasion:—Their security very materially depends upon the Navy, and the vigilance of our Cruizers in the Bay of Fundy.

The core of Prevost's defense troops, the Forty-First and the Forty-Ninth, were due to go back to England soon, but he did at least know that, if war broke out, he could keep them, together with those regiments sent out as their replacement.

Lieutenant General Sir George Prevost came, like Brock, of a military family. His father had been wounded at Quebec in 1759, and had fought gallantly at Savannah against the French and the Americans in 1778, although he was a French-speaking Swiss by nationality. The family was Protestant, however, so this may at least partially explain their allegiance. Prevost's father was a lieutenant colonel in the Royal American regiment, whose officers were mostly Swiss, and stationed in New Jersey, in 1767, when his eldest son was born on May 19. The boy was sent to England and educated there, with the customary Grand Tour, and commissioned in the army a month after his sixteenth birthday; he fought in (among other places) the West Indies, where he did well enough to become a full colonel in 1798, then a brigadier general, and Governor of St. Lucia. After that island was returned to France by the 1802 Treaty of Amiens, Prevost led the successful defense of Dominica in 1805, for which he was made a major general and a baronet. He spent two years in England and, after the *Chesapeake* incident, was sent to Nova Scotia as a lieutenant governor and commander. He had married an Englishwoman. He was appointed to Craig's place not only because of the turbulent events in Lower Canada but because of the turn for the worse in Anglo-American relations, for the government in London believed, with good reason, that his unhurried temper, his suavely diplomatic manner, and his natural charm would help to stave off, if not to prevent, an open breach. He arrived in Quebec on September 13, 1811 as

Captain-General and Governor in Chief in and over the Provinces of Upper and Lower Canada, New-Brunswick, and Nova-Scotia, and the Islands of Prince Edward and Cape Breton, and their several Dependencies, Vice-Admiral of the same, Lieutenant-General and Commander of all His Majesty's Forces in the Provinces of Lower and Upper Canada, Nova-Scotia and New-Brunswick, and in the Islands of Prince Edward, Cape Breton, Newfoundland and the Bermudas.

Craig wearily gave up that resounding position to Prevost, and before sailing back to England issued a parting warning to the British Chargé in Washington about the Indian menace. This, he said, should be passed on to the United States government. It was hardly necessary: the Lexington *Reporter,* of December 10, 1811 sounded a blast that referred to this in conjunction with American economic problems:

The SCALPING KNIFE and TOMAHAWK of *British savages, is now again devastating our frontiers. Hemp* at three dollars. *Cotton* at twelve dollars. *Tobacco* at nine shillings. Thus will our farmers, and wives and children, continue to be *ruined* and *murdered,* whilst those half-way, *quid,* execrable measures and delays preponderate.

Craig had honestly believed that he was administering a conquered country which had to be taught to be English. Prevost, a good deal more farseeing, calmed matters down considerably during his first months in office. He called off the pro-British campaigners, appointed many French Canadians to the army and the bench, and placated the militants enough to make sure that Lower Canada stayed loyal in 1812.

Three of Prevost's new members of the Legislative Council were French Canadians, and two of the seven new members of the Executive Council. He enlarged the status of Bishop Plessis as head of the Catholic clergy in the province, though this move provoked the enmity of the Church of England Bishop Mountain. He went out of his way to meet the principal traders and merchants of Montreal. Behind his placid, chubby face his mind shrewdly acknowledged that all these persons were more or less self-seeking opportunists, but he moved as smoothly as events would permit him on his diplomatic path. At the same time he had to hold back the impetuous Brock and look at the defenses for himself. He toured the forts, got London's permission to carry on Craig's defensive works, asked for two hundred extra saddles and bridles and sabers, and for ten thousand more muskets. He was somewhat disconcerted to learn that most of the

Canadian military supplies were bought from the Americans. But all the time he knew that the central dilemma of his position was the eternal colonial governor's problem, the question that was to bedevil (for example) Singapore in 1941: not enough strength to hold on against invasion until reinforcements could be spared, equipped, and sent to the rescue. And the St. Lawrence was full of ice in winter.

James Madison—N.Y. *Public Library Picture Collection*

James Monroe–N.Y. *Public Library Picture Collection*

POLICE.

WHEREAS authentic intelligence has been received that the Government of the United States of America did, on the 18th instant, declare War against the United Kingdom of Great Britain and Ireland and its dependencies, Notice is hereby given, that all Subjects or Citizens of the said United States, and all persons claiming American Citizenship, are ordered to quit the City of Quebec, on or before **TWELVE** o'clock at Noon, on **WEDNESDAY** next, and the District of Quebec on or before 12 o'clock at noon on **FRIDAY** next, on pain of arrest.

ROSS CUTHBERT,
C. Q. S. & Inspector of Police.

The Constables of the City of Quebec are ordered to assemble in the Police Office at 10 o'clock to-morrow morning, to receive instructions.

Quebec, 29th June, 1812.

A Proclamation—*McCord Museum, Montreal*

Henry Clay–N.Y. *Public Library Picture Collection*

Winfield Scott–N.Y. *Public Library Picture Collection*

Lieutenant General Sir George Prevost–*The Public Archives of Canada*

Sir Isaac Brock–*The Public Archives of Canada*

The Battle of Queenston, October 13, 1812–*The Public Archives of Canada*

Lieutenant General Sir John Cope Sherbrooke–*The Public Archives of Canada*

Oliver Hazard Perry–*N.Y. Public Library Picture Collection*

Vice Admiral Sir Alexander Inglis Cochrane–*The Public Archives of Canada*

Rear Admiral George Cockborn–*The National Maritime Museum, London*

Brigadier General William H. Winder–*N.Y. Public Library Picture Collection*

The capture of the city of Washington by British forces, August 24, 1814–*Courtesy of The New York Historical Society, New York City*

Francis Scott Key—*N.Y. Public Library Picture Collection*

A view of the bombardment of Fort McHenry by the British fleet, September 13, 1814—*Courtesy of the New York Historical Society, New York City*

The Battle of New Orleans–*N.Y. Public Library Picture Collection*

Andrew Jackson–*N.Y. Public Library Picture Collection*

Letter from John Quincy Adams to his mother on the Treaty of Ghent–*Massachusetts Historical Society*

N. 67. Mrs A. Adams. Quincy.

Ghent 24. December 1814.

My dear and honoured mother.

A Treaty of Peace between the United States and Great Britain has this day been signed by the British and American Plenipotentiaries at this place. It is to be dispatched to morrow, by Mr Hughes the Secretary of the American Mission, who is to sail in the Transit from Bordeaux – I have not time to write a single private Letter excepting this, but I request you to inform my brother that I have received his Letter of 2. October brought by Mr William Wyer to France. I was much disappointed in not receiving either by him, or by the Ajax, the second Dutch vessel arrived from Boston, any Letter from you – I have none later than that of 1. May.

You know doubtless that heretofore the President intended in case of Peace, to send me to England – If the Treaty should be ratified I am uncertain whether he will still retain the same intention or not – I have requested to be recalled at all Events from the Mission to Russia. I shall proceed from this place, in a few days, to Paris, to be there, in readiness to receive the President's orders; and I shall write immediately to my wife, requesting her to come and join me there. If we go to England I beg you to send my Sons George and John there to me – After the Peace there can be no want of good opportunities for them to come, and I wish them to embark at the most favourable Season for a safe passage. If any other person should be sent to England, I intend to return as soon as possible to America, and shall hope before midsummer to see once more my beloved Parents.

Of the Peace which we have at length concluded, it is for our Government, our Country and the world to judge – It is not such, as under more propitious circumstances might have been expected, and to be fairly estimated must be compared not with our desires, but with what the situation of the parties and of the world at and during the Negotiation made attainable – We have abandoned no essential right, and if we have left every thing open for future controversy, we have at least secured to our Country the power, at her own option to extinguish the War.

With my duty to my dear father, I remain your ever affectionate Son. John Quincy Adams.

John Quincy Adams on the Treaty of Ghent, 1814

FIVE

§

Outbreak

Of course anybody whose fate it is to succeed a great man has a hard time of it. James Madison has been described as high-principled and honest, distinguished for his work on the Constitution, a thinker, a scholar, a well-read man of learning—all admirable qualities, but following Jefferson without any of Jefferson's flair and forcefulness, he failed to impress. He has been described as having a puzzled look, and at no time did he appear likely to take America by the scruff of the neck, a quality usually looked for in a wartime leader. This lack of obvious leadership struck some Republicans even before the inauguration, and one of them, Nathaniel Macon, wrote despondently on February 28, 1809: "The Lord the Mighty Lord must come to our Assistance, or I fear we are undone as a nation."

Madison was seen to be pale and trembling with nerves as he began his inaugural speech, and tiredly spiritless at the ball that night. He displayed a lack of resolution in making his cabinet appointments, antagonized many by leaving Albert Gallatin at the Treasury and by appointing Senator Samuel Smith's brother, Robert Smith, utterly incapable according to majority opinion, to the State Department, which meant in practice that the President would have to do much of the work. Madison is described by the historian Bradford Perkins as reluctant to do this. Congress was divided as badly as was the Whig party in England. Madison himself, writing to William Pinkney on February 11, 1809, remarked upon it.

> You will see with regret the difficulty experienced in collecting the mind of Congress into some proper focus. On no occasion were the ideas so unstable and so scattered.

The luckless embargo was repealed, to the accompaniment of many predictions. Some men expected war to follow; some dreaded that it might; some feared that after all, America might not be able to save face by fighting. The disgrace of America's quick knuckling-down, as most men in government saw America's eagerness to make a settlement with the high-handed demands of Britain, stung many into proposing fresh plans, and by the end of February the Non-Intercourse Act had passed both Houses. It was passed by default rather than by any particular merit, or even support, it could claim to have, being a kind of lowest common denominator of what Congress as a whole might be induced to accept for lack of anything better.

The Act, while it killed off the embargo, stopped trade with British and French possessions, yet permitted it with either as soon as American ships were not violated anymore, and closed American ports to armed ships of both nations. It was a compromise measure, patched up out of pieces of various proposals, and it at once called out the stern disapproval of John Randolph:

> We have trusted our most precious interests in this leaky vessel, and now, by way of amendment, we are going to bore additional holes in this machine, which, like a cask, derives all its value, if it have any, from being water-tight.

Certainly the Act allowed greater latitude to Britain than had the embargo, and it restricted the French as well, so it was not surprising to know that Englishmen considered it something of a moral victory. American ships once again entered British ports. The reconstruction of the British government under Spencer Perceval in the summer of 1809, however, pushed American affairs into the background for a time in London. Meanwhile, the French went on seizing American ships, and once again America's warlike emotions cooled against Britain, aided by the hope that the new British Administration might prove to be more favorably disposed toward America than its predecessor had been.

By November 1809, when Gallatin's annual Treasury statement showed a trade deficit for the first time for years, it seemed depressingly clear that America must either return to complete embargo or give up trying to restrict the trade of foreigners with the United States. Gallatin drafted a bill which Nathaniel Macon introduced, so that in time it became known as Macon's Bill Number One. It allowed United States merchant ships to go freely anywhere, and allowed British and French goods to be imported in American ships, but closed

American ports to both British and French vessels. This prohibition would be relaxed if either power repealed its decrees; presumably, that is, relaxed in favor of the repealing power. This part of the bill was unrealistic in that French ships did not come to America because of the Royal Navy, and, indeed, British ships did not come all that frequently. On the other hand, Macon's Bill Number One did give the chance of raising more money by allowing American ships to trade anywhere, but many were doing this already, permission or not.

Peace-loving Federalists opposed the bill because of the measures they feared England might take against it. War-hoping Republicans opposed the bill because it was not spirited enough in matter and tone. Others, however, backed it, either because it might provoke war with England through American commerce with France, or because it would mean that the English, with their victorious navy, could get goods through while the French could not, a situation that rejoiced the pro-British Federalists.

The bill was passed by seventy-three votes to fifty-two after three weeks' discussion. The Senate, who received it next, tore it to shreds and, after five weeks' deadlock, a miserable new compromise, called Macon's Bill Number Two,* although he had little or nothing to do with it, was drafted. This compromise bill was based upon proposals made by Congressman John Taylor of South Carolina. He suggested abolishing all trade restrictions and promising to re-introduce a trade ban against any European power that continued to harass American shipping. It seemed to many Americans that this bill was an unhappy blend of surrender and bribery in that it promised rewards for good behavior after letting down trade barriers. To the satisfaction of nobody, as Josiah Quincy said, came

> a sort of bargain that, if the Senate would agree not to protect commerce, the House would agree not to burden the people with an additional tax;

and the new Act passed both Houses in May 1810. The British Consul at Norfolk, Virginia, commented:

> After the Hurricane of Passion in which the Congress opened their Session, it is truly laughable to witness the miserable feeble Puff, in which they evaporated.

The British, thinking the new Act humiliated America (as many

* See Appendix VI

Americans themselves thought too), looked forward to increased profits.

Napoleon, after one clear look, proclaimed the Rambouillet Decree (March 23, 1810), ordering all American ships seized that entered French ports, whether or not they had previously entered British ports or been searched by the Royal Navy. He followed this on August 5, 1810 with the Trianon Decree, in which he said that United States ships so seized by the French would be sold, and their cargoes too. For some reason this decree was not made public to the Americans (indeed, Gallatin himself never received a copy until 1821) and only vague rumors reached America that United States ships would find themselves in trouble if they visited French ports. There was nothing in Macon's Bill Number Two, or in the reports of the new Napoleonic decrees, to make the British readier to repeal their Orders in Council. After all, as one American gloomily remarked, it was impossible to seize the trident from George or the thunderbolt from Napoleon.

Madison's whole attitude had been shaped by his belief that America could only expect humiliation if she tried to take on both great powers at once; he found that she was going to feel humiliated anyway. The French grew increasingly hostile, the British became more finicking in their insistence on details of American conduct and attitudes. By the end of 1810 England had stumbled into one of her periodic economic crises, which caused Congress to consider a revised Non-Intercourse Act, proposed by Congressman John Eppes. This assumed on no secure grounds that France was willing to modify her blockade of neutrals trading with the British and to reassert the rights of neutral ships whether searched by the Royal Navy or not (thereby abandoning great parts of the Berlin and Milan decrees), and assumed, also, that everyone concerned would allow America to prohibit British trade until the Orders in Council were repealed yet, somehow at the same time, continuing to send goods to England in American ships and to bring produce back. The Eppes Act was heatedly debated but, after an all-night sitting, was pushed through the House of Representatives at dawn on February 28, 1811, and then passed the Senate and received the President's signature within a matter of hours.

The newspapers of both Britain and the United States now adopted a more consciously pugnacious tone. The Washington *National Intelligencer* said that if both France and England continued their aggressions "we must eventually set them both at defiance." The London *Courier* snapped: "As long as BONAPARTE persists in his present system, we warn all Powers that the Continent is in a state of blockade, and they must not presume to trade with it without our leave."

English merchants, alarmed for their trade, asked for the Orders to be repealed, but the British government refused. Persistent rumors and unofficial confidential statements–oral or written–suggested that the French had decided to relax their decrees; but the British government never quite accepted these. Madison, in the eyes of many of his countrymen, appeared weak, vacillating, and far too ready to conciliate the French. Many Americans believed that war was now inevitable: either the British would declare it, or America's refusal to stand boldly against the French would provoke the British to believe that America had forfeited her neutrality once and for all. No face-saving way out except through war seemed possible to many Americans. As a result of this hardening of opinion, the elections, which followed the Eleventh Congress's leaving of office in March 1811, showed that those who preached negotiation were now unpopular, and those who stood for war were higher in the people's favor.

Not to everyone, though. Thomas Jefferson, who had signified his retirement by cutting down his newspaper subscriptions, wrote to Monroe that "the people are unmoved by these clamours"; and, if some observers said that new thrusting young men were coming in on the waves of the people's will, the figures showed that the average age of the Twelfth Congress was almost exactly that of the Eleventh (forty-six instead of forty-seven) and that it had returned eighty-three former members and fifty-nine new ones, three old members fewer than its predecessor. The actual composition of the new Congress was mixed; but assemblies carry their own dynamic, and the Twelfth Congress certainly gave an impression of fresh vigor. In one important respect at least the United States government was truly more vigorous: the unfortunate Robert Smith had left the State Department. He had leaked his government's secrets, openly criticized his government's policy, given unfair preference to his brother's group, and quarreled face-to-face as well as in the newspapers with Gallatin, even encouraging a running battle between his wife and Gallatin's wife. Smith's place was taken by the future fifth President, James Monroe.

Monroe, a big, well-proportioned fellow with chiseled features and a mobile mouth that could readily twist in contempt or sardonic amusement, had served with dashing competence in the War of Independence and was, indeed, a born man of action. The bustle of politics was a magnet to him: he longed to be of use. In accepting Madison's offer he knew that it would bring him into a position to try for the presidency, that he could help to restore party unity, and that Madison really needed him. In addition he believed that he could genuinely affect American policy toward Britain. He hoped to bring about a peaceful settlement.

Monroe began work at the State Department on the morning of April 6, 1811. In just over a month a spectacular clash at sea pulled the new secretary into his first real test.

Senator Samuel Smith, brother of the ex-Secretary of State Robert Smith, described the situation in a letter to his son John.

> We are all in a Bustle in Consequence of the Cruel Conduct of Four British Cruizers who have been off the Coast for these few weeks. They press the Young Men from our Coasters and in one Instance a Young Man who had never been at sea before. Indeed the Impres$ments can no longer be tolerated. Pusyllanimity has been Charged on the President. Few desire that War should follow, but if it should, the Nation will meet it on this Ground with Alacrity. All parties are outraged. . .

Impressment went back, with the British, at least unofficially, into the mists of time; with the Americans, for the better part of twenty years. On this occasion, in obedience to presidential standing orders, Commodore John Rodgers, the lively, aggressive commander of one of America's few warships, the USS *President,* sailed out of Norfolk, Virginia, to recover, if he could, the impressed Americans. It appears unlikely in the extreme that he had been told to take them by force, but the newspapers thought he had, and simmered accordingly. Rodgers had a long way to sail before he came up with the British ships, but just after sunset on May 16 he overhauled the British sloop HMS *Little Belt,* and the two vessels exchanged shots. After a short time the *Little Belt* struck her colors. Nine of her crew were dead and twenty-three wounded. When the reports reached America, the facts were obscured by rumor and speculation, for it was impossible to determine which ship had fired first, and it was widely believed that the *President* had mistaken the *Little Belt* for HM frigate *Guerrière,* though how an experienced captain like Rodgers could mistake a sloop for a frigate *, even in the fading light of a spring evening, is hard to understand. No doubt, however, existed about the reactions on both sides of the Atlantic. America believed that the Englishman had fired first, and crowed with delight at the salutary lesson he had been given; Britain thought that the big American bully had (typically) started the attack on the smaller ship. English papers morosely reported the offensive American statement that

She Stoops to Conquer, or the Mistakes of a Night, a new play with an old title, was performed with *loud* applause off the Capes of Virginia, by the frigate *President,* and a British picaroon, to the gratification of all America.

Undeniably this event gave both nations one more push toward an eventual state of war.

Madison's message to Congress seemed to have paved the way. He had asked for increased military forces and supplies, saying:

The period is arrived, which claims from the legislative guardians of the national rights a system of more ample provisions for maintaining them. Notwithstanding the scrupulous justice, the protracted moderation, and the multiplied efforts on the part of the United States to substitute for the accumulating dangers to the peace of the two countries, all the mutual advantages of re-established friendship and confidence; we have seen that the British Cabinet perseveres, not only in withholding a remedy for other wrongs so long and so loudly calling for it; but in the execution; brought home to the threshold of our territory, of measures which, under existing circumstances, have the character, as well as the effect, of war on our lawful commerce. With this evidence of hostile inflexibility, in trampling on rights which no independent nation can relinquish,–Congress will feel the duty of putting the United States into an armour, and an attitude demanded by the crisis.

With these words from the thoughtful little President, it is not surprising that the more belligerent members of Congress had leaped into a warlike posture. The War-Hawks, as they were called, bugled for action and action, to them, meant striking at the one readily available piece of British territory–Canada. The events at Tippecanoe brought

* According to the dictionary definition, a frigate was a warship next in size to a ship of the line, with anything from 28 to 60 guns, and a raised quarterdeck and forecastle, while a sloop was a small one-masted vessel, with fore-and-aft rigging, mainsail, and jib.

the Indian menace into the scales, and the press clamored for action against

> the tomahawk and scalping knife, which for many years past, and at this very moment the inhuman blood-thirsty Cabinet of St. James had incessantly endeavoured to bring on the *women* and *children* of our western frontiers,

asserting that "British intrigue and British gold" had more power over the Indians than (despite Tippecanoe, presumably) "American justice and benevolence." The Lexington *Reporter* announced that "The *whole* body of Western citizens call for the probing of this British villiny to the bottom."

The Philadelphia *Aurora* chimed in:

> War has been begun with British arms and by the Indians instigated by British emissaries. The blood of American citizens have already been shed in actual war, begun undeclared.

A man called Andrew Jackson blamed "Secrete agents" of Britain; and Monroe, listening to the gathering storm, commented:

> War, dreadful as the alternative is, could not do us more injury than the present state of things, and it would certainly be more honourable to the Nation, and gratifying to the publick feelings.

With the War-Hawks shouting more and more loudly for action, which they emphasized would be easy, the French minister in Washington, Louis Sérurier, cheerfully wrote to his chief, the French Minister of Foreign Relations:

> That which pleases me most in these people, Monseigneur, is the tranquil confidence they have in their means of aggression and resistance.

The Americans believed, or professed to believe, that the Indians would not attack them unless "instigated by British mercenaries." Actually Britain was more concerned with keeping the Indians friendly to themselves than with urging them on against others, for they knew only too well that yesterday's allies can easily become tomorrow's foes. Castlereagh summed up the government's views in his note: "We are to consider not so much their Use as Allies, as their Destructiveness if Enemies."

Sir Isaac Brock told Indian chiefs that British supplies to them would be cut off if they fought against the Americans; presumably this meant if they fought on their own account, because no one discounted the possibility of the Indians being incorporated in British forces, if war with America did come. Also, it is clear that to draw the line between keeping the Indians friendly, and encouraging them to repel anyone who seemed to threaten them, was difficult, perhaps impossible.

Madison's call for men and arms was answered by various authorizations from Congress to call out volunteers for both the regular army and the militia in huge numbers: over 30,000 short-term enlisted men, up to 80,000 militia. Practice fell short of theory. By the eleventh hour–early June 1812–the United States Army consisted of 6,744 officers and men and the newly recruited groups had not passed 5,000, many of whom in both categories were entirely without experience or completed training.

It did not look like this to Sir George Prevost. By the time the reports from the United States reached him, they sounded positively menacing, and he worriedly counted his forces. Like those of Madison, these were mostly on paper, but Prevost did not realize that the unfortunate facts facing him applied equally to his potential adversary. Much of the Canadian militia, where it existed in flesh and not just on lists as unreliable in their analysis as election canvassing returns, was untrained, poorly equipped, and scattered piecemeal over miles of country. Prevost accordingly put the pressure to draw up a new Militia Act on his government superiors, who responded by allowing him two thousand bachelors selected by lot from Lower Canada's 18–25 age range, to train for ninety days in two successive summers and, if war came, to serve thereupon for two years; they also voted him twelve thousand pounds for defense spending, and another thirty thousand if war broke out. On his own responsibility Prevost ordered the raising of a new battalion of Fencibles in Glengarry County, Upper Canada, under Captain "Red George" Macdonell of the King's regiment. Captain Macdonell set to work with such a will that the recruitment soon totaled 600 instead of the 376 originally asked for: a force this size meant that they had to have a colonel in command, so Prevost, instead of promoting Macdonell, named his own adjutant, Colonel Edward Baynes, to the post, with Major Francis Battersby of the King's regiment as lieutenant colonel. He promoted Macdonell to the rank of major.

Prevost also ordered a Provincial Corps of Light Infantry to be raised. His principal military aide was a colorful figure with a resounding title: Major General Franz de Rottenburg, a German baron born in Danzig fifty-four years before, who had fought in Louis XVI's and Kościuszko's armies in Europe. A soldier of fortune, he had come into the British Army in 1795 by way of one of its foreign corps, and in 1798 had raised, and commanded, a battalion in the British Royal American regiments. He was the author of a book, written in German, on rifle and infantry drill, which had come to the favorable attention of the Duke of York. Now he was very close to the peak of Canadian military power. His aide-de-camp was a French-speaking captain with the rank of brevet-major, Charles Michel de Salaberry, who with other members of his family, had an excellent record of service on behalf of the British government. Prevost picked de Salaberry to raise the new Provincial Corps, choosing his six captains and eighteen lieutenants from "the most respectable Families in the Province," each captain to recruit thirty-six men, each lieutenant to find sixteen, all between the ages of seventeen and thirty-six, and all taller than five-feet-three. Every recruit would get a bounty of four pounds, and a promise of fifty acres of land on eventual discharge. Major de Salaberry had no trouble at all (to judge by the Quebec *Gazette)*:

> This Corps now forming under Major De Salaberry, is completing with a dispatch worthy of the ancient warlike spirit of the Country. Captain Perrault's company was filled up in 48 hours, and was yesterday passed by His Excellency the Governor; and the companies of Captains Duchesnay, Panet, and L'Ecuyer, have very nearly their complement. The young men move in solid columns towards the enlisting officers, with an expression of countenance not to be mistaken.

But as a matter of cold fact, only 309 of the required 538 men had moved toward the enlisting officers by the first week of June 1812.

Brock, who tried to prod Upper Canada into making similar pledges to those of Lower Canada, thought his comparative lack of success was because of "the numerous settlers from the United States" who dwelt there, but at least he was authorized to form flank companies. (A flank company had forty-one men, a captain, two lieutenants, two sergeants, a drummer, and thirty-five other ranks.) Their main use was, he wrote:

> to have constantly in readiness, a force composed of Loyal, Brave, and Respectable Young Men, so far instructed as to enable the Government, on

any emergency, to engraft such portions of the Militia as may be necessary, on a stock capable of giving aid in forming them for Military service.

They were to parade three times a month, and train six days a month, unpaid, but with one strong allurement:

A volunteer should not be liable to any personal Arrest on any Civil Process, or to serve as Juror, or to perform duty as a Town or Parish Officer, or Statute labour on the Highways, during the time he shall continue in such flank Companies.

In addition they were to be uniformed: each man should equip himself with "a Short Coat of some dark coloured Cloth made to button well round the body, and Pantaloons suited to the season, with the addition of a Round Hat."

Prevost prepared a statement on the military situation as he saw it, which he sent to the Earl of Liverpool in May 1812.* It set out his appreciation of the position in detail, both in matters of defense and of readiness, and showed his own qualities as well as how thorough he was. He felt sure that if the Americans attacked Canada they would head first for Montreal. That was why the city bristled with guns; but Prevost knew that the safety of the city depended on an outer defense line of soldiers and supply, and a large enough flotilla of ships to protect the St. Lawrence. Here, surely, the Americans could not put up much of a challenge.

By 1811 the main issues between Britain and the United States were Canada, and the Orders in Council, the first stemming from the other. Loss of trade and falling markets and profits alerted more Americans to think of war than did impressment, though the steady trickle of seizures still found newspaper space. The tone of this had changed, however, and editors grumbled that Americans were taking the capture of American citizens for granted. Ship actions, if accompanied by a little drama, could still whip up sentiment. When HMS *Tartarus,* looking for deserters, captured two American merchant vessels off Norfolk in August 1811 and then sailed into the port to restock, the British Consul, alarmed by the angry crowd gathering in the streets, scribbled a note which he managed to get to the commander of the *Tartarus,* saying: "For God-sake if you are not already gone–get to sea as fast as you can," whereupon the commander

* See Appendix VII

prudently made off. But the War-Hawks' threats to Canada made, in general, the loudest sound. Repeatedly they stated that "the object of all our military preparations" was to retaliate against Britain by "an invasion of her provinces, as the only quarter in which she is vulnerable," and that unless Britain repealed the Orders "the most valuable of all her colonies" would be "torn from her grasp." When in 1811 it was seen, for example, that the price level of exports from the port of New Orleans alone had fallen by one-third in four years, these clamors resounded more steadily and noisily than ever.

It was at this point that a new personage appeared upon the stage of events: the new British envoy in Washington. Since the recall of Erskine and Jackson the post had been held by a stopgap, John Philip Morier, an agreeable and well-connected young man who had behaved with moderation in Washington in spite of having written, when appointed: "I had rather get into a soupe, by a conduct spirited and spurning at their infamous proceedings towards us, than by one of the milk and water kind," meaning that he would rather cause trouble by positive reactions to American hostility than by insipid behavior. But Morier was a mere Chargé; and this was not good enough for America. In fact Madison considered it so derogatory that he recalled William Pinkney from London. Just as Pinkney left, the new minister to Washington was appointed and, six weeks after the *Little Belt* affair, Augustus John Foster arrived on board the *Minerva,* bringing with him seven servants and Anthony St. John Baker, his Secretary of Legation. The *Minerva* was approaching Annapolis on June 29 when (symbolically, as it might seem) a deserter jumped overboard to swim ashore, a distance of more than three miles; and on the same day the USS *Essex* brought William Pinkney home. Foster spent a few days in Georgetown before settling in to the new legation, which was housed in the Seven Buildings on the corner of Pennsylvania Avenue and Nineteenth Street. He chose the site himself, saying that the old legation was too small for him as well as too far from the center of events. He wasted no time in presenting his credentials to Monroe, for he was introduced by Monroe to the President on July 2; he tactfully stayed clear of the Fourth of July festivities, but on July 6 he was courteously received at the White House, after which he began a round of visits to other government leaders. He had several talks with Monroe, of whom he reported: "I found in the American Secretary, a tone and manner of the most mild and conciliatory nature."

Augustus John Foster, a good-looking thirty-three-year-old with confident, polished manners and an unquenchable zest for enjoying himself, had been in the United States before, serving as a junior attaché under the ill-fated Merry. He had then been sent as Chargé to Stockholm, but had asked to be returned to Washington. He was even more well-connected than Morier. His father had been a member of Parliament, his mother an earl's daughter. When Mr. Foster, Senior died, Lady Elizabeth became the mistress of the Duke of Devonshire, who later married her. One of his aunts was the wife of the Earl of Liverpool, then in the cabinet and a future Prime Minister. Young Foster had been educated at Oxford and then, as a matter of course, made the Grand Tour. The discreditable Francis Jackson said maliciously that "Foster is a very gentlemanlike young man, quite equal to do nothing at his post"; and the fat Federalist Congressman Samuel Taggart thought him "a pretty young gentleman" but far too boyish in appearance to make a really impressive Minister Plentipotentiary, rather better suited to a ballroom or drawing room.

Young Mr. Foster took a clear look at the sketchy contours of the capital, with its unfinished roads, its scattered houses, its incomplete public buildings, and its general air of a raw design in a swamp, and decided that if he was living in a wild colonial encampment he might as well make the most of it, and at the same time live it up a little. He estimated that during his term in Washington he spent nine thousand pounds on entertainment. It amused him to give his guests caviar, which they mistook for jam and spat out, and he noted with ironic pleasure that one congressman had relieved himself in the legation fireplace. He kept a diary full of such agreeably indiscreet comments, and his regular letters to his mother, like her replies to him, were equally outspoken. After all, a diplomat on a delicate mission has to cut loose somewhere.

Foster's instructions were to back-pedal on the question of the Orders in Council, to see whether the French might not do something that would antagonize America again; to protest mildly against the proposed American takeover in Spanish West Florida, while remembering that Britain would not fight for Spain in this connection; to guard against America's possible adoption of the French view that a true blockade must include land as well as sea restriction; and to bear in mind always, as the final sentence of Foster's briefing stated:

> No Extremity can induce His Royal Highness to relinquish the ancient and established Rules of Maritime War, the maintenance of which is indispensable, not only to the Commercial Interests, but to the Naval Strength, and to

the National Honour of Great Britain, as well as to the rights of all Maritime States, and to the general prosperity of Navigation and Commerce throughout the Civilised World.

Monroe might appear friendly, but it was soon clear that he was prepared to take a stand on behalf of his government. In his correspondence with England, he was firm about the *Little Belt* and *Chesapeake* questions, brushed aside the Florida issue by saying in a casual tone that of course sooner or later Florida would become part of the United States, and told Foster that his government would absolutely refuse to admit that the French had *not* repealed their decrees against American shipping. He obviously believed that the French had not repealed them, however, for he suggested to Foster that "if Great Britain would issue such a conditional and ambiguous promise of a revocation of Her Orders as France did of the Decrees last August, that it will be considered enough to authorise the cessation of the operation of the Non-Importation Act against her Commerce." In other words, France's repeal was pretense, so if Britain made an equal pretense at repeal, the two would cancel out.

It was not a bluntly honest solution, but it would probably have prevented war between Britain and America. Behind a mist of uncertainty, negotiations could continue. Foster naturally did not feel bold enough to agree to this step on his own responsibility. He asked for guidance and of course it took months before Britain was ready to make a gesture in pretense of repeal; by that time America had drawn back from it. To Monroe's suggestion, Foster, remembering that he had been told to make a show of firmness, asked for proof that the French had repealed their decrees. This request sent even Federalist pro-British stalwarts into gasps of astonishment, and caused Monroe to write to Lord Holland:

A demand so entirely inconsistent with the rights of the U States, and degrading to them as an independent nation, has been viewed in no other light than that of evidence of a determined hostility in your government against this country.

Such overreaction prompts the modern reader to suspect that the French repeal had indeed been no such thing.

What with this British intransigence, the Indian menace as typified by Tippecanoe, the War-Hawks' mounting cries for advance against Canada, and the continued French seizure of American ships and bland disregard for American feelings, tempers rose dangerously in the United States, and the newspapers printed editorial comments such as:

Things have now arrived at that crisis, that something spirited must be done, or the United States will become proverbial for servility and debasement.

Of course no international situation ever moves smoothly and consistently: it is much more like the course of a sailing ship in a strong sea, yawing now one way, now another, and during the last part of 1811 and the first part of 1812 the American government found itself torn in exasperation and rage between both Britain and France. Napoleon, growing more hostile toward the czar of Russia, ordered that all American ships going up the Baltic toward St. Petersburg should be seized and, for good measure, clapped fresh restrictions on American trade with French ports. He would not allow sugar, coffee, or tobacco, in case some of these products had come originally from British traders, and he insisted that America should take from France only those goods of which he had a surplus, particularly wine and silk.

At one point it looked as though American opinion had swung right around: when it was known that only forty-nine (instead of the usual hundreds) American cargoes had entered French ports in the year following the supposed French repeal, Jonathan Russell wrote that it was hardly worthwhile going to war with England now, and Augustus Foster said that a few minor concessions on the part of Britain would "render the whole Country cordially united with Us." But as autumn came in, golden and beautiful, suspicion and anger against both powers still gripped Congress, as its members packed the Representatives' Chamber on November 5, 1911 to hear what the President had to say. Some newspapers were frankly suspicious of Madison's motives. The Lexington *Reporter* declared that if any president stood "as a mere stock, or block, or statue" then it made no difference "if we have a *British agent,* a *monarchist,* or *federalist* for president."

Madison's speech contained a summary of the events of the past year, saying nothing about impressment and very little about Tippecanoe, but asking for "putting the United States into an armour and an attitude demanded by the crisis." Copies of the speech, reaching (for example) Philadelphia in ten hours and Boston in sixty, produced, on the whole, a favorable response, only the most dedicated War-Hawks and peace doves standing out against it: the War-Hawks because they wanted war at almost any price, and the peace doves because they wanted peace at almost any price. The President's words seemed to promise the certainty of neither.

During 1810 and 1811 a serious trade depression slowly mounted in Britain. Seven thousand business firms failed, exports to America fell from 17 percent of Britain's total to less than 5, her overall trade was three-quarters of what it had been, and the developing industrial areas, notably in the northwest and the midlands, suffered so acutely that factory owners complained to Parliament and mobs rioted in the streets. Blame for this alarming situation was placed by many on the Orders in Council. Some members tried to brush it off, saying that "We have so often been threatened and then forgiven by the American democratics, that we have our doubts whether they are really in earnest"; or that America "could not do without Birmingham–she could not even shave herself, or catch her mice without their aid." (To which the Boston *Independent Chronicle* snapped back: "If America cannot shave *herself,* she can *shave old England,* as the battles of Bunker-Hill, Saratoga, &c. plainly evince:–And as to *mousing,* we ask, who manufactured the *mouse-traps* in which BURGOYNE and CORNWALLIS were taken?" Even so, it is true that the United States did need industrial products from Britain. Madison's message provoked scornful comment in London but, apart from a suggestion that Canada should perhaps look to her defenses, it was not taken as a serious threat of war. The effect of the Orders upon British trade, however, touched British sensibilities on a vital point, and it was this rather than any notion of danger from America that led to the increased demand in London for their repeal.

The diffuse and divided Whig Opposition, aptly described as an army without generals, spoke, as it had always done, for repeal, its chief, indeed almost only, spokesman being Henry Brougham. Lord Auckland, who might have added much weight, was too unwell to attend the House much; Lord Grenville preferred living in Cornwall; Erskine, Baring, and Whitbread did not command close attention or respect in Parliament. On the government benches, Spencer Perceval presided over a reshuffled cabinet in which the most significant new appointment was the Foreign Office. Lord Wellesley had resigned, and the new Foreign Secretary was Robert Stewart, Viscount Castlereagh.

Castlereagh, a forceful, clear-sighted Ulsterman with a natural flair for foreign affairs, had held cabinet office, on and off, for ten years. He had a high reputation as a watchdog of the British empire, fervently believed, as he had written as early as 1802, "that France should feel that Great Britain cannot be trifled with," and was upheld in any crisis by a practical, quiet optimism. Yet the instability that was to make him die by his own hand in 1822 was already there; it led him into his bitter clashes with Canning, whose lively impulsiveness grated on him just as his caution rasped Canning's volatile nature. The differences between the two men led to their absurd duel on Putney Common in September 1809, when Castlereagh wounded Canning in the thigh and Canning demanded: "Now, pray, tell me what we have been fighting about?" Indeed it is difficult to determine this, apart from its having been an outburst of mutual detestation. Shelley wrote that Sidmouth and Castlereagh were "two vipers tangled into one," and, even more savagely,

> I met Murder on the way–
> He had a mask like Castlereagh;

but far more common, at least in 1812, was the judgment of a contemporary in the House that Castlereagh was "a splendid summit of bright and polished frost which, like the travellers in Switzerland, we all admire, but no one can hope, and few would wish to reach." He was a poor speaker, long-winded and tedious, he never lacked for enemies, but he unwaveringly supported and admired Wellington, and he believed in Britain and the capacity of her people with a steadfast faith. Shy, awkward, speaking very bad French, vainly trying to arrange his long legs whenever he sat down, he was nonetheless so striking a personality that when he came into a room every eye turned in his direction, and he commanded respect and unwilling admiration from those who thought him gauche. Talleyrand, who had seen hundreds of vivid personalities, exclaimed when he first met Castlereagh's frank stare: "What a distinguished air he has!"

Castlereagh took office quietly, wishing, it seems, to have a good look at the state of affairs before making any decisions, but he was well aware that the majority of businessmen, anxious for trade development, opposed the Orders in Council, that the press was partly hostile and gathering support, and that the shipowners themselves, while still largely in favor of the Orders, were losing ground. One shipowner who testified in favor of the Orders was a certain John Gladstone, father of William. Not one manufacturer spoke up for the Orders, and even some members of Parliament on the government side were beginning to oppose them.

Parliament held a full debate on the Orders, the first on the subject for three years, on March 3, 1812. The House was full when Henry Brougham, speaking for the Opposition, opened the debate. He was an imposing speaker, with his dark, glowing face, heavy black brows, and rough black hair. Although the debate went on throughout the night, more than three hundred and fifty members stayed in their places to listen. Apart from Brougham's reference to war with America, which he called the last of disasters, and his loud denunciation of the cabinet's "mean and profligate" policy, there was only one really lively and dramatic speech, for all the rest quoted interminably from customs reports, listing shipping statistics, which went on, it seemed, for hours. It was Canning who struck a spark, as might have been expected, when he caught the Speaker's eye in the middle of the night, sprang to his feet, and accused the government of using the Orders to change from a blockade of United States ports into a commercial competition. What he wanted, and had wanted for years, was to operate the Orders in the clear, vigorous way in which they had first been planned. "They were most perfect," he said, "as they approached toward a belligerent measure, and receded from a commercial one." The House divided at half past four in the morning and, although the government won the vote by 216 to 144, not only was this not an overwhelming victory, but various prominent members–Wilberforce, Sidmouth, and Melville–led their bands of adherents into the anti-government lobby. Brougham expressed his pleasure, and went home convinced that he had started the movement snowballing.

Spencer Perceval, seeing his uneasy Administration wavering more obviously than before, tried to strengthen it by inviting Viscount Sidmouth to join the cabinet. Sidmouth agreed on condition that Britain should abandon her system of issuing trading licenses for ships taking goods to America, and Castlereagh accordingly wrote to Augustus Foster on April 10 offering to abandon the licenses if America would reopen trade with Britain. This statement amounted to a genuine, and considerable, British climb-down, but its effect was spoiled on April 21 when the government made another statement, saying that France was trying to deceive the United States and that the Orders would exist until Britain had clear information that the French had repealed theirs. Taking this to mean that, after all, the government was going to cling to the Orders, Parliament broke into fresh uproar, and Perceval was forced to approve the formation of a special committee to examine the whole question of the Orders, a step he had absolutely refused to consider only a few weeks before.

By this time, Britain was ready to talk more toughly than she had been for a long time. The news from Europe was better. In March 1812 Wellington had done what Napoleon had flatly declared impossible: he had captured the great fortress of Badajoz. It was a terrible assault, with troops storming, or attempting to storm, sheer walls a hundred feet high in places and protected by an unbridged ditch thickly sown with mines, iron harrows, and bristling *chevaux-de-frise* of bayonets and sword blades. With astonishing speed and endurance, at a terrible cost–almost four thousand, so that next morning the ditch was still steaming with blood in the chill misty air–the British troops, led by the incomparable Light Division whose spearhead was the Rifles, smashed and wrenched their way into the fortress. The French, demoralized by their enemies appearing where no enemy could possibly be, collapsed and fled; the exhausted survivors found themselves master of the city; and in a violence of reaction from the violence of the attack, they sacked Badajoz with brutal ferocity for two days and nights. On the third day Wellington rode in with fresh troops, had a gallows set up in the square and restored order.

He then went to give the bride away at a wedding. It was one of the best known military weddings in British history. During the sack, British officers struggled as best they could to protect Spanish women and children who turned to them for sanctuary. One Spanish lady brought along her young sister, a girl of fifteen named Juana de Léon. She came up to two officers standing outside their tent, and asked them to see that Juana was safe. Both officers fell in love with Juana on sight, but John Kincaid was too self-conscious to speak of it; Harry Smith was not. Two days later he married her, and she happily followed the drum with him for the rest of the Spanish campaign.

Brigade Major Harry George Wakelyn Smith of the Rifles, a wiry, dark, spirited man of boundless vitality and restless charm, was described by official historians later as the preeminent fighting soldier of his generation. He fought in Portugal, in Spain, at Waterloo; and he fought in America in the War of 1812.

Wellington, with both Ciudad Rodrigo and Badajoz in his hands, could now take the initiative in driving back the two French armies, one under Soult and one under Marmont, that stood between him and the frontiers of France. The two could communicate only through Madrid; neither could reach the other in time to help in an attack; the tide had turned at last. Napoleon's troops in Spain numbered a quarter of a million; Wellingon had forty-five thousand British and twenty-five thousand Portuguese. But Wellington was sure now that he could not be dislodged and Napoleon obliged him by angrily refusing to mention Badajoz. Instead, he took a fatal step, and ordered his army, the quarter of a million veterans of the *Grand Armée* plus 120,000 fresh conscripts, and hundreds of thousands of Germans, Poles, Italians, Dutch, Austrians, to move east against Russia. He could not crush the English, whose navy had made Europe the Emperor's cage; the only other way out was toward the east. He had declared, years earlier, when he was simply a brilliant, clear, competent general of genius, that the greatest of military follies was a campaign against a desert; now he launched just such a doomed campaign. So the long, long columns wound across every road leading to Poland, over the vast flat plains of northern Europe; and Britain took a deep breath. With all this drama developing in Europe what was this upstart little American colony–oh, all right, then, ex-colony–doing, tapping Britain impatiently on the shoulder? What was the fuss about?

"The present Congress," wrote young Mr. Foster, "has certainly brought with it a considerable accession to both Houses of men of talents and respectability, although there still continue in it too many low and uneducated Individuals who are too ignorant to have any opinion of their own."

One of the most striking new appointments of November 1811 was the election of Henry Clay as Speaker of the House. It did not look like it at first, for the "Kentucky gamecock" was not well known: the *Columbian Centinel* confused him with a cousin, Matthew Clay of Virginia. But very soon Henry Clay was known throughout the land. He combined debonair manners, a sleepy appearance, a marked talent for gaming, much of the equipment of a Mississippi riverboat gambler, in fact, with a zest for the political rough and tumble, powerful public speaking, belief in both industry and farming, and an unabashed patriotism. After one or two experiences of him, the House came to attention when he rose to speak. He was no remote, quiet figure, presiding from the Speaker's chair over debates which he controlled in a dimly godlike way: he took firm controversial decisions, set up committees packed with War-Hawks, came down onto the floor of the House to take a partisan role, and brought forward several vigorous young men entering Congress for the first time. As a sign that new strong hands grasped the congressional tiller, he told John Randolph that from now on he must not bring his big pet dog into the House.

Randolph was now somewhat overshadowed by the leading War-Hawks. On the Foreign Affairs Committee he was an odd man out, as was the solitary Federalist, Philip Barton Key, who had fought on the British side in the War of Independence and who had a son called Francis Scott. The Republicans were still divided, for among their ranks sat one group that wished to preserve peace above all, and a middle group, described by Samuel Taggart as

> those who vote for war without any sincere intention to go to war, but in hopes that Great Britain may be intimidated by the din of our preparations to relax her system so that they will eventually come off with flying colours.

Taggart called these "the scarecrows." Other Republicans clamored for military readiness more from a wish to annoy the President, or to jolt him into more resolute action, than to bring about war, or to try to bluff the British. But the War-Hawks were unquestionably the leaders. Four of them—Henry Clay, George Bibb, Langdon Cheves, and William Lowndes—shared a Washington boardinghouse, which Lowndes called "the strongest war mess" in the capital. But this is perhaps a little misleading. The War-Hawks did not want war at any price; what they cared about was the national honor, and if they could maintain that without war, meaning that the British should repeal the Orders and stop impressment, they would be quite satisfied. If not, then war was the answer. One War-Hawk, David Rogerson Williams, said that a new peace would be easier to settle than an old quarrel.

A few Republicans clung to their belief that commercial pressure alone could push Britain into repeal, and two or three Quids, led by Randolph, represented the extreme, almost Federalist anti-war position. Yet it is essential to remember that all these categories were mutable, with members of each shifting on one point or another as the debates eddied. The closest one can come to an exact appreciation is to say that, on the whole, the War-Hawks plus the Scarecrows could usually carry the House, and that the President stood to the rear of the War-

Hawks but in front of those who wanted to bluff, at any rate until the end of the year 1811.

The Republicans in the Senate were impossible to group even to that limited extent. They ranged from the War-Hawk George Washington Campbell to the weak, amiable, usually drunk Richard Brent, and were a collection of individuals whose political ambitions were aimed at curtailing the President's political future. This can be taken to mean that they hoped to hold the supreme office, or something very close to it, themselves in time, and their actions in the Senate were prompted by self-interest to an unusual degree even for politicians.

There were at this time thirty-seven Federalist members of the House and seven Federalist senators. On the whole they took the War-Hawks' speeches as examples of crying wolf, and they followed the lead of Josiah Quincy, who, fearing that his party might "degenerate into a mere faction" and make fools of themselves, proposed a policy of watching, waiting, letting the Republicans quarrel, and voting for military preparation while avoiding, if possible, provoking Britain; though two members called on Augustus Foster to say that Britain ought to hang on to the Orders so that the Republicans would be forced to the wall, and another wrote that the only way to dislodge the Republicans from office was by saddling them with a war which they could not conduct, or from which they would have to back down. In general, though, the Federalists refrained from taking a clear line. They sat in their little groups–nine were living in Birch's boardinghouse and five in Coyle's–and hoped devoutly that there would be no war, and that the Republicans would make fools of themselves.

The long debate on military measures jerked on its way for weeks–Taggart noted that the war fever "had its hot and cold fits"–handicapped by proposals far too grandiose for reality as well as by internal squabbles and divisions. In December 1811 Monroe went so far as to pledge a declaration of war in the spring if Britain had not backed down by then, but even this failed to move the House to anything resembling a united front. Randolph, though tired and ill, fought against too easy a view of potential war, saying that if war came, it would not be a war "for our homes and fire-sides" with "manly sentiments," but "a scuffle and scramble for plunder." He said that greed, not righteousness, urged the War-Hawks on, and bitterly remarked that during the debate "We have heard but one word–like the whip-poor-will, but one eternal monotonous tone–Canada!–Canada!–Canada!"

A bill to expand the army, an impractical affair accurately described by Foster as electioneering rather than a war measure, was passed, but the bill to expand the navy was defeated by sixty-two votes to fifty-nine. Those against it said that the American Navy could never meet that of Britain, ships could not be built in time, and the expense was ruinous. Now that it was clear, or ought to have been clear with these two bills that the army was too loosely planned and the navy too small to deal competently with a war, the question of paying for war had to be dealt with, and the debate on taxation opened in January, dragging on even longer than had the military discussion preceding it.

There are few things more certain to lower fighting tempers than a statement of costs, and Congress moved toward the spring in an increasingly sulky mood. Tax proposals were tossed about the chamber, as members discussed, if that word is not too dignified, a possible import tax, salt tax, stamp tax (shades of 1776!), a tax on sugar, on carriages, on wine, on distilleries and taverns, even on marriage licenses in the District of Columbia (to which one member jovially suggested that people taking these out should get a bounty rather than have a tax slapped on them). The debate was additionally bedeviled by the increasing awareness on the part of many members that France had behaved toward America quite as badly as had Britain, and that, if Congress passed the bill to increase taxation in order to finance military supplies, it would mean the government was in earnest about facing the prospect of war. The Tax Bill passed the House on March 4, 1812, with forty Republicans absent. Five days later, Madison placed the Henry letters before Congress and, reflecting on the explosive effect of this apparent evidence of British subversive activity in New England, Augustus Foster (gloomily) and Louis Sérurier (gleefully) both commented: "If this event does not produce a war nothing will do so."

Yet the furor soon died down. Partly because Henry was so quickly discredited, partly because his letters were too vague to incriminate individuals, partly because the Federalist press started up a fresh fuss over alleged agents of Madison busily working to undermine Spanish Florida. Foster recovered his spirits and resumed his cheerful evenings in War-Hawk and Federalist taverns and his lavish parties, overrunning his expense account to entertain as many as two hundred people at a time. Accusations of War-Hawk bluff rose higher than ever, alarming

Ambassador Jonathan Russell in London so much that he wrote to Pinkney's Chargé d'Affaires, John Spear Smith:

I hope it will not prove to be merely a show. I should indeed hang my head if there were any retrograde movement after so much blustering.

And Federalist Congressman Abijah Bigelow wrote to his wife, Hannah:

The poor souls have got themselves into a sad dilemma, they know not how to go forward, or how to retreat, and what is still more disgraceful they have no settled plan which they mean to pursue, they depend upon the chapter of accidents.

James Bayard, another Federalist congressman, who went pheasant-shooting with Augustus Foster, noted:

One can discover very little war spirit in either House of Congress. And yet the members will tell you very coldly, that war is inevitable. But I have found no one willing to declare war and very few to adopt any measure of hostile character.

James Kelly commented in a letter to Senator Timothy Pickering:

What a Ridiculous Farce has been played off in the Face of the Nation. Why Sir, Congress have made themselves so Ridiculous and insignificant that all their War Measures are regarded just as men would Regard Boys cracking Nuts at a Distance.

Now it was March in Washington. The winter, unusually cold that year so that sleighrides had been possible in the District of Columbia, was over; a newspaper called the *Sentinel of Freedom* said that the spring sun had dried the roads, it was excellent weather for campaigning, therefore why were troops not moving north already? A British ship, the *Gleaner,* specially chartered at a cost of five thousand pounds, brought dispatches for Foster from the retiring Foreign Secretary, Lord Wellesley, virtually his last act before quitting office. In the middle of the afternoon of March 20 one Lieutenant Green presented the dispatches, which contained the old statements that the French had not repealed their decrees and so Britain could not repeal her Orders. Meanwhile, various members of Congress were writing privately to the President imploring him to give the country a clear lead, while others suggested that the quickest way to bring Britain down would be to stop the enormous, essential grain supplies from America to the British troops in Spain and Portugal, which had grown to 835,000 bushels in 1811 and were still increasing. On March 30 Peter Porter, the War-Hawk congressman from Buffalo, asked Monroe when the Administration would "be ready to proceed to ulterior measures." That afternoon Monroe tentatively proposed a sixty-day embargo to give America time to receive further news from Europe and, amid some belated misgivings from the War-Hawks, a bill was drawn up during the next few days designed to show that America was in earnest. It scraped past the House, whereupon the Senate modified it to a ninety-day embargo, passed it by twenty votes to thirteen, and Madison signed the bill on April 4.

Foster wrote to his mother, the Duchess of Devonshire, next day:

> The Embargo has put us all in a fuss. Great Quantities of corn and flour have gone off so I hope Spain and Portugal will not suffer. Theres hardly enough left in New York for the bakers.

Rumors of the embargo had sped north, where the Boston Collector of Customs kept his office open until nine o'clock at night so that all who wished could clear their ships' papers, and in spite of a sea fog some eighty vessels slipped out. More than a hundred got clear of New York. Congressmen and editors alike stated that British reaction to this new embargo would make war now inevitable, but the Administration shuffled and staved off its questioners, waiting for news from Europe. What it was particularly waiting for was the return of the *Hornet,* which had sailed in December for England laden, according to the Baltimore *Federal Republican,* with "paper bullets, bloody messages, war resolutions and frightful speeches." Speculation and false news of the *Hornet*'s return kept everyone jumpy. Throughout April and the first half of May the country buzzed with contradictory words.

Josiah Quincy observed on April 15: "The levies do not progress, no important strength is proposed to the fortification of our seaboard, no addition to our navy, no plan for arming our merchantmen," and wanted to know whether any man could believe "an Embargo, accompanied by such a state of things is preparatory to war?" Hermanus Bleecker, of Albany, a good-looking and vigorous young Federalist, said in the House on May 4: "No, Sir, rely upon it there will be, there can be, no war within sixty days." Jonathan Russell wrote in London on April 22: "I am convinced that whoever wishes for the respect of this highminded people must occasionally fight them." Foster, who had noted on May 3: "Mr Monroe in a conversation which I lately had with him, expressed his wish that we would exchange our Orders for blockades [meaning, presumably, that the tensions resulting from a blockade would be easier to bear than the effects of the Orders in Council] which might answer the purpose," added two days later: "The Bubble will soon burst. I am assailed on every Side with tremendous Stories but the ruling party seems to be in a State of Desperation." The Republican congressman John Taylor of Caroline County, Virginia, said that none of his neighbors wanted war; but the Virginia House of Delegates had resolved that "the period has now arrived when *peace, as we now have it,* is disgraceful, and war is honourable." The New York *Herald* of May 19 said: "Nothing was ever so universally execrated as is the projected war." Joseph Nicholson told his brother-in-law Gallatin on May 7 that "The apathy of the Nation is not thrown off and never will be"; yet Jefferson had said on April 2: "All regret that there is cause for war, but all consider it as now necessary." On May 13 a friend from Baltimore wrote to Henry Clay:

> We are a Humbled and degraded Nation, and If the Stand that is now Taken is departed from, Without bringing England to Justice, we may as well give up our Republican Government and have a Despot to rule over us.

Matters reached such a pitch that a triangular war between America, France, and Britain was seriously discussed, particularly after a spate of French seizures of American grain ships; but even the hottest War-Hawks hesitated, and Madison wrote to Jefferson:

> To go to war with England and not with France arms the Federalists with new matter, and divided the Republicans some of whom with the Quids make a display of impartiality. To go to war against both, presents a thousand difficulties.

But the talk of triangular war confused issues still further. The *Columbian Centinel* of May 6 remarked acidly that rich people in Boston would not lend money to "the ruling faction, for the same reason that they would not lend swords to the tenants of a lunatic hospital."

On May 22 the *Hornet* sailed in. Crowds crammed Monroe's office to suffocation point clamoring to know whether the news she carried would let America out gracefully. Castlereagh's words were eagerly scanned. He had written:

It is impossible America should not feel under these Circumstances that She has not only an Act of Justice to perform by Great Britain, but that France has deliberately attached Conditions to the Repeal of Her Decrees which she knew Great Britain could never accept, hoping thereby to foment Disunion between Great Britain and America. America can never be justified in continuing to resent against Us that failure of Relief, which is alone attributable to the insidious Policy of the Enemy. We are entitled to claim at Her Hands, as an act not less of Policy, than Justice, that she should cease to treat Great Britain as an Enemy.

Hoping that America could now "recede without disgrace from the precipice of War," he said that "to rescue America from the influence of France, is of more importance, than committing Her to War with that Power." He offered to regulate trading licenses so that Britain and America might share the European trade, or even abandon the licenses entirely.

The tone of this well-meant dispatch was, to American eyes, unbearably highhanded and condescending, as from an elderly relation pontificating on conduct to a young man. What seemed natural, practical, and sensible in London was maddeningly lofty and overbearing across the Atlantic. The Administration hardened against Britain, ignored the offer about the licenses, stubbornly insisted that the French *had* repealed their decrees though no American in calmer mood could possibly have believed this, and said that Britain was trying to extend her demands. Years later, Madison recalled that any chance of conciliation was, or seemed to be, at an end, and that now "no choice remained but between war and degradation, and degradation inviting fresh provocation and rendering war sooner or later inevitable." But he delayed sending a War Message to Congress. They fretted, waiting for it, drafting replies in anticipation, expecting it any minute; Henry Clay told a companion on a morning ride to Georgetown that it would come on the first of June. Augustus Foster's guests began casting a speculative eye on his livestock, his ornaments and pictures, and the big marquee he used for his garden parties, deciding how much they would offer him for them when he had to leave.

The London hearings concerning the Orders in Council sedately went on, until, on May 11, an incident unique in Parliamentary history took place. Spencer Perceval, arriving at the House of Commons a little after five in the afternoon, hurried alone into the lobby. A deranged commercial agent named James Bellingham, armed with a pistol, came out of the shadows to meet him, and fired at pointblank range, killing the Prime Minister instantly. Bellingham walked to the fireplace, and stood there waiting, apparently, to be arrested, which promptly happened. Panic swept the building in the echoes of the shot: Lords and Commons alike rushed into the corridors, caught up arms, flung open doors, looked inside cupboards, and searched the rambling building from roofs to cellars in scenes unparalleled since the arrest of Guy Fawkes over two hundred years earlier. The resulting government crisis lasted for a month. Perceval received the usual glowing official obituaries, though, as Lord Grenville wrote within four days: "I confess I am a little sick of the Apotheosis of a man whom I believe to have been a very good, moral, and charitable man in private life, but as factious a partisan in opposition, and as bad a Minister of Government as the Country ever saw"; but Parliament voted pensions to his widow and his crowd of children, while town mobs applauded his death. It was impossible to form a government except by asking Lord Liverpool to lead the rest of Perceval's Administration; and by the time these had pulled themselves together sufficiently to assume office, the sands had run out in Washington.

The formal motion to repeal the Orders was announced on June 16, and one week later repeal was a fact. Brougham, who thought the repeal was his greatest achievement, was given a testimonial dinner; factories set up extra shifts to produce goods for America; within two weeks fifty ships left Liverpool carrying more than two million yards of calico and a supply of English cheese; and news of the new embargo was brushed aside with scornful comments like Brougham's "Jealousy of America! I should as soon think of being jealous of the tradesmen who supply me with necessaries."

But it was all too late. Madison, who had told Foster that the Orders were "tantamount to Letters of Marque," duly sent his War Message * to Congress on June 1, where one of the clerks read it out in a monotonous voice. The House debated behind closed doors for three rumor-filled days, and finally passed the War Bill on June 4 by seventy-nine votes to forty-nine. One member had been sworn in the day before; another, on leave, dashed into the House with an hour to spare before the vote.

* See Appendix VIII

Reaction was mixed. In New England, flags were lowered to half mast, church bells tolled, two War-Hawks were hissed in Boston and one was mobbed at Plymouth, and the Connecticut *Courant* said that the war had "commenced in folly, it is proposed to be carried on with madness, and (unless speedily terminated) will end in ruin." One New York lady, Maria Austen, told her husband, Moses, that the war had come "like an Electrick shock"; one New York gentleman, Arthur Roorbach, wrote that "there are not wanting those who rejoice" in war-hating New York; and John Jacob Astor (who had emigrated from his German village of Waldorf with twenty-five dollars and seven flutes and who had made a quarter of a million dollars in furs by 1800) wrote with endearing misspelling on June 27 to Gallatin that "Pepal here are more reasonable about the war measure than what I esspected, and alltho many disapprove of the manner and time it was declared all agree that we have plenty cause." But the Philadelphia *Aurora* sounded its trumpets predictably, in reporting a speaker at Germantown who declaimed:

It hath pleased the Almighty Ruler of the universe to suffer the perfidious outrages of the British Government to render it necessary, once more, for the American people to struggle for their sovereignty and independence.

Congressman William Pope of Virginia told Madison that he had "politically regenerated the nation, and washed out the stain in their national character, inflicted on it by England"; a Federalist newspaper plant in Baltimore was demolished, and some of the editor's friends, who had taken refuge in the jail, were dragged out by a mob led by a Frenchman, and beaten up so savagely that one of them died–an episode which turned the State of Maryland Federalist for years. One happy celebrator, a drunken passenger in a gig, tipped the driver into the ditch twice: the driver was young Lieutenant Winfield Scott.

The commander of the Western Tennessee Militia stated:

We are going to fight for the re-establishment of our national character, misunderstood and vilified at home and abroad; for the protection of our maritime citizens, impressed on board British ships of war and compelled to fight the battles of our enemies against ourselves; to vindicate our right to a free trade, and open a market for the productions of our soil, now perishing on our hands because the *mistress of the ocean* has forbid us to carry them to any foreign nation; in fine, to seek some indemnity for past injuries, some security against future aggressions, by the conquest of all the British dominions upon the continent of north america.

His name was Andrew Jackson, and that passage just about summed up the case for the United States.

Congress declared war on June 18–three years to the day before Waterloo–on these four grounds; the Orders, just then in process of repeal; impressment; the blockade, often declared in being when it was not maintained in fact; and violations of American territorial waters. "Free Trade and Sailors' Rights!" shouted congressmen from inland areas, whose electors would have subscribed to the London *Times* more readily than they would have enlisted in the United States Navy. News of repeal reached America at the end of July, and the *Aurora* exclaimed: "The *Leviathan* of the sea has floundered and crouched to the *terrapin!*" But on declaration day itself, John Taylor of Virginia wrote soberly to Monroe: "May God send you a safe deliverance."

SIX

§

North

There seems little sense in calling this conflict the Anglo-American War of 1812. To be sure, it started in the summer of 1812, but its final engagement was fought in January 1815. If we say it lasted for two and a half years, that is misleading also. A number of scuffles and skirmishes, few of which would qualify as full-scale battles, took place at separate times over widely separated areas. Its pervading air of faint absurdity is demonstrated by the facts that fighting started only because the news that might have prevented it came too late, and its last battle was fought after the peace treaty was signed.

The first news that a state of war existed reached Sir George Prevost in a letter to his secretary from the trading firm of Forsyth, Richardson and McGillivray on June 24. It politely said: "You will be pleased by an express which left New York on the 20th and Albany on Sunday last at six a.m., the account that war against Great Britain is declared." Prevost's adjutant general, Colonel Edward Baynes, wrote at once to Brock, saying that Prevost was "inclined to believe the report" and adding that "Sir George desires me to say that the present Order of the Day with him is *forbearance.*" Brock, whose one idea was to move fast, set off at once from York in an open boat across Lake Ontario to Fort George, where he set up his headquarters. On the way he composed messages to be delivered at top speed to key forts: George, Chippawa, and Erie.

Both sides overestimated the numbers at the disposal of the enemy as well as his state of readiness. Brock had about eight hundred militiamen to reinforce the five hundred regulars of the Forty-First Foot whose duty it was to man the defenses of Fort George, Fort Erie, and Chippawa. The militia had no tents, and Brock had to buy hammocks, blankets, and kettles himself. He thought that his opponent at Fort Niagara had twelve hundred men at complete readiness, while in fact the United States commander was nervously expecting a full-scale attack every hour and was frantically sending appeals for more troops to reinforce his little garrison. Both sides found themselves in the awkward position of having to let large numbers of their militiamen go, they hoped temporarily, in order to get the harvest in. The reports of these departures were exaggerated when they reached the enemy, so that the Fort Niagara commander wondered whether it might lead to a kind of secession on the part of the Canadians: perhaps they might "declare themselves an American State," he noted hopefully. He was wrong.

The Americans had already snatched the first success of the war on the St. Lawrence, but news of it took a long time to reach either American or British headquarters. Three local farmers, acting entirely without orders, had surprised the four soldier caretakers at the tiny British base on Carleton Island and had taken it over without bloodshed. The farmers came under the direction of Brigadier General Jacob Brown, aged thirty-seven, who, after a mixed career as a schoolteacher and a land speculator, had founded the settlement of Brownville where he was of course the leading citizen. A son of Quaker parents, he had proved to be a somewhat un-Quakerly belligerent; during the embargo periods his exploits, which had caused a particular route to be named "Brown's Smugglers Road," had become notorious or famous according to which side one was on. His militia brigade was supposed to cover the line from St. Regis to Sackets Harbor near Brownville. Refusing to place his men thinly all along the line, Brown concentrated them at Sackets Harbor, where he found Colonel Thomas Benedict of Ogdenburg busily digging rough emplacements for two six-pounder guns. Brown detached a sizeable group of his force and stationed them at Cape Vincent on the St. Lawrence, where they discovered on arrival the successful coup of the three farmers.

Brock meanwhile had received reports from Colonel Robert Lethbridge, the elderly commanding officer at Kingston, who had also released many of his militia to get the harvest in. He said that his men, who came from Glengarry, Dundas, Stormont, and Grenville counties, were eager to fight, so he anticipated no trouble in asking them to return, but that their supplies were poor. The posts under his command were widely scattered and communication between them was not easy, so he had been told to use his own judgment "under all circumstances not expressly provided for," and above all he was not to provoke hostile action. He kept his volunteer flank companies to guard the river, especially at its narrowest points, and let off the rest.

The British commander at Amherstburg heard the news of war on June 28, thanks to Brock, who warned him while his future adversary, General Hull, was still pushing stolidly overland toward Detroit in steady rain. Prevost, who like everyone else was worried about reinforcements and supplies, heard from Lord Bathurst in London that two infantry battalions were on their way, one to Quebec with ten thousand stands of arms and one to Halifax with five thousand and, as Bathurst kindly pointed out,

> Your own Military Experience and local information will make you the best judge of the mode in which these means can be supplied with the greatest Prospect of ultimate success. It is sufficient for me to express my concurrence in the general Principles upon which you intend to conduct operations, by making the Defence of Quebec paramount to every other consideration, should the Threat of Invasion be put into Execution.

Quebec was, as we know, the only permanent Canadian fortress. It had about 2,300 regular soldiers in its garrison; the total of regulars and Fencibles in all Canada numbered 5,600, and of these the twelve hundred whose duty it was to defend Upper Canada were widely scattered across that enormous region. Many parts of the country were impassable in wet weather; in winter, horsedrawn sleighs or boats could move about more easily than could men on foot. Only near the St. Lawrence were roads better: the Montreal-Kingston road, which had the river in sight almost all the way, was "good enough." Some tiny townships were quite progressive, with wide streets, neat wooden houses, a church, a courthouse and a lock-up, while out in the open "long stretches of corduroy bridge the swamps and low grounds, bridges remarkably solid, some long and lofty, span creeks and fairly wide rivers," wrote one observer. All correspondence was, of course, written out in longhand and painstakingly copied by clerks, with the result that officers kept their writing to a minimum (though one would hardly guess it from their classically rolling periods) and were not swamped by paperwork.

One arm of the fighting forces that attracted special attention in this war was the militia. It was not long before zealous civilians created, or helped to create, the legend that the militia had done most of the fighting with a little help here and there from the regulars. On November 22, 1812, after five months of fighting, the Reverend John Strachan of York proclaimed that

> the Province of Upper Canada, without the assistance of men at arms, except a handful of regular troops, repelled its invaders, slew or took them all prisoners, and captured from its enemies the greater part of the arms by which it was defended . . . they have emulated choicest veterans, and they have twice saved the country.

But this was too sanguine a judgment. At least Brock placed his trust in the regular troops. One message he sent immediately on arrival at Fort George was directed to Captain Charles Roberts at Fort Joseph; Brock had barely landed before the messenger was spurring on his way.

Fort Joseph, on St. Joseph's Island in the St. Mary's River between Lake Huron and Lake Superior, was about forty miles northwest of Mackinac Island, where the Americans had set up a small stronghold called Fort Michilimackinac, commanded at this time by Lieutenant Porter Hanks with sixty-one United States regular soldiers. It was not much of a stronghold: a structure of logs overlooking the small harbor, fortified with a few nine-pounder guns not powerful enough to command the channel between Lake Huron and Lake Michigan or even to protect the spring on which the garrison depended for its fresh water, and it was overlooked by a hill less than a mile off. The fort stood on a limestone bluff, but the hill was not defended. Lieutenant Hanks was unaware of the declaration of war.

Brock's message to Roberts told him to look quickly to his defenses, but also to take "the most prompt and effectual measures" to capture Fort Michilimackinac. The messenger came ashore on St. Joseph's Island on July 8, having taken twelve days to make the journey north from Fort George, arriving shortly before another courier scrambled up to the fort with a dispatch from Prevost urging "the greatest vigilance and Caution," all possible help and protection to the officials of the North West Company, "Consistent with a due regard to the Security of the Post and," the dispatch went on ominously, "in Case of Necessity the ultimate retreat of your Party."

Roberts had at his disposal some 50 soldiers; Robert Dickson, with more than 100 Indians who were trading there; nearly 300 other Indians also trading; and a mixed bag of 180 Canadian and half-breed employees of the North West Company. He naturally preferred Brock's instructions to those of Prevost, especially since he knew that his fort was even weaker than the American, but he hesitated to move against Prevost's orders for a few days. On July 15, however, a fresh dispatch from Prevost, telling him to use his own discretion, let him off the hook. He left one officer and 6 of his 10th Royal Veterans to man his fort and set off next morning with 45 soldiers, all the Canadians, and some 400 Indians, crammed aboard the company's schooner *Caledonia* and in a flotilla of canoes.

Lieutenant Hanks, hearing rumors of an Indian concentration at Fort St. Joseph, sent a local islander to reconnoiter. This man was captured by Roberts's advancing force, which landed on Mackinac Island just after three in the morning of July 17 and at once set the prisoner free to warn the local population to place itself under British protection. The local doctor alerted the fort, but by then the Canadians had managed to get a six-pounder gun to the top of the hill, and Hanks surrendered. The terms were worked out in a gentlemanly manner: the Americans were granted the honors of war and allowed parole provided they would agree not to fight again until they could be exchanged for any British prisoners captured elsewhere; and Roberts took over a quantity of ammunition and supplies from the fort, along with three British deserters. Roberts, setting up his new headquarters in the fort, wrote delightedly to Brock: "It is a circumstance without a precedent, and demands the greatest praise for all who conducted the Indians, that although these people's minds were much heated, Yet as soon as they heard the Capitulation was signed they all returned to their Canoes, and not one drop either of Man's or Animal's Blood was Spilt, till I gave an Order for a certain number of Bullocks to be purchased for them." But he had doubts about his own troops, who, "tho' always ready to obey my orders are so debilitated and worn down by unconquerable drunkenness that neither the fear of punishment, the love of fame or the honour of their Country can animate them to extraordinary exertions."

There is always a right way and a wrong way of preparing to attack anywhere. If, as several commentators have said, the Canadian sealanes are the roots of the Canadian tree, the St. Lawrence is the trunk, and the Great Lakes the branches, it is true that the British conquered Canada in the first place by grasping the roots and grappling the trunk. In 1812 the United States had no navy capable of seizing the roots but the army could have chopped the trunk by strongly attacking Montreal or Quebec, either of which the British rather expected them to do. Instead of the bold stroke, however, they made a number of weak and haphazard loppings at the branches. The first of these loppings began three weeks before the declaration of war when a sixty-year-old veteran of the War of Independence, Governor William Hull of Michigan Territory, newly created a brigadier, was ordered to cut his way through the wilderness from Dayton, Ohio, to Detroit, from which fort he would be in a position to invade Upper Canada.

Hull, a gray-haired, tobacco-chewing, heavy man with an amiable expression, is described by one historian, C. E. Carrington, as an incompetent braggart, and by another, Admiral Mahan, as a soldier "on occasion" who "probably never had the opportunity to form correct soldierly standards." He had twice refused command of the Western Army, and when he eventually accepted it he did so on the unusual condition of remaining governor, thus drawing his salary for both posts at the same time. He was given the 4th United States Infantry regiment which had fought at Tippecanoe, and the remaining three-quarters of his force was to come from civilian volunteers. Hull chose as his aides-de-camp his son Abraham and his son-in-law Harris Hickman, and took over his new command at the end of May in Dayton where the governor of Ohio, picturesquely named Return Meigs, handed over three volunteer regiments armed with a mixed collection of muskets and sporting rifles and dressed in homespun jackets and breeches and felt hats. The three regimental commanders were men who had enjoyed positions of some eminence in private life: Duncan McArthur was a rich speculator who had served in both Houses of the state government; James Findlay had been mayor of Cincinnati and a U.S. marshal as well as an Ohio legislative councillor; and Lewis Cass, also a former marshal, was prosecuting attorney of his county. McArthur and Findlay were approaching forty, Cass thirty, and all three were now, of course, full colonels, without any previous military experience.

On June 1 Hull led his militia off into the wilderness knowing, or at any rate hoping, that the regulars would soon catch up, which they did at Urbana ten days later. The 4th Infantry Commander, James

Miller, was only a lieutenant colonel, but when a large group of volunteers refused to go on until they were paid, Miller's men had to advance on them with leveled muskets and arrest three ringleaders for court-martial. Hull told Miller: "By God, sir, your regiment is a powerful argument," yet he did not promote Miller to equal the other three commanders. On June 17, having made surprisingly good time, the column passed the last outpost of Ohio and entered Indian country, straggling along with its motley of troops, ox and mule wagons, herd of cattle, bandsmen, army wives, mounted scouts, and its chief guide Thomas Maxwell, aged seventy. Ahead lay two hundred miles of forest, marsh, stream, and swamp, all of it potentially hostile, all of it unmapped and unbridged and, just then, soaking under a steady fall of rain that lasted for several days. All the same, they reached the Miami Rapids on June 28, and on July 1, found Captain Cyrenius Chapin whose schooner *Cayauga* would take Hull's sick men, the army wives, and bandsmen who could act as nursing orderlies, and the heavy baggage on to Detroit for a fee of sixty dollars.

Hull agreed to this offer, and Captain Chapin set off, entering the Detroit River next morning. At Amherstburg he came under the guns of Fort Malden, a barracks and stores surrounded by loopholed fencing with powerful bastions at each corner and a dry ditch, defended by a battery of mounted cannon and three hundred men under Lieutenant Colonel Thomas St. George. Moored below lay a flotilla of British ships, one of which, the *General Hunter,* spoke the *Cayauga* and ordered her to heave-to. In the face of the guns from the ships and the fort, Chapin complied, and Lieutenant Charles Rolette, RN, came aboard, announcing that as a state of war existed between Britain and the United States he was empowered to seize all military personnel and supplies. The Union Jack was raised at the *Cayauga*'s masthead, Hull's bandsmen played the British national anthem, perhaps a lesser offense than it might have been since the tune is the same as that of *My Country 'Tis Of Thee,* and Rolette's sailors, bringing off the Americans' supplies, found a wooden box containing copies of Hull's correspondence with Washington, his instructions, and the muster roll of his troops.

It was not the prize from heaven that seizure of enemy dispatches often is, for there could be no doubt where Hull was going. Fort Detroit was obvious: Brock, who had rapidly alerted Amherstburg a week before, knew this perfectly well. Hull himself had received the

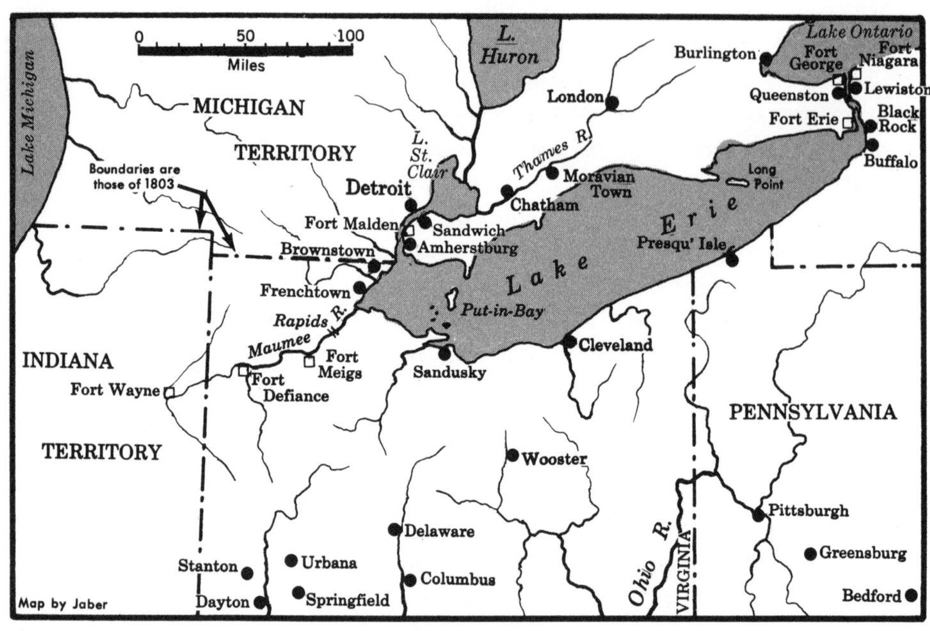

0 50 100
Miles
Lake Michigan
L. Huron
Lake Ontario
MICHIGAN
TERRITORY
Boundaries are those of 1803
L. St. Clair
Thames R.
Burlington
Fort George
Fort Niagara
Lewiston
Queenston
Black Rock
Fort Erie
Buffalo
London
Moravian Town
Chatham
Detroit
Sandwich
Fort Malden
Amherstburg
Brownstown
Frenchtown
Long Point
Lake Erie
Presqu' Isle
Put-in-Bay
Rapids
Maumee R.
Fort Meigs
Fort Defiance
Fort Wayne
INDIANA
TERRITORY
Sandusky
Cleveland
PENNSYLVANIA
Wooster
Pittsburgh
Greensburg
Delaware
Ohio R.
VIRGINIA
Stanton
Urbana
Columbus
Dayton
Springfield
Bedford
Map by Jaber

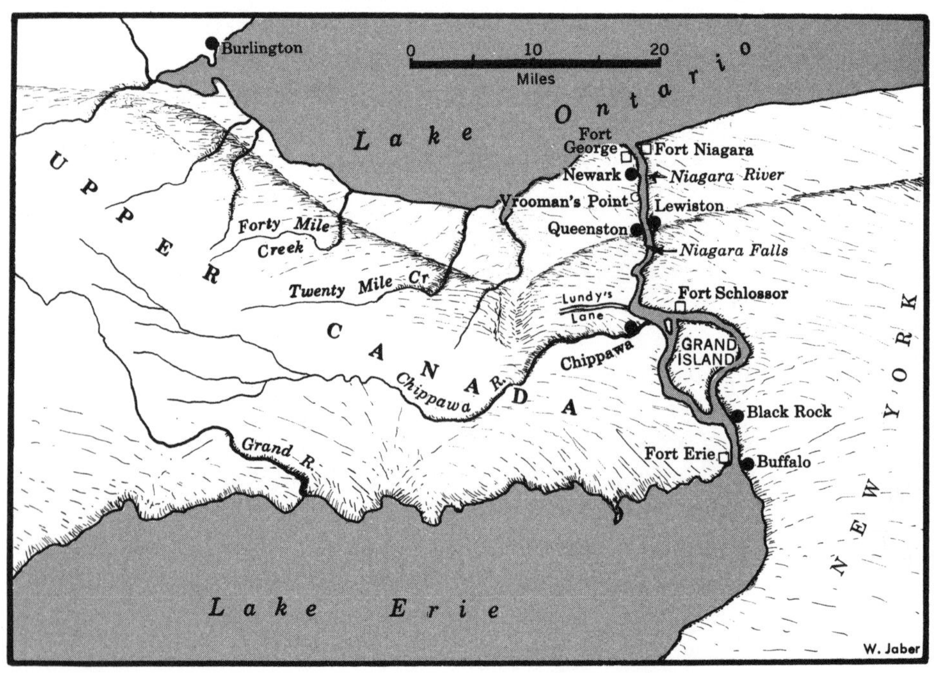

Burlington
0 10 20
Miles
Lake Ontario
Fort George
Fort Niagara
Newark
Niagara River
Vrooman's Point
Lewiston
Queenston
Niagara Falls
UPPER CANADA
Forty Mile Creek
Twenty Mile Cr.
Lundy's Lane
Fort Schlossor
Chippawa
GRAND ISLAND
Chippawa R.
Black Rock
Fort Erie
Buffalo
Grand R.
NEW YORK
Lake Erie
W. Jaber

war news in camp early that same morning, and now went on more apprehensively than ever. Sixteen miles north of Fort Malden was the settlement of Sandwich, facing Fort Detroit across the river. The fort, originally built by the British, resembled Fort Malden, but the population of Detroit was eight hundred, much bigger than that of Amherstburg. The equally small population of Sandwich had started to leave as soon as Hull's troops were reported on the river, and by the time Hull's outriders caught sight of the flag of Fort Detroit above the trees the opposing village was utterly deserted, its inhabitants having taken refuge, with their livestock, in the woods or at Fort Malden.

Hull, of course, did not know this and, finding Detroit short of all supplies except for whisky and soap, determined to capture Sandwich if he could. He ordered all available ferryboats assembled, tried to put some nerve into his quaking militia (many of whom kept mumbling that their call of duty did not include service in a foreign country, which was true), told the villagers not to add to his problems by encouraging the reluctant militia to desert, court-martialed one recalcitrant captain whose men promptly reelected him and, covered by every cannon that could be trained on the river, took the bulk of his force across. The Americans found Sandwich silent and empty. Hull set up his headquarters and issued a proclamation, unconsciously comic in view of his position and blithe in tone:

> In the name of my Country and by the authority of my Government I promise you protection for your *persons, property* and *rights.* Remain at your homes. Pursue your peaceful and customary avocations. Raise not your hands against your brethren, many of your fathers fought for the freedom and *Independence* we now enjoy. Being children therefore of the same family with us, and heirs to the same Heritage, the arrival of an army of Friends must be hailed by you with a cordial welcome. You will be emancipated from Tyranny and oppression and restored to the dignified station of freemen. Had I any doubt of eventual success I might ask your assistance, but I do not. I come prepared for every contingency. I have a force which will look down all opposition and that force is but the vanguard of a much greater. If, contrary to your own interest and the just expectation of my Country, you should take part in the approaching contest, you will be considered and treated as enemies, and the horrors and calamities of war will Stalk before you.

Despite the bold tone of this, Hull stayed in Sandwich and contented himself with sending out foraging parties. When these returned with supplies pillaged from government and North West Company stores, they brought along little groups of settlers who volunteered to form a cavalry troop. Some of Colonel St. George's militia from Fort Malden came too. Hull at this point was not seeking action, but Hull's old opponent, Colonel Lewis Cass, fidgeting for a crack at the redcoats, led his own militia regiment south on July 16 toward the little Canard River midway between Sandwich and Fort Malden. Here they found a party of British soldiers guarding the single bridge, and in the first land action of the war drove the British off. Cass sent a note back to Hull asking for authority to consolidate this gain; Hull, characteristically wavering, replied that Cass and Miller could decide the matter between them. Furious at being placed on a level with a mere lieutenant colonel, Cass drafted a letter to the American Secretary of War, William Eustis, threatening to disband and go home, and McArthur and Findlay signed it with him. Next day, Cass and McArthur, again disobeying orders, fired on the British brig *Queen Charlotte,* to which the ship briskly (and more heavily) replied. Neither party to this exchange appears to have thought of following it up. Hull, taking Miller with him, crossed to Detroit to see how soon his cannon would be ready to move on Fort Malden, leaving McArthur in charge at Sandwich.

Trouble now struck Hull from all sides. The cannon were not ready, and when they were they would have to be transported by water, and rafts would have to be built. McArthur, hearing that Indians were moving up from the Canard River, sent Major James Denny with 120 militiamen to ambush them, but a small party of Indians put them to undignified flight, running back to Sandwich ahead of the Major. Two Chippewa Indians arrived in Detroit with the news from Mackinac Island; scouts reported that a force of Wyandotte Indians across Hull's line of communication, opposite Amherstburg, had joined forces with Fort Malden. Hull, apprehensive lest all the Indians in the region might descend upon him, sent letters begging for help to the governors of Ohio and Kentucky, along with orders to abandon the lonely outpost of Fort Dearborn, built where the city of Chicago is now.

Brock had ordered his most capable officer, Colonel Henry Procter, to take over from St. George at Fort Malden: arriving there on August 4, Procter next day sent an Indian party of about two dozen men led by our old acquaintance Tecumseh across the river with orders to ambush a supply train coming north to Fort Detroit. Hull meanwhile had detached about two hundred militia to move south to escort the supply train, and the Indians ambushed the lot with complete success close to a small settlement called Brownstown, where ten rankers and seven officers were killed. The Indians captured the supplies and Hull's dispatches, and the militia commander, Major Thomas Van Horne, ordered a withdrawal which at once turned into a headlong flight back to Detroit twenty miles away, most of the men, like those of Denny, arriving ahead of their commanding officer.

On the following day, August 6, Hull held a Council of War, at which the majority, bolstered by the knowledge that the siege cannon were ready to be floated down the river on rafts, voted for a quick attack on Fort Malden. News came in that caused Hull to override this decision. Brock himself was on the way. He had flung together a force of 300 men–40 regulars and 260 energetic young militiamen from York–and the expedition had set out on that same day, August 6. Hearing that the formidable Brock was after him, Hull withdrew into Fort Detroit and began to plan a further withdrawal toward the Raisin River in order to repair his supply route and, with luck, meet his longed-for reinforcements. He disliked the prospect of making a stand at Detroit, for the village lay between the fort and the river, and this meant that the fort's guns had to fire at long range. His fire-eating colonels, however, wanted to stay where they were, so Hull selected the best of his troops, about 600, and sent them off under Miller to convoy another supply train. They went off on August 8, and next day, near a village called Maguaga or Monguagon (the accounts do not agree), they blundered into a British ambush set up behind brushwood screens under Captain Adam Muir who had planned to carry this out with 150 British soldiers and Canadian militia together with a party of Indians again led by Tecumseh. One volunteer, John Richardson, wrote later:

> Here it was that we had first an opportunity of perceiving the extreme disadvantage of opposing regular troops to the enemy in the woods. Accustomed to the use of the rifle from his infancy–dwelling in a measure amid forests with the intricacies of which he is wholly acquainted, and possessing the advantage of a dress which renders him almost indistinguishable to the eye of a European, the American marksman enters with comparative security into a contest with the English soldier whose glaring habiliment and accoutrements are objects too conspicuous to be missed,

while his utter ignorance of a mode of warfare, in which courage and discipline are of no avail, renders the struggle for mastery even more unequal.

These words, which could have applied equally well to the Boer War at the other end of the century, were followed by others which would have been appropriate even later, to the Singapore campaign of 1941. Saying that the Ohio militiamen were barely less skillful than the Indians, Richardson went on:

Dressed in woollen frocks of a gray colour, and trained to cover their bodies behind the trees from which they fired, without exposing more of their persons than was absolutely necessary for their aim, they afforded us, on more than one occasion, the most convincing proofs that without the assistance of the Indian Warriors, the defence of so great a portion of Western Canada would have proved a duty of great difficulty and doubt.

The Americans drove Muir's force off at a cost of eighteen dead and sixty-four wounded, while Muir's casualty list noted six dead, twenty-one wounded (including himself), and two captured. Miller's men, who, properly led for once, had faced up to battle with a good deal of resolution, claimed forty Indian scalps. They reassembled and made camp in the middle of a violent thunderstorm. Hull recalled them, and by August 12 they were back in Detroit, having done nothing to follow up their surprising victory.

Next day, Brock arrived at Amherstburg, after an unpleasant journey five days of which had been spent tossing in open boats on Lake Erie. When he arrived the Indians shot off their rifles in welcome, which caused Brock to suggest that they had better save their ammunition for the attack on Detroit. It was almost midnight when Brock arrived, so he did not review his troops until morning, which dawned sunny and warm with a clear blue sky. The person who interested Brock most was Tecumseh, whom he met for the first time. History has decorated their meeting with grandiloquent speeches, and it is a fact that Brock wrote afterward: "A more sagacious or a more gallant Warrior does not I believe exist."

Brock, aware from Hull's captured dispatches that he was expecting reinforcements, overrode his subordinates' caution and resolved to attack quickly. He issued an Order of the Day praising the troops and showing indulgence to deserters, saying that he "was willing to believe that their conduct proceeded from an anxiety to get in their harvests and not from any predilection for the principles or

Government of the United States." He organized his 300 regulars and 400 militia into three groups, with St. George and two captains promoted to majors from the Forty-First Foot in command, with Procter above all, directly under Brock himself. Next day, August 15, he sent his aide-de-camp under a flag of truce to Fort Detroit, requesting Hull to surrender, with a powerful threat:

It is far from my intention to join in a war of extermination, but you must be aware, that the numerous body of Indians who have attached themselves to my troops will be beyond control the moment the contest commences.

Hull, worried by this, took his time to refuse. It was not his only worry. He knew that his three Ohio colonels were circulating a round-robin to depose him; two of them, Lewis Cass and Duncan McArthur, had reluctantly gone off with 400 picked men to meet another supply train which was supposed to be coming forward from the Raisin River but which in fact had not moved from there; Miller was ill. There was plenty of ammunition–twenty-six large cannon with four hundred rounds of twenty-four-pounder shot, a hundred thousand cartridges and a large quantity of powder–but Hull had not enough troops to deploy fully. He regarded the Indian menace as the worst that faced him, and posted his remaining militia around the picket fence that sheltered the village on the landward sides, stationed his regulars in the fort and at the shore batteries, put the women and children in a root cellar in an orchard, and knew that he could not place any troops at all to guard the likeliest place for Brock's men to cross the river, Spring Wells, three miles below the fort, where the river was narrowest.

Cass and McArthur, finding no one at the rendezvous point, decided to go back, but they sent no message to inform Hull of this fact nor did they make haste to return, making camp that night barely three miles from Detroit although they could hear desultory cannon fire in the distance. It came from the shore batteries of Sandwich and Detroit, exchanging shots across the river without doing the slightest damage because neither side could get the range.

During that Saturday night of August 15, Tecumseh led a file of about six hundred Indians across the river and, at six on Sunday morning, a hot hazy dawn, Brock's troops, wearing worn red tunics and carrying cold breakfasts with them, crossed in boats and canoes, Brock in the foremost boat and his seven hundred men crowding behind him, under cover of fire from the guns of Sandwich and of the two ships, *General Hunter* and *Queen Charlotte.* All, Indians and troops, crossed at Spring Wells, and came ashore in a warm, flower-scented silence. Within a short time the Indian scouts reported the absence from Detroit of Cass and McArthur with their four hundred and, gambling coolly on Hull's irresolute bearing and his officers' dissension, Brock led his men forward on a narrow approach between the river and "a chain of houses and fences" where there was no room to deploy. John Richardson wrote:

> When within a mile and a half of the rising ground commanding the approach to the town, we distinctly saw two long, heavy guns, afterwards proved to be 24-pounders, planted in the road, and around them the gunners with their fuses burning. At each moment we expected they would be fired.

Hull, who did not seem to think that Brock's frontal advance was likely to succeed, was still preoccupied in worrying about the possibility of war-whooping Indians rushing his picket fence. He sat chewing "quid after quid" of tobacco while he tried to decide what to do. It was abruptly decided for him when one of the Sandwich guns, finding the range at last, lobbed an eighteen-pound shell into the officers' mess in the fort, killing four men, one of whom was the luckless Lieutenant Hanks of Michilimackinac. Hull at once hoisted a flag of truce and asked for an hour's grace. Brock, going forward with no hesitation whatever, made terms, and soon after midday the Union Jack was hoisted over the fort.

Hull surrendered his entire force, including the troops of McArthur and Cass, just then waiting in their camp for an ox to be roasted, and including the supply train on the Raisin. The militia were disarmed and turned loose to find their way home; Hull and his 582 regulars were shipped to Canada pending future exchange, and Brock wrote delightedly to Prevost:

> When I detail my good fortune, Your Excellency will be astonished. Detroit is ours and with it the whole Michigan territory, the army prisoners of war. Rejoice in my good fortune, and join with me in prayers to heaven.

The other area of war at this time was Niagara, to which Brock now hurried back.

He went in the knowledge that he left no menace behind him. The only other American positions in the old Northwest were two little forts, Fort Wayne on the Miami River and Fort Dearborn on Lake

Michigan. When the Detroit situation began to look difficult, Hull had sent a message to Captain Nathan Heald at Fort Dearborn ordering him to evacuate the fort and take his people—fifty-four regular soldiers, a dozen militiamen, nine women, and eighteen children—to seek shelter either at Detroit itself or at Fort Wayne. Heald led his sixty-six men and twenty-seven dependents off on the morning of August 15. The local Indians of the Potawatomi tribe, led by a chief called Black Bird, having joyfully received the news from Mackinac Island, formed up, four hundred in number, and met the little column in sandy scrubland not far from Fort Dearborn. In a savage scuffle, all twelve militia, twenty-six regulars, two women, and twelve children perished; the rest, rather surprisingly in view of reputed Indian battle fury, were taken prisoner. Some escaped later, and the rest were ransomed by the British. Soon after, Fort Wayne, garrisoned by seventy regulars under an officer reputedly drunk much of the time, was attacked and occupied by Indians. Brock was enabled by these two swift and brutal actions to concentrate singlemindedly on the position at Niagara.

Madison's Secretary of War, William Eustis, was just then a kind of Lord High Everything Else, carrying out, or attempting to carry out, the duties of quartermaster general, commissary general, Commissioner of Indian Affairs, Commissioner of Public Lands and Commissioner of Pensions. To discharge these varied functions he had a staff of about a dozen. Administrators and staff officers alike kept their paperwork to a minimum, not only because it was handwritten, but because dispatches had to be carried at a pace no swifter than that of a good horse or an Indian runner over huge undeveloped distances. Eight days after Madison's war message, that is on July 9, Eustis wrote to his senior combat officer, Major General Henry Dearborn, aged sixty-one and stationed at Boston, ordering him to move his troops to Albany from where they would strike into Canada by way of Lake Champlain. Eustis rather unwisely included the phrase: "You will take your own time."

Dearborn, who had served for eight years in Jefferson's cabinet and for three years as Collector of Taxes for the Port of Boston, before being appointed Major General on January 27, 1812, was known to be a slow mover. He replied to Eustis that he doubted the wisdom of leaving his work in Boston just then, to which Eustis replied: "Go to Albany or the Lake! The blow must be struck. Congress must not meet without a victory to announce to them." Dearborn waited a week after receiving this appeal, then hauled his advance column onto the road—if the tracks it had to follow merited that name—reached Albany, and camped there throughout the month of July.

On the evening of August 1 a ship from Halifax came into the dock at Quebec with the news that the British government had repealed the Orders in Council. The dispatch suggested that Prevost might try to open peace moves with the Americans, so Prevost sent Colonel Baynes to Albany under a flag of truce. Baynes arrived at Dearborn's headquarters, at Greenbush across the river from Albany, on August 8. Dearborn, who was not at all loth to abandon his military prospects, nonetheless knew that he did not possess the authority to call off the war on his own in the name of the United States government, and suggested that he should give orders to officers commanding frontier posts to take only defensive action until orders to the contrary came, if they did come, from Washington. He told Baynes that he had no authority over Hull but that he would suggest the same course of action to him (at that time Hull was still hesitating at Sandwich). Dearborn's promised letter to Hull had gone no farther than Niagara by August 17, by which time Detroit and Fort Dearborn had both been lost. Hull did know before then, however, that the troops at Albany had not moved toward his assistance. On August 9 Dearborn wrote to Eustis, presumably to excuse his lack of decisive action:

I consider the agreement as favourable at this period, for we could not act offensively except at Detroit for some time, and there it will not probably have any effect on General Hull or his movements.

Prevost, hugely encouraged by events, reported on August 17 to Lord Bathurst in London:

Another consequence of the Mission of Col. Baynes and of the arrangement resulting from it, has been a Discovery of the inability of the Government of the United States to overrun the Canadas and of their unprepared state for carrying on the war with vigour; this has become so manifest that His Majesty's Subjects in both Provinces are beginning to feel an increased confidence in the Government protecting them, and as the means and resources which have been displayed appear to have far exceeded their expectations, so has it effectually secured their best exertions for the defence of their Country against any tumultuary force—In the mean time from a partial suspension of hostilities I am enabled to improve and augment my resources against an Invasion, whilst the Enemy distracted by Party broils and intrigues are obliged to remain supine and to witness daily the diminution of the Force they had so much difficulty in collecting.

Brock, who as a victorious general naturally wished to clinch matters with another quick victory, had doubts. He wrote to his brothers: "Should peace follow, the measure will be well; if hostilities recommence, nothing could be more unfortunate than this pause." He was particularly troubled in case the Indians, stimulated by action, might feel that the British had let them down by seeming hesitant. In this belief he was reinforced by the comment of one officer who wrote in picturesque style:

Tecumseh now openly holds that the Great Spirit intended the Ohio River for the boundary between his white and red children, but that a cloud hung over the eyes of the tribes and they could not see what the Great Spirit meant. General Brock has now torn away the cloud.

But, like so many successful commanders, Brock had trouble with the civilians upon whom he depended. He noted that the Upper Canada legislature, though "a more decent House had not been elected since the formation of the Province," seemed passive:

If I have recourse to the Martial Law I am told the whole armed force will disperse. The population, though I had no great confidence in the Majority, is worse than I expected to find it–And all Magistrates &c &c appear quite confounded and decline acting–the consequence of the most improper conduct is tolerated–The officers of Militia exert no authority, everything shews as if a certainty existed of a change taking place soon. But I still hope the arrival of reinforcements may yet avert such a dire calamity–

This was a natural reaction in an eager soldier confronted with an Assembly which persisted in debating a school bill instead of voting him the orders and supplies he needed. They did not seem to realize that the effective military frontier of the United States was now back on the Wabash and Ohio rivers, and that a splendid opportunity existed to make capital of that advantage. For the Americans were wavering badly. An elderly American, Major General Samuel Hopkins, had been told to take four thousand militiamen of Kentucky from Vincennes to attack the Indians who had captured Fort Dearborn;

within a few days the Kentucky men refused to move, and when Hopkins called for five hundred volunteers not one stepped forward, so the project came to nothing. On the other hand the army in Canada was enjoying unusual prestige. The Reverend Michael Smith, a Baptist Minister, wrote:

> The surrender of the fort at Detroit and all the Michigan Territory, were events which the people of Canada could scarcely believe, even after they were known to be true. Indeed, when I saw the officers and soldiers returning to Fort George, with the spoils of my countrymen, I could scarcely believe my own eyes.

Smith, who had moved to Canada from the United States in 1808, saw that "the Army now became respectable, and a dread fell on those who had opposed the Government."

But Prevost, aware that Brock's twelve hundred men could have more than six thousand moving against them, viewed the campaign as a defensive one, and cautioned delay. Neither he nor Brock realized that Dearborn was a delaying general, nor were they fully informed about the sluggish response of many Americans to the war. On paper, America could easily raise and maintain an army of a hundred thousand; in practice, few men were eager either to enlist with the regulars for five years in return for steady pay, a bounty, and a good-sized piece of land at the end of it, or to join the militia for a year. The most Congress could hope for was a six-months' term of militia service, and even that was far from satisfactory, for without hesitation men would go off to fetch the harvest in.

President Madison had replied quickly to Dearborn's note about peace moves. The repeal of the Orders might be revoked at any time, Britain had said nothing about impressment, and to back down now might lose face. Madison therefore told Eustis to order Dearborn into battle: "After the receipt of this letter and allowing a reasonable time in which you will inform Sir George Prevost thereof, you will proceed with the utmost vigour in your operations." Dearborn notified Prevost that the war was still on, with effect from September 4, on which day Brock arrived in Kingston to inspect the forces. The news of the supposed resumption of hostilities reached him there, and that night he sailed across Lake Ontario for Fort George, where the commanding officer, Major General Sheaffe, told him that American strength on the opposite shore was increasing far beyond the numbers under his own command. Brock, not stopping to count, sent a hurried appeal for more men, which angered Prevost because for several weeks past he had been sending a steady stream of troops, more than ten companies in all. By the time he had mastered his temper sufficiently to write back telling Brock he could spare no more troops, Brock had taken a good look around, decided that he could afford to reinforce Amherstburg and Michilimackinac, and tackle the Niagara Americans as well, especially now that he had more than half his own Forty-Ninth Foot with him, even though, as he wrote home, "the regiment has been ten years in this country, drinking rum without bounds."

Facing Brock on the opposite bank of the Niagara River, which was two hundred and fifty yards wide at that point, were Dearborn's troops, plus 900 regulars and 2,650 militia under Major General Stephen Van Rensselaer and 1,650 more regulars under Brigadier General Alexander Smyth, known as "Apocalypse" Smyth because he had written an "explanation" of the Book of Revelations. He had reached his eminent rank more for his reputation as an orator in his native Virginia than for any military talents he had. Van Rensselaer's men were grouped at the village of Lewistown, situated below the Falls and opposite Queenston on the Canadian side. The sheltering Queenston Heights, running east and west on both banks, formed, in Van Rensselaer's opinion, an excellent objective from which, if he could capture that ground, he could sweep up resistance throughout the whole area. Smyth, who had never done any fighting in his life, decided that a crossing above the Falls, where the banks were lower and the river slower, would be more sensible, and did not condescend to discuss this view with his opposite number, who was a mere militia officer from New York. The consequent ill feeling between the two generals caused them to act independently and without any coordinated plan.

Brock's troops were dispersed, part of them at Fort Erie and Chippawa above the Falls, part at Fort George, and a small force at Queenston. At this village of less than a hundred houses he had about three hundred men with one three-pounder gun and an eighteen-pounder in a small earthwork on the north slope of the Heights above the village. A mile down the river at Vrooman's Point was a twenty-four pounder overlooking the river. Queenston lay approximately midway between Fort George and the Falls, a distance of about seven miles in either direction.

On the night of October 9 a a band of soldiers and sailors led by Lieutenant Jesse Elliott, USN, captured two vessels from under the guns of Fort Erie: the *Detroit,* surrendered earlier by Hull, which ran aground and had to be burned; and the *Caledonia,* which Elliott's men sailed safely away. This was a distinct success on the part of the Americans, and Brock was worrying about it all next day and into the night, when Van Rensselaer attempted a crossing from Lewiston. It was a fiasco: the men had not been drilled or properly briefed; the plan was imprecise; several boats were found to have no oars; and a tremendous downpour of rain soaked the whole force; so that Van Rensselaer ordered everyone back to camp. Brock assumed that the move was a feint, but in the morning sent a staff officer to Queenston, partly to sort our mutinous rumbles in the British troops, partly to make a duty call at American headquarters to arrange for an exchange of prisoners. On his return to Fort George the officer reported that he had found some of the British mutineers under arrest but had released them "on the specious plea of their offense proceeding from too free an indulgence in drink," with the underlying reason that he was sure that another American foray upon Queenston was certain within a very short time.

Van Rensselaer, in the unfortunate position of being ignored by his closest colleague and prodded to action by his superiors in Washington as well as by Governor Daniel Tompkins, his political opponent in his native New York, ordered another river crossing for the early hours of Tuesday, October 13. Of some eighty boats at his disposal he employed thirteen; of his five thousand men he took about six hundred, half of them militia. He employed every gun he could bring to bear on the river for a bombardment to cover the crossing. Three of his boats found the current too strong for them and were swept downstream, but the rest managed to come ashore at the right place, just above Queenston. Brock, roused from a troubled sleep by the gunfire, scrambled out of bed, flung on his clothes, called for a horse and, without waiting for his aide-de-camp to be ready, set off as fast as the horse could go in the darkness toward the sound of the guns seven miles away.

Ven Rensselaer's cousin and chief of staff, Colonel Solomon Van Rensselaer, had been seriously wounded in the first moments of the assault, and his militiamen had been halted by the 49th regiment's fire. Captain John Wool and a company of the 13th US Infantry regiment, striking out on their own, found the twisting path that led up the Heights and climbed it. This was so unlikely a thing to do that its possibility did not occur to Brock, who, as soon as he galloped into Queenston, ordered the company of the 49th positioned on the Heights to come down into the village for support. He rode alone up to the gun in its earthwork, from where he could see in the faint light of dawn the shadowy groups of Americans across the river waiting to enter the boats, and the splashes of cannon shot hitting the water from both guns, the one where he stood and the one on Vrooman's Point. Without warning Captain Wool's party appeared on the crest above and charged yelling down the slope. Brock's gunners hastily put the eighteen-pounder out of action by ramming a spike into the touch-hole and fled down into the village, with Brock running along beside them, leading his horse. Here Brock rapidly ordered about a hundred of the 49th and about a hundred militia into line and led them back toward the Heights.

In that uncertain light the determined figure in red coat trimmed with gold with cocked hat set firmly on his head, coming steadily foward waving his sword, was unmistakable: Wool's men had no doubt where to aim. Brock was shot in the wrist, stumbled, and went on; a moment later a bullet struck him in the chest, and he died instantly–or, according to legend, after having just enough time to gasp out: "Push on, the York Volunteers."

The York Volunteers were two companies of militia from York who had been hurriedly ordered up by Brock in his rapid commands before spurring off from Fort George. His aide-de-camp, Lieutenant Colonel John Macdonell, had brought the York militia into Queenston moments before his chief fell; Brock's men stood for a minute or two irresolutely looking down at their dead leader, then turned and retreated down the hill, where Macdonell drove them back to recapture the gun, which they did, though Macdonell was fatally wounded in the charge. Captain Wool had received reinforcements which enabled him to order a fresh attack from the Heights, but he was wounded too seriously to continue, and the leadership passed to a young lieutenant colonel of the regular army, Winfield Scott. Scott regrouped his men and sent them down the slope again, this time to such good effect that the British withdrew from Queenston altogether and went back as far as Vrooman's Point to rearrange themselves and wait for reinforcements in their turn. The twenty-four pounder on the

Point kept on stolidly banging away at the American position across the river, where the American militia were refusing to cross on the grounds that their terms of reference did not include military service outside United States territory, but actually because they disliked the prospect of battle. Meanwhile, the garrison at Fort Erie remained poised to beat off a possible attack from Black Rock, and the guns of American Fort Niagara and British Fort George, facing each other, continued the exchange of fire that they had been carrying on all morning, in the course of which the American shots managed to set several houses in the nearby village of Newark on fire.

Van Rensselaer, who had briefly visited his troops on the Heights where they numbered about six hundred and were running short of ammunition, found on returning to Lewiston:

> To my utter astonishment, the ardour of the unengaged troops had entirely subsided. I rode in all directions, urged the men by every consideration to pass over; but in vain.

He was now forced to stand on the Lewiston Heights watching helplessly as the British reinforcements from Fort George, whose gleam of distant scarlet had revealed their approach for some time, came up and dislodged the Americans, who backed down to the edge of the water. Here they found no boats ready to receive them; they surrendered. They had lost sixty killed and a hundred and seventy wounded. Their total losses for the day were more than three hundred killed and wounded, and nearly a thousand taken prisoner. The British losses were, apparently, fourteen dead, seventy-seven wounded, and twenty-one missing. It is illuminating that among so small a number of the dead were two of their commanders, Brock and Macdonell. No one could accuse the generals of leading their troops from behind. The successful push from Vrooman's Point had been led by Sheaffe, who was rewarded by London with a baronetcy; the British government had created Brock a Knight of the Bath for capturing Detroit, but of course he was dead long before the news of this could have reached him.

Van Rensselaer had had enough. He arranged a truce with Sheaffe, an offer that Sheaffe promptly accepted because he was in the somewhat awkward position of having more prisoners than troops, and the American commander instantly sent in his resignation to General Dearborn, which was as instantly accepted. The American command thus passed to Apocalypse Smyth. Both sides were glad of a breathing space.

The Americans made curiously little use of the breathing space once they had it. The first three weeks of November were marked by many fiery speeches and little else. Much of this inactivity was caused by the militia's cheerful assumption that they could refuse to go on whenever it suited them. On November 19 General Dearborn took his troops north from Plattsburg on Lake Champlain and, after going about twenty miles, the militiamen declined to go farther. Dearborn accepted this and marched them back again, for all the world like the Grand Duke of York in the nursery rhyme.

Apocalypse Smyth had been making many loud pronouncements. On assuming command he had said that his predecessors had been "popular men, destitute alike of theory and experience." His men, he said, were used to "obedience, silence, and steadiness"; they would conquer or die. He made two attempts to cross the river. Just before dawn on Saturday, November 28, an assault force landed two and a half miles from Fort Erie, at a point where there were some fifty British soldiers with two guns; meanwhile a second assault wave went to destroy the bridge over Frenchman's Creek toward Chippawa, but failed to do so. Smyth had managed to embark, in all, twelve hundred men by midday, but a force of British regulars and militia commanded by Lieutenant Colonel Cecil Bisshopp repelled the Americans and drove them back across the water at a cost of seventeen dead, forty-seven wounded, and thirty-five missing. Smyth held a council of war and canceled the action. The following night, in sleety rain, he embarked fifteen hundred men to spend most of the hours of darkness in the boats, encouraging them with the words: "Hearts of War! Tomorrow will be memorable in the annals of the United States!" When tomorrow came, Smyth sent a message demanding the surrender of the British position on the opposite bank. It was refused. He called off the action again and ordered the boats unloaded.

The troops, astounded by this, broke into wild disorder: "A scene of confusion ensued which it is difficult to describe, about four thousand men discharging their muskets in every direction," wrote one officer. Many of the shots happened to be fired in the direction of Smyth's tent. Smyth sent his resignation to Dearborn, whereupon the War-Hawk Peter Porter, who now commanded a militia regiment with the rank of brigadier, called Smyth a coward in public. The two of them then fought a duel, with pistols at twelve paces, but contrived to avoid actual bloodshed. Smyth in due course got himself elected to Congress, where he made loud statements for a long time. Winfield Scott summed him up rather kindly when he wrote in his memoirs that Smyth, "though well read, brave and honourable," showed "no talent for command, and made himself ridiculous on the Niagara frontier." Smyth published a reply to his critics on December 3, 1812, in which he made a number of interesting points:

My orders were to pass into Canada with 3,000 men *at once.* On the first day of embarkation not more than 1,100 men were embarked, of whom 400, that is, half the regular infantry, were exhausted with fatigue, and want of rest. On the second embarkation, only 1,500 men were embarked, and these were to have put off immediately, and to have descended the river to a point where reinforcements were not to be expected. On both days, many of the regular troops were men in bad health, who could not have stood one days march; who, although they were on the sick report, were turned out by their ardent officers.

The affair at Queenston is a caution against relying on crowds who go to the bank of Niagara to look on a battle as on a theatrical exhibition; who if they are disappointed of the sights, break their muskets: or if they are without rations for a day, desert.

Smyth's comment on his near-civilians who thought that a battle might be a very fine sight reminds the reader of the picnic parties in their carriages who drove lightheartedly out of Washington nearly fifty years later, to watch the battle of First Manassas, and who, finding the experience less agreeable than they had expected, turned hastily for home, blocking the road, so that the soldiers' retreat became a rout.

Although the creation of the police force in Britain cannot be dated earlier than 1829, the term, at least, was known and used in Canada by 1812. In Quebec on June 29 of that year a notice headed by the British coat of arms and the word POLICE in large letters announced that:

WHEREAS authentic intelligence has been received that the Government of the United States of America did, on the 18th instant, declare War against the United Kingdom of Great Britain and Ireland and its dependencies, Notice is hereby given, that all Subjects or Citizens of the said United States, and all persons claiming American Citizenship, are ordered to quit the City of

Quebec, on or before TWELVE o'clock at Noon, on WEDNESDAY next, and the District of Quebec on or before 12 o'clock at noon on FRIDAY next, on pain of arrest.

ROSS CUTHBERT,
C.Q.S. & Inspector of Police.

The Constables of the City of Quebec are ordered to assemble in the Police Office at 10 o'clock to-morrow morning, to receive instructions.

Not everyone who could do so had obeyed this order, for on November 9 another proclamation announced that every citizen of the United States who did not report to the examination boards meeting at York, Kingston, or Niagara before the first day of 1813 would be "considered as an alien enemy and become liable to be treated as a prisoner of war or a spy as circumstances might dictate."

Running parallel with the difficulty of weeding out those American-Canadians who might prove dangerous was the practical need to prevent unnecessary conflict in a territory which had tiny scattered settlements dotted thinly over huge stretches of undeveloped country. Cultivation and trade had to go on, war or no war. Independent plans for mutual convenience were worked out in places where commerce between Canada and America was essential. The citizens of Eastport in Maine agreed with the citizens of New Brunswick not to do any damage to one another's property or goods, and New Brunswick asked for permission to receive imported supplies in unarmed American ships. Permission was given by the man who had succeeded Prevost as governor of Nova Scotia, Lieutenant General Sir John Coape Sherbrooke, to whom the military commanders of New Brunswick, Newfoundland, Cape Breton, and Bermuda were directly responsible. Sir John's order read in part:

I have therefore thought proper by and with the advice of His Majesty's Subjects under my Government, to abstain from molesting the Inhabitants living on the shores of the United States contiguous to this Province and New Brunswick: and on no account to molest the Goods, or unarmed Coasting Vessels, belonging to the Defenceless Inhabitants on the Frontiers, so long as they shall abstain on their parts from any acts of Hostility and Molestation towards the Inhabitants of this Province and New Brunswick, who are in a similar situation.

Sherbrooke had made gestures of defense, mounting guns in all his principal harbors, but he hoped that nothing would interfere with the arrival of necessary goods. He was relieved of some anxiety by the fact that the Royal Navy could spare few ships to patrol ports in his area: only one ship of the line with six frigates and sixteen small ships could be called upon between Nova Scotia and Bermuda, and the British Consul * in Boston could, and did, recommend American merchants who were carrying supplies to the British Army in the Peninsula for permits to proceed freely. Vice-Admiral Herbert Sawyer issued a license "given under my hand and seal, on board His Majesty's ship *Centurion,* at Halifax, this fourth day of August, 1812", to

> require and direct all captains and commanders of His Majesty's ships and vessels of war, which may fall in with any American, or other vessel bearing a neutral flag, laden with flour, bread, corn and pease, or any other species of dried provisions, bound from America to Spain and Portugal, and having this protection on board, to suffer her to proceed without unnecessary obstruction or detention in her voyage: *Provided,* she shall appear to be steering a due course for those countries, and it being understood this is only to be in force for one voyage, and within six months from the date thereof.

It is curious that after war had broken out, the manners of both sides toward each other improved considerably.

When the war broke out, the Canadian Provincial Marine had, in addition to the *Queen Charlotte* (sixteen guns) and the *General Hunter* (six guns), a twenty-two gun corvette, the *Royal George,* and four armed schooners, three of them on Lake Ontario and one on Lake Champlain. These four were neglected, however, and the Provincial Marine was undermanned, partly because sailors could earn more under better conditions in the merchant vessels, and partly because the commanders clung on like barnacles and would not retire: one of them was eighty-seven. There were as a result few opportunities for promotion.

The Provincial Marine still heavily outnumbered anything that the Americans could put on the Great Lakes against it. The American Secretary of the Navy, Paul Hamilton, had asked Congress for twelve ships of seventy-four guns each and twenty frigates, a request that Congress had refused on the grounds that shipbuilding was a slow and

* It may seem peculiar to modern readers that there were still Consuls of enemy powers staying at their posts after the outbreak of war, but nevertheless it is a fact that they were not recalled. It is, of course, equally strange that American merchants continued to supply British troops. One can only assume (perhaps in both cases?) that the profits outweighed any possible heroics.

costly process and the new ships would not be ready soon enough to have a decisive effect in the war. The United States Navy had ten frigates at that time: five of them laid up for repairs, three sloops, seven brigs, and sixty-two of Jefferson's ill-fated gunboats; there were about four thousand seamen and boys in the American Navy and some eighteen hundred enlisted marines. All that Congress would agree to do was to authorize repairs to the five frigates. The three best frigates, beautiful ships with fine clear lines and plenty of canvas, were the USS *Constitution, United States,* and *President.* On June 22, 1812 these three, with a couple of sloops and brigs, put to sea from New York harbor as two squadrons commanded by Commodore Rodgers (of the *Little Belt* affair and still on board the USS *President)* and Commodore Stephen Decatur on the *United States.* The captain of the *Constitution* was Isaac Hull, nephew of the general.

Decatur, a bold and dashing officer despite his slight figure and dreamy-eyed delicate face with its aquiline nose, had already proved his quality in battle. In 1804 he had gone to Tripoli to recapture the frigate *Philadelphia,* seized as a prize vessel by the piratical Bashaw of Tripoli as part of his running war against all ships sailing close to his coast. Decatur began by capturing a Turkish ketch, the *Mastico,* remnaming it *Intrepid* but changing nothing else in the appearance of the ship, cramming it with seventy-five American sailors and marines and, in a twenty-minute action of daring brilliance, sailing into Tripoli harbor, grappling a line to the *Philadelphia,* setting her on fire to make her useless to the enemy, pulling clear with Decatur himself one of the last men to jump before the ropes were cut, and getting clean away with the ship and without the loss of a single American life. Decatur, then a lieutenant, was promoted the youngest captain in the United States Navy for an exploit that won warm praise from Nelson himself. Later in 1804 Decatur took part in the American attack on Tripoli in which he acquitted himself with such distinction that he was awarded a Congressional Sword of Honor. For years after that, he increased his reputation on almost every voyage, and now his squadron consisted of the *United States* with the three smaller ships, *Essex, Hornet,* and *Argus.*

The two American squadrons attracted so much attention from the Royal Navy that the American Merchant Marine enjoyed a period of unusual calm. An officer on board HMS *Guerrière* wrote: "We have been so completely occupied in looking for Commodore Rodgers that we have taken very few prizes." Admiral Sawyer ordered a squadron out from Halifax to search for him, led by HMS *Shannon,* commanded by Captain Philip Bowes Vere Broke, and including HMS *Belvidera* and HMS *Africa.* They did not find Rodgers, but on July 19, off the coast of New Jersey, they saw the USS *Constitution,* which had just taken on a fresh crew at Annapolis and was making what speed she could toward New York. The very slight breeze fell and for two days all the vessels were becalmed. When on the afternoon of July 19 a wind sprang up, the big American frigate was able to draw away and easily outdistance her pursuers.

Captain Isaac Hull, pleased by this, put into New York for supplies and sailed again without waiting for orders. But for seventeen days he saw no sign of the enemy. Then, near Bermuda on August 20, he encountered the *Gurrière,* a ship captured by the British from the French, and "in less than thirty minutes, she was left without a spar standing, her hull cut to pieces." The hulk, floating helplessly, was blown up. It was the first single-ship victory of the war.

Two other naval encounters followed. In September the American sloop *Wasp* fought the British sloop *Frolic* in a drawn action on the same Halifax-Bermuda run, and in October USS *United States,* with accurate use of long-range guns, outfought and captured HMS *Macedonian* midway between the Canaries and the Azores. For this exploit Decatur was granted the freedom of the city of New York, swords of honor from Pennsylvania and Virginia, a congressional gold medal, and a sword of gold from his native city of Philadelphia. Americans and Britons alike were stunned to find that the supreme Royal Navy was not, perhaps, quite as supreme after all. The flag of the *Macedonian* was presented to Mrs. Madison at a celebration ball in Washington "amid the loud exclamations of the company and national music" by Paul Hamilton's son, a lieutenant in the United States Navy. Hamilton, Secretary of the Navy, was so delighted that he got drunk. The President sent for him on December 29 and asked for his resignation, apparently on the grounds that his conduct in public (for this was not his only appearance in that condition) had become sufficiently scandalous to outweigh his usefulness. On the very same day, as if to underline the sequence of American victories at sea, the *Constitution,* now commanded by Captain William Bainbridge, reduced HMS *Java* to floating debris in forty-three minutes. Captain James Lawrence of USS *Hornet* sank HMS *Peacock* in a quarter of an hour off the Demerara River on February 24, 1813. These stirring events prompted Congress to vote provision for four new ships of the line and six heavy frigates for the United States Navy, though none of these reached blue water before the war was over, and the military value of the victories was only slight, for the Royal Navy, stung to action by them, mounted a new and effective blockade on the Delaware and Chesapeake bays from the end of 1812 and extended this during 1813 to all ports from New York southward and to Long Island Sound. USS *Constellation* and *Constitution* were bottled up for months to come.

James Madison's first message to Congress after the outbreak of the war had been the kind that all, or nearly all, national leaders feel compelled to announce at such moments:

> To have shrunk under such circumstances from manly resistance would have been a degradation blasting our best and proudest hopes; it would have struck us from the high rank where the virtuous struggle of our fathers had placed us, and have betrayed the magnificent legacy which we hold in trust for future generations. It would have acknowledged that on the element which forms three-fourths of the globe we inhabit, and where all independent nations have equal and common rights, the Americans were not an independent people, but colonists and vassals.

And at the Fourth of July celebrations in Boston the toast had been proposed: "The war—the second and last struggle for national freedom—a final effort to rescue from the deep the drowning honour of our country." The theme of the "second struggle" was widely embroidered.

Across the Atlantic the British, who had taken on Napoleon, could hardly be expected to flinch at a small war far away. The *Times* took a lofty tone: "We cannot fear a war with any Power in the world." But, it continued, "It is not unmanly to say, that we regret the sad necessity of carrying the flame and devastation of war to a part of the world which has not seen a hostile foot for thirty years." The *Caledonian Mercury* had declared that "impressment was too paltry an affair for two great nations to go to war about" now that the Orders having been repealed were no longer an issue. It took time, and some uncomfortable events, to make the British angry. The defeats at sea, the tentative moves in Canada, helped to change the mind of London.

SEVEN

§

From a Find to a Check

When Hull surrendered at Detroit and Dearborn showed no disposition to remedy his mistakes, Madison and his cabinet decided that the little United States Navy should be brought into the game. Command of the Lakes was what they were after. Command of the sea was too much to expect, but the Lakes might be possible.

They sent one hundred and seventy sailors and marines with a hundred and forty ships' carpenters, more than a hundred guns, and a wagon train of supplies to Sackets Harbor by a meandering river route up the Hudson, Mohawk, and Oswego rivers to Lake Ontario. Sackets Harbor had a small navy yard where Lieutenant Melancthon Woolsey, USN, was busy superintending the conversion of several schooners into warships and transports. Brigadier General Jacob Brown had his militia brigade there, to which was added a rifle company under the big, dashing North Carolina Captain Benjamin Forsyth. During July and August a couple of harmless skirmishes had taken place at Sackets Harbor, but little other action. On September 3, 1812 the order to "assume command of the Naval forces on Lakes Erie and Ontario, and to use every exertion to obtain control of them this fall" was sent to Captain Isaac Chauncey USN, who was given the courtesy rank of commodore. Chauncey, who had a high reputation for practical, versatile competence, had just turned forty and had been for the last four years in charge of the New York navy yard. He reached Sackets Harbor on October 6.

Sackets Harbor was a good base for attacks on Canadian supplies moving along the St. Lawrence from Montreal to Lake Ontario. For safety, such supplies went in convoy, escorted by Canadian militia or, if possible, by regular troops, but the way was complicated by the sequence of rapids on the river. At the rapids, the boats had to be dragged by ropes pulled by teams of men on shore, and it is clear that these would be particularly easy to attack. One try was made on September 16 near Prescott, but the British-Canadian escort troops drove the Americans off; a week later Captain Forsyth took his American riflemen and about thirty militiamen to Cape Vincent, across the St. Lawrence, and up to the western edge of the small staging-post of Gananoque in the Thousand Islands, seventeen miles from Kingston. As Forsyth made his dawn landing, the alarm was raised in Gananoque, but the local militia could do no more than fire their muskets and retreat, for the place was not fortified. One American died, one was wounded; four Canadians were wounded, eight captured. Some of the Canadians had been wearing discarded British Army red coats, so Forsyth naturally assumed that he had beaten off real British regulars. His men took what arms they could find, set fire to a small storehouse with some meat and flour in it, and fired on the house of one Colonel Stone, wounding his wife who was alone there. "They broke open and ransacked his Trunks, and had his Bedding and other articles carried down to the shore with an intention of carrying them off with them; but this was prevented by their officers," reported the Kingston *Gazette.* Brown paid Forsyth's men a bounty for their exploit, and went up to Ogdensburg to reinforce its garrison, taking Forsyth's riflemen with him. The river at Ogdensburg was two thousand yards wide, and Brown found to his horror that the citizens on both banks were pretending that the war did not exist, crossing from one side to another under flags of truce, with Canadians from Prescott coming over to shop at Parish's store and have tea or dinner with him. This happy state of affairs appealed to David Parish who had made a fortune in his early days by smuggling Mexican gold to upper New York by way of Paris. Brown stopped all this unseemly fraternization by filling up the shore batteries and ordering them to fire on all convoys, and by sending Forsyth's men out on quick forays against the opposition militia.

The British commander at Prescott was Colonel Lethbridge, who had been transferred there from Kingston, and who now decided on a bold stroke: a frontal attack. He collected every Canadian militiaman he could muster, their arrival in Prescott being hopefully observed by Brown with an excellent telescope in one of Parish's upstairs windows,

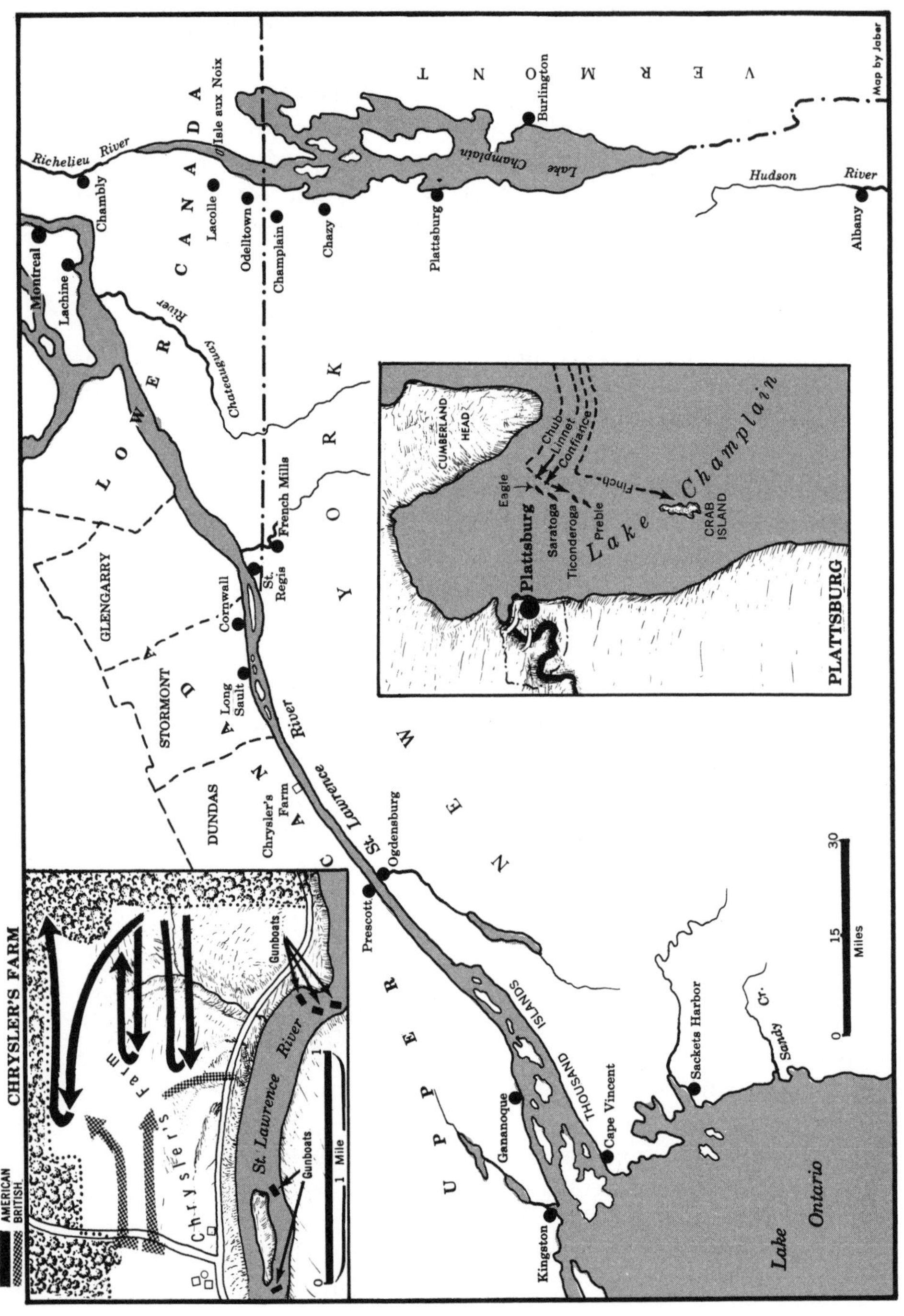
LOWER CANADA
UPPER CANADA
NEW YORK
VERMONT
Richelieu River
Chambly
Isle aux Noix
Lacolle
Odelltown
Champlain
Chazy
Plattsburg
Burlington
Lake Champlain
Hudson River
Albany
Montreal
Lachine
Chateauguay River
French Mills
St. Regis
Cornwall
GLENGARRY
STORMONT
DUNDAS
Long Sault
Chrysler's Farm
St. Lawrence River
Ogdensburg
Prescott
THOUSAND ISLANDS
Gananoque
Kingston
Cape Vincent
Sackets Harbor
Sandy Cr.
Lake Ontario
0
15
30
Miles
Map by Jaber
PLATTSBURG
CUMBERLAND HEAD
Chub
Linnet
Confiance
Finch
Eagle
Saratoga
Ticonderoga
Preble
CRAB ISLAND
CHRYSLER'S FARM
AMERICAN
BRITISH
Chrysler's Farm
Gunboats
0
1
1 Mile

for Brown looked forward to action. On the morning of Sunday, October 4, two companies of Fencibles and six hundred militia set out in a swarm of boats to cross the river; the Americans opened fire with grapeshot; the attackers turned back in midstream; and Colonel Lethbridge was recalled to Montreal.

Just before dawn on October 23 the American militia at French Mills made an unexpected attack on the Canadian outpost across the river at St. Regis, which was manned by thirty men under an ensign named Pierre Rototte. This was successful: Rototte and seven of his men were killed and the rest were captured, but the Americans made the mistake of taking away with them a supply of guns and blankets intended for the nearby Iroquois reservation, so that the Iroquois became, and remained, anti-American from that time on.

The opposing navies were, for the most part, continuing to evade one another. But the Royal Navy, emboldened by Napoleon's disastrous foray into Russia, had increased its power in what it lumped together as the North America and West Indies Command. This now numbered ninety-seven vessels: eleven ships of the line, thirty-four frigates, thirty-eight sloops, and fourteen other ships. Their overall commander was Sir John Borlase Warren, aged fifty-eight, MA of Cambridge, who had served in the War of Independence and then, in 1802, had been sent to Russia as ambassador-extraordinary. He arrived in Halifax on September 26 with instructions to explore the possibilities of a settlement between the two warring nations.

It was, of course, too late. Neither side could then afford to lose face, or so each thought. Neither could accept, or even consider for more than a token pause, the conditions proposed by the other. Yet Warren obediently tried. The British government, in the meantime, took the unusual step of authorizing piracy by permitting the governor of Nova Scotia, Sir John Sherbrooke and his administrator, General G. S. Smyth, to give their local shipowners letters of marque to fit out privateering vessels. This of course was not to be official, and the normal trading licenses would continue to be issued as before.

Meanwhile, on the American side, Chauncey at Sackets Harbor had been busily working away at plans that were going to change the situation on the Lakes considerably. He had about a dozen ships to deploy, the biggest of which was the US brig *Oneida.* The rest were armed schooners. All were armed with carronades rather than orthodox cannon. Carronades could fire heavier shot than cannon, yet they were smaller and lighter, required fewer men in the gun crews, and had never been known to explode. It is only fair to point out that these advantages had been appreciated by the officers of the Canadian Provincial Marine, whose *Royal George* and *Earl of Moira* were also equipped with carronades.

On November 8 Chauncey was ready for his first attack, which was aimed at three ships, the *Royal George, Prince Regent,* and *Duke of Gloucester,* en route for Kingston harbor. He set out in USS *Oneida* with an escort of six schooners, caught up with the British on November 10, and came under fire from the British guns at Point Henry. The town of Kingston was crammed with troops, alerted hours in advance, but the exchanges of shot were too far apart to do much damage. After two hours of lobbing across the water, Chauncey withdrew, leaving one Briton dead and a handful wounded, and one dead and three injured on his own ship, reporting to the Secretary of the Navy that she had only

> a few shot through her sails. The other vessels lost no men and received but little injury in their Hull and sails with the exception of the *Pert,* whose gun bursted in the early part of the action [presumably it was not a carronade] and wounded her Commander, sailing master Arundel, badly, and a midshipman and 3 men slightly. Mr. Arundel who refused to quit the Deck although wounded, was knocked overboard in beating up to our anchorage and I am sorry to say was drowned.

Despite the low-key quality of this action, it had a considerable effect. The *Prince Regent* and the *Duke of Gloucester* made haste to take shelter in the harbor of New York and stayed there for the rest of the winter; the *Earl of Moira* crept quietly into Kingston and stayed there; Chauncey kept a blockade going at that port, and received a fine reinforcement, the corvette *Madison,* built at Sackets Harbor in forty-five days and launched on November 26.

Three days before the launching, the militia of Cornwall and Glengarry counties had attacked French Mills in revenge for the American attack a month before at St. Regis. Luckily they had placed themselves under the command of Captain Andrew Gray who with seventy regulars was escorting a convoy. The militia had wanted to attack head on in a blaze of enthusiasm, but Gray

> saw what would happen by following their advice. The only difference between us was, that I saw it before, and they after the capture of the place.

They were all fully convinced that their error—had we gone by the River, we would have been shamefully beaten, as they expected us in that direction, and had a Picquet of 20 men on the River banks, that might have killed the whole Party.

But, wrote Gray cheerfully, the militia had done very well once he had "got them in motion, and all properly arranged"—which meant that they were operating to his own satisfaction.

At this time, Dearborn had experienced another fiasco. He had slowly moved six thousand men, half of them regulars, up to the Canadian border close to the village of Champlain, so slowly indeed, that Major de Salaberry, who held the grand-sounding command of the "forward defences of the Eastern Townships," had plenty of time to move his defense troops into position. In the early morning of November 20 Dearborn's advance guard crossed the border, and met firm resistance, helped, in the dim light, by one group of Americans firing on another by mistake. The militiamen of New York and Vermont refused to cross into Canada. Dearborn's troops retreated to Champlain; Dearborn sat still for three days, then ordered the whole force back to Plattsburg, where they went into winter quarters.

The British Army might feel reasonably cheerful, but the British Navy was despondent: one report commented that at Kingston they were dispirited, low in numbers, and jeered at by "all who know them." As the year drew to an end, the only American soldiers in Canada were prisoners of war in Quebec. Yet the United States was big and could be powerful; so Prevost asked London, once again, for more men.

For the first time America held a presidential election in the middle of a war. In the late autumn of 1812 Madison had to put his reputation, and that of his government, to the test of the ballot box. He did it to the accompaniment of harshly critical newspaper comment. The Alexandria *Gazette* remarked:

Should the obnoxious and fatal administration of Mr Madison continue, we may bid adieu to the Union and prepare for the horrors of intestine commotion, civil war, and all the calamities that have desolated the Old World.

And the *Gazette* was not alone in its abuse. Against Madison stood those who opposed the war and those who opposed the conduct of it.

His rival for the presidency was the mayor of New York and governor of New York State (another traditional American candidature), De Witt Clinton, who hoped to weld together both factions into enough votes to defeat Madison. In those days before radio and television, before transcontinental flights of hopeful candidates, it was possible to say one thing in one place and contradict it in another. Clinton therefore made anti-war speeches in New England and pro-war speeches in the South and the frontier states. Madison's election strategy, utterly beyond the reach of any politician today, was to keep quiet and say nothing, or at least as little as possible, and wait for Clinton to tie himself in knots. Madison's supporters implored him to speak. The Reverend David Jones, chaplain to the forces, wrote: "My dear Sir, if you must die politically, die gloriously." Madison waited until the last minute to say anything in public. In those days the states did not all vote on the same day and, with two states left to cast their verdict, Madison addressed Congress, saying that the war, which was "neither of ambition nor vainglory," must be carried through to "peace with justice." He may have been anxious about the outcome. Indeed he was returned with only a slender majority.

One macabre incident ended the diplomatic year for the American government. Ambassador Joel Barlow, under Madison's instructions to tell the French government in the clearest possible terms that once Britain made peace there would be trouble between France and America unless Napoleon changed his attitude, went in search of the Emperor, who was retreating from his disastrous expedition to Moscow. Barlow was elderly, and his health was failing, but he went on the long, cold, exhausting journey across Europe, from Paris to Berlin, Königsberg, and Vilna, taking three weeks, fairly fast going in 1812. At Vilna he was told that Napoleon was moving toward Warsaw; at Warsaw he found that Napoleon had left for Paris. Barlow, by now in seriously weakened health, started back, but collapsed near Cracow and died on December 26. Among his papers was found the draft of a poem called *Advice to a Raven in Russia.* It was a strange, sad end for the man who had written so utterly American a piece as *Hasty Pudding.*

By this time the reelected President was reshuffling his cabinet appointments. The War and Navy Departments received new men. The Secretary of War was John Armstrong, who had been a soldier and a diplomat. He came from Pennsylvania, of partly Irish descent, and combined, apparently, a quick temper with a lazy, easy-going charm. The Secretary of the Navy was also a Pennsylvanian, William Jones of Philadelphia, a former sea captain and congressman. Both men realized, of course, that no attack could be made along the St. Lawrence until the thaw, so there was time, they thought, for a new shipbuilding plan to be put into operation. While this was going on, two lines of assault by land could be developed: one against Fort George and Fort Erie on the Niagara, leading, with luck, toward Kingston and York; the other to recapture Fort Detroit.

It is important to remember, however, that this war (like many another) saw critical differences between plans worked out on paper in peaceful offices and plans put into practice on the spot by fallible humans beset with difficulties of finding enough supplies, keeping their volunteers, and (if possible) defeating the enemy.

Prevost was told in a regular flow of letters from London to expect big military reinforcements but, since these would have to travel from Europe (except for a comparatively small force from Bermuda), they could scarcely be expected to arrive in Canada before the summer of 1813 at the earliest. News of the proposed reinforcements for the American campaign had reached England's most famous soldier, and Wellington wrote from Portugal to Lord Bathurst on February 10 with all his usual prudence and hard common sense:

> I only hope that the troops will go in time; and that Sir George will not be induced by any hopes of trifling advantages to depart from a strong defensive system. He may depend upon it that he will not be strong enough either in men or means, to establish himself in any conquest he might make.

Lieutenant Colonel John Harvey, newly appointed deputy adjutant general to Prevost, traveled by the same route as Prevost's letters from London–across the Atlantic to the port of Halifax, by sleigh to the St. John valley, on snowshoes to Rivière-du-Loup, and by boat along the St. Lawrence to Quebec–and proposed that reinforcements from New Brunswick should come as soon as possible by the same way. On February 16 the first party set off from Fredericton, north of St. John in New Brunswick, followed by five other companies on the next five days. It had been a severe winter and enough snow was still steadily falling to make each group break trail afresh every day. There were five hundred and fifty men and they advanced on snowshoes. At first they were able to find barns, or even houses, to sleep in, but as they moved out of the settled region into the wilderness they had to sleep out, around their campfires, huddled closely together behind the dubious shelter of roughly built windbreaks, much in the way of the earliest settlers. One young officer wrote:

> No dinner that day, no supper that night, no breakfast the next morning; but in the afternoon, we were agreeably surprised, when crossing the River du Loup, to find two men, with bags of biscuits and two tubs of spirits and water, handing out a biscuit and about a half pint of grog. I found it very acceptable after a march of two days and a fast of upwards of thirty hours.

The worst was over by then, for there was a road, of sorts, from there to Quebec, with farms and tiny hamlets so that food could be found. The total distance was more than three hundred and fifty miles and the men covered it in twenty-four days with the loss of twenty-one lives, only one of which occurred during the actual march: the other twenty died subsequently of frostbite. It is worth remembering that the troops concerned had served in Canada for eight years and that they had not been harassed by enemies apart from ice and snow. As things turned out, the long march proved unnecessary: reports of Dearborn's massing of sleighs at Plattsburg for a winter attack on Canada led to no more action than had Napoleon's massing of flat-bottomed boats in the Channel ports for the invasion of England.

On February 6 Admiral Warren gave orders for "the most strict and rigorous" naval blockade of Chesapeake Bay and the Delaware River. This was partly designed as a diversion, partly to show that, if need be, the Royal Navy could carry the war to the very doorstep of the American government. A month later a powerful body of British seamen set sail from England for Quebec: four hundred sailors and eighteen midshipmen with two master mates, two masters, two gunners, two boatswains, six surgeons, two ships's carpenters, two pursers, eight lieutenants, and three commanders, all under Captain Sir James Lucas Yeo, RN, aged thirty. Yeo had joined the Royal Navy at the age of ten, and had served with distinction in small ships. He had been knighted for the successful siege of Cayenne in French Guiana in 1809, had been promoted to captain at twenty-five, and only the previous year as commander of HMS *Southampton* had captured the United States brig *Vixen* off the West Indies. He was under Admiralty orders to defend the North American provinces in full cooperation with Prevost and to do nothing without Prevost's knowledge and consent. Yeo could, if need be, ask for extra help from Warren.

While all this was going on, Prevost's assistants were working hard to increase the numbers of the militia at their disposal, and all troop movements were reported on both sides of the border by the swarms of smugglers who were crossing backward and forward to trade. So many American farmers came into Canada because the prices were better on the northern side of the border that Prevost commented that two-thirds of his army were "eating Beef provided by American Contractors, drawn principally from the States of Vermont and New York." Quite often an American farmer would have his sleigh commandeered by the British for assistance with troop transport, or the running of a supply train.

In spite of the increased activity, or the promise of it, on the Atlantic seaboard (with a number of towns and cities hastening their plans for defense and eventual attack), Canada remained the magnet for American military hopes. John Randolph put it into words: "Go, march to Canada! Leave the broad bosom of the Chesapeake and her hundred tributary rivers unprotected!"–though whether this stirring comment was delivered in an ironic tone is impossible to know. There can be no doubt that the recapture of Fort Detroit was a matter to rouse American emotions, and the man selected to lead the way back to the fort was the hero of Tippecanoe.

He did not enjoy an undivided command. Brigadier General William Henry Harrison was to march alongside Brigadier General James Winchester, an elderly man recalled to the colors after a long retirement in Tennessee. A stern leader of the old type, with a grizzled mane and keen dark eyes, he rather unwillingly agreed to cooperate with Harrison. Harrison, a slight figure with neat plain clothes, was far more flexible and adaptable than was Winchester. Between them the two men commanded more than ten thousand troops, which were to advance north in three sections. The right wing, regiments from Virginia and Pennsylvania, would move up the Sandusky River; the left wing, many of them from Kentucky, would move along the Miami River to Fort Wayne; the center, mostly from Ohio, would go from Urbana along the trail that Hull had followed the previous autumn. All would converge at Miami Rapids and regroup to attack Detroit.

The big force set off in midwinter, knowing that the Detroit River would be frozen and therefore easy to cross. Winchester's Kentuckians approached the Canadian outpost of Frenchtown on January 18 and their advance guard of about nine hundred men quickly drove the comparatively few Canadian and Indian defenders out. Detroit was only twenty-six miles from Frenchtown, and it was likely that Colonel Procter's men from there and from Fort Malden would counterattack at once. This possibility does not seem to have occurred to Winchester. It happened nonetheless. Before dawn three days later Procter grouped a force of about three hundred and fifty mixed soldiers, twenty-eight sailors, and a large body of Indians and moved on Frenchtown, attacking it at dawn on January 22. Procter's impetus was weakened by his opening fire with his three-pounders, mounted on sleighs, rather than attacking hand-to-hand. His men in consequence suffered one hundred and eighty-five casualties. Even so, they overcame the nine hundred Americans, capturing more than half of them; some three dozen got away somehow through the deep snow. Winchester was among the prisoners. His casualty list totaled almost four hundred killed or wounded. Procter paroled the Kentuckians to their homes, on their promise that they would not serve again until they were exchanged in the normal way. Prevost promoted Procter to the rank of Brigadier General.

Harrison's men were some twenty miles off when news of Winchester's defeat was brought to him by Colonel Samuel Wells, who had feared the worst when Winchester had not prepared for a counterattack. Winchester wrote later: "Neither night-patrol nor night-pickets were ordered by me, from a belief that both were matters of routine and in constant use." At Miami Rapids, Harrison ordered his stores burned and retreat to begin, though when Procter fell back on Fort Malden Harrison brought his men up again to build a properly defensive post which he named Fort Meigs. He promised to attack Detroit as soon as he could be ready, but the ice had melted before he could begin. John Armstrong in Washington noted that the cabinet was willing "with perhaps less patriotism than of prudence, to leave the question of continuing the winter campaign exclusively with the General."

Meanwhile, Chauncey had been busy on the Great Lakes. He had set up a new naval base at Presque Isle, near the town of Erie in Pennsylvania, because this was a more accessible place than Black

Rock, the base previously suggested. On January 19 he returned to Sackets Harbor where, he reported, "altho' I think the Vessels with their crews are fully competent to protect themselves against any attacks of musketry, yet if the Enemy by any desperate effort should succeed in obtaining possession of the Forts in this Town, the Vessels must fall of course, as they could not be moved for the ice." He expected a hostile force of up to four thousand men to gather at Kingston, less than thirty miles away, and move by way of Wolfe Island and Gravelly Point to Chaumont Bay and so "to this Harbour in about 12 hours as all their Troops are exercised to walk with Snow Shoes. Now, Sir, suppose 2 or 3000 men cross in the way pointed out, what can save us here? Nothing but a re-enforcement of Regular Troops . . ."

This idea had struck others besides Chauncey. On January 22 the New York *Evening Post* printed the following comment:

Look out: From information we have received, we think it highly probable, that the British are preparing to make a descent on Sacket's Harbour with a view of destroying the American vessels which are hauled up there for the winter.–Their destruction, would be important to the British, as thereby they may retain the command of Lake Ontario, which they cannot do, if our little fleet is *well* found in the spring. A great number of sleighs, loaded with British troops, have been seen to pass up on the other side of the St. Lawrence, and as soon as the river is frozen over, it is apprehended they will cross.

Prevost sent six companies of soldiers as reinforcements, four to Kingston and two to Prescott, and he also reshuffled his commanding officers. Sir Roger Hale Sheaffe, who had replaced the dead Brock, had fallen ill, so during his period of sick leave Colonel John Vincent was sent to the Niagara, Lieutenant Colonel Thomas Pearson to Kingston, and Major "Red George" Macdonell to Prescott. Finally, Prevost came to see for himself. Traveling with Pearson, he made the journey to Prescott in four days, very good going indeed from Quebec at that time of year, arriving on Sunday, February 21.

He found both Pearson and "Red George" anxious to stop the Americans across the river at Ogdensburg. That these had been troublesome, no one could deny. Two weeks before, the dashing Captain Forsyth had led his riflemen over the ice to Brocksville in a surprise dawn raid, taking fifty-two prisoners, whom he had promptly paroled to their homes, as Procter had done the other way round at Frenchtown. Forsyth had been promoted to the rank of major for this successful exploit. Soon afterward, a small American patrol, moving by night, had captured three Canadian farmers with a team of horses. "Red George" himself had crossed the ice under a flag of truce to protest about this, and had been received with jeers and insults.

Prevost's presence in the locality could hardly be hidden: if the Americans had not actually seen that someone of particular importance was traveling just over a mile away, they would have heard news of him from two soldiers who had deserted from Prescott that day. Prevost did not want to order a full-scale attack, but he thought it might be helpful if "Red George's" men made a show of attacking across the river while he and his escort set forward for Brockville. Prevost left Prescott just before dawn, having spent less than twenty-four hours there, and "Red George" ordered his troops onto the ice, with something more in mind than a mere feint.

They often drilled there, so the Americans suspected nothing at first. "Red George" ordered Captain John Jenkins, with his company of Fencibles from Glengarry and about seventy militia, to attack the fort and barracks housing Forsyth's men on the west of Ogdensburg, and led his own troops–one hundred and twenty officers and men of the 8th regiment, thirty Fencibles from Newfoundland, and two hundred and thirty militia–to cross the river farther down and attack on the flank. Both sets of advancing soldiers took with them small field guns mounted on horse-drawn sleighs.

The British force was halfway across the frozen river before the American sentries grasped the fact that this was not just another exercise. Hastily they alerted the Ogdensburg garrison, which equally hastily opened fire, though, as Sergeant James Commins of the 8th wrote later, "their firing had not much effect as their gunners were undisciplined, most of their shots going over our heads. On our nearer approach their soldiers abandoned their posts, leaving the inhabitants to Protect their own Property; some of them fired upon our men from their windows, but they suffered for their Temerity, every one was bayoneted; all this time the soldiers were retreating and some of ours was ordered to pursue them while others took possession of the town."

Forsyth's men were holding out easily in the barracks, and their firing was more accurate than that of their comrades, for Captain Jenkins had one arm shot away. But Forsyth soon realized that he and his men would be cut off, so he ordered the retreat from the barracks and withdrew into the forest toward Black Lake. "Red George," slightly wounded himself, entered Ogdensburg and counted his casualties: seven dead, forty-eight wounded. A message was handed to him from Prevost, written on the road to Brockville, telling him not to make any attack of any kind without first consulting de Rottenburg in Montreal, "unless the imbecile conduct of your enemy should offer you an opportunity for his destruction and that of his shipping, batteries, and public stores, which does not admit of any delay in availing yourself of it." It is easy to picture the satisfied grin on the face of "Red George" upon reading this dispatch.

The captured shipping and stores were attended to at once: the nearby American vessels, locked into the ice, were set on fire, and the military stores were carried away on sleighs. Along with them went a quantity of stuff from Parish's store, to which the local inhabitants also helped themselves. Parish's local agent, Joseph Rosseel, said:

> At one time they were carrying off some of my property and hurrying my person off to Canada when a British officer who knew me, happening to pass by my house, perceiving my embarrassment, rushed in, bid the ruffians desist and dispersed them.

Forsyth quartered his men at Sackets Harbor and for the rest of the war no American troops were posted to Ogdensburg. The happy civilians quickly reopened trade with the Canadians, and resumed their visits across the river, Rosseel himself going over to Prescott from time to time to dine with "Red George." Prevost received the news in Kingston that night and, forgiving "Red George" for his insubordination (as he saw it), reported to Lord Bathurst that Lieutenant Colonel Macdonell,

> in consequence of the Commands of His Excellency to retaliate, under favourable Circumstances, upon the Enemy for his late wanton aggressions on this Frontier, this morng about 7 o'clock cross'd the River St. Lawrence on the Ice & attacked & carried, after little more than an hour's action, his position in & near the opposite Town of Ogdensburg.

The news reached Albany on February 25, and the lethargic Dearborn creaked into action, placing Jacob Brown's militia on standby, ordering eight hundred regulars under Colonel Zebulon Pike up to Sackets Harbor, and even setting out for there himself, under the mistaken impression that Prevost had arrived at Kingston with a total force of more than six thousand men, half of them regulars. Dearborn's panic, for that is what it was, affected Chauncey, who noted that attack was hourly expected:

> Sir George Prevost is to command in person and has assured his friends that he will destroy our little Fleet here or perish in the attempt. The latter I have no objection to, but the former I shall endeavour to prevent.

Chauncey wrote those words on March 5 on which day Prevost, having inspected all the posts and the little capital of York, returned to Kingston. Two days later he left for Montreal. His departure was unknown in Sackets Harbor for a week, by which time Chauncey had regained his philosophical outlook, for he wrote on March 14:

> I presume that the truth is that the people on the other side are as credulous as our own countrymen, and that they magnify a few Sleighs loaded with stores and accompanied by guards into a Brigade of Regular Troops.

By now, the new Secretary of War, Armstrong, had worked out the United States' war plan for 1813, at least in broad outline. More than one-third of the army, then numbering close to nineteen thousand men, were to go to Buffalo and Sackets Harbor by the beginning of April. Their briefing was to capture Kingston, then York, then forts George and Erie. At any rate, that was Armstrong's original idea. He was persuaded to alter it by Dearborn, who said that the seizure of York would give the Americans control of the Lake, while other troops advanced against the forts, after which all could join together for the massed assault on Kingston. Armstrong agreed.

The British had been thinking along the same lines. Sheaffe warned Prevost that York's rudimentary defenses ought to be strengthened before the spring. Lieutenant Colonel Bruyères of the Royal Engineers wrote that he was sure that Chauncey meant to attack York "previous to the Ice being dispersed in the narrow part of the Lake," adding: "Nature has done very little to the position as a Military Post, or to the Harbour for the purpose of a Dock yard; everything must be created which will require considerable time, and Expense." A huddle of barrack huts and a small blockhouse stood overlooking Old Garrison Point east of Garrison Creek; west of the Creek was Government House Battery with two twelve-pounder guns, but neither the fort on the Point nor the Western Battery overlooking a wide beach half a mile west of York was completed. The garrison totaled less than eight hundred men, of whom a few dozen were Indians. A mile to the west stood the ruined French Fort Toronto.

On the afternoon of Monday April 26, 1813 the sentries gave the alarm as Chauncey's assault force in fifteen ships came in sight of York. For some unknown reason, and contrary to British expectations, the Americans had not attacked while the ice was still on. The ships carried seventeen hundred regulars, and Sheaffe thought it likely that they would land by Fort Toronto; so he ordered one infantry company and the Indians to go to the ruined fort. The infantry lost their way in the forest, and only the Indians were on the spot to face Forsyth's riflemen, who had overshot the fort and landed farther east, where the beach was steeper. Zebulon Pike, now a brigadier general, brought three infantry companies ashore on the heels of Forsyth's men, but Sheaffe, whose appreciation of the state of affairs was imprecise, sent his men up in small groups, so that the Americans were able to push each lot back without too much trouble. The British fell back upon the Western Battery, harassed all the time by steady fire from the American ships which stayed as close inshore as they dared. Suddenly the open magazine in the Western Battery exploded with a deafening roar, blowing twenty men to pieces, and badly wounding others. Under cover of the confusion, Pike brought up his field guns, and the Western Battery fell to the Americans.

The action had opened at eight in the morning of Tuesday and it was now just past eleven. Sixty-two British were dead and ninety-four wounded. Sheaffe decided to withdraw, leaving the flag flying above York as a deceptive measure, and ordering the senior militiamen to set fire to the half-built storehouse and blow up the Grand Magazine. He then took his troops out, leaving the senior militia to arrange surrender terms.

Pike was questioning a prisoner when the Grand Magazine exploded, hurling stones and debris among the Americans and killing a number of them, Pike included. Dearborn, on board USS *Madison,* came ashore at once to take command, in a great rage at finding that American casualties numbered three hundred and twenty–more than those of the British. He managed, however, to restrain his troops so that they behaved reasonably well in the captured town, looting only those houses which stood empty and murdering or raping nobody. One lady, Penelope Beikie, wrote later:

I kept my Castle, when all the rest fled, and it was well for us I did so–our little property was saved by that means. Every house they found deserted was completely sacked.

On Friday evening, April 30, the capital city's Parliament buildings were set on fire, and on Saturday the Government House and the rest of the military buildings were burned. The Americans planned to leave York that night, but a storm blew up and Chauncey's ships had to wait, crammed with men so that only half their number could go below at any one time to escape the fury of the rain and the lashing waters of the lake. Eventually they went off on the following Saturday, many of the troops suffering from seasickness. Chauncey and Dearborn decided that the men were in no fit state for an assault on Fort George, so the flotilla returned to base at Sackets Harbor.

Meanwhile, William Henry Harrison had been slowly building up strength at Fort Meigs. In late April, Brigadier General Procter moved against him, setting out on Wednesday April 28 with a mixed force of over a thousand men in a fleet of small ships, augumented by twelve hundred Indians led by Harrison's old enemy Tecumseh. The British opened fire on May Day and the Indians surrounded the fort, but not before Harrison had managed to send a messenger to twelve hundred Kentuckians along the Miami River, asking them to hurry to his support. Nine hundred of them arrived at nine in the morning on Wednesday, May 5, and at first plunged in among the British besiegers to great effect, but were soon attacked in their turn by Tecumseh's Indians, who killed many and captured nearly all the rest. The British meanwhile regrouped to deal with a force of American defenders, who had come out of the fort on the opposite side, and drove them back in again in disorder. Altogether about four hundred Americans were killed and six hundred captured at the comparatively small cost of fifteen British dead and forty-six wounded. After this action was over, Procter's militia, thinking presumably that they had done enough for the war effort, went off to plant their spring crops, and Procter broke off the siege of the fort and withdrew on Sunday, May 9, noting as he did so: "Daily experience more strongly proves that a regular force is absolutely requisite to ensure the Safety of this District."

Sir James Yeo now reentered the picture. He heard the news from York in Quebec on May 5 and set off next morning for Kingston with one hundred and fifty officers and ratings, at such a good speed that he caught up to Prevost, who had left on the same journey the day before.

The two men entered Kingston together on May 15. There, to their delight, they found "two Ships of 23 and 21 guns, a Brig of 14 and two Schooners of 14 and 12 guns, comprising every sort of calibre," one ship building, and six gunboats on order. Even so, Yeo knew that his vessels were no match for the heavier guns of Chauncey's fleet, especially once his new corvette was ready. And Chauncey was too quick for Yeo, taking his ships up to the north of the Niagara on May 25 to bombard Fort George, where he started promising fires in many of the wooden buildings. In the early hours of May 27 the American assault force scrambled ashore, led, while Dearborn lay ill in bed, by his chief of staff, Colonel Winfield Scott, not quite twenty-seven years old.

Winfield Scott, born on June 13, 1786 at Laurel Branch, near Petersburg in Virginia, is one of the very few Americans who took part in the War of 1812 whose name is internationally famous. Of Scottish descent, an orphan at seventeen, he was at first distinguished by his colossal size: six feet five inches tall, two hundred and thirty pounds in weight by the age of nineteen. After a few months at the College of William and Mary in Virginia, he spent a longer period studying law in Petersburg. The *Chesapeake* affair inflamed his patriotism and he enlisted in the Petersburg cavalry; in March 1808 he received his commission as a captain, recruited a company, served in New Orleans, and was court-martialed and suspended for a year for criticizing his superior officer. In the autumn of 1811 he set out with four companions to rejoin his regiment, traveling by wagon and cutting the first roads to Baton Rouge, learning on the way something of the customs of the Creek and Choctaw Indians. In New Orleans, he served under another man who was to win fame, Brigadier General Wade Hampton, and went, with Hampton, to the city of Washington in February 1812. The authorities ordered him to recruit a regiment in Philadelphia, and by September he had obtained permission to report for duty to Alexander Smyth at Buffalo. Arriving on October 4, he came under fire four days later. His quality was first recognized after Van Rensselaer was wounded at Queenston, for he was captured and, disarmed, was set upon by two Indians with knives and tomahawks. His quick wits, huge strength, and the well-timed intervention of a British officer saved his life. On November 20 he was paroled and taken to Boston, and in March 1813 he arrived in Philadelphia as an adjutant general with the rank of colonel. Now here he was, leading the attack on Fort George.

Major General John Vincent had divided his mixed force of

thirteen hundred into three, with orders to counterattack at any point where the Americans might land, or try to land, but the firing from Chauncey's ships swept the spaces between the fort and the beach so thoroughly that the British had no choice but to remain on the defensive. The Americans killed fifty-two and wounded or otherwise put out of action three hundred and six before Vincent withdrew his men from the fort out of range of Chauncey's guns. After an hour's wait Vincent was told that an enemy force of four or five thousand men was approaching on the flank, whereupon, without confirmation of this information, he ordered the fort evacuated, the guns spiked, the ammunition destroyed, and marched his men away "across the Country in line parallel to the Niagara River, towards the position near the Beaver Dam beyond Queenston Mountain," where, some time before, he had set up a supply post in a big stone house. Here he found Lieutenant Colonel Bisshopp and Captain Barclay with their troops. After sending the militia off home, the sixteen hundred regulars and Fencibles followed Vincent into camp at the town of Burlington in Vermont.

The Americans had lost forty killed and one hundred and twenty wounded in the action.

Meanwhile, Prevost ordered seven hundred and fifty troops from Kingston, under Colonel Baynes, to move off in a fleet of forty boats to attack Sackets Harbor. They waited throughout the day of May 28 for the wind to change, by which time the British had captured a string of twelve barges loaded with supplies and the Sackets Harbor garrison, informed of the British movements, was on full alert. Militiamen were flocking in from the surrounding countryside to reinforce the four hundred men in the garrison, and Jacob Brown himself rode in to take command. Expecting the British to attack by way of Horse Island, from which they could ford the narrow water to the southwest of the town, Brown placed five hundred militia facing the ford. Soon after dawn on May 29 Baynes led his assault troops off and, in spite of the complete lack of surprise and the lowering effects of a steady drizzle, the British pushed the Americans back toward their blockhouses, where Captain Andrew Gray, among others, was killed. But the fighting became confused, and the cautious Prevost "reluctantly ordered the Troops to leave a Beaten Enemy, whom they had driven before them, for upwards of three hours." Sergeant Commins remembered afterward:

We brought all our wounded away it was possible to remove, and embarked on board ships tired, hungry, wet and thirsty, highly mystified and looking very sheepish at one another; you would hardly have heard a whisper until that powerful stimulant grog was served out when the Tower of Babel was nothing like it, everyone blaming another, nay some of them were rash and imprudent to lay the blame on any one but themselves. As for my part, I thought much but said little, having got a wound in my thigh which began to pain me as soon as I got cold.

The losses were disproportionate: twenty-one dead and eighty-five wounded on the American side; forty-seven dead, sixteen missing, and nearly two thousand wounded on the British. Jacob Brown was made a brigadier general.

It was as certain as anything can be in war that the British must try a return match for this humiliation. When the Americans moved "a Corps of 3500 Men with 4 Field Guns and 150 Cavalry to Stoney Creek," Lieutenant Colonel John Harvey obtained permission from Vincent at Burlington to see what he could do. Harvey had reconnoitered during the night of June 5 and reported back to Vincent that the Americans were encamped beside the road in an exposed position with few sentries and those badly placed, so a swift night attack seemed a good idea. A paroled prisoner had divulged the American password. Vincent agreed, let Harvey have seven hundred men—almost half his force—and they crept up toward Stoney Creek at two in the morning of June 6 under orders of strict silence. The sentries were quickly killed with the bayonet, and the British penetrated the camp, where, forgetting their instructions in the excitement of battle, they fired off their muskets with loud yells of premature triumph. The Americans were quick to react, and a welter of confused fighting followed, in which many died by accident at the hands of their own side. As daylight appeared, Harvey broke off the engagement and retired into the forest, with twenty-three of his men dead and one hundred and thirty-four wounded compared with fifty-five American casualties, though the British had managed to capture the two American generals, John Chandler and William Winder, future defender of the city of Washington. This left Colonel James Burn as senior American officer and, after a brief consultation with his fellow officers, he withdrew to Forty Mile Creek. Yeo shelled that position the next day, at the same time seizing sixteen supply boats, so the Americans fell back again, this time to Fort George.

On the night of June 8 the Americans evacuated Fort Erie and Chippawa, leaving them burning, and joined the garrison at Fort George, where everyone was working hard preparing for a probable siege. Vincent promptly moved his British troops up to Forty Mile Creek in order, as he put it, to encourage

the Militia and Yeomanry of the Country who are everywhere rising upon the fugitive Americans, making them Prisoners and *withholding* all Supplies from them and lastly (perhaps *chiefly)* for the purpose of sparing the resources of the Country in our rear and drawing the Supplies of the Army as long as possible from the Country immediately in the Enemy's possession.

Commodore Yeo meanwhile cruised backward and forward along the American side of Lake Ontario, capturing supply boats and stores and burning the empty storehouses to great effect. All this time Chauncey stayed at Sackets Harbor, debating with himself whether to seek naval immortality by a heroic foray or to play for safety and live to fight another day, while his new ship was in preparation. His perhaps excessive prudence was balanced by the excessive rashness of Lieutenant Thomas Macdonough, USN, who on June 3 had taken two schooners, USS *Eagle* and *Growler,* into the Richelieu River where they were engaged by British troops rowing out in gunboats from the British post on the Isle aux Noix. The low-set gunboats made a poor target for the American guns and the schooners were forced into the steep river bank, where they surrendered. The British took over, renamed the schooners *Broke* and *Shannon,* and consequently ruled supreme on Lake Champlain. The Americans lost one man dead and nineteen wounded, the British had three wounded only, and won warm praise from the Quebec *Gazette,* which stated that the militia who had taken part conducted themselves "in a stile honourable to themselves and to the Canadian Character."

On June 23, Prevost reported directly to the commander in chief, the Duke of York, that he had again reshuffled his principal officers, mainly because Sheaffe, a stiff, difficult man with a reputation for parsimony—not the type to inspire heroic action—had proved inadequate.

The support I have received from the General Officers in command since the Death of Major-General Sir Isaac Brock, I am sorry to say has not always corresponded with my expectations. Circumstances indicating an insufficiency on the part of Major-General Sir R. H. Sheaffe to the arduous task of defending Upper Canada, have induced me to place Major-General de Rottenburg in the Military Cmd and civil administration of that province.

In a letter to Bathurst he stated bluntly that Sheaffe had "lost the confidence of the Province."

Exactly the same thing was happening at exactly the same time on the American side, where Dearborn was losing the confidence of his superiors. A group of almost six hundred American infantry and cavalry had been sent to attack the Beaver Dam post, and had done so in so relaxed a manner that the local inhabitants had hours of warning, and a housewife from Queenston called Laura Secord went off on foot to warn Lieutenant James Fitzgibbon at Beaver Dam. She reached Fitzgibbon after a journey of more than twelve hours in the evening of June 22, and the Americans did not appear until the early morning two days later, when some four hundred Indians under captains Dominique Ducharme and William Kerr attacked from behind and frightened the Americans into nervously firing at movements and war cries among the trees. After three hours of this, Fitzgibbon rode up at the head of fifty troopers and called on the Americans to surrender, a thing Ducharme had been unable to do because he did not speak English well enough. Fitzgibbon reported that the British never fired a shot, that the Indians "beat the Americans into a state of terror, and the only share I claim is taking advantage of a favourable moment to offer them protection from the tomahawk and the scalping knife." One officer commented later: "The Caughnawaga Indians fought the battle, the Mohawks got the plunder, and Fitzgibbon got the credit." On July 6 Armstrong wrote to Dearborn:

I have the President's orders to express to you the decision that you retire from the command of District Number 9, and of the troops within the same, until your health be re-established and until further orders.

In the spring of 1813 the Russian minister in Washington, André de Dashkoff, had suggested to the President that, now that Napoleon had been defeated in Russia, it might be wise for the United States to explore the possibilities of making peace with Britain and, if so, Czar Alexander I would be prepared to act as mediator. Madison reacted to this suggestion with his usual caution, but for some reason, when John Jacob Astor, David Parish (of the Ogdensburg store) and Stephen

Girard, scenting peace prospects, invested sixteen million dollars among them in War Loan, he agreed to send a mission to St. Petersburg. Three men were chosen to go: Albert Gallatin, Secretary of the Treasury; John Quincy Adams, American minister to Russia and future sixth President; and Senator James Bayard, an anti-war Federalist. With them as secretary he sent Mrs. Madison's twenty-one-year-old son, John Payne Todd. The three members of the peace mission were instructed to ask for specific guarantees against impressment.

Unfortunately, the plan came to nothing. Before the mission had crossed Central Europe, Russia and France signed an armistice agreement, thereby causing the British to revive their old mistrust of the Czar. The Prince Regent made a speech in which he let fly at America for "assisting the aggressive Tyranny of France"; Lord Liverpool, apparently still regarding America as an ex-colony, said that America ought to have looked to Britain as "the guardian power to which she was indebted not only for her comforts, not only for her rank in the scale of civilisation, but for her very existence," contradicting the words of Castlereagh who seemed to have accepted the results of the War of Independence when he said that "the conduct of the American Government was unworthy of any State calling itself civilised and free."

If the war had been a boxing match, the British would by now be leading on points; not, perhaps, by a very wide margin, but by enough to feel fairly confident. The Americans had scored successes at Carleton Island, Sandwich, Monguagon, Queenston where Brock had been killed, Gananoque, St. Regis, and York; they had pushed the British out of Fort George and beaten them off at Sackets Harbor; they had captured or destroyed five British ships. But the British held Lake Champlain; and their land actions, including Michilimackinac, forts Dearborn, Detroit, Wayne, and Meigs, the recapture of Lewiston, and the repulse of the enemy at Chippawa, Prescott, Frenchtown, Brocksville, Ogdensburg, Stoney Creek, and Beaver Dam—often with the capture or surrender of very large bodies of American troops—put them sufficiently ahead on land to take the worst sting out of their undoubted humiliations on water. What was more, they had their blockade, tightening upon American ports from New York to the Gulf of Mexico. It did not, interestingly enough, stretch up the coast of New England, because, as Admiral Mahan explained many years later, the hope of embarrassing the general government by the disaffection of New England, and of possibly detaching that section of the Country from the Union,

seemed more valuable to the British than a blockade would have been.

During 1813 the cotton and rice of the South failed to find buyers; the price of imported tea doubled; the price of sugar more than quadrupled. If American ships were to dodge or even successfully engage the British, they would have to do so in the North, possibly as far north as the St. Lawrence and the Lakes.

Off Boston in May 1813 HMS *Shannon* was cruising, under the command of Captain Philip Vere Broke, RN, rather to challenge American warships than to interfere with peaceful trading vessels.

In Boston Harbor rode USS *Chesapeake* of great fame, now about to experience new adventure. Freshly refitted and commanded by Captain James Lawrence, USN, she was under orders from the Secretary of the Navy, William Jones, to proceed north and intercept ships headed for Quebec. Captain Broke actually sent a challenge to Lawrence for a ship duel, but this had apparently not reached him when, on the afternoon of June 1, Lawrence put to sea, flying a flag emblazoned with the words "Free Trade and Sailors' Rights." A swarm of small boats escorted the *Chesapeake* down the Boston Roads, while crowds watched from the shore, and officers on the roofs of Fort Warren and Fort Independence looked through their telescopes. The sun shone, the sky was blue; across the blue water stood the enemy in plain sight. Broke moved away to make room for a fight; Lawrence followed. At just after half-past four, Broke opened fire; a quarter of an hour later, *Shannon* ran close alongside *Chesapeake* and grappled, and a boarding party of about sixty men, headed by Broke himself, scrambled across. Lawrence, mortally wounded, gasped out: "Don't give up the ship!"–a saying that became immortal among Americans, most of whom could not always name the occasion or the speaker. At one point the grappling irons loosened and the ships drifted apart, leaving Broke's men temporarily marooned, but in less than an hour the Americans surrendered, with forty-eight dead to the British twenty-six and ninety-nine wounded to the British fifty-six.

Strong reaction in both countries greeted this engagement. The American attorney general Richard Rush recalled years afterward:

I remember the first rumour of it. I remember the startling sensation. I remember at first the universal incredulity. I remember how the post-offices were thronged for successive days by anxious thousands; how collections of citizens rode out for miles on the highway, accosting the mail to catch something by anticipation. At last, when the certainty was known, I remember the public gloom.

In England, the exploit won the accolade of a popular song, so persistent that over forty years later Thomas Hughes quoted it as heartily sung at Rugby in *Tom Brown's Schooldays:*

> Brave Broke he waved his sword, crying, now my lads aboard,
> And we'll stop their playing Yankee-doodle-dandy-oh!

Shannon led *Chesapeake* up to Halifax. Within a few days, Madison fell ill: the newspapers called it "bilious fever"; the rumors multiplied; Congressman Thomas Grosvenor of New York predicted that the President would "soon appear at the bar of Immortal Justice"; the Federalist press hinted that Henry Clay would murder the old Vice-President, Elbridge Gerry of Massachusetts (who gave the language the word "gerrymander") in order to seize the presidency for himself. But, thanks to his own resilience, his wife's devoted nursing, and a period of convalescence at Montpelier, Madison recovered steadily through the summer.

On July 21 Commander Thomas Everard, RN, brought his ship, HMS *Wasp,* into Quebec for a two-week refit and offered to spend that time in leading an expedition on Lake Champlain. He set off on July 22 with fifty members of his own crew and thirty volunteers to join up in Montreal with Lieutenant Daniel Pring, RN, newly appointed commander of the Lake Champlain naval base. From the Isle aux Noix came Lieutenant Colonel John Murray with more than a thousand troops and a couple of field guns. The whole party traveled in the schooners *Broke* and *Shannon,* three gunboats, and forty-seven small boats to Plattsburg, landing on July 30 to find that the little garrison of American militia had fled. The British systematically destroyed the blockhouse, barracks, and stores, sent parties up to Swanton to destroy military property there (though some soldiers exceeded their instructions), and Everard captured four small ships off Burlington before returning via the Isle aux Noix to Quebec.

On Lake Ontario, Sir James Yeo was trying to find an opportunity to attack Commodore Chauncey's new corvette, USS *General Pike,* which, when finished, would have twenty-six twenty-four-pounder guns and thus be heavier than anything Yeo could bring out against it. Yeo tried to lure Chauncey out on the lake, but in vain. The Kingston *Gazette* reported on July 7 that on July 1

our brave tars, with a detachment of the Royal Scots, and 100th Regiment, lay concealed in the woods, within ten miles of the Enemy's squadron the whole of Thursday, and the attack was to have taken place on that night.

Reports of two deserters caused Yeo to cancel the operation. On July 16 Yeo realized that the *General Pike* was almost ready for service and, indeed, on the evening of July 21 Chauncey led his squadron off. He had planned to attack Vincent's base at Burlington but, finding it too well defended, turned instead to unprotected York, where he seized supplies and burned stores, before sailing back to Niagara. Here Yeo appeared with six ships early on August 7, and a full clash seemed imminent, but a storm sprang up in which two of Chauncey's schooners were lost, and Yeo prudently held off for four days, at the end of which he captured two other schooners that had become separated from the rest of the American flotilla. Both commanders explained their caution to their superiors: Chauncey thought that Yeo "thinks to cut off our small dull sailing schooners in detail." Naturally Yeo's evasions suited Prevost, who ordered Vincent to make what he called "a general demonstration" before Fort George on the morning of August 24. Prevost was present that Tuesday, and described what he saw.

The Picquets were driven in, a great part of them being taken, with a very trifling loss, and I found myself close to the Fort, and the new entrenched Camp which is formed on the right of that Work, both of them crowded with men, bristled with Cannon, and supported by the Fire from Fort Niagara on the opposite side of the River; but no provocation could induce the American Army to leave their places of shelter, and Venture into the Field, where alone I could hope to contend with it successfully–having made a display of my force in vain, a deliberate retreat ensued without a casualty;–I am now satisfied that Fort George is not to be reduced, strengthened and supported as it is by Fort Niagara, without more troops, the Co-operation of the Fleet, and a battering Train–to accomplish this object a double operation becomes necessary, Fort Niagara must be invested and both places be attacked at the same moment, but my resources and means do not allow me to contemplate so glorious a termination to the Campaign in Upper Canada.

What Prevost had actually done was to take a good look at the formidable American defenses, and decide that it would take a lot more power than he had under his command just then to stand a chance of successfully attacking; so he had made a dignified withdrawal and sent another appeal for extra forces on a truly ambitious scale, including ships of the Royal Navy as well as a "battering Train."

While Prevost was seeing for himself what the position was like at Fort George, Lieutenant Colonel Bruyères on his instructions was rebuilding the fort at York and strengthening the defenses at Burlington. Prevost went to Kingston and told Commodore Yeo to find Chauncey's fleet and put it out of action; Yeo, in his evasive way, moved about the lake for days until Chauncey's ships came in sight on September 7, whereupon both commanders sailed more or less in parallel for five days, first one coming nearer while the other drew away, then the second turning to approach while the first backed off and for one night both lying becalmed and immovable just outside striking distance. Even Prevost protested against this lack of decisive action, though he was no doubt impelled to do so by his anxiety over the situation on Lake Erie.

Oliver Hazard Perry now enters the scene of action. A compactly built, active figure, with a youthfully good-looking face and an attractive speaking voice, he was twenty-eight years old on August 20, 1813. Born in the village of Rocky Brook in Rhode Island, the eldest son of a naval officer, he was appointed to midshipman at the age of fourteen and served on his father's ship, the *General Greene,* in the West Indies, then in the Mediterranean on the *Adams* and the *Constellation,* becoming a lieutenant in 1807. He was employed in New England for two years, first in building gunboats and then in commanding a flotilla during the embargo. In command of the *Revenge* in 1810 he captured the *Diana,* an American ship sailing under British colors. In 1811 he was once again in command of gunboats at Newport in his native Rhode Island, where, in May of that year, he married a young lady named Elizabeth Champlin Mason. When war with Britain seemed likely to start at any moment, he applied to the

Secretary of the Navy for a posting on active service, even traveling to Washington to ask in person; he was promoted to the rank of master commandant in August 1812 and, being persuaded that his work on the gunboats did not afford him enough scope, volunteered for service on the Lakes with Chauncey, who wrote to him saying that he was the very man for the particular job of commander on Lake Erie. He reported for duty at Sackets Harbor on February 8, 1813 and reached his own headquarters at Fort Erie on March 23. Apart from one break when he joined in the attack on Fort George, he stayed on Lake Erie for five months, making ready a fleet for action, a difficult task as everything had to be transported for his use across a vast distance, most of it wilderness. Chauncey mentioned him in dispatches after the capture of Fort George, saying that he had been "present at every point where he could be useful, under showers of musketry," and that he had "fortunately escaped unhurt."

Perry was ready for action by early August. He had ten ships, of which the largest were 480-ton brigs, *Niagara* and *Lawrence.* Perry made the *Lawrence* his flagship, and flew on it a special flag emblazoned with the words "Don't give up the ship." His principal opponent, Commander Robert Barclay, was hampered by shortage of both men and supplies: in July only one hundred and sixty soldiers and Fencibles, and seven British sailors with one hundred and eight members of the Provincial Marine were on hand to defend his base at Amherstburg, man his ships, and attack the enemy. Once again Prevost appealed for reinforcements. "Even an Hundred Seamen pushed on here immediately would, in all probability, secure the Superiority of this Lake," he wrote to London. "I am already weakened on Shore by my Efforts to enable Captain Barclay to appear on the Lake." To Barclay he wrote: "The Ordnance and Naval Stores you require must be taken from the Enemy whose resources on Lake Erie must become yours."

General Procter had thought it a good idea to make a raid on General William Henry Harrison's supply depot on the Sandusky River. It was not very strongly guarded and the project was a practical one, but Procter yielded, unwisely as it turned out, to the protests of the Indian members of his force, as he was afraid that they might otherwise desert him. He moved instead against Fort Meigs, but on the way there allowed the Indians to persuade him into an attack on Fort Stephenson, garrisoned by the American Major George Croghan with one hundred and sixty men. The attack, on the afternoon of August 2, cost ninety-six British casualties before Procter called the retreat, explaining later:

> The men displayed the greatest Bravery, the greater part of whom reached the Fort and made every effort to enter: but the Indians who had proposed the Assault, and had it not been assented to, would have ever stigmatized the British Character, scarcely came into Fire, before they ran off out of its Reach.

To this, Prevost sent a sternly disapproving reply:

> I cannot refrain from expressing my regret at your having allowed the clamour of the Indian Warriors to induce you to commit a part of your valuable force in an unequal and hopeless conflict.

On the same August 2, and during the two days following, Perry's men at Presque Isle removed the guns from their two large brigs, mounted the brigs on floats, and got them over the sandbar at the harbor mouth. Perry, who, like Barclay, was short of men, took his mixed force, numbering almost five hundred, to set up a new base at Put-in-Bay in the Bass Islands about thirty miles from Amherstburg. In his opinion attack would be easier from the new base. On both August 25 and September 1 the garrison of Fort Malden saw Perry's squadron. Procter, still smarting from Prevost's rebuke, urged Barclay to reopen, if he could, the line of communication with the supply depot at Long Point. Barclay, well aware of the risk he was running, for Perry had six schooners to his three and he was desperately short of supplies, decided to make a try. On the morning of Thursday September 9 he set off from Amherstburg in the *Detroit,* escorted by the *Queen Charlotte,* the *Lady Prevost,* and the three schooners, and sailed toward Put-in-Bay. It was not long before the two flotillas drew together, and at noon Barclay opened fire on the *Lawrence.* The wind chopped around in the Americans' favor so that Perry was able to close, and by two in the afternoon both flagships were battered, the *Lawrence* so badly that Perry struck his colors, had himself rowed over to the *Niagara,* and bored in afresh. Barclay was carried below, severely wounded and, a short time later, with every British captain and second-in-command out of action, the British flotilla surrendered. Perry's jubilant ships escorted them into Put-in-Bay, and Perry dashed off reports to Harrison: "We have met the Enemy and they are Ours"— and to Washington, saying: "It has pleased the Almighty to give to the arms of the United States a signal victory over their enemies on this Lake." By return dispatch the Secretary of the Navy, William Jones, wrote that the President had promoted him Captain USN.

Barclay, too, gained promotion, although he had to return to England and face court-martial because he had lost his squadron. This was a formality, for his bravery could not be doubted: Yeo had reported that he had acted heroically, and the court-martial "fully and honourably" acquitted him. Both commanders, in their separate ways, were now heroes to their countrymen.

Presumably still being extra cautious, Procter now withdrew from Fort Malden, to the horrified wrath of Tecumseh and his fellow Indians or, at least, to those who were ready to fight. Many were not. To Procter, the Indians, unless Tecumseh was there in person, were all too willing to sit back, or even to run away, and let the British do their fighting for them; to Tecumseh, the British were letting the Indians down and scuttling away when there was not an American in sight. Procter wrung a reluctant consent from Tecumseh to go with him to Moravian Town about seventy miles up the Thames River, and on September 24 the Fort Detroit garrison withdrew to Sandwich after setting fire to the fort's installations. Two days later Fort Malden was similarly evacuated, and Harrison brought his men cautiously into the deserted ruins on September 27, reporting carefully: "I will pursue the enemy to-morrow, although there is no probability of my overtaking him, as he had upwards of 1,000 horses, and we have not one in the Army." He had five hundred four days later, when Lieutenant Colonel Richard Johnson rode in with his mounted riflemen.

Harrison's pursuit was slow and reluctant, but the British seemed almost to be dawdling. They did not destroy bridges behind them, and by the evening of October 2 the Americans had reached the mouth of the Thames where Perry was waiting for them with his gunboats. The gunboats accompanied the troops for a distance along the river next morning, but Perry went on "as a volunteer." (Nowadays he would be called an observer.) Early on October 5 Procter made a stand a couple of miles out of Moravian Town with the river on his left and a swamp on his right. The Indians manned the swamp; the British infantry spanned the road. Harrison swung his cavalry at the redcoats, quickly routing them, and then sent Johnson and his men, dismounted now of course, into the swamp. The fight was stiff but decisive: Tecumseh and his nucleus of particularly warlike braves died; the rest of the Indians melted away into the woods; twenty-eight British officers and six hundred and six men were killed or capured. Harrison lost seven dead, twenty-two wounded.

Harrison, after proclaiming that the civil servants in the Western District could continue in their posts provided they pledged fidelity to the United States government during the period of occupation, signing a truce with the Indians at Detroit, and promising safety of persons and property, discharged his militia and went up to Buffalo with Perry, who journeyed on in a triumphal progress to Baltimore. About seventeen hundred American troops were left to guard Detroit, Sandwich, and Amherstburg. Procter reestablished his command at Burlington, much chastened. The Americans had won their victories by land and water at last.

EIGHT

§

From a Check to a View

The autumn of 1813 saw English eyes gazing upon the beguiling ridge of the Pyrenees, as the last of Soult's army trailed away from Roncesvalles. The peninsula was clear of the French after six years; and Wellington was considering how best to lead his valiant veterans into France itself. The Emperor stood at bay in a ring of enemies before Leipzig, facing as best he might his second full defeat. In London, the social round went on as ever: the Prince Regent squeezed himself into his corsets; young Lord Palmerston prepared the army estimates for 1814, and the red head of Robert Peel bent over papers in the Irish Office. In Washington, everyone danced the waltz: at balls and levées and gala receptions crowded with "the youth and beauty of the City"; young ladies gathered at "fringe parties" whose purpose was to sew uniform epaulettes; and Mrs. Samuel Smith wrote to her sister Jane that there was "so little apprehension of danger in the city that not a single removal of person or goods has taken place. You see, we are esteemed quite out of danger." Everybody said it was "impossible for the enemy to ascend the river." An anonymous correspondent, signing himself "Old Soldier," wrote fiery letters to the papers pressing for measures proposed by the Secretary of War, Armstrong, and the whisper ran through the capital that "Old Soldier" was Armstrong himself, although, as Secretary of the Navy, William Jones, sardonically said, "Old Soldier" was "not a legitimate son of Mars."

Armstrong had written to his old colleague James Wilkinson, who had fought with Armstrong at Saratoga and was now general officer commanding at New Orleans, asking him to go to Canada. "The men of the North and East want you," he wrote. Wilkinson accordingly traveled up to Sackets Harbor where, in due time, he set down his plan of attack on paper:

> To rendezvous the whole of the troops on the Lake in this vicinity and, in co-operation with our squadron, to make a bold feint at Kingston, slip down the St Lawrence, lock up the enemy in our rear to starve or surrender, or oblige him to follow us without artillery, baggage or provisions, to sweep the St Lawrence of armed craft and, in concert with the division under Major-General Hampton, to take Montreal.

But it was not as clear-cut as that. The decision to employ Hampton was unfortunate. Hampton and Wilkinson disliked one another so heartily that neither would take orders from the other without recourse to the Secretary of War. Armstrong came up to Sackets Harbor to sort matters out with Wilkinson in person, but only made them worse, delay followed delay, and by the first week of November the invasion fleet of three hundred boats had reached a point only twenty miles below Ogdensburg, with the hardest stretch of the river yet before them. Wilkinson wrote:

> I speak conjecturally, but should we surmount every obstacle in descending the river, we shall advance upon Montreal ignorant of the force arrayed against us, and in case of misfortune, having no retreat, the Army must surrender at discretion.

This doubtful attitude did not promise well, but Wilkinson's senior officers believed they should press on, mainly because there appeared to be "no alternative." At this point, Armstrong left them to it. He had told Wilkinson that he would meet him on the way,

> but bad roads, worse weather and a considerable degree of illness admonished me against receding further from a point where my engagements call me about the 1st proximo.

So instead he traveled the four hundred miles back to Washington.

The summer had passed quietly at Kingston for the British. Chauncey's ships had twice brushed with Yeo's, with modest failure on September 28 and modest success on October 5, but little else of note happened. Prevost had gone back to Montreal on September 25, leaving his aide, de Rottenburg, to reinforce the defenses of Kingston, which he did with, among others, several companies of French-Canadian militia. Dr. William Dunlop, meeting these on the road, praised their neat appearance in "capots and trowsers of home-spun stuff" and their vigorous attitude:

They marched merrily to the music of their voyageur songs, and as they perceived our uniform as we came up, they set up the Indian War-whoop, followed by a shout of *Vive le Roi* along the whole line.

General Wade Hampton had been summoned to the scene of action by this time. Finding his troops running short of water in country parched after a dry summer, he took them forty miles out of their direct route to the Chateauguay River, where fresh water was plentiful. No doubt this natural concern on his part gave rise to many jests because Hampton was known throughout the army for his "too free use of spirituous liquors." His men numbered about four thousand, most of them inexperienced. Prevost knew their total, but not their quality, and believed them to be more of a menace to Montreal than they were. Armstrong ordered Hampton to hold the British in check at the mouth of the Chateauguay, to which point he brought his troops in a straggling movement taking four days, whereupon his New York militia refused to cross the border. By the evening of Sunday, October 24, Hampton was in position alongside the river close to a bend where the former recruiter of Quebec, Colonel de Salaberry, had prepared a fairly satisfactory defensive emplacement.

American reconnaissance patrols reported a light force in front of them and Hampton decided that a flank attack would be a good idea. He sent Colonel Robert Purdy with fifteen hundred men across the river to execute this, a distance of fifteen miles in pitch darkness. They lost their way and when it was light they blundered into two sets of enemy fire, while Hampton held his own troops back until Purdy had successfully made his move. Purdy, however, had not only de Salaberry's men firing in front of him but a deliberately noisy movement behind him from a British detachment under "Red George" Macdonell. With his main force virtually untouched, Hampton withdrew, and Purdy got out as best he could, with fifty casualties as opposed to de Salaberry's twenty-five.

This reverse caused Armstrong to believe that it would be unwise to press home, or attempt to press home, any attack on Montreal. He did not say this to Wilkinson, who had moved his troops, eight thousand strong, out of Sackets Harbor on the night of October 17 in three hundred boats guarded by a dozen gunboats. Gales raged and bottled them up among the Thousand Islands for nearly three weeks. It was here that the dispirited commanders saw "no alternative" but to go on, which they did in intermittently vile weather, camping miserably within sight of the Long Sault Rapids on the night of November 10. Close behind them came the British pursuit, led by Lieutenant Colonel Joseph Morrison, who made his headquarters in a farmhouse belonging to John Crysler. His position covered the road to Montreal between the river and an impassable swamp half a mile inland.

At eight in the morning of November 11 an Indian fired at an American scouting party, which made both sides spring to battle stations. Wilkinson sent his two thousand regulars in, in three columns, under Brigadier General John Boyd, and these easily pushed back the British skirmish line, but when he tried to turn the British left flank, his men were taken aback to find that the opposition were gray-coated regulars, not raw militia, and the Americans were driven off by half past four in the afternoon. During the day Captain William Howe Mulcaster, RN, kept up a steady rain of shells from his gunboats on the river, much of it aimed at Wilkinson's headquarters. Morrison reported that the Americans had been

> received in so gallant a manner by the Companies of the 89th under Captn. Barnes and the well directed fire of the Artillery that they quickly retreated and by an immediate charge from those Companies one Gun was gained. The Enemy immediately concentrated their Force to check our advance but such was the steady countenance and well directed fire of the Troops and Artillery that about ½ past four they gave way at all points from an exceeding strong position, endeavouring by their Light Infy. to cover their retreat, who were soon driven away by a judicious movement made by Lt. Col. Pearson.

British casualties were twenty-two dead, one hundred and forty-eight wounded, and nine missing; the Americans lost one hundred and two dead, two hundred and thirty-seven wounded, and more than a hundred prisoners. During the battle of Crysler's Farm Jacob Brown had cleared the bridge at Hoople's Creek and opened the road to Cornwall, but Prevost had massed a considerable force in front of Montreal, and Hampton, unwilling to face this, told Wilkinson, in a letter dated November 12, that he did not propose to rendezvous with him at St. Regis. Hampton then sent in his resignation, and Wilkinson took his men into winter quarters at French Mills.

The British had their problems too. Commodore Yeo wrote to the First Lord of the Admiralty on December 6:

> Had any part of this Squadron been lost, taken, or rendered unserviceable, nothing could have saved Upper Canada. Your Lordship can have no idea what a wretched class of Vessels I found on this Lake–all with flat bottoms like our River Barges, and no one in good property belonging to them. Gun Brigs are very far superior to them. The *Moira* has at least 24 pdr Shot thro her Hull, and I verily believe not a shot of hers ever reached the Enemy.–I have always been obliged to tow her in, and out of action to prevent her being cut off by the numerous small Vessels of the Enemys Squadron.

Chauncey transferred to Sackets Harbor the brigade brought by Harrison to Niagara, leaving only a few hundred New York militia to patrol the whole Niagara frontier, whereupon, on December 10, Brigadier General George McClure prudently decided that he had better withdraw his troops from Fort George and retire to Fort Niagara, a better defensive position. For some reason, perhaps to show that he was not to be trifled with, perhaps to impress his superiors, perhaps out of spite or sheer bad temper, he burned the village of Newark, and a large part of the town of Queenston, on a cold night after only a few minutes' notice to the people living there. These sheltered in nearby farms as best they could. McClure, possibly with a view to defending this action, wrote to Armstrong:

> This step has not been taken *without counsel, and is in conformity with the views of your Excellency expressed in a former communication.*

This sounds as if Armstrong had actually ordered McClure to burn Newark or at least to burn something. In fact he had only said that as a defense measure it might become necessary to put Newark out of action. Naturally, the United States government promptly disowned responsibility, but it left great bitterness, which, added to the anger caused by the burning of York, has been judged by various commentators as a strong factor in the later burning of Washington by the British.

Again a change of command took place in Canada. Lieutenant General Gordon Drummond, aged forty-one, with a good record of command behind him including service in the Netherlands, Egypt, and Ireland as well as three years in Canada itself, arrived on the Niagara to relieve de Rottenburg. He brought with him, as a relief for Vincent,

Major General Phineas Riall, aged thirty-eight, an Irishman who had served in the West Indies. De Rottenburg took up again his former command in Lower Canada; Vincent commanded Kingston and the Upper St. Lawrence; Riall was to be in charge of everything west of Kingston. Sheaffe was retired to England, whither Procter was due to go to face the court-martial that normally awaited a general who had blundered. Drummond and Riall arrived to take command on December 16, and were delighted by a rapid success. Three days later Lieutenant Colonel John Murray with five hundred and fifty soldiers recaptured Fort Niagara without firing a shot, losing five dead and three wounded to the Americans' sixty-seven dead and eleven wounded. Riall, following up, destroyed the village of Lewiston. Ten days later Riall again crossed the river with some fifteen hundred men, who burned Black Rock and Buffalo, destroyed four armed schooners and carried away or set fire to a quantity of American supplies. This sequence of actions brought a courteous protest from Prevost, who invariably objected officially to British acts of violence, though he pointed out at the same time that the Americans had brought it on themselves. The local Canadians, he said, would find that

prompt and signal vengeance will be taken for every fresh departure by the Enemy, from that system of warfare, which ought alone to subsist between enlightened and civilised nations.

Lord Bathurst sent words of comfort to Prevost:

I am aware of the weight of your Responsibility, of the Clamour which will at times arise at any failure, or the advance of the Enemy on any part of the wide extended frontier of the Canadas.

But Justice will always be done you. The Result of Campaigns is that to which the Public will always look. Against occasional failures no man can guard. An extended line of frontier cannot be everywhere defended, against the Troops which the Enemy may be able, with their resources on the spot, to collect; with a force double what you have, if Great Britain could afford it, it might be imprudent to undertake it. The very advance of the Enemy to a given point may in many Cases be desirable, as furnishing the fairest opportunity of bringing on a decisive engagement in an open country, where your collected force might have the means of being employed to the greatest advantage.

The peace commission sent to Europe by Madison in May 1813 had achieved nothing, but its members were still in Europe, watching what looked ominously like the last act of the Napoleonic drama. Castlereagh, who had told the Czar of Russia that Britain would prefer to make her own peace terms direct, without mediation–for he trusted no third party to settle the question of maritime rights–sent a letter to Washington on the subject. It suggested that selected British and American spokesmen should meet to discuss terms. This letter, together with a bundle of London newspapers reporting Napoleon's defeat at Leipzig, crossed the Atlantic in the *Bramble,* which came into harbor at Annapolis in Maryland on December 30, 1813.

At that moment, affairs on the frontier were at something of a draw. The Americans had the Detroit part and the upper hand on Lake Erie, but the British had the Niagara part, and Montreal was as far away as ever. If Napoleon lost the German territories, as he had already lost Spain, then all the coasts of Europe apart from France would be open to British trade. As the power of France declined, so Britain could send greater reinforcements to fight in the New World. Perhaps indeed it was time to negotiate. At any rate, nothing could be lost by trying. Accordingly, Madison proposed the four eminent Americans already in Europe–Albert Gallatin, John Quincy Adams, Jonathan Russell, and John Bayard–as peace commissioners, and sent over no less a person than the redoubtable Henry Clay to join them. Clay sailed on January 9, 1814. It would, of course, take time to assemble the mission and to begin the talks; meanwhile there might be a chance of a truce. Feelers were put out to arrange a more complete exchange of prisoners, as an opening move, but London told Prevost to go on as before and not precipitate any concessions, or apparent concessions, until the peace commission had started its work.

Prevost was still preoccupied with his need for more troops, particularly since he had many sick and wounded men who were not yet fit for action. He was troubled, too, by the bickering and niggling of the Lower Canada legislature, which was preventing a good deal of necessary business from going forward. Its members would not amend the Militia Act to prevent substitutes from taking the places of balloted men, and spent days trying to impeach two chief justices, Jonathan Sewell and James Monk, for alleged misdemeanors dating back to the time of Craig. The Upper Canada legislature gave no trouble, but the farmers in that province were raising their prices so high that martial law and a list of fixed prices had to be proclaimed.

The Americans at Sackets Harbor were busy hunting spies, of which there seemed to be dozens, and the small United States posts along the St. Lawrence were plagued by British raids, which carried off supplies at several places during February. Meanwhile, one person received a positive lightening of his load: Sir James Yeo, whose force was augmented by two hundred and sixteen officers and men of the Royal Navy and Royal Marines from New Brunswick. The New Brunswick House of Assembly gave three hundred pounds toward their journey, an amount equaled by that of the citizens of St. John. Under the command of Edward Collier, the men made the journey in fifty-three days, arriving at Quebec in the last week of March. By now, Yeo's frigates *Prince Regent* and *Princess Charlotte* were almost ready, and he had asked for sixty new guns and carronades, which he seemed likely to receive.

In that month of March, General Wilkinson made what was to be his final try, and it did not succeed. Mustering his full effective force of about four thousand men, he set off from Lake Champlain and on March 30 occupied Odelltown and moved forward to the banks of the Lacolle River, where a small enemy garrison guarded the crossing some ten miles from Isle aux Noix. The garrison made its headquarters in a sturdy stone mill, upon which Wilkinson's twelve-pounders made little impression. The snow lay thick on everything, impeding troop movements, and the defending garrison used rocket artillery to good effect. At least Wilkinson did not lead his men from behind. One newspaper report stated:

> Gen. Wilkinson seems to have exposed his life with great prodigality. By a flag that came in, it appears the British officer enquired what person it was they had so repeatedly fired at, who it seems was the general.

This failure was the end of Wilkinson's military career. He was replaced on May Day by Major General George Izard, aged thirty-seven, and considered in influential quarters the most promising officer in the United States Army. Harrison similarly decided, or was persuaded, to retire, and among other new promotions were those of Jacob Brown, who became a major general, Winfield Scott, who became a brigadier general, and Harrison's replacement in Military District number 8, Major General Andrew Jackson.

Jackson has been described, and with reason, as one of the most astonishing men in American history. His father, a poor linen-draper of

Ulster Scottish birth, had come to South Carolina, where he cleared a small farm, and died before Andrew was born. His mother kept house for her brother-in-law. During the War of Independence she died of fever while nursing in Charleston, and her two elder sons were killed in action, so that at the age of fourteen Andrew Jackson was alone in the world, and very poor. Frail-looking, nervous and sensitive, yet with a quick temper, he had the unbreakably durable quality that earned him his later nickname of "Old Hickory." He never lost his sympathy for the oppressed, his liking for plain people, his fighting nature, and his utter distrust of Eastern business and everything to do with it. Like another plain man of the frontier, Abraham Lincoln, he studied law, and settled in Tennessee where he bought and sold land, horses, and slaves, and (temporarily) owned a store. Here he learned just how completely the eastern states dominated western trade. He also acquired one unwavering belief, which was that all things are possible for a frontiersman, a creed from which later events did nothing to dissuade him. He had already won his spurs in two separate ways. He had been a senator representing the state of Tennessee, and he had fought against the "Red Sticks"–the Creek Indians–who, by his efforts, had been practically wiped out. A tall, commanding figure, with a harsh face redeemed by an appreciative twinkle in his eye, and volcanic energy, he still spelled Europe without the initial E, swore cheerfully, and had a wife who smoked a corncob pipe. A personality so striking would be an automatic choice for command.

For most of April all the rival commanders were planning a variety of offensives which did not take place, either because a plan stipulated more troops than were available just then, or Prevost or Armstrong counseled caution, or conditions at the target changed before an assault could be started. But with Yeo's frigates ready on May 3, Yeo and Drummond in consultation decided to attack Oswego. Gales delayed the ships for twenty-four hours, but on the morning of Friday, May 6 Lieutenant Colonel Victor Fischer landed with four hundred marines and one hundred and forty soldiers, Captain Mulcaster brought ashore two hundred sailors armed with pikes, and they stormed a long steep hill under fire. As they crested the top, the Americans fled, leaving six dead, thirty-eight wounded, and twenty-five missing. The British lost eighteen dead and seventy-three wounded. However, they captured not only the fort but also twenty-four hundred barrels of pork, salt, bread, and flour, seven guns and much ammunition, which they loaded onto captured boats and took back to Kingston next day. Yeo then mounted a blockade on Chauncey's new ships at Oswego Falls, causing Chauncey to report ruefully: "This is the first time that I have experienced the mortification of being blockaded on the Lakes."

Master Commandant Melancthon Woolsey now determined to try to reach Sackets Harbor with a large supply of ships' guns and heavy cables. With eighteen small boats escorted by riflemen and Indians he began his journey on the night of Saturday, May 28, and on the Sunday morning reached Sandy Creek, eight miles from his destination. Here he was attacked by a small force under Commander Stephen Popham, RN, who did not know how strong the American force really was. Popham ran into what amounted to a sizeable ambush on Monday, May 30, where, after losing fourteen men killed and twice that number wounded, he surrendered. This meant that Yeo's available force had lost two hundred men, three gunboats, and four small boats, all of which could ill be spared, and the blockade had been broken. Yeo would now have to go back on the defensive until the hoped-for reinforcements arrived from Europe.

In Europe, spring had come, with its fresh blossom and green leaves and birdsong, but something else was new, something not known for years. The roads of Europe no longer rang and jingled to the passing of the armies. Instead, detachments in green and blue and scarlet lined up, looking unnaturally neat, on sunny paradegrounds, to be reviewed by jovial monarchs. France seemed to have lapsed into a trance. The Emperor, no proper emperor now, paced the ramparts above the blue Italian waters at Elba; and the Duke of Wellington came up a gangway at Calais to return, after six years and much glory, to an admiring England. Peace had come to Europe. Now there was just that silly, small war, so scattered and so very far away, in America.

Lord Bathurst had asked the Duke for advice about this, and Wellington had replied that naval superiority on the Lakes came first:

> But even if we had that superiority, I should doubt our being able to do more than secure the points on those lakes at which the Americans could have access. In such countries as America, very extensive, thinly peopled, and producing but little food in proportion to their extent, military operations by large bodies are impracticable, unless the party carrying them on has the uninterrupted use of a navigable river, or very extensive means of land transport, which such a country can rarely supply.

The larger the British forces, said the Duke, the more they would depend upon the Lakes, and the same objections applied to the possibility of landings on the coast. "I do not know," the Duke wrote firmly, "where you could carry on such an operation which would be so injurious to the Americans as to force them to sue for peace." Reflecting on these sensible comments, Bathurst came to the conclusion that Britain must do three things: make Canada safe from invasion; hold on to conquered territory until proper boundary lines could be established; and bring over to Canada a large force, perhaps ten thousand, drawn from Wellington's most experienced veterans. Translated into practical terms, the first step was to destroy American strength at Sackets Harbor and on lakes Erie and Champlain, then to reinforce Fort Niagara, retake Detroit, and occupy as much as possible of the Michigan Territory. After the war was over, Detroit and the Michigan Territory would be restored to the Indians.

Bathurst explained all this to Prevost, adding that four regiments of troops from Europe would be sent to invade America, with a follow-up operation by "a considerable force" later. On July 5 he wrote that fourteen regiments were on their way, led by four major generals selected by the Duke himself: Thomas Brisbane, James Kempt, Manley Power, and Frederick Robinson.

Of course rumors of all this circulated in the United States, affecting the American war plans which, after some delay, finally gained Congress approval on June 7. The Americans were to attack the Niagara peninsula, as they held Lake Erie, and were then to press on against Burlington and York. Some speakers had proposed recapturing Michilimackinac, but Armstrong had opposed this, on the grounds that it was "perfectly useless" once Burlington and York lay in American hands: "On the other hand, take Mackinac, and what is gained but Mackinac itself?" Other cabinet members thought that Izard should lead a feint from Plattsburg as if threatening Montreal. No orders to this effect went out. The cabinet overestimated the number of troops available to Jacob Brown, believing that he could have five thousand regulars and three thousand militia at his disposal, whereas in fact he had less than half that total. During the summer, a number of small raids took place along the Niagara River, more, it seemed, to convince the Americans of the good intentions of various deserters from Canada than for any other reason. The British troops on the Niagara were suffering from sickness and low spirits that even an issue of rum could not lighten. Major General Phineas Riall wrote:

> The Men are Sick of the place, tired & disgusted with the constant labour to which they see no end & have got sulky & dissatisfied.

At dawn on July 3, Brown moved across the river. Winfield Scott's brigade landed below Fort Erie. Eleazer Ripley's brigade landed above it. Brown's Indians came around behind it. The fort surrendered. Next day, Scott led the American force toward Chippawa, approaching the Chippawa River that afternoon. Here he found Riall with about two thousand men, and camped his own men at Street's Creek, two miles from Chippawa, for the night. The Chippawa River was one hundred and fifty yards wide, spanned by one bridge, which Riall crossed on July 5. For the first time in the war, two forces approximately equal in numbers met on an open plain in broad daylight. The two generals, however, were unequal in quality: Riall's Royal Scots and 100th regiment charged "with the greatest Gallantry, under a most destructive fire," but "I am sorry to say, however, in this attempt they suffered so severely that I was obliged to withdraw them, finding that their further Efforts against the superior numbers of the Enemy would be unavailing." With one hundred and forty-eight dead and three hundred and sixty-seven wounded or missing, Riall withdrew across the Chippawa River. Scott reported forty-eight dead and two hundred and twenty-seven wounded. The Americans began what looked like a flanking movement and Riall went back to Fort George. Here he took a breathing space. Scott, quartering his men in Chippawa, did the same.

General Brown went up to Queenston, but receiving no supplies along the river, for Chauncey was immovably staying in Sackets Harbor, retired to Chippawa on July 24. Riall at once moved up a defensive force of a thousand regulars under Colonel Pearson to Lundy's Lane, a long crest of trackway running west from the river road. A mile off, across the river, roared the Niagara Falls. Twelve hundred regulars were coming up behind Pearson as well as the 89th regiment under Joseph Morrison, and some eight hundred regulars recently disembarked from Europe under no less a person than Drummond himself, who had reached Fort George only that morning.

By early evening, in clear sunlight, Scott's advance guard had come within sight of the Falls and of Riall's troops on the crest. He decided to attack at once, although he had no idea of the strength opposing him. Neither had Riall, who, mistakenly believing that the whole of Brown's army was in front of him, prepared to retire. Before he could do so, Drummond came up and quickly ordered Riall's men to open fire upon the Americans.

Scott and his men fought stubbornly, but they were outgunned and outnumbered, and by nine in the evening fewer than half were still on their feet, still trying to push back the left flank of the British side. On the right, by the river, the Americans had fared slightly better, pushing a wedge into the British line and seriously wounding Riall. Jacob Brown's reinforcements now came charging up in the center, aiming at Drummond's battery on the crest which had so far commanded everything in front of it. The right pressed on, the center fell back, and Ripley, in command of both, had to halt and regroup, or attempt to do so, while at the same time Colonel James Miller infiltrated his men through the trees and captured the guns. The British fell back from the crest just as Colonel Hercules Scott's twelve hundred British regulars arrived from Fort George and restored the balance. It was now ten o'clock on a hot night and for two more hours the battle swayed backward and forward, men firing every time they saw the flash of a musket and often hitting an ally rather than a foe.

Winfield Scott and Jacob Brown were severely wounded by now, and sheer exhaustion on both sides combined to bring a stalemate. In the early hours of the morning, each army disengaged, the Americans struggling back to camp and the British sinking to the ground where they stood. Casualties were approximately equal, almost nine hundred on each side. Both claimed to have repulsed the enemy. Brown wrote:

> While retiring from the field, I saw and felt that the victory was complete on our part, if proper measures were promptly adopted to secure it.

Drummond wrote:

> The Enemy abandoned his Camp, threw the greater part of his Baggage, Camp Equipage and Provisions into the rapids, and having set fire to Streets Mills, and destroyed the Bridge at Chippawa, continued his retreat in great disorder, towards Fort Erie.

This made the battle of Lundy's Lane a tactical British victory, though Drummond did not follow it up. Brown retired upon Fort Erie which, just then, could have been easily retaken, but in the ensuing five weeks Brown had time to strengthen it, so that when Drummond began a siege of the fort on August 15 he was hurled back with heavy losses. For over a month, mostly in wet weather, Drummond tried to reduce the fort, losing more and more men in every foray, and putting them to the hardship of camping in the open, for there were no tents, and the few huts he had were small and dilapidated. Dr. William Dunlop described the situation as more like a bivouac than a camp, with

> the troops sheltering themselves under some branches of trees that only collected the scattered drops of rain, and sent them down in a stream on the heads of the inhabitants, and as it rained incessantly for two months, neither clothes nor bedding could be kept dry.

On September 16 the Americans emerged for attack, inflicting six hundred casualties to their own five hundred and capturing three of Drummond's six siege guns. Drummond had already lost nine hundred men, ten times the American losses, so he now felt impelled to give up the struggle. At eight in the evening of September 21 he withdrew to Chippawa.

Despite Armstrong's opinions, a move against Michilimackinac was made that summer. Prevost had taken precautions by sending Lieutenant Colonel Robert McDouall to the fort in May, after a winter journey during which his thirty carpenters paused at the little post at the mouth of the Nottawasaga River and built thirty small boats. Four of these were armed. The only other British vessel in the district was the schooner *Nancy,* commanded by Lieutenant Miller Worsley. By the end of May, McDouall, with one hundred and forty regulars, twenty sailors from Kingston, and about three hundred local militia and Indians, was quartered in Fort Michilimackinac and building a new blockhouse on the highest point of the island.

Four hundred miles to the southwest, a force of about sixty American soldiers now seized the fur-trading post at Prairie du Chien on the Mississippi River, in the course of this killing some local Indians, whose brethren asked the British for aid and vengeance. McDouall commissioned a fur trader named William McKay to the rank of lieutenant colonel and sent him off with a small force that gathered strength on the way, so that he reached Prairie du Chien, finishing the journey by canoe, with one small gun, manned by a professional royal artilleryman, a dozen Fencibles, one hundred and twenty Canadian volunteers, and more than five hundred Indians.

After three days of waiting and parley at the trading post, the Americans surrendered, on condition that they would be protected from the Indians and paroled to their homes. The operation was concluded on July 20.

On that same day, an American officer, Lieutenant Colonel George Croghan, with seven hundred men in five ships, reached St. Joseph's Island, after a seventeen-day voyage from Detroit. The Americans set fire to the deserted buildings, captured a ship belonging to the North West Trading Company, and burned the trading post at what is today Sault Ste Marie. On July 26 they dropped anchor off Mackinac Island, where their guns could not be trained on the fort or the new blockhouse, so Croghan moved to the other end of the island and attacked from there. McDouall was ready for them, with his men spread out behind a low earthwork in an open space which the Americans had to cross as they emerged from the woods. Thirteen Americans were killed and fifty-one wounded, and Croghan, deciding that the fort was too expensive a luxury at that price, withdrew to the ships and sailed off next day, on the way back stopping only to shoot up the little post at the Nottawasaga and to destroy the *Nancy.* They had left behind two schooners, *Tigress* and *Scorpion,* to blockade Mackinac Island, and one Lieutenant Worsley, arriving with the rest of the *Nancy*'s crew at the fort, captured both in two bold night attacks. The schooners were thenceforth used by the British on Lake Huron.

After all these scattered efforts, the Americans still held the Detroit forts on one frontier and Fort Erie on the other. Now in their turn they were finding out what a little invasion is like—the other way round.

During the previous year, Sir John Borlase Warren had sailed up and down the eastern coasts of America, making occasional forays into Chesapeake Bay, as he had been ordered to do. He was enthusiastically seconded in all he did by his second-in-command, Rear Admiral Sir George Cockburn, a tough forty-two-year-old who could inspire hero-worship in his men. One young midshipman later recalled:

> It is almost impossible to depict my boyish feelings and transport when I gazed for the first time in my life on the features of that undaunted seaman with his sunburnt visage and his rusty gold-laced hat.

In a single week in early May 1813 Cockburn had raided Havre de Grace, destroyed a cannon foundry on the Susquehanna River and an arms store on the Elk, and wiped out two villages on the Sassafras, all without the loss of a man on either side. He and Warren had spent the spring and early summer of 1814 in Chesapeake Bay or off the Delaware Capes, landing frequently to steal livestock and burn a building. Sometimes his men did the kind of wanton damage that simply infuriates the opposition to no good purpose, stealing books, cutting beds to pieces, looting a cemetery, chopping down trees. One angry lady left bottles of poisoned whisky on her porch. Naturally enough, the British laid hold of all the tobacco they could find, for they could sell that for five hundred dollars a barrel on the British market in Bermuda.

The Americans Cockburn saw seemed astonishingly unprepared for real warfare. He wrote in July: "It is impossible for any country to be in a more unfit state for war than this now is."

Most of the inhabitants of Washington remained unwilling to think that they might be in any danger. The only citizens of the capital who gave it much thought were the President and James Monroe, who between them during June drew up a plan for the local defenses. Two to three thousand soldiers, backed by ten to twelve thousand militia, should be put on standby to protect the cities of Washington and Baltimore. To command these, Madison selected Brigadier General William Henry Winder, aged thirty-nine, who had seen brief service in Canada, was a native of Baltimore, and the nephew of the Federalist governor of Maryland, and who was willing to take the command. Madison explained his plan to the cabinet on July 1 at the presidential mansion, which people were now calling the White House. On July 2 the tenth Military District–the District of Columbia, Maryland, and Northern Virginia–came into being, Winder's appointment was announced, and orders prepared for extra militia to be called up in all the fifteen states of the Union.

Within a few days, Winder realized that his command existed mainly on paper. He sent a stream of appeals to Armstrong, who ignored most of them, though they bristled with urgent questions, such as: "What possible chance will there be of collecting a force after the arrival of the enemy? He can be in Washington, Baltimore or Annapolis in four days after entering the Capes." He toured his area with great energy, but little result. The only other person who seemed prepared for action was the commander of the District of Columbia militia, a banker called John Van Ness, who persuaded his fellow bankers to offer the government a loan of two hundred thousand dollars for the fortification of Washington.

The government in London, or at least some of it, together with the press and some sections of the armed forces, now had leisure to turn their full, and scornful, consideration toward the United States. To the newspapers, Madison was malicious and corrupt, his country an uncivilized wilderness. The *Times* stated that "only two motives can with the least show of plausibility be assigned to Mr Madison's conduct—venality, or malice," and that the British should "chastise the savages." Colonel Henry Torrens, Military Secretary at the War Office, wrote: "The Government have determined to give Jonathan a good drubbing."

New leaders were chosen to carry through this program. Admiral Warren had been replaced by Vice-Admiral Sir Alexander Inglis Cochrane, aged fifty-five, who had first served in the Royal Navy during the War of Independence and who, after action in many waters, had become governor of Guadeloupe and commander of the Leeward Islands station. He used the same terms as had Torrens in referring to his new post:

> I have it much to heart to give them a complete drubbing before peace is made, when I trust their northern limits will be circumscribed and the command of the Mississippi wrested from them,

he wrote to Bathurst. He proclaimed asylum and freedom for any American slaves who sought it on his ships, and a large number did so, to the alarm of plantation owners; he declared a blockade of the New England coast, hitherto clear of this particular scourge; he sent a string of British barges on a raid up the Connecticut River in April, where they destroyed twenty ships; and, to the fury of many men on both sides, he canceled the trading licenses that had allowed warm profits on the northeast frontier. The precise demarcation of the border was, as always, a sore point, and in June 1814 Bathurst wrote to Sir John Sherbrooke telling him to occupy "so much of the District of Maine, as shall ensure an uninterrupted communication between Halifax and Quebec." Sherbrooke privately thought that this was too big a task, preferring to try for the Penobscot River, the old Massachusetts boundary. While waiting for approval for that, he sent an expedition to occupy Moose Island in Passmaquoddy Bay. The troops sailed in ships commanded by Captain Thomas Hardy—Nelson's Hardy—and

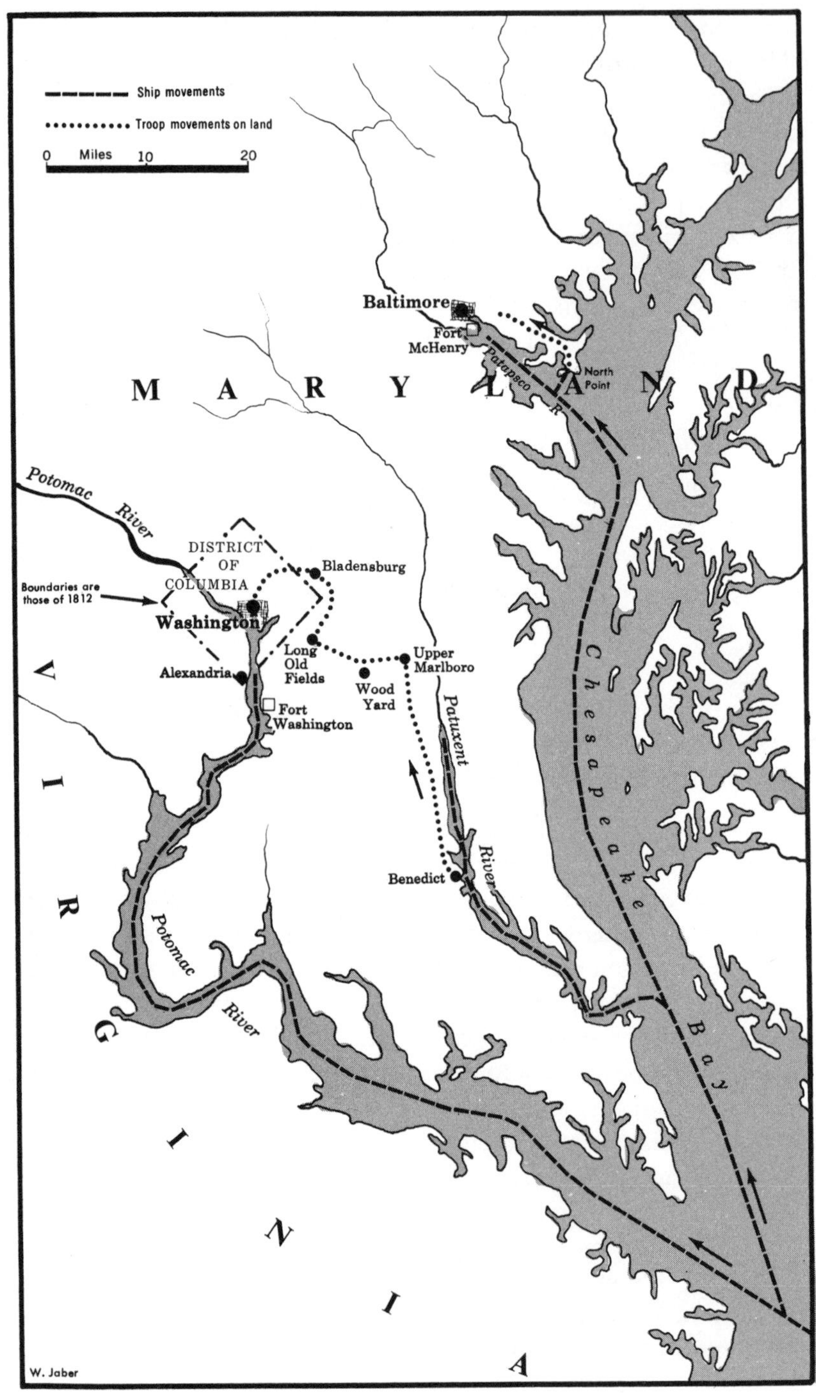

Ship movements
Troop movements on land
0 Miles 10 20
Baltimore
Fort McHenry
North Point
Patapsco R.
M A R Y L A N D
Potomac River
DISTRICT OF COLUMBIA
Boundaries are those of 1812
Washington
Bladensburg
Long Old Fields
Upper Marlboro
Wood Yard
Alexandria
Fort Washington
Patuxent River
Benedict
Chesapeake Bay
Potomac River
V I R G I N I A
W. Jaber

landed without resistance on July 11. Their military leader, Lieutenant Colonel Andrew Pilkington, gave the island population a week to decide whether to take the oath of allegiance to the King or to leave. Most of them took the oath.

On July 24 the new commander of the American coastal raiding force arrived in Bermuda with orders to "effect a diversion on the coasts of the United States of America in favour of the Army employed in the defence of Upper and Lower Canada." He was Major General Robert Ross, aged forty-seven, who had served under the Duke with credit and was respected by his men for his courage, energy, and discipline. His smiling Irish face, with its keen blue eyes, concealed a character reputedly as tough as that of Cockburn. Ross had sailed in the *Royal Oak,* flagship of the seventeen vessels bringing 2,814 men of the 4th, 44th, and 85th regiments, some of them packed in forty to a cabin. The fleet commander, Rear Admiral Poultney Malcolm, was a friendly person reputed to talk in his sleep. During the seven-week journey he gave a party during one period when the ships were temporarily becalmed; his officers produced a newspaper called *The Atlantic News;* on one of his ships, the *Weser,* the men produced a performance of Sheridan's play *The Rivals;* on another, the *Menelaus,* the ship's band played on calm nights. Now the two groups of ships, Malcolm's and Cochrane's, had linked at Bermuda, where, on July 26, the sloop *St Lawrence* arrived with despatches from Cockburn, which informed the commanders:

> I feel no hesitation in stating to you that I consider the town of Benedict in the Patuxent, to offer us advantages for this purpose beyond any other spot within the United States. Within forty-eight hours after the arrival in the Patuxent of such a force as you expect, the City of Washington might be possessed without difficulty or opposition of any kind. If Washington (as I strongly recommend) be deemed worthy of our *first* efforts, although our main force should be landed in the Patuxent, yet a tolerably good division should at the same time be sent up the Potowmac with bomb ships etc, which will tend to distract and divide the enemy, abuse Fort Washington, if it does not reduce it, and will most probably offer other advantages.

On July 29, two more ships sailed in, carrying three regiments, two for Canada and one for Ross. On August 1, Ross came aboard Cochrane's flagship, the *Tonnant,* and at noon the fleet set off, with Captain Edward Codrington writing in a letter to his wife: "We are on our way to the Chesapeake–mind you don't tell the Yankees." Even as early as this, the characteristic British mistake of lumping all Americans together under the name of Yankees, hardly calculated to endear them to citizens of the South and West, appeared to be a fixed practice.

On August 11, the *Tonnant* passed the Capes, entering the sweltering summer weather of Virginia (next day Captain Wainwright placed a thermometer on the deck and it registered 133 degrees) and on August 14 they saw Cockburn's ships ahead in the bay. The rest of Malcolm's fleet was some way behind; it approached the coast soon after dawn on August 16, where it was observed first from the Pleasure House Inn near Cape Henry at half past eight. As the fleet passed up the Chesapeake, they were noted from many points and from each of these, a rider was sent to the nearest town to report the sighting. The full assembly of the fifty-one vessels took place off Smith Point at the mouth of the Potomac on the evening of August 16, with a roar of gun salutes. At dawn on August 17, a militia observer, Thomas Swann, a Washington lawyer, counted the combined fleet as best he could through the heat haze, and as they began to move soon after eight in the morning, Swann wrote a dispatch and sent a young man called Carmichael off with it to Washington, a distance of seventy miles.

The plan worked out by the combined chiefs was that the main part of the fleet would go up the Patuxent River, and that two small detachments would carry out separate assignments: Captain James Alexander Gordon would take the frigates *Seahorse* and *Euryalus* with six little ships up the Potomac to destroy what fortified posts he could find there, and Captain Sir Peter Parker would go in the *Menelaus* with two schooners up the Chesapeake to a point above Baltimore, to cut, or appear to be able to cut, the lines of communication between that city and Philadelphia. On August 17 all three groups moved toward their objectives, and after a tricky negotiation of the winding Patuxent River, by sunset on August 18 the main body lay off Benedict, placed well apart so that they occupied miles of water. Ross's assistant adjutant, observing the river banks thick with trees, recorded an impression of ships moving through woods rather than across water. The assistant adjutant was Brigade Major Harry Smith.

Harry Smith had crossed the Atlantic in the *Royal Oak,* an excellent passage under Admiral Malcolm, to whom he had taken a great liking. Ross, he thought, was friendly and kind but, in Smith's opinion, overcautious. The only cloud on Smith's horizon was his separation from his wife: Juana had accompanied him right through the Spanish campaign ever since their drumhead wedding at Badajoz over two years before, and now he had been forced to leave her in England. His fury and sorrow matched hers. Now, as he gazed out from the deck of the *Tonnant* at the uncannily quiet woods, where no one, nothing, stirred, or appeared to stir, the twenty-seven-year-old brigade-major reflected that the men had been told to land at dawn on August 19. Indeed they did so, each man carrying sixty pounds' weight of clothes and equipment in the shimmering heat. At first they did not go far. They made camp close to Benedict, and stayed there for over twenty-four hours, still without incident of any kind.

The news of the British arrival in the Patuxent swept across Washington on that Friday. Commodore Joshua Barney, stationed with a flotilla of gunboats higher up the river, was ordered to move as far up as possible, burn his boats if the British came near, and bring his men into Washington. Jones and Armstrong both thought that the British objective must be Baltimore. They alerted it, at the same time calling out all the local militia and asking for reinforcements wherever they thought they could get them. General Winder, in command of the District of Columbia, issued a proclamation exhorting the Americans to "teach our haughty foe that free men are never unprepared to expel from their soil the insolent foot of the invader." More than a thousand militiamen were marched to the Wood Yard, where, because their equipment had not arrived, they had to sleep in the open. Monroe had set off on horseback to see for himself, but had neglected to bring a telescope. He saw, from a hill three miles from Benedict, the masts and sails crowding the river, and detected the buzz of troop movement, but could not accurately judge the numbers involved. He sent off a note to Madison, containing the alarming words: "The general idea is that Washington is their object, but of this I can form no opinion at this time."

Monroe spent the night at the Charlotte House near Benedict, and spent much of the next day trying to find the British. He made several casts across country which actually took him around the entire British force, but he never realized this. At about four in the afternoon of Saturday, August 20, Ross took his troops off on the road to Nottingham, a road running parallel with the river, so that Admiral Cockburn, still looking out for Commodore Barney's flotilla, could move level, more or less, with Ross (the Admiral had a string of small vessels in which he was transporting all the sailors and marines who could be fitted into them). It was again bakingly hot, and Ross halted after six miles to camp for the night. Stragglers had been falling out of the line of march to break into any isolated house they passed, in search of something to drink. Relief of a sort came at midnight, with a violent thunderstorm accompanied by sheets of rain.

At dawn on Sunday, Ross set off again, and so did Monroe, who had stayed that night also at the Charlotte House. Riding to the river bank, he saw that the British had vanished. Once more by circuitous routes he set out to look for them. The country through which they were now moving was more thickly wooded, and it was harder to see any distance, but the British met hardly a soul. Once an advance patrol found two men, carrying muskets with bayonets attached, sitting under a tree; blandly they said that they were merely shooting squirrels. By five in the afternoon the British entered Nottingham village, and found it deserted.

Monroe had reached Nottingham while the British were still a few miles away, but at last he saw them, and rode to the Wood Yard to report to Winder. He arrived at about eight in the evening, closely followed by Colonel William Beall of the Maryland militia, who had been out scouting too, and had seen the enemy in the distance. Neither man agreed about the probable strength of the British troops, but Winder was sufficiently alarmed to send a dispatch to some militia units then coming south from Baltimore, ordering them up as far as the village of Bladensburg. He added to Monroe and Beall that his men at the Wood Yard would march next morning. Monroe slept for several hours.

Reveille sounded in the Wood Yard at two in the morning, and by sunrise the Americans were on their way toward Nottingham, with Winder and Monroe riding ahead of the column. Five miles away they approached Benjamin Oden's farm, lying at a fork in the road. The west prong of the fork, down which the Americans had marched, came from Washington; the east prong came from Upper Marlboro. From the farm, the single track led to Nottingham. It seemed, and was, a good strategic point, and here Winder and Monroe stopped, quartering themselves in the farmhouse, from which they could see some distance along the road. The British, who had marched from Nottingham at seven in the morning, came into sight an hour and a half later. They glimpsed a few United States cavalry, who promptly retired into the woods.

Ross's advance guard probed a little way along the west fork, which was quite enough to convince the watchers from the farmhouse that they were intent on attacking the capital. Ross, however, did not want to cut himself off from Cockburn's boats, so he backed his column and headed it along the east fork in the direction of Upper Marlboro. Soon he was in sight of the river once again, and there were the boats, as before. But others were just visible ahead, on the far side of Pig Point and, even as the British looked, these began to blow up with a series of loud explosions. Barney had scuttled his flotilla. He had in fact left a skeleton crew on board each ship during the night, and had marched his four hundred men away to the Wood Yard to join their fellows there.

Monroe, naturally, had no idea of all this. As soon as Ross's vanguard made its turn on to the west fork, he had scribbled a note and sent a rider off with it at top speed to carry the news to the President, while he and Winder withdrew their troops under the assumption that they were heavily outnumbered. The message was clear cut: "The Enemy are in full march to Washington."

At first, the tone of comment in the capital had been determinedly optimistic. The *National Intelligencer* stated calmly: "All look with confidence to the capacity and vigilance of the Commanding General." Mrs. Samuel Smith wrote: "Our troops were eager for an attack, and such was the cheerful alacrity display'd, that a universal confidence reign'd among citizens and people." Yet a few began to take quiet precautions. Washington has always been noted for redoubtable ladies, and several wives of prominent men calculated quickly that the safest place in the city was the French ministry, which had diplomatic immunity. Consequently they wrote polite notes asking Madame Sérurier if they might lodge their valuables with her. She courteously replied that of course they could, "although she is in hopes that it will be no occasion for it." This leaked out, and Colonel John Tayloe asked Louis Sérurier to take over his whole house, one of the most striking Washington buildings, named The Octagon House. Sérurier agreed, and the colonel flew a sheet from a flagstaff on his roof, the nearest he could get to the white Bourbon banner.

But ominous signs that all was far from well were showing to the increasingly alarmed eyes of the population. Refugees were coming in from Maryland; wagons were leaving, loaded with furniture and domestic treasures; men in offices were stuffing papers into sacks for removal to safe hiding places; Colonel Decius Wadsworth took two hundred men to dig entrenchments at Bladensburg. Rumors abounded: the redcoats were coming (that old cry), the slaves were going to rise in revolt, the army was scattered. Monroe's message redoubled the panic, so that one New York correspondent wrote: "The distress here and in Georgetown is beyond description," and Mrs. Richard Rush sent a pathetic note to her husband:

> Remember that the happiness of your wife and helpless little boys are bound up in you, and do not expose yourself unless impervious duty demands it. I am all anxiety to hear from you, really think of nothing else.

Richard Rush, attorney general, had gone with the President to visit the army. Armstrong, Jones, and several aides went too. They reached Winder's camp at Long Old Fields, a crossroads eight miles east of the city, by nine in the evening of August 23, and stayed the night. Winder had three thousand men, more than four hundred cavalry, and twenty guns, a good-sized force, but they were all jumpy, and there was a false alarm during the night to which they reacted in a panicky way. Colonel Allen McLane noted sourly: "If General Ross does not rout us this night, it will not be our fault."

At six next morning, Madison held a conference, during which all those present advanced different theories about what the British were going to do. At eight the President reviewed his troops. Winder behaved irresolutely, plagued by jittery doubts. As scouts came in throughout the morning with reports, mostly vague and contradictory, his plans veered wildly in response. The British were moving—they were not—they were heading for Washington—for Annapolis—they were still in Upper Marlboro—they were going to withdraw. Armstrong in particular was most emphatic that Washington could not possibly interest the enemy.

Ross had spent a comfortable night at Upper Marlboro in the house of the one local man still there, sixty-five-year-old Dr. William Beanes, an affable Federalist with British sympathies. Ross would indeed have liked to withdraw, having made his gesture along the river. His officers, and Admiral Cockburn, who came ashore in the morning to talk to him, persuaded him to go on. At two in the afternoon of Wednesday, August 24, the British moved off along the road that led to Washington.

At exactly that same moment, Madison mounted his horse and started for the capital, convinced that it was safe, at least for the present. Winder wanted to mass all his available forces together for a full attack, and sent messages to the commanders of all his dispersed units. He also sent Major George Peter with a small company to see where the British now were. Monroe went with them, and so did another scout, Thomas McKenney, a draper by trade. Not far out of Upper Marlboro, Peter's men brushed against the flank of the British march and, at last, in this peculiar campaign, shots were exchanged deliberately between opposing troops.

Little damage was done, for Peter sensibly retired, and McKenney, observing the enemy preparing to make camp at Melwood, rode back to Long Old Fields where he announced dramatically that the British were "within a mile." They were, of course, over three miles away, and stopping there, but McKenney's words made it sound as if the enemy were hard behind him, and Winder's deputy, Brigadier General Walter Smith, strung out his men across the road, expecting an attack at any moment. Winder was riding toward Bladensburg, and a message was sent to recall him to the scene of action.

Only there was no action. Winder rode back, praised Smith for his sensible arrangements, and decided, in view of all the varying reports he had received that day, to fall back on Washington to guard its bridges. By eight in the evening his weary men were stumbling into the city.

Here, tension had mounted. Belatedly, squads of militia were drilling on the open space in front of the White House. Every wheeled vehicle in the city was on the move, carrying government papers and personal possessions to supposedly safe places in the Virginia countryside. The banks sent their gold stocks away. Large numbers of people left, too. Mrs. Madison, told in a hurried note by her husband to be ready to go "at a moment's warning," filled all the trunks and boxes that her carriage would hold with cabinet papers, and sat down to wait until she could "see Mr Madison safe, and he can accompany me." Her majordomo, Jean Pierre Sioussa, suggested spiking the cannon at the White House gates and laying a train of gunpowder that could be exploded as the British came in, but Mrs. Madison forbade it. During the day a note arrived for her from William Jones's wife, Eleanor, saying:

> In the present state of alarm and bustle of preparation for the worst that may happen, I imagine it will be more convenient to dispense with the enjoyment of your hospitality today.

To this, Mrs. Madison replied that of course she would excuse Mrs. Jones from dining at the White House that evening.

As a matter of fact the night of Tuesday, August 23 passed peacefully among the encamped British. The only person to move among them was Lieutenant James Scott, RN, one of Admiral Cockburn's aides. He carried a message from Captain Codrington at Benedict to the Admiral and Ross at Melwood, cautioning them against risking an attack on the American capital. They had made a positive demonstration, they could easily be outnumbered, it would be prudent to withdraw. Scott, riding through the warm darkness with a marine captain called Robyns, delivered the note at Melwood soon after two in the morning. Ross, as usual, hesitated; Cockburn, also as usual, observed that they had come too far now to turn back. A glow in the sky to the west showed that something, probably a bridge, was on fire. The decision was taken, and by five in the morning of Wednesday, August 24 the British troops were on the road. They were heading not directly toward Washington, but toward the village of Bladensburg, where, if the bridge had gone, there was a ford.

The glow in the sky was indeed a burning bridge. At that time there were two bridges leading out of Washington into Maryland: an upper and a lower. The lower was the main one, and Winder posted soldiers there, ready to defend it or destroy it, while he ordered the upper bridge, Stoddert's Bridge, to be burned at once. This was done between three and four in the morning, while, all over the District of Columbia, groups of soldiers were alerted, moved, settled, alerted, moved again, apparently without any decisive kind of plan, and commanding officers and government officials in twos and threes debated what to do. One citizen offered to blow up the Capitol; Madison replied that it would do more to "arouse the Nation" if the British did so. The newspapers appeared in the morning, full of hopeful statements. The *National Intelligencer* said: "We feel assured that the number and bravery of our men will afford complete protection to the City"; the *Federal Republican* said: "It is highly improbable that the enemy would advance nearer to the Capital." Winder, who had fallen into a ditch during the night and wrenched his ankle so that he was limping painfully, sent a note to Armstrong asking what to do; the note was delivered by mistake to the President, who instantly went to the Navy Yard. He found Winder in temporary headquarters at the Griffith Coombs House near the lower bridge. Here, from seven until ten in the morning, eminent men argued and messengers came and went with reports of British movements, most of them wrong. Finally, however, Winder decided that the latest news, that the British were moving on Bladensburg, must be true.

Winder now ordered every unit in the District to go as fast as possible to Bladensburg. Except one: he forgot, or thought it better not, to send Barney's troops, which remained guarding the eastern branch of the Potomac. Historians have wondered whether the safety of the lower bridge was the preoccupation in Winder's mind. Barney himself was furious at being kept there "with five hundred of the precious few fighting men around to do what any damned corporal can better do with five." Winder appears to have given way to pessimism: to his aide-de-camp he said: "I am but nominal commander. The President and the Secretary of War have interfered with my intended operations, and I greatly fear the success of the day."

The village of Bladensburg lay where five roads converged on the single bridge. West of the river ran the roads to Georgetown and Washington; east of it were two routes to Upper Marlboro, one direct, one not, and the turnpike to Baltimore. A rider coming from Washington would crest a gentle hill from which he could see the river, shallow at this point, the mildly decaying little brick houses clustered on the far side of the bridge, apple orchards below him on the slope and, on the far side, the undulating country that, somewhere, concealed the British Army. Monroe, who had galloped ahead of Winder's force, saw exactly that sight soon after eleven o'clock. He also saw Brigadier General Tobias Stansbury's two thousand militia milling about in the field between the two roads, shifting positions as various officers suggested.

This is the really surprising thing about the battle of Bladensburg, that all sorts of people–generals, colonels, cabinet ministers, anybody–could, apparently, walk up and move troops, or suggest moving troops, piecemeal. One young man who offered his opinions to Winder himself was a lawyer from Georgetown named Francis Scott Key. Stansbury had placed some of his men in the orchard near the river; Monroe moved them back up the open hill. The troops from Washington were arriving, each unit adding to the confusion: it seemed as if each commander had to decide for himself, or follow someone's hastily expressed opinion, where to put his men. Winder, ordering up three guns to flank the orchard, said with a sad lack of commanding fire: "When you retreat, take notice you must retreat by the Georgetown road."

The President, with his small escorting group, rode in at noon, almost unremarked, and led the way down to the river bank to water the horses. He crossed the bridge, where stood a scout, William Simmons, just dismounted after riding up the hill for a look around. Simmons shouted: "Mr. Madison, the enemy are now in Bladensburg!" and the group hurriedly rode back.

It was true: a cloud of dust on the road from Upper Marlboro revealed, now, the gleam of musket barrels, the flash of scarlet, the steady tramp of marching boots. The British had come.

Ross, who had fallen-out his men for a short rest before noon, had reconnoitered his position, and had realized that the Americans had the advantage of the rising ground. They also appeared to outnumber him. On the other hand, his men were veterans of the Peninsula, and he had, among his armaments, some of the Congreve rockets, which, he thought, might well strike terror into the unseasoned militia. One of his officers recorded his impression of the Americans that day:

> A few Companies only, perhaps two or at the most three battalions, wearing the blue jacket which the Americans have borrowed from the French, presented some appearance of regular troops. The rest seemed country people who would have been more appropriately employed attending to their agricultural occupations than standing with muskets in their hands on a bare hill.

Ross ordered his light brigade of about twelve hundred men to attack the bridge. As they advanced in sixes, yells could be heard from the Americans. One infantryman remarked: "Let's see what you'll say when we've been at it half an hour or so!" The worst problem, for the British, was the heat, the heavy steamy weight of summer in the District of Columbia. Many suffered from heat exhaustion, including one of Ross's aides, Captain Tom Falls. The Americans opened fire, too soon: their first shots hit nothing. They got the range within a few minutes, however, and began to register on the redcoats stolidly coming up to the bridge. Men fell, others drew back, cannoning into those behind them, and some began to sidestep the bridge, splashing across through the shallow water. Marines, clustered in little bands to the right of the bridge, set off several rockets, which caused little damage but a good deal of alarm. Winder rode up to the President, who was sitting watching on his horse in the center, and suggested that he should draw back. As Madison wrote afterward:

> When the battle had decidedly commenced, I observed to the Secretary of War and the Secretary of State that it would be proper to withdraw to a position in the rear, leaving military movements to the military functionaries.

The little party did this. Armstrong commented: "I now became, of course, a mere spectator of the combat." He did not have to watch long. The practised, disciplined attack of the British, now in three prongs, right and left fording the river and threatening both American flanks, the screeching rockets, the badly spaced American lines, all contributed to a rout. Within half an hour, the American troops were in full retreat, scrambling back toward Washington as best they could, and setting such a pace that the British referred to the battle afterward as "Bladensburg Races."

There was one shot left in the American locker. Barney's men had come out of the city as fast as they could, but of course they were late starting, and they reached the highest ridge of hills on that side of the eastern branch just in time to form a second line there. Winder had not named a rallying point in case of retreat; his men were scattered all over the landscape by now. But Barney stood. At half past two the British came in sight, and Barney, encouraging his men with naval cries, made a stiff fight of it in spite of a wound in the leg and his horse shot under him—as Ross's had been. His ammunition wagons, manned by civilians, did not like being fired at, and turned for home; Barney could do nothing but surrender. Captain Wainwright of the *Tonnant* brought Cockburn up, and there was an awkward moment when Wainwright named the admiral, naturally, as "Co'burn," to which Barney pugnaciously insisted on "Cock-burn." Cockburn sent Barney, carried by several soldiers, to have his wound dressed at a nearby tavern.

It was a real victory for Ross: with 2,600 men he had routed more than twice that number, captured 10 guns, 220 muskets, 120 prisoners, and inflicted 150 casualties. But he had lost 250 himself, of which Harry Smith said: "The times I have sighed, Oh, for dear John Colborne! At Bladensburg we licked the Yankies and took all their guns with a loss of 300 men, whereas Colborne would have done the same thing with a loss of forty or fifty at most!" The Americans were well impressed, even so, by the British demeanor: "The militia ran like sheep, chased by dogs," wrote one of Barney's men; "Our militia dispersed like a flock of birds assailed by a load of mustard seed shot," said the Philadelphia *General Advertiser;* the Norfolk *Herald* reported the British moving "as steadily and undismayed as though there were no opposition"; Colonel Joseph Sterett said: "We were outflanked and defeated in as short a time as such an operation could well be performed."

The Americans scampered clear of the battlefield, then headed instinctively for Washington or Baltimore, whichever seemed the better. Cockburn commented that "the victors were too weary and the vanquished too swift" for close pursuit; Ross ordered a rest for a couple of hours. He set up temporary headquarters in the house of Thomas Barclay, HM Commissioner on Prisoner Exchanges. Barclay had reluctantly left for Baltimore that morning, but his assistant, George Barton, was there, and made the British welcome.

In Washington all was quiet. At three in the afternoon Mrs. Madison wrote in a long letter to her sister that she was writing in fragments, like a journal, over several days: "Will you believe it, we have had a battle near Bladensburg, and I am still here within sound of the cannon! Mr. Madison comes not. May God protect him! Two messengers, covered with dust, come to bid me fly; but I wait for him."

The messengers had galloped up to the White House. One of them shouted: "Clear out, clear out! General Armstrong has ordered a retreat!"

NINE

§

A Little Trip

One of the shouters (and it is noticeable that he was named Armstrong, not Winder) was Jim Smith, a freedman servant of the President. He carried a note from Madison to his wife, stating simply that the battle was lost and that she should "fly at once."

Mrs. Madison was never the type to panic. She was in no hurry. She ordered more goods to be loaded on a wagon, silver, books, more papers, a small clock, and the red velvet curtains from the drawing room. Helping her was quite a crowd of people, including the servants; a presidential aide named Charles Carroll; her sister and brother-in-law Mr. and Mrs. Richard Cutts; and two New Yorkers, the banker Jacob Barker and a young man, Robert de Peyster. Mrs. Madison kept adding bits to her letter to her other sister, Lucy Washington Todd. She wrote:

> Mr Carroll has come to hasten my departure and is in a very bad humour because I insist on waiting until the large picture of General Washington is secured, and it requires to be unscrewed from the wall.

The combined efforts of everyone present could not unscrew the painting. In the end they cut the frame to bits, lifted out the canvas, and laid it carefully on the floor. Mrs. Madison entrusted it to the two New Yorkers, saying that all that mattered was not to let it fall into British hands. They were also to carry away the four remaining boxes of presidential papers and the ornamental eagles in the drawing room. Having arranged these details, she was ready to go. Three vehicles set off: two carriages, one containing Mrs. Madison and her maid Sukey, one the Cutts couple, and lastly the "coachee" driven by the butler,

John Freeman, with his family packed inside and a featherbed strapped on the back. They headed toward Georgetown.

The retreating troops assembled bit by bit in the grounds of the Capitol, where Monroe, Armstrong, and Winder met to plan, or discuss whether they could plan, what to do. Armstrong wanted to use the Capitol as a fort, and fight it out there; the other two preferred Winder's idea of retiring to the heights, such as they were, behind Georgetown, and making a stand if they could. Rumors of the discussion reached the weary troops, who, believing that no real attempt was going to be made to hold the city, began to look after themselves, many of them going off to see to their homes and families. At half past four, about half an hour after Mrs. Madison had driven away, Madison, with Richard Rush, entered the White House. Here he found Barker and de Peyster, still packing up in, apparently, a most leisurely manner, for the Washington portrait still lay on the floor, and the two men had been refreshing themselves with glasses of the President's brandy. From time to time passing soldiers wandered in, had a look around, helped themselves to a drink, and wandered off again. The President sat down for an hour to rest and chat—he was, after all, sixty-three, and it had been a long, hot, trying day—and the four men talked of where they should go and what they should do. Madison had proposed (and had told his wife) to seek refuge at Salona, the Virginia estate of the Reverend John Maffitt, a friend of his. At sunset, they collected themselves, left the house, and rode to the riverside, where Madison and Rush took a ferryboat over to Analostan Island. From there they walked across the causeway to the Virginia shore. Barker and de Peyster went back to the White House, where they loaded the portrait on a cart, along with some silver urns, and set off up Pennsylvania Avenue. All around them straggled a fleeing crowd, clutching bags and bundles, heading, generally, for the long bridge over to the spot where Robert E. Lee later made his home, and beyond that to the open country.

Sioussa, left in the White House, hid some showy-looking gold and silver objects, set out water and wine for any one who might walk in, especially, he thought, the poor thirsty soldiers, and took Mrs. Madison's pet macaw in its cage along to the Octagon House, where he asked the French chef to take care of it. He then returned, closed all the doors and windows, locked up at the back, and took the front door key to the house of the Russian minister, Dashkoff. The minister was in Philadelphia, but his staff took the key and promised to keep it safe.

In the worry of trying to decide what to do, Winder had forgotten about Barney's men, just as he had forgotten them that morning. He had also overlooked Captain Thomas Tingey at the Washington Navy Yard. Armstrong belatedly remembered, and sent a note to say: "The Navy Yard cannot be covered." Tingey, a resolute but temperamental character, had virtually created the navy yard, and it went to his heart to think of destroying it. He was appalled to see that Captain John Creighton was blowing up the lower bridge, close by; the explosion shattered the shore end, and the timbers began to burn along their full length. Tingey prepared for demolition of the navy yard, then stood irresolute as messengers came in and out, bearing conflicting tidings of where exactly the British were. Finally Tingey's chief clerk, Mordecai Booth, offered to go find out. He rode to the turnpike gate and gazed toward Bladensburg, where a single horseman was riding hard in his direction. It was a butcher from Georgetown, Thomas Miller, and he said the British were not far behind him. The two men rode to the top of the hill and, sure enough, there was a marching column. But they were dressed in blue. How could they be the British? A shot was fired, and passed unpleasantly close. Booth, from the navy yard, had forgotten the Royal Navy.

He reported back to Tingey, who was relieved to hear that the enemy was still some distance off. Booth went on to the White House. A United States cavalry colonel stood by the steps, but the house was dark, silent, and empty. The two men went back to the Capitol, picking up a few others on the way; one of them pointed out some cows near Long's Hotel on A Street; then, close by, a dim glow of red coats. The Americans dashed away, Booth heading for the navy yard. At twenty past eight, Tingey gave the signal, and the yard exploded and began to burn, lighting up the sky.

The British seen by Booth and his companions were, first, the 1,460 men of the Third Brigade, consisting of sailors and marines and most of the 21st Regiment of Foot; the few near the hotel were, had he known it, Ross and Cockburn with a small advance guard. They had entered the dark and silent city with feelings of puzzlement. It did not look like a city; rather it was "as if some giant had scattered a box of child's toys upon the ground." There were open spaces, and there were black bulks of building, but not many, so that, to commanders fresh from the huddled towns of Europe, it seemed weird and alarming. Ross told his drummer to sound the parley and, as the brisk tattoo died on the hot air, they stood and listened. Nothing happened. They rode slowly on toward the Capitol, halting beside Robert Sewall's house. Here they paused again. They wanted to find someone to speak to, because they intended to levy an indemnity on the city as the price for sparing it. No one appeared.

Suddenly a flurry of shots startled everyone. One soldier fell dead and so did Ross's horse, the second he had lost that day. Lieutenant Scott led several men to break down the door of the Sewall house: they found no one inside. They came out, and fired in a few rockets. Cockburn rode away to fetch the rest of his troops. At the same time the bright light of flames rose into the sky from the burning navy yard, lighting up, it seemed, miles of space. Tingey, having given the signal, stepped into a gig and was rowed across the river to Alexandria.

It is not clear exactly who determined to burn various buildings in Washington that night, though Harry Smith was convinced it was Cockburn. Also that it was the gentler Ross who laid down the principle that private houses, whose inmates made no resistance and concealed no arms, would not be touched. Smith considered the whole thing barbarous: "It made one ashamed to be an Englishman. We felt more like a band of Red Savages from the woods." Wellington, he said, would never have done such a thing.

Sewall's house was burned, and then the Capitol, through which the soldiers explored first. It impressed them with its imposing design, incomplete though it was. Many picked up small objects as souvenirs: Cockburn himself kept a bound copy of a Treasury report. The Capitol was a solid structure, not easy to set alight, but its furnishings would burn, and burn they did. The clock over the Speaker's chair said ten exactly as the fire took hold. After that came several more buildings, including two houses on North Capitol Street built under the direction of George Washington himself. From time to time, groups of British soldiers knocked at doors, explaining to terrified inhabitants that they would like something to eat and drink. Dr. James Ewell thought his own house was on fire until he realized that it was the burning Capitol reflected in his windows; he promptly sought out Ross and offered him hospitality, a neat way of making sure that his house would be safe. Ross accepted, saying that he would return later, and he and Cockburn, with one hundred and fifty men, went to the White House, pausing on the way to arrange for a meal for his own party at the boardinghouse belonging to Mrs. Barbara Suter. Near the White House they halted again, while Cockburn sent an officer with a message to Mrs. Madison, offering her an escort to any place of safety she cared to name. The officer came back, reporting that the President's house stood empty; the British approached, trod up the front steps, and walked in. Sioussa had not locked the front door, in order to allow "the poor thirsty soldiers" to get in.

The biggest surprise they found there was the dining room, with its long table set for forty people, in perfect order, with wine bottles in coolers–Harry Smith said it was "super-excellent Madeira"–and they drank "to the health of the Prince Regent and success to His Majesty's arms by sea and land." Again they went all over the building, picking up souvenirs. Harry Smith, with his usual practical campaigning sense, changed his shirt, putting on a fresh one that presumably belonged to Madison. The soldiers cleared the dining table, putting the china, glass, and silver into a tablecloth. A messenger arrived from the Octagon House, asking for protection for Sérurier "against an accident or a mistake, which," the note went on, "could easily happen despite the intentions of His Britannic Majesty's officers." If it seemed comical to Ross to protect a Frenchman, he did not show it, but replied: "The French King's House will be as respected as if His Majesty were there in person." The messenger went away. Ross, Cockburn, and the rest took a last look around. Then the fire was lit.

As soon as it had got hold of the President's furniture, the British moved on to the Treasury Building, where, perhaps not unnaturally, they expected to find money. They found none. That building, too, was set alight, and that concluded the business of the evening: five private houses and three public buildings burned, or at least gutted. Contemporary illustrations do not suggest so modest a total; they make it look as if acres of houses were leveled to the ground. Ross, Cockburn, and their staffs returned to Mrs. Suter's and ate a chicken supper. During it, however, Cockburn appeared to have an afterthought, for he asked, on leaving, to be directed to the offices of the *National Intelligencer.* It stood opposite McKeowin's Hotel, and a soldier, running in, came back with a copy of the latest edition, which informed the reader that the capital was safe. Cockburn wanted to burn the offices, but two ladies who lived nearby, and who had evidently been not only watching the admiral but listening to him, asked him not to do it, as their houses would burn too. Cockburn agreed, saying he would come back and wreck it in the morning, and that, meanwhile, the ladies would be "as safely protected under my administration as under that of Mr Madison." He went away, bidding everyone good night, and leaving a soldier on guard outside the newspaper building; strangely enough, this man was the only British occupying force in the middle of Washington that night.

The rest of the troops camped on Capitol Hill or at the edge of the District by the tollgate on the Bladensburg road. The flames from the various fires still lit up the dark sky. They could be seen from Baltimore, forty miles away. The officer of the watch on HMS *Meteor,* miles down the Potomac, noted in his log "a large fire NNW." They could be seen by the scattered members of the Administration, many of whom were still moving through the countryside. Winder had collected the remnants of his army at Tenleytown; Monroe was at Wiley's Tavern near Great Falls; William and Eleanor Jones had caught up with Mrs. Madison, who realized that her husband was heading for Salona. Despairing of getting as far as that, she and the Joneses stopped at Mrs. Matilda Lee Love's house, Rokeby. The President had reached Salona, and Armstrong was on his way there.

In the early hours of August 25 a thunderstorm broke, heavily enough to put out the fires. By half past five Cockburn rode up Pennsylvania Avenue on a "borrowed" gray mare, with her foal trotting behind. He watched while the newspaper offices were systematically wrecked, the presses smashed, and the type broken up. Captain Wainwright took a working party to the navy yard to complete Tingey's work of destruction, and found it swarming with American looters. Major Timothy Jones led another group to blow up the office building that housed the Departments of War, the Navy, and the State (it is pleasant to think that these three giants could all fit under one modest roof), and then went on to perform the same function at the Patent Office. Here, however, they were stopped by Dr. William Thornton, Superintendent of Patents, who ingeniously pointed out to them that almost everything in the place was private property, inventors' models mostly, and to destroy "what would be useful to all mankind" would be "as barbarous as to burn the Alexandria library, for which the Turks have been condemned by all enlightened nations." This argument was decisive, and the Patent Office was spared.

Only two other things were burned: three ropewalks–long narrow enclosures where ropes were twisted–and the Long Bridge. This last was burned by both sides, from both ends. As the British applied the torch, a woman with several children ran through onto the bridge; three British soldiers ran after her and, at the risk of their lives, got her and the children safely through at the already burning other end, and darted back. One thing was exploded: the American ammunition dump at Greenleaf Point, which contained one hundred and fifty barrels of powder. Four officers with two hundred men went off to detonate it, but while they were rolling the barrels into a well in preparation for blowing them up, the whole thing went off prematurely, killing thirty men and injuring forty-four.

During the afternoon a terrific storm drenched the city with sheets of rain, blew the roof off the Patent Office, threw three-pounder guns about the streets, and rattled windows all over the District. It also soaked to the skin several tiny groups of Americans who were making their way across Washington, trying to find somebody to whom to surrender. The officers they met put up a convincing pretense of being interested, finding out what they could, saying that they would let them know later and, meanwhile, with an eight o'clock curfew imposed, the British were preparing to leave. Apparently their commander felt that they had done enough, or perhaps they were wary of pressing the advantage in case enemy reinforcements came up to take them by surprise. They left that night, very quietly, under cover of a rearguard which lit campfires and moved about as though the whole force were still there. From eight in the evening they marched out, back along the Bladensburg road, taking with them a herd of sixty cattle and many bags of flour, some of which were dropped by exhausted men on the march. Harry Smith said that his part of the column found its way back by following the trail of flour. At Bladensburg they rested, went on at one in the morning, stopped for five hours at seven, and reached Upper Marlboro at sunset on August 26. Next day they moved on again, taking three days to reach Benedict. For the whole of that five-day march they tramped through what might have been a deserted landscape: they saw no one, heard nothing, from beginning to end. As the twelve-day foray ended, one young officer, back on board his ship in the Patuxent, noted that "the luxury I enjoyed in turning into clean sheets is beyond description."

Among the Americans, the situation was chaotic. Winder tried to find a focal point to which all his troops could rally, but as fast as one group reached him, another melted away, and he had moved back as far as Montgomery Court House, twelve miles north of Washington, before any persons of authority reached him. Colonel Allen McLane noted:

> I find the road full of straggling militia looking towards Baltimore. I have prayed, I have begged, I have threatened, all to no purpose. Those drones on the public persist in running away. From a disorganised militia, Good Lord deliver us.

Throughout Thursday and Friday, August 25 and 26, the various members of the Administration were dispersed all over the countryside, looking for one another. Madison had suggested reconvening at Frederick in Maryland; Armstrong got there and found nobody. The Madisons missed each other as they searched from Rokeby to Salona, from Salona to Falls Church, held up for hours by the great storm, until at last they met at Wiley's tavern on suitably named Difficult Run late on Thursday evening. All the time reports and rumors reached all the principal actors in the drama: the British were here, there, marching on Baltimore, massing for a fresh attack; the slaves were rising (the recurrent nightmare, one that never came true); Washington lay in ashes. Madison set off at midnight to rejoin Winder if he could find him, but did not reach Montgomery Court House until six in the evening of Friday, by which time Winder had moved to Snell's Bridge, and Madison spent the night at Brookville, a small Quaker village where Mrs. Caleb Bentley said: "It is against our principles to have anything to do with war, but we receive and relieve all who come to us."

Monroe had been to Snell's Bridge, and he rode to Brookville early on Saturday to suggest going back to Washington; a note to him from Madison saying the same thing reached him on the road. Madison had sent similar notes to Armstrong and Jones, and one to his wife at Wiley's tavern, telling her that Washington was safe so "we shall accordingly set out thither immediately; you will of course take the same resolution." At noon, Madison, with Monroe, Rush, and an escort of twenty cavalrymen, started off.

The main problem on Friday in the city was looting, which went on from the moment the citizens knew that the enemy had left. The first person to try to restore order was the gallant Dr. Thornton, who, once he was sure that his beloved Patent Office was more or less all right, placed guards and organized street patrols, including some British soldiers who were still in the city, and called upon every responsible person he could think of to help. The worst was over by the time the mayor, Dr. James Blake, came back to Washington at about three in the afternoon, and resumed authority, to the accompaniment of sardonic remarks by Thornton about mayors who left their cities in time of danger. The President rode in at five o'clock. What he saw is described by Margaret Bayard Smith, wife of Samuel Smith, who, in a letter to her sister, set down her impressions.

We pass'd several dead horses. The poor capitol! nothing but its blacken'd walls remained! 4 or 5 houses in the neighbourhood were likewise in ruins. Some men had got within these houses and fired on the English as they were quietly marching into the city, they killed 4 men and Genl Rosse's horse. I imagine Genl R. thought that his life was particularly aim'd at, for while his troops remained in the city he never made his appearance, altho' Cochburn and the other officers often rode through the avenue. It was on account of this outrage that these houses were burnt. We afterwards look'd at the other public buildings, but none were so thoroughly destroy'd as the House of Representatives and the President's House. Those beautiful pillars in that Representatives Hall were crack'd and broken, the roof, that noble dome, painted and carved with such beauty and skill, lay in ashes in the cellars beneath the smouldering ruins, were yet smoking. In the P.H. not an inch, but its crack'd and blacken'd walls remained. That scene, which when I last visited it, was so splendid, throng'd with the great, the gay, the ambitious placemen, and patriotic Heros was now nothing but ashes, and it was in these ashes, now trodden under foot by the rabble, which once posses'd the power to inflate pride, to gratify vanity.

The Madisons had taken refuge in Richard Cutts's untouched house, which became the Executive Mansion for the time being, for, as Mrs. Smith pointed out, the White House was a forlorn, roofless shell. The Smiths called there:

Mrs. M. seem'd much depress'd, she could scarcely speak without tears. She told me she had remained in the city till a few hours before the English enter'd. She was so confident of Victory that she was calmly listening to the roar of cannon, and watching the rockets in the air, when she perceived our troops rushing into the city, with the haste and dismay of a routed force. The friends with her then hurried her away, (her carriage being previously ready) and she with many other families, among whom was Mrs. Thornton and Mrs. Cutting with her, retreated with the flying army. In George town they perceived some men before them carrying off the picture of Genl Washington (the large one by Stewart) which with the plate, was all that was saved out of the President's house.

When, eventually, the Capitol was rebuilt, the winning design was Dr. Thornton's, though the end result was a modified version of his plan. From Mrs. Thornton, Margaret Bayard Smith heard further details about the burning of the White House.

We drank tea at Mrs Thornton's, who described to us the manner in which they conflagrated the President's H. and other buildings,–50 men, sailors and marines, were marched by an officer, silently thro' the avenue, each carrying a long pole to which was fixed a ball about the circumference of a large plate,–when arrived at the building, each man was station'd at a window, with his pole and machine of wild fire against it, at the word of command, at the same instant the windows were broken and this wild fire thrown in, so that an instantaneous conflagration took place and the whole building was wrapt in flames and smoke. The spectators stood in awful silence, the city was light and the heavens redden'd with the blaze! . . . Cochburn paid this house a visit and forced a young gentleman of our acquaintance to go with him,–on entering the dining room they found the table spread for dinner, left precipitally by Mrs. M.,–he insisted on young Weightman's sitting down and drinking Jemmy's health, which was the only epithet he used whenever he spoke of the President. After looking round, he told Mr W. to take something to remember this day. Mr W. wished for some valuable article. No, no said he, that I must give to the flames, but here, handing him some ornaments off the mantlepiece, these will answer as memento. I must take something too. He seized an old hat a chapeau de bras of the President's and a cushion off Mrs M's chair, declaring these should be his trophies.

The city was quiet; but, during the evening, the ominous rattle of gunfire from the Potomac alarmed everyone. They suddenly remembered the British naval squadron under Captain James Gordon, which had been making a slow, uncomfortable journey up the river for ten days, and had now begun to bombard Fort Washington. The rumble of cannon went on for two hours or so, until, at half past eight, there was a shattering explosion. Then silence. In the city, people felt a spasm of terror; on the river, Gordon and his men watched in disbelief as the fort blew up before their eyes. The commander of the fort, Captain Sam Dyson, had been told by Winder to blow up the fort and withdraw if he was attacked by land. For some reason, never clear even after Dyson's court-martial, he blew it up now, after spiking his unfired guns and leading out his sixty men. More than three thousand pounds of powder went up and, next day, the British landed and captured twenty-seven guns and a stock of muskets.

At ten on Saturday morning a boat from Alexandria, flying a flag of truce, approached Gordon's ships, and a deputation of three came on board the *Seahorse* to ask for surrender terms on behalf of the town. Gordon said he would think it over, and sent them back, perhaps to gain time, perhaps because he thought that an attitude of stern reserve on his part might make the citizens of Alexandria quicker to make concessions. During the afternoon he sailed slowly up to the town quay. A fresh deputation waited upon him that night and, by threatening, or appearing to threaten, dire consequences unless the Alexandrians purchased their immunity with gifts, Gordon persuaded the delegation to let him take over all the naval stores and a full supply of merchandise, together with goods destined for export, and any vessels not previously scuttled. On Monday morning the work of loading began, and lasted three days, during which, wrote the mayor of Alexandria, "it is impossible that men could behave better than the British behaved while the town was in their hands." Well they might. Their haul was rich by any standards.

The surrender of Alexandria further dispirited Washington. Margaret Bayard Smith noted on August 30:

> Alexandria has surrendered its town and all their flour and merchandise. What will be our fate I know not. The citizens who remained are now moving out, and all seem more alarmed than before.

And Dr. Thornton's wife wrote that "the people are violently irritated at the thought of our attempting to make any more futile resistance." Everyone believed that the British were going to make another assault on the city. It was Monroe who saved them and, in doing so, rescued his own reputation, which was a little tarnished by his blunders at Bladensburg. He said that he would bayonet any deputations he saw going to treat with the British; he set up three defensive batteries aimed down the river, placed militia on the heights, resited guns on the opposite shore, and put new heart into his fellow countrymen. It is possible that his resolute, clear actions now ensured him the presidency in succession to Madison, who had appointed him to take charge of the city's defenses.

As Monroe's star rose, Armstrong's fell: everyone blamed him for the defeat. The *Federal Republican* stated that "the movements of this fiend should be narrowly watched." When he appeared in public, he was jeered at, men refused to shake his hand, officers threatened to "tear off their epaulettes" rather than serve under him. Madison suggested that he should stay away from local forces, and perhaps take a holiday visiting his family in New York. On August 30, twenty-four hours after his return to Washington, Armstrong left it for Baltimore, where he brooded over his wrongs, as he saw them, writing to the papers to announce his resignation and then, and only then, submitting the same officially in a brief note to the President.

On that same day Sir Peter Parker in the *Menelaus* landed near Moorfields on the eastern shore of the Chesapeake with a small force of seamen and marines and led them against a larger body of local militia; the British were beaten off, and Parker was killed.

While Washington looked to its defenses and scoured the city for traitors and spies, Gordon began the dangerous passage back down the shoal-ridden, fort-dotted Potomac, taking with him twenty-one captured ships and enormous quantities of flour, beef, sugar, cotton, tobacco, and tar. He sailed at five in the morning on September 2, pursued the next day by Commodore John Rodgers with a flotilla including fireships. These were pushed back in disorder, and Gordon went on. He next had to pass a bluff on the Virginian shore called (interestingly) the White House, where Commodore David Porter had posted ten guns, entrenched infantry, and a banner reading "Free Trade and Sailors' Rights." Gordon had sixty-three guns, the trajectory of which he raised by loading his ships to one side, and successfully blasted his way past. This was on September 5. One final obstacle stood in his way: Commodore Perry, brought down from Lake Erie to take his station at Indian Head. But Perry had only one heavy gun, and little ammunition for it, so, early on September 6, Gordon ran clear of the last guns.

The rest of the habitable United States had learned the news of the capital's fall, and newspapers thundered denunciations of those whose fault, as they saw it, it clearly was. "The blush of shame, and of rage, tinges the cheek," said the Richmond *Enquirer.* The Philadelphia

United States Gazette said that if the government did not resign, its members "must be constitutionally impeached and driven with scorn and execration from the seats which they have dishonoured and polluted." The *Gazette* of Winchester in Virginia commented: "Poor, contemptible, pitiful, dastardly wretches! Their heads would be but a poor price for the degradation into which they have plunged our bleeding country." The distinguished writer Washington Irving said: "The country is insulted and disgraced by this barbarous success," but he went on: "every loyal citizen would feel the ignominy and be earnest to avenge it."

And, as late as September 10, came the trumpet blast of Niles' *Weekly Register:*

> The hate with which *we* have always said *Great Britain* regarded us, is now exhibiting by a Goth-like war, which the late strange events in *Europe* enables her to carry on with extraordinary force and energy. The barriers with which civilised nations have circumscribed their military operations, are cast down by the foe; and the contest, begun for unalienable rights on the sea, is becoming a struggle for liberty and property on the land. The shores of the *Chesapeake* are lighted by the flames of farm houses and cottages, hitherto respected in war; and the fruits of the earth are wantonly consumed by the invader's torch. Whatever of private property pleases him, he lays hold of as a prize; and wickedly destroys what he cannot carry away. Household furniture has been a favourite object of his vengeance, and *negroes* and *tobacco* are his darling spoils! His late capture of *Washington City* is an honour to the valour of his soldiery; but his conduct in burning the capitol, the president's house and the public offices, is a disgrace that he will not wipe away . . . The *outlaw, Bonaparte,* entered *Lisbon, Madrid, Amsterdam, Berlin, Vienna, Moscow, Turin, Rome, Naples,* and the capitals of ten or fifteen of the minor states of Europe, but never, in the case of the *Kremlin* excepted, destroyed a public building undevoted to military purposes . . .

On September 3, sailing down the Patuxent, Admiral Cochrane wrote to the First Lord of the Admiralty: "As soon as the Army is all re-embarked, I mean to proceed to the Northward and try to surprise Rhode Island."

Matters had been quiet in Canada while all these events were going on, both sides looking to their troops, their ships, and their defenses. Prevost had received his longed-for reinforcements at last, and had more than ten thousand regulars ready by September 1 to cross the border at Lake Champlain. Yeo at Kingston was superintending work on an enormous ship of war, the *St. Lawrence,* while at the Isle aux Noix HMS *Confiance* was slowly building. Yeo and Chauncey had established an unspoken convention of letting one another cruise up and down Lake Ontario in the largest ship each had, without any threat of confrontation. On Lake Champlain, Thomas Macdonough, now master commandant, had fifteen ships, USS *Saratoga* and *Eagle* with a schooner, two sloops, and ten gunboats, easily outweighing the British brig *Linnet,* three sloops, and twelve gunboats, but once the *Confiance* appeared the balance would change. Prevost saw Lake Champlain, backed by the American base at Plattsburg, as the focus of possible operations, though he did not want to upset the traders and smugglers too much:

> The State of Vermont having Shown a decided opposition to the War, and very large supplies of Specie coming in daily from thence, as well as the whole of the Cattle required for the use of the Troops, I mean for the present to confine myself in any offensive Operations which may take place to the Western side of Lake Champlain.

Major General George Izard had refortified Plattsburg during the summer, but on August 10 he had received a letter from Armstrong suggesting that he should move his army, or a good part of it, toward the St. Lawrence as if to threaten the Montreal-Kingston road, as a diversion, to assist Jacob Brown at Fort Erie. Knowing that Prevost had massed troops on the border nearest to him, Izard nevertheless obeyed, and on August 29 left Plattsburgh for Sackets Harbor with four thousand regulars, leaving about three thousand men under Brigadier General Alexander Macomb to man the stronghold he had created.

Prevost's large force crossed the border on September 1, irritated by all sorts of small matters, notably Prevost's own disapproval of the casual dress and manners of the Peninsular veterans, and those veterans' contempt for Prevost's methods. Some of the leading commanders were far less experienced in the field than most of the officers they had to command, while, as Major General Frederick Robinson wrote in his journal,

> It appears to me that the army moved against Platsburg without any

regularly digested plan by Sir George Prevost. There were neither Guides, Spies or Plans.

He also disapproved of the lack of reliance on intelligence work, saying that Prevost apparently thought "it was throwing money away to attempt it–for which reason Secret Service money was with-held from the Generals commanding at the out posts." Wellington had never failed like that. But the British came on, and Macomb, doing the best he could with his depleted forces, tried desperately to block the road with chopped-down trees. On September 6, reported Macomb, his men skirmished with the British advance, but "except a few brave men, fell back most precipitately in the greatest disorder, notwithstanding the British troops did not deign to fire on them, except by their flankers and advanced patrols." He went on: "So undaunted was the enemy, that he never deployed in his whole march, always pressing on in column."

Macomb, whose position was indeed hopeless, withdrew across the Saranac River, and that evening the British entered Plattsburg. Macomb disposed his men, had the planking removed from the two bridges spanning the river and, no doubt thankfully, noted the presence of Macdonough's flotilla in the bay. He reported later:

> The enemy was employed in getting on his battering-train, and erecting his batteries and approaches and constantly skirmishing at the bridges and fords. By this time the militia of New York and the volunteers of Vermont were pouring in from all quarters. I advised General Mooers to keep his force along the Saranac to prevent the enemy's crossing the river, and to send a strong body in his rear to harass him day and night, and keep him in continual alarm. The militia behaved with great spirit after the first day, and the volunteers of Vermont were exceedingly serviceable.

Prevost, not knowing where the fords were nor exactly where the Americans had placed themselves, waited to make liaison with the British ships, commanded by the young Captain George Downie, RN, before ordering an attack. He sent a note to Downie at Isle aux Noix:

> Your share in the operation in the first instance, will be to destroy or to Capture the Enemy's Squadron, if it should wait for a Contest, and afterwards Co-operate with this division of the Army, but if it should run away and get out of your reach, we must meet here to consult on Interior Movements.

Downie, of course, knew that HMS *Confiance* was not yet ready, and hastened on the work on her as fast as he could, bringing her down to the level of the Chazy River on the night of September 9 while workmen still toiled on board, and sending a note to Prevost saying that he hoped to set off again at about midnight "in the Expectation of rounding into the Bay of Plattsburg about the dawn of day," whereupon he would attack at once "if they should be found Anchored in a position that will offer chance of success." He was held back by a strong unfavorable wind, which produced a note from Prevost written in a slightly less urbane tone than usual:

In consequence the Troops have been held in readiness since 6 o'clock this morning to storm the Enemy's Works at nearly the same moment as the Naval Action should commence in the Bay.

Downie irritably commented that he was responsible for his squadron and "no man shall make me lead it into action before I consider it in a fit condition," by which he meant that the ship and his men must be in battle readiness and the weather suitable for attack. He thought that Prevost's "Letter does not deserve an Answer but I will convince him that the naval Force will not be backward in their share of the attack." Downie, who seems not to have liked punctuation, noted his plan:

When the Batteries are stormed and taken possession of by the British Land Forces which the Commander of the Land Forces had promised to do at the moment the naval action commences the Enemy will then at all events be obliged to quit their position whereby we shall obtain decided Advantage over them during their Confusion.

Early on the morning of Sunday, September 11, Downie moved his ships twelve miles along the river until he was just off Cumberland Head, across the bay from Plattsburg. From here he reconnoitered the American position. Macdonough had placed his four biggest ships—*Eagle, Saratoga, Ticonderoga,* and *Preble*—in a line between Downie and Plattsburg, facing north, with his ten gunboats to port of them, and Downie decided to sail in an arc across the bay and pass the American ships from north to south, head to tail like sardines in a tin, firing a broadside at *Eagle* as he passed in *Confiance* and then making his main attack on the big *Saratoga.* HMS *Linnet* and *Chub,* following, would attack *Eagle,* and HMS *Finch* and the eleven British gunboats would go for *Ticonderoga* and *Preble.* Downie returned to his ship, and gave the order to sail at half past eight.

Prevost's plan was that, while the ships engaged, the army would attack in three places: at the two bridges, which, it will be remembered, had now no planking, and where the British were primarily to make a diversion and, with a bigger force under Robinson, from the flank and rear after crossing the Saranac River at the ford three miles away, for which purpose Robinson's men had been standing by at combat readiness since an hour before dawn. Prevost, despite Downie's belief that both land and water attacks were to start together, told Robinson not to move until ten o'clock, which makes Downie's order to his men particularly ironic: "There are the Enemy's Ships; our Army are to storm the Enemy's works at the moment we engage, and mind don't let us be behind."

Success depended upon two things, both of which were open to chance, and both went wrong. Robinson's troops, faced with several sets of cart-tracks in the woods, could not be sure which was the right one, and took much longer than they should have done to reach the ford. By the time they did so, cheering sounded across the Saranac, for Downie had become embroiled in action without the promised army support, and without the right wind to bring his ships into alignment, for the wind had suddenly dropped. Downie opened fire at about nine in the morning at a range of five hundred yards, and his first broadside put one-fifth of *Saratoga*'s crew out of action. Macdonough of course replied at once, and within a quarter of an hour Downie fell dead on the quarterdeck of *Confiance,* leaving his second-in-command, Lieutenant James Robertson, to take over. *Linnet,* with sixteen guns, fought the twenty-gun *Eagle* so hard that *Eagle* moved out of the line of battle.

But not for long. Her commander simply wanted to turn her to face the other way, so that her undamaged port side with its fresh guns could be brought to bear. At the same time, Macdonough turned *Saratoga* and, although Robertson in his battered ship did the same, it took a long time, and *Confiance* was heavily pounded, so that Robertson, faced with the choice of sinking or surrendering, chose to give up the unequal struggle. *Linnet* struck her colors a few minutes later. *Chub* for some reason had gone adrift, veering through the American line of battle and surrendering on the far side, and *Finch* also went off course, running aground on nearby Crab Island. As for the gunboats, only four of them joined in the fight; half of each of their crews consisted of militia, who apparently lost their heads completely, and lay flat inside the boats, not firing a shot. The gunboat commander made no attempt to rally his men and after the battle was sent to Kingston for court-martial; on the way there he escaped and vanished.

Prevost had been watching the action from the shore and, when he saw the British débâcle, he sent a message to Robinson at Pike's Ford, telling him to come back as "it will no longer be prudent to persevere in the Service committed to your charge." Robinson was at that moment in a most favorable position, his men having easily splashed across the shallow ford, chased off the American defenders, and seen that the way lay clear before them. Robinson, however, obeyed orders, and told his troops to retire. In the evening, Prevost said that surplus equipment should be destroyed and that the whole force should withdraw across the border. The British had lost just under one hundred killed and just over one hundred wounded altogether, two-thirds of these on the water. American losses were very slightly less, a difference of not more than a dozen in either case. Macomb reported his part of the action in terms that sounded like a considerable victory, but it was Macdonough who had really achieved that. Acrimonious comments now appeared in private letters and in official dispatches on the British side, criticizing Prevost for overcaution, lack of coordination, and general blundering; these comments no doubt were sharper than before, not only because of the unaccustomed sting of naval defeat, but also because the troops now included many officers who had served under Wellington.

In England a number of influential people wanted to send the Duke to the American war. The Prince Regent was one of them, urging his Prime Minister that

> nothing should be neglected to induce the Duke of Wellington to accept of the Chief Command in America as soon as possible, as his name alone will reconcile the whole view & opinion of the Country, & at the same time be the means of obviating as well as removing many difficulties which may afterwards arise.

Lord Liverpool suggested it to the Duke, whose main objection was that he felt his presence was needed in Europe still. The Duke summed it up:

> That which appears to me to be wanting in America is not a General, or

General officers and troops, but a naval superiority on the Lakes; without it I could do little more than sign a peace which might as well be signed now.

Admiral Cochrane, according to his original plan, intended to land his men in Rhode Island and give them six weeks' rest, by which time fresh reinforcements would have arrived from England. He would then, he said, come south to capture Baltimore. It was not surprising that the British felt vengefully about Baltimore, that "nest of pirates" which had furnished 126 pirate ships to harass the Royal Navy. It was also, Cochrane believed,

the most democratic town and I believe the richest in the Union. As this Town ought to be laid in ashes, if the same opinion holds with H. Maj.'s Ministers, some hint ought to be given to Gen'l Ross, as he does not seem inclined to visit the sins committed upon H. Maj.'s Canadian subjects upon the inhabitants of this State. When he is better acquainted with the American Character, he will probably see as I do that like Spaniels they must be treated with great severity before you even make them tractable.

Once Baltimore had fallen, the admiral continued in his letter of September 3 to Bathurst, "as the season advances, I propose going to the Carolinas, Georgia, etc., and ending at New Orleans, which I have not a doubt of being able to subdue and thereby hold the key to the Mississippi."

This plan had much to recommend it: removing the British from the Chesapeake during what they all called "the sickly season," diverting American troops from Canada, and clinching the victory at Washington by two stunning blows: Baltimore and New Orleans. Cockburn, however, did not agree entirely, preferring to attack Baltimore at once while the British were in the area and the Americans disheartened. Ross, somewhat unhappily, sided, or seemed to side, with Cochrane. The letter went off that same day in a box of dispatches carried on board HMS *Iphegenia* by Harry Smith. Saying goodbye to Ross on the *Tonnant,* Smith asked: "May I assure Lord Bathurst you will not attempt Baltimore?" Ross replied: "You may." Smith crossed to the *Iphegenia* with Captain Wainwright and Captain Tom Falls, the latter now on sick leave after the heat exhaustion he had suffered ever since reaching America.

Cochrane had drawn up plans for redeploying his forces, and the orders were issued on Sunday and Monday, September 4 and 5. Admiral Malcolm with most of the ships as a troop convoy was to sail to and anchor at the south of Tangier Island in the Chesapeake, Captain Sir Thomas Hardy with thirteen ships was to relieve Cockburn in the Chesapeake, and Cockburn, giving up at least for the time being his idea of going to Rhode Island, was to sail to Bermuda in the *Albion* loaded with tobacco, unship his cargo, and return. At half past eight on Tuesday morning, Malcolm led off in the *Royal Oak* down the Patuxent, moving very slowly, the rest of his troop convoy strung out behind him.

Baltimore at that time was the third largest city in the United States, with a population of forty-five thousand. The British press referred to it as "Mobtown" because from its streets had come so many clamors for war. But in these recent weeks the mood had changed: the defeat in Washington had struck cruelly home, many citizens had left or wished to leave, many urged surrender. Alarmed by this defeatist spirit, so different from that which had created the Great Republic, a few more martial individuals had formed, by the time of Bladensburg, a Committee of Vigilance and Safety. As the news came quickly in of the divided counsels in the capital, these men resolved that Baltimore should have one officer in overall command of its defenses, and named as their choice Major General Samuel Smith, sixty-two years old, born in Pennsylvania, and with twenty years' experience behind him in the United States Congress as well as a record of active service in the War of Independence.

Smith was ambitious and tough, but he was also shrewd enough to know that he had not much time (the British were expected to turn their attention toward Baltimore as soon as they had finished with Washington) and, if he accepted office, he must have proper authority. He told the committee that he required the sanction of the governor of Maryland, perhaps a stiff hurdle to jump, for the governor was Levin Winder, uncle of the unfortunate general who had failed so sadly in the capital. Uncle Levin wrote a typically evasive note of agreement that was good enough, apparently, for both Smith and the committee, and Smith within a matter of hours hurled himself into a whirl of activity that heartened his fellow citizens and stiffened their spines remarkably quickly. He was well aware that his militia rank was lower than that of the regular soldier General Winder in Washington, so he wrote asking the general, in rather curt terms, for details of the forces at his disposal. This brought Winder in person and in an angry temper, but Commodore John Rodgers, who witnessed the interview, noted later that "General Winder has in a manner much to his honour I conceive, consented to waive his pretensions to rank for the present." On August 28, bands of citizens started digging fortifications along the eastern side of Baltimore, where the broader water and lower shoreline invited attack in their opinion, and advertisements appeared in the papers, asking militiamen to reassemble, and also inviting "elderly men, who are able to carry a firelock, and willing to render a last service to their Country." Despite the lugubrious word "last," in this, elderly men, roused no doubt by echoes of Seventy-six, did rally to the colors and, in addition, many members of the Pennsylvania and Maryland militia came flocking into the city during August 29. From the dawn reveille until seven in the evening of August 30 they were mercilessly drilled, while Rodgers went off to pursue Gordon's ships down the Potomac. Smith, cutting ruthlessly through red tape, diverted five guns intended for the District of Columbia to Fort McHenry, the fort protecting the harbor of Baltimore, obtained a loan of one hundred thousand dollars from the local banks to buy supplies and pay his men and, perhaps the most important, was seen working everywhere. Baltimore, within the space of four days, had quickly filled up with men, goods, offers of help, and a spirit of pugnacity.

On September 4, General Thomas Forman wrote in a letter to his wife:

> We have assembled seven generals: Smith, Winder, Stricker, and Stansbury of Baltimore, Douglass and Singleton of Virginia; and your humble servant. This morning all the general officers and their aides and brigade-majors assembled at six o'clock to view the grounds and country surrounding Baltimore. The parade was splendid and interesting.

One of the seven generals, Winder, was still angry: treated as merely one of seven, given the western part of Baltimore to defend, not the place of honor and, above all, surrounded with people who were deaf to his complaints, including Smith, to whom he wrote appeals for better consideration, but who was too busy to bother. Smith had posted lookouts at all suitable places and eagerly scanned their daily reports, which told him literally nothing. From the dome of the State House at Annapolis, Commodore Barney's son, Major William Barney, sent every day: "There is nothing in sight"; from the Goodwin House near North Point, Major Josiah Green reported rather more elegantly: "There is nothing of the Enemy below."

On Tuesday, September 6 at soon after one in the afternoon an American sloop sailed down the river and approached the *Royal Oak,* flying a flag of truce. Two men in civilian dress came aboard to speak to Admiral Malcolm. They were John Skinner, the United States agent for the exchange of prisoners of war, and Francis Scott Key, the young lawyer. They wished, they said, to negotiate for the release of Dr. William Beanes.

The doctor, who had been perfectly willing to accommodate Ross and Cockburn in his house, had subsequently rounded up half a dozen stragglers from the British Army and put them in jail. Ross, furious at this entirely logical action on the part of his former host, sent a detachment of cavalry to arrest the doctor, which they did in the early hours of August 28. Along with the doctor they also seized the former governor of Maryland, Robert Bowie, and two or three other men staying in the doctor's house, and brought them all back to the ships, where the American prisoners were confined in the brig of the *Tonnant.*

On receiving the request of Skinner and Key to release the doctor, Malcolm explained that he was not the commander in chief of the British expeditionary fleet, for that was Cochrane, now anchored off Tangier Island in the Chesapeake, but he sent Skinner's request in writing on ahead by a fast dispatch boat, and sent the American sloop along behind, escorted by HM frigate *Hebrus,* to report to Cochrane in person. *Royal Oak* then resumed her slow passage down the river.

At noon on Wednesday, September 7 *Tonnant,* having left Tangier Island, came into view, moving up the Chesapeake. *Hebrus* spoke her, she hove-to, and the two Americans went on board, where Cochrane, Ross, and Codrington entertained them to dinner. Ross, despite his bitterness about Beanes who had uttered friendly sentiments and then had arrested the British stragglers, agreed to release the doctor. He expressed courteous appreciation of the kindly way in which the Americans in general had treated their British prisoners, and emphasized that he was agreeing to Beanes's release because the other Americans he had encountered had behaved decently throughout. But it did not suit him to let the Americans leave just yet, because at some point on that Wednesday Cochrane changed his mind and decided not to go to Rhode Island after all, but to head for Baltimore instead. If the Americans were set free too soon, any advantage of this move might be lost. Cochrane therefore suggested that Skinner and Key should transfer to the frigate *Surprise,* commanded by his son, Sir Thomas Cochrane, on the ground that *Tonnant* was overcrowded. Skinner and Key agreed and, in preparation for the eventual approach to Baltimore, the British ships moved to meet Gordon's detachment. On Thursday, September 8, with *Surprise* towing the American sloop, they entered the Potomac, and slowly negotiating the tricky reaches of that river, had covered twenty miles by dawn on Friday, when they thankfully observed Gordon's ships, safe out of reach of the American guns. The whole fleet now turned and sailed back to the Chesapeake, from which they moved northward, anchoring for the night at the familiar mouth of the Patuxent.

By now, many Americans were scurrying about in various stages of alarm, wondering what to do. The town of Annapolis in particular was gripped by panic, observed by Major Barney from the dome in the intervals of counting the British sails. By eight in the evening he had seen fifty vessels, all moving up the river under full canvas. He sent on this news to Baltimore where, by now, Smith's defenders numbered 16,391, most of them allocated to positions on the east and south of the city. He had sixty-two guns, and he had sealed off one arm of the river. Baltimore stands at the fork of the Patapsco, twelve miles from the Chesapeake. The river divided at Whetstone Point, on which was Fort McHenry, built in the shape of a star fifteen years before. The western fork was the Ferry Branch, the eastern (somewhat illogically) the North West Branch. A boom ran across the mouth of the North West Branch, and Smith had stationed a line of armed barges along it. He had also quadrupled the fort's garrison so that it numbered one thousand men, and they had fifty-seven guns.

Technically, Winder was responsible for the fort, and for its two little supporting works a mile farther west, Forts Babcock and Covington, but, as the defense preparations went on, and he was never consulted, he realized that his was a paper command. The actual commander was Major George Armistead, and he was on the spot in the fort. Commodore Rodgers, writing on Friday, observed that the city now had "nothing to fear even should the enemy make his appearance tomorrow." Certainly, when the reports began to come in on Saturday, there was little or no panic, and on Sunday morning people went to church as usual.

Or almost as usual. Toward the end of the services, the congregations heard three loud bangs, for all the world like the three knocks that signal the start of a French play in the classic manner. They came from the cannon mounted on the courthouse green. In one church, the minister paused, listened, and piously commented: "May the Lord bless King George, convert him, and take him to heaven, as we want no more of him." Hastily, clergymen brought their services to a close, and the congregations surged out into the crowded, sunlit streets, making for home, or for their posts of duty, or to wagons and carriages that would take them out of town. From the observation post on Federal Hill, watchers could see, dim in the heat haze, the British ships approaching North Point, a narrow peninsula between the Patapsco and the Back rivers. As fast as possible, news of this was brought to Smith, who ordered Brigadier General John Stricker to move his three thousand men toward North Point. They set out at three in the afternoon, following a winding road called Long Log Lane, where, by eight that night, they paused at the narrowest point of the peninsula: a very good defensive position between two inlets, the wide Bear Creek and the narrow Bread and Cheese Creek. They were seven miles from North Point. Smith, who had realized that this spot was readily defensible, had stored rations for three thousand men and hay for two hundred horses there. Stricker sent his cavalry three miles on, to a farm belonging to one Robert Gorsuch, his riflemen two miles on, to a forge, and bivouacked the rest where they were.

Cochrane had transferred the three Americans–Skinner, Key, and Dr. Beanes–to their own boat, but insisted that it must remain with the British ships. The British intended to land their soldiers at North Point, then sail on up the Patapsco and start bombarding the fort. They began putting the men ashore at three in the morning, and by half past six they stood ready to march. There were between four and five thousand of them. They began to walk forward at seven on Monday, September 12, less than twenty-four hours after the British defeat on Lake Champlain.

Stricker's cavalry reported the British landing to him soon after it took place, their rear unit telling him that they had stopped for breakfast close to the Gorsuch farm. His riflemen, misled by a rumor that they were being outflanked, also came back. Stricker set up his force in battle order and waited all morning. At noon, troubled by fears of a night assault on his notoriously unreliable militia, he determined to force a battle now. He selected about two hundred and fifty of his best men with one field gun and a few cavalry, and sent them forward under Major Richard Heath. The British had started to advance by this time, but the advance was strung out, and when each side caught sight of the other and exchanged the first shots, the Americans were firing at about sixty men, including Ross and Cockburn. Ross turned back to call up his main force quickly, when more ragged shooting from the Americans who had faded back into the trees caught him. He lay in the road, mortally wounded, for a few minutes, before the vanguard of the Light Companies came up, whereupon he gasped a request for his second-in-command, Colonel Arthur Brooke. According to Brooke's account, "the General lived long enough to recommend [his] young and unprovided-for family to the protection of his King and Country." Ross's body, wrapped in a Union Jack, was carried down to the beach.

Brooke quickly mounted a full attack, which the troops pressed home with professional confidence. The Americans fired canisters loaded with nails, broken bits of metal and horseshoes, and inflicted over 300 casualties, but the British came on, knocking out 163 of their opponents, and the American militia broke and fled. But Stricker had learned from Winder's mistakes. He had kept one regiment in reserve a mile to the rear, and he rallied his stragglers behind them. There must not be another "Bladensburg Races." He took them back as far as Worthington's Mill, near the northeast end of the Baltimore earthworks.

Brooke halted his army close to the little bridge carrying Long Log Lane over Bread and Cheese Creek, and camped there for the night. Meanwhile, Cochrane was making his way up the river as best he could–a hard task, for the Patapsco was shallow and full of shoals. HMS *Seahorse* ran aground; it took nearly four hours to refloat her. At half past three the *Surprise* dropped anchor about five miles from the fort, followed by the rest of the ships. Lookouts saw that the Americans were sinking hulks across the mouth of the North West Branch. Cochrane studied through his glass the crowded earthworks on Hampstead Hill, and noted that they seemed comparatively shallow, which led him to believe that they could be flanked. He wrote:

> At daylight we shall place the Bombs and barges to bombard the fort. You will find them over upon the eastern shore, as the enemy have forts upon the western side which it is not necessary to encounter.

He addressed the note to Ross, and sent it off. It was returned unopened at half past seven with the news that Ross was dead. Cochrane readdressed it to Brooke, and added a paragraph:

It is proper for me to mention to you that a system of retaliation was to be proceeded upon in consequence of the barbarities committed in Canada–and if General Ross had seen the second letter from Sir George Prevost he would have destroyed Washington and Georgetown. Their nature are perfectly known to Rear Admiral Cockburn and I believe Mr Evans.

Major Armistead, surveying the formidable mass of ships in the river, wrote to Smith at soon after four in the afternoon, "From the number of barges and the known situation of the enemy, I have not a doubt but that an assault will be made this night upon the Fort." The year before, he had expressed a wish to have "a flag so large that the British will have no difficulty in seeing it from a distance," and he certainly had that–a huge flag with stripes two feet broad, stars (fifteen of them) two feet across, the whole measuring forty-two feet by thirty. It flew now from the flagstaff in the parade ground.

The bombardment opened up at soon after seven. By that time the British ships had brought their range down to less than two miles. Armistead brought all his own guns to bear, but they lacked the range, and at ten in the morning he ordered them to cease firing: it was using ammunition for nothing. Cochrane worried on two counts: first, that the bombardment seemed to be achieving very little and, second, that there was no sign of the British attack by land being resumed. At two in the afternoon a shell exploded on the southwest bastion of the fort, killing a gun crew; another came through the roof of the powder magazine, but failed to go off; after this, Armistead ordered his men to move the powder barrels outside and place them under the rear walls of the fort. About an hour later, he saw three of the bomb ships and the rocket ship moving in closer. As soon as they were within range, Armistead's gunners fired off every gun that would bear, and the British, damaged and startled, retired.

Actually, both Cochrane and Brooke were facing stalemate. Neither could succeed without the other, and the admiral was blocked by sunken hulks, while the colonel was deterred by reports of the crammed defenses of the city which had left little room for maneuvering. It had poured with rain all night and well on into the next day. The ships kept up the shellfire, however, right into the early hours of Tuesday morning; Captain Charles Napier took a body of sailors and marines in small boats with muffled oars into the Ferry Branch to make a diversion, which he duly did, only to retire as no responding gunfire from the east signaled the expected advance of the army at last. The army was in fact retreating to North Point, as Brooke had decided it would be unwise to press the attack further. The bombardment stopped at four in the morning. Standing on the deck of the American sloop in the damp light of dawn, Francis Scott Key looked through his spyglass, as he had anxiously done so often during the hours of Monday's daylight, to see whether the flag was still there. If it was, it would mean that the British had failed in their attack on Baltimore. He saw it. He was so overwhelmed by the sight that the only way he could express his feelings was in verse. He used the back of a letter in his pocket to draft out the first version of what is known today as *The Star-Spangled Banner.*

Oh! say can you see, by the dawn's early light,
What so proudly we hailed at the twilight's last gleaming?
Whose broad stripes and bright stars, thro' the perilous fight,
O'er the ramparts we watched were so gallantly streaming?
And the rockets' red glare, the bombs bursting in air,
Gave proof thro' the night that our flag was still there.
Oh! say does the star-spangled banner yet wave
O'er the land of the free and the home of the brave?

On the shore, dimly seen through the mists of the deep
Where the foe's haughty host in dread silence reposes,
What is that which the breeze, o'er the towering steep,
As it fitfully blows, half conceals, half discloses?
Now it catches the gleam of the morning's first beam,
In full glory reflected now shines on the stream:
'Tis the star-spangled banner! O long may it wave
O'er the land of the free and the home of the brave!

And where is that band who so vauntingly swore
That the havoc of war and the battle's confusion,
A home and a country should leave us no more?
Their blood has washed out their foul footsteps' pollution.
No refuge could save the hireling and slave
From the terror of flight, or the gloom of the grave:

And the star-spangled banner in triumph doth wave
O'er the land of the free and the home of the brave!

Oh! thus be it ever, when freemen shall stand
Between their loved homes and the war's desolation!
Blest with victory and peace, may the heav'n-rescued land
Praise the Power that hath made and preserved us a nation.
Then conquer we must, when our cause it is just,
And this be our motto: "In God is our trust."
And the star-spangled banner in triumph shall wave
O'er the land of the free and the home of the brave!

On the afternoon of Tuesday, September 20, the *Iphegenia* approached the south coast of England and anchored off Spithead. Three officers, one of the Royal Navy and two of the army, came ashore in the captain's gig, walked to the George Inn, arranged transport and, by five o'clock, were driving out of Portsmouth along the London road in a postchaise drawn by four horses. It was just past midnight when the chaise reached Downing Street. Captain Wainwright walked off to leave his box of dispatches at the Admiralty; Harry Smith lodged his at the Prime Minister's house and, with the sickly Captain Falls, found a room for what remained of the night at the Salopian Coffee House in Parliament Street. Early next morning, Harry set off to find his wife, with whom he had a joyous but brief reunion before going back to Downing Street to report in person to Lord Bathurst. This gentleman took him to Carlton House, to acquaint the Prince Regent with tidings from America, and invited him to dine at his house on Putney Heath that night.

The English newspapers were full of strong criticisms of the Washington fires, either in their editorial columns or contained in the Parliamentary reports. Samuel Whitbread, for example, told the Commons that the burning of buildings was "abhorrent to every principle of legitimate warfare," and the *Statesman* commented:

The Cossacks spared Paris, but we spared not the Capitol of America. Is it certain, that the destruction of the public edifices for destruction-sake alone, is a legitimate method of warfare?

All the government could do in reply was to cite the American burning of York: "Although a small town, it was a capital, and among other public and private buildings, the House of Assembly and the House of the Governor had been burnt to the ground."

Harry Smith had been back in England for less than four weeks when news from America reached him from the Horse Guards. It was a mixed budget of information. After withdrawing from Baltimore, the British ships had gone to Jamaica to repair their damage, except for Cochrane's ship which carried the admiral to Halifax, Nova Scotia. Here he heard consoling news: Sir John Sherbrooke and Rear Admiral Edward Griffith had sailed with two thousand regular soldiers in a flotilla of ships to the Penobscot River in Maine, arriving at its mouth early on September 1; their approach caused the American garrison in the Castine Fort to withdraw in a hurry. The British wanted to capture US frigate *Adams,* then under repair thirty miles up the river at Hampden, so an expeditionary force sailed up to a point three miles from Hampden by September 3, and put to flight a force of fourteen hundred American militia at the cost of one dead and eight wounded. At this, the captain of the *Adams* set his frigate on fire and retreated, the British followed, taking twenty American guns along with them and, according to Captain Robert Barrie, RN: "On approaching Bangor, the Inhabitants who had opposed us at Hampden, threw off their Military character, and as Magistrates, select men, &c. made an unconditional surrender of the Town." Everyone behaved very well: the British paroled all the citizens, did no looting, and gladly accepted supplies of fresh bread, fresh meat, wine, and spirits, before retiring down the river with the honors of war on September 9.

On that same day another British company left the mouth of the Penobscot to capture "the only place occupied by the Enemy's Troops, between this and Passmaquoddy Bay," the town of Machias. The troops landed close by on the evening of September 10 and spent the night blundering about in the woods in order to attack Machias from behind but, when they reached it, the Americans had fled, and it too was occupied without firing a shot. The leader of the British expedition, Colonel Pilkington, intended to press on after a couple of days, but on the morning of September 13 he received a letter of surrender from the county militia making further advance unnecessary. The most striking consequence of this campaign was the spread of rumors that citizens of Maine were swearing allegiance to King George, and that parts of New England were planning to secede from the Union.

On Friday, September 16 the Kingston *Gazette* reported that "the fine Ship St. Lawrence, of 104 Guns" had been launched at Point Frederick "on which occasion a Royal Salute was fired from the Batteries." Other ships were building: three frigates and two brigs at Isle aux Noix, two ships of the line and a frigate of fifty-five guns at Kingston, two schooner gunboats and a frigate at Chippawa, while the Americans were working on two large warships at Sackets Harbor. General Izard took an army of over six thousand, most of them regulars, to the Niagara front at the beginning of October, and found to his dismay that the British were far stronger than he had been led to believe, that Yeo was hovering menacingly off the mouth of the Niagara, and that Chauncey was barricading himself in at Sackets Harbor. Izard wrote:

> I confess I am greatly embarrassed. At the head of the most efficient army the United States have possessed during this war, much must be expected from me; and yet I can discern no object which can be achieved at this point worthy of the risk which will attend its attempt.

On October 21 he withdrew; Jacob Brown took his division to Sackets Harbor; the rest went into winter quarters at Buffalo, blowing up Fort Erie on the way, perhaps as a precaution, perhaps as a gesture.

Cochrane, meanwhile, was planning the attack against New Orleans. The British fleet was supposed to assemble in Jamaica on November 20. In the words of a revived old American song, based upon a tune known as "Bonaparte's Retreat":

> In eighteen-fourteen we took a little trip
> Along with Colonel Jackson down the mighty Mississipp';
> We took a little bacon and we took a little beans
> And we beat the bloody British near the town of New Orleans.*

The American version of the battle as expressed in those lines was, more, or less, what was about to happen.

* "The Battle of New Orleans," words by Jimmy Driftwood, copyright © 1957 and 1959 by Warden Music Company, reproduced by permission of Acuff Rose Music Limited.

TEN

§

The Cousins

In England the European situation continued to overshadow the American war. In August 1814 a great festival in London signified official rejoicing at Napoleon's defeat. By happy timing it was also able to celebrate the centenary of the House of Hanover's occupation of the throne and the sixteenth anniversary of the Battle of the Nile. A reproduction of this, enlivened by fireworks, was mounted on the Serpentine. A lavish display of more fireworks delighted crowds in the Green Park, where a "Gothick castle" more than one hundred feet square had been set up. Colored lamps shone in the trees, fairground swings and carousels, booths and ornamental kiosks, filled Hyde Park. The bridge in St. James's Park had sprouted a Chinese pagoda and ornamental railings in yellow with a blue roof and Japanese lanterns. Windham Sadler made a balloon ascension; and the Prince Regent gave a fête for two thousand guests in a specially built polygonal pavilion in the garden at Carlton House.

All this time the peace commission to try to end the war between Britain and the United States had been meeting, talking, and failing to reach agreement. Their meeting place was in the old town of Ghent in–the Austrian Netherlands–what is now Belgium. The delegates saw the castle of the counts of Flanders and the Marché du Vendredi, crossed bridges spanning tranquil canals and the River Scheldt, heard the bells of St. Bavon's Cathedral, and wrestled with the problems of an acceptable settlement. The Americans–John Quincy Adams, Albert Gallatin, James Bayard, Henry Clay, and Jonathan Russell–and the British–Admiral Lord Gambier, William Adams, and Henry Goulburn, who was Parliamentary Under-Secretary of State for War and the Colonies–found, of course, their attitudes influenced by the news from the war zones. But the eternal dilemma underlying their discussions was that neither side was prepared to admit the first claims of the other.

Acting on Castlereagh's instructions, the British were expected to press for retention of conquered territory. They would naturally wish to keep Plattsburg, Fort Niagara, Michilimackinac, the northern part of Maine, but rather surprisingly, since Britain did not then hold them, she was likely to ask for Sackets Harbor and Detroit, though these two places would presumably fall to Britain if the proposed new boundary lines were accepted. It was believed that an Indian state ought to be created across today's frontier line in the old Northwest to act as a buffer between the British and the Americans, and to deter American frontiersmen from encroaching into Canadian territory.

The Americans had been told to put an end to impressment by the Royal Navy, to clarify the issues of blockade, contraband, and the right of neutrals and, perhaps surprisingly, to try to secure a large area of Canada to the United States. Gallatin, realizing how far these instructions, or much of them, belonged to a cloud-cuckooland of international diplomacy, wrote to Madison as early as June, saying:

> Under the existing unpropitious circumstances of the world, America cannot by a continuance of the war compel Great Britain to yield any of the maritime points in dispute, and particularly to agree to any satisfactory arrangement on the subject of impressment; and that the most favourable terms of peace that can be expected are the *status ante bellum.*

Even this might not be enough to expect, for Britain was more and more irritated by the American privateers operating against unprotected merchant ships in British waters. Their activities had provoked indignation meetings in British ports and a note to the Admiralty on September 7:

> That the number of American privateers with which our Channels have been infested, the audacity with which they have approached our Coasts, and the success with which their enterprise has been attended, have proved injurious to our Commerce, humbling to our Pride, and discreditable to the Directors of the Naval Power of the British Nation, whose flag of late waved over every sea and triumphed over every rival,–there is reason to believe, in the short space of twenty-four months, above eight hundred vessels have been captured

by the Power whose maritime strength we have hitherto impolitically held in contempt.

This agreed with the "mortifying reflection" of the *Annual Register* that, with peace in Europe, and a Royal Navy of nearly a thousand ships, it was still unsafe for "a vessel to sail without convoy from one part of the English or Irish Channel to another." The news from Washington stiffened the British attitude; the news from Lake Champlain hardened that of the Americans. The talks went on, though, unlike international talks of the present day, they were not regular or frequent. Ten days, or even longer, would elapse between meetings of the delegates. One must remember, too, how long it took for dispatches from Washington to arrive in Ghent.

Matters were uneasy in the United States. Trade was sagging badly, banks failing, paper money losing its purchase, subscriptions to War Loan falling off sharply, recruitment lapsing to a trickle. Moreover, there were critical stirrings in New England that lent color to the belief that these states might secede from the Union. Unaware of all these things, Bathurst wrote to Goulburn: "I hope you'll be able to put on a face of compress'd joy at least, in communicating the news [of Washington] to the American Ministers," but he did not suggest any change in the British terms. The British government wanted to end the war, as Lord Liverpool put it, "if it can be done consistently with our honour and upon such terms as we are fairly entitled to expect." The French newspapers, sounding the full gamut of outraged sympathy with the citizens whose capital had been burnt by the wicked British, did not make the negotiations easier. They described Washington as swept from the face of the earth, and compared the British with the barbaric "old banditti of Attila" in "this act of atrocious vengeance." But some British newspapers were no better when they were trying to cover up the withdrawal from Baltimore. They tried to pretend it was a victory, and the *Morning Post* loudly proclaimed:

All the victories of Alexander, Caesar, Scipio, and Hannibal are dimmed by the resplendent glories of the heroes of our Isle. It is hard, then, it is indeed distressing that their immediate duty requires them to contend with a set of creatures who take the field only to disgrace the musket.

But the *Statesman* kept its head: "Victories which have effects like these, we think Britain had better be without."

Goulburn wrote to Bathurst on October 21:

> The news is very far from satisfactory. We owed the acceptance of our article respecting the Indians to the capture of Washington; and if we had either burnt Baltimore or held Plattsburg, I believe we should have had peace on the terms which you have sent us in a month at least. As things appear to be going on in America, the result of our negotiation may be very different.

One of the things "going on in America" was the overnight popularity of Francis Scott Key's verse. He had left it untitled and, according to some historians, intended it to be sung to the tune of a well-known drinking song called "To Anacreon in Heaven." Within a few days of its first draft the verse had been delivered at the Baltimore offices of the *American and Commercial Daily Advertiser* with orders to print it as a handbill. Key did not send it; either John Skinner or Judge Joseph Nicholson, to both of whom Key showed the completed verse, did that. It was printed with the title "Defence of Fort McHenry" and the suggested tune, and every member of the fort's garrison received a copy. Ten days later the Baltimore *Patriot and Evening Advertiser* printed it with the comment that it "is destined long to outlast the occasion, and outlive the impulse, which produced it." People sent copies to other cities, and within a month it was appearing in newspapers from Georgia to New Hampshire. Key himself later explained how he came to write it in terms so grandiloquent that they irresistibly suggest afterthoughts:

> In that hour of deliverance and joyful triumph, my heart spoke; and "Does not such a country and such defenders of their country deserve a song?" was its question.

But the American government was troubled, busy, and deep in discussion of plans. Madison worried about the reports of disaffection in New England, stating that "the greater part of the people in that quarter have been brought by their leaders, aided by their priests, under a delusion scarcely exceeded by that recorded in the period of witchcraft; and the leaders themselves are becoming daily more desperate in the use they make of it. Their object is power."

Some Republicans were sure that unless peace came soon the Union would not last for another year; others advised Monroe not to try to build up the regular army he wanted, saying, "It is nonsense to talk of regulars. They are not to be had among a people so easy and happy at home as ours. We might as well rely on calling down an army of angels from heaven"; or "States must and will take care of themselves."

Monroe, shouldering the double burden of office as Secretary of War and Secretary of State, staggered with fatigue: "I had a couch in a room in my house on which I occasionally reposed," he wrote later, "but from which even in the night I was called every two hours, when the expresses arrived."

The government was also preoccupied by the repairs and rebuilding necessary in Washington and Baltimore. Bit by bit the damage was set right.

With the death of Ross, a new commander had to be found for the British Army in America. Partly because the Duke was all-important in Europe, where the Congress of Vienna was doing its best to work out the European settlement, which involved a brave attempt to return to the status quo as if 1789 had never happened, the government in London selected Pakenham.

Major General Sir Edward Pakenham, an elegant gentleman of thirty-eight, was not only one of a family that has gained, and continues to gain, notable distinctions in many fields; he was also the brother of Kitty Pakenham, Wellington's wife. He had served in the Peninsula with the Duke. Indeed, at the Battle of Salamanca in 1812, he had commanded the leading column of attack, and his redoubtable brother-in-law had ordered him simply: "Ned, move on with the Third Division; take the heights on your front; and drive everything before you." Pakenham had answered: "I will, my lord, if you will give me your hand." The attack "beat forty thousand men in forty minutes," Pakenham noting that "our Chief was every where and Sadly Exposed himself" to every risk. But he had contributed greatly to the victory and, as Harry Smith wrote later, when he was Pakenham's aide-de-camp: "I am delighted with Sir Edward; he evinces an animation, a knowledge of ground, of his own resources and the strength of the enemy's position, which reminds us of his brother-in-law, our Duke. I do believe I am more attached to Sir Edward, as a soldier, than I was to John Colborne, if possible!"

The situation facing Pakenham as the year moved into its last month was one of peculiar difficulty. Admiral Cochrane was making his push for New Orleans. That evocative city, reputedly the liveliest and most civilized in the New World, situated about one hundred miles from the Gulf of Mexico on the east bank of the Mississippi River, bulged with rich stores of cotton and sugar, estimated to be worth three and a half million English pounds, as well as possessing a busy harbor crowded with profitable shipping. Prospects for prize money lured Cochrane, as they had done ever since he took over command seven months before. He had in the early summer sent a frigate under Captain Pigot to the mouth of the Apalachicola River on the Gulf, to see what he could find out. Pigot reported that local Indians had told him that New Orleans could be captured by a small number of British, as it was absolutely undefended. Cochrane obtained approval from London to send an expeditionary force, and on December 10, 1814 the advance guard of sixteen hundred men under Major General John Lambert began to go ashore.

Cochrane, who had anchored off Ship Island in the Mississippi Sound two days before, thought it foolish to try to sail straight up the river under the guns of the forts, so he proposed that the attack should be made overland. The route he selected went across a shallow lagoon, Lake Borgne, from the head of which the Bayou Bienvenu led to a point near New Orleans and less than five miles from the Mississippi. Lake Borgne was defended by half a dozen gunboats and a number of smaller vessels, all of which Cochrane captured on December 14 with troops in forty-five rowboats after a sharp but brief engagement. The British pushed on to the swampy island called the Ile aux Poix (with a touch of symmetry unusual in war there were nuts in the north and peas in the south), where they were twenty miles from the mainland but from which they could, Cochrane thought, make a reconnaissance of the Bayou Bienvenu. Scouts, nosing ahead, reported the island deserted, and the rest of the force followed up into Lake Borgne, where the larger ships ran aground.

The leaders of the combined naval and military expedition were a Scot and an Irishman, Admiral Malcolm of the *Royal Oak* and the Irish Major General John Keane, who had risen from the rank of lieutenant to the command of a brigade under the Duke. Theirs was a tiring journey. It rained most of the time, with flurries of icy sleet. The British sailors had to row in open boats with little pause, for the journey from Ship Island to the mouth of the bayou took thirty-six hours and each boat had to make the trip three times to bring up the whole force. This part of the operation took eight days, during which the British were constantly wet, cold, and fatigued. Spanish fishermen acted as guides, and recommended that the British should press forward onto better ground before the Americans had time to look to their defenses. Keane, expecting Pakenham to arrive and take over the command at any moment, did not hurry: he apparently did not realize that every hour counted in getting his troops in a position to rest and organize themselves before the fighting started. Meanwhile the Americans had become aware of the British approach.

As the leading boats moved into the bayou, the riflemen in the first boat saw a glimmer of light ahead. It proved to come from a tiny fishing village from which the inhabitants had gone, leaving a picquet of eight United States soldiers on guard. The picquet had stationed themselves on a small artificial mound surrounded by reeds and rushes ten feet high. Despite their admirable concealment, the British detected their presence, crept up as silently as possible, and captured them. The British boats rowed on up the bayou, first between tall reeds blocking out the view on either side and then, as the water narrowed, between the characteristic cypress trees of the region, until at last they came to firm ground, where the prospect opened out to disclose orange groves, fields of sugarcane, and a glimpse of distant houses. By the morning of December 23 more than sixteen hundred men had come ashore. With difficulty the scouts found the right direction in which to look for the city of New Orleans and the road leading toward it. Across their path lay a plantation belonging to Major General Jacques Villeré, who was not at home when the British surrounded his house, but his son, Major Gabriel Villeré, was actually smoking a cigar on the veranda when he was taken prisoner. He was questioned, seated in a chair in one of the ground-floor rooms, and it was then that he showed something of the quality that was to make the South a legend fifty years later. During the questioning he suddenly sprang up and leaped through the open window and away, so fast that his astonished questioners could not see where he went. They fired after him, of course, but after shooting his favorite dog, which might have betrayed his position, the Major made his way into the woods, borrowed a horse, and galloped to the city, rushing into Andrew Jackson's headquarters soon after noon with the news that the spearhead of the British column had reached the Villeré plantation. Jackson, springing up with sparkling eyes, exclaimed: "By the Eternal, they shall not sleep on our soil! We must fight them tonight!"

Jackson's appearance–a tall, bony figure with a graying mane of hair under a leather cap, a worn Spanish coat, and high cavalry boots—fitted the hunter's zest with which he set his plans into motion. He had the alarm gun fired, and sent his motley force of just over two thousand men on their way by five o'clock. There were mounted riflemen in Davy Crockett caps, Mississippi Dragoons, marching riflemen from New Orleans, two hundred "free men of colour" from Haiti, men of Tennessee, and even some Choctaw Indians in warpaint. Jackson also ordered up the armed schooner *Carolina,* which was to fire on the British from the river. The schooner reached the right place by about seven, and opened fire within half an hour, and the British scrambled to action stations as best they could without artillery. The fighting that followed was confused, both sides misunderstanding orders, starting at shadows, grappling with foes who proved to be friends, but neither had gained any appreciable ground before the mist came up and the fighting fizzled out. As soon as they could, both armies encamped within sight of each other, and during the next day they worked to strengthen their own positions, while sporadic firing came from the *Carolina.* It was Christmas Eve. Late on that day, Sir Edward Pakenham reached the British lines to take up his new command.

At the Hotel des Pays-Bas in Ghent on that same day, after more than four months of talks, the British and American peace delegations set their names to the treaty * that would end the war. In present-day terms, it was all over; in the terms of 1814, it was over on paper but not in fact, for the armies would not stop fighting until they were told to do so, and any instructions could reach them only by a long sea voyage and a journey up the Mississippi to the city of New Orleans. The Americans had been instructed to settle for a restoration of pre-war conditions, as far as this was practicable.

The Treaty of Ghent embodied eleven articles, stating that all conquests on both sides were to be returned, acts of hostility to the Indians were to end, the British were to give up the idea of the Indian buffer state, and the border from the Bay of Fundy to the Isle of the Woods was to be marked out precisely by international commissions to be formed as soon as possible.

It is not clear why the British concessions at the end of the war

* See Appendix IX.

were considerably greater than those they might have made before it broke out, nor why the treaty made no mention of "free trade and sailors' rights," no reference to impressment nor, indeed, to any of the incidents that had started the war in the first place. One can only conclude that the treaty was as dogged by illogicality as the war itself had been.

When Pakenham entered the British lines, after an Atlantic crossing taking eight weeks and a trip up the narrow waters lasting nearly twenty hours, the gunners fired a salute which made the American troops believe they were about to start a new assault. Pakenham, who had brought some artillery with him, began in spirited style by blowing up the *Carolina* on December 27. Jackson meanwhile was sending another boat down, the USS *Louisiana,* to back her up. At dawn on December 28 Pakenham started to advance, but the *Louisiana* was in position by then, and shot so strongly at the British flank that Pakenham thought better of it, and drew back. For three days the armies waited, uncertain, apparently, what to do next, while the British floated fourteen naval guns and carronades up in canoes, and then dragged them by main force over the swampy ground, to place them in position.

New Year's Day, 1815, opened with a thick white fog over the shivering troops among the sugarcane. On their left the great Mississippi curved around behind them; on their right lay a stretch of treacherous ground with water lying either on the surface or not more than nine inches below it–lagoons, cypress trees, bayous so narrow that two boats could barely pass, and alligators reported lurking in the pools. The British were now eighty miles from their base at Ship Island, with such supplies as they had reaching them in open boats and then across four miles of land. The Americans, who had been preparing for a New Year's Day review, saw the fog lift just before nine in the morning, and instantly the British guns opened fire. The Americans rushed to reply, which they did with such a will that after six hours of bombardment Pakenham stopped, and Jackson ordered his bands to strike up "Yankee Doodle." Both sides again set to work on their defenses.

Major General John Lambert brought his reinforcements up on January 6 to find that the British had deepened the bayou, widened the channel, and carved out a breach in the levee. Jackson had by then placed two new defense lines nearer to the city, altered his gun emplacements, and built up the embankment. He too had received fresh troops, some of the Kentucky militia, but they were short of guns, which caused Jackson to comment that never in his life had he seen a Kentucky soldier "without a gun and a pack of cards and a bottle of whisky." He spent some time scanning the British lines through his spyglass, and came to the conclusion that they would attack on January 8, which indeed they did.

And fatally. All kinds of things went wrong: fourteen hundred men were supposed to cross the river, capture the guns on the redoubt there, and turn them on to the Americans, but the channel bank had fallen in at one place, and the boats were so seriously delayed that by zero hour only one-third of the men were ready. Their commander took them forward nevertheless. Captain John Henry Cooke of the 43rd regiment, in the main part of the army, wrote:

When people talk of the field of battle, and the heat of the fight, how little do they know how many tedious hours the troops of outpost duties have to undergo, waiting for the whispers or the tread of an armed foe, or in momentary expectation of a flash of fire, or a discharge of bullets, and how often these troops are exposed to straggling and single combats for whole days. This was the case with the Rifles, for they had always been in front, and always called for, and before New Orleans were much cut up. . . . How can I convey a thought of the intense anxiety of the mind, when a solemn and sombre silence is broken in upon by the intonation of cannon, and when the work of death begins? Now the veil of night was less obscured, and its murky mantle dissolved on all sides, and the mist was sweeping off the face of the earth; yet it was not day, and no object was very visible beyond the extent of a few yards. The morn was chilly—I augured not of victory, an evil foreboding crossed my mind, and I meditated in solitary reflection. All was tranquil as the grave, and no camp-fires glimmered from either friends or foes.

Soon after this the two light companies of the seventh and ninety-third regiments came up without knapsacks, the Highlanders with their blankets rolled and slung across their backs, and merely wearing the shell of their bonnets, the sable plumes of real ostrich feathers brought by them from the Cape of Good Hope, having been left in England. . . . I asked Lieutenant Duncan Campbell where they were going, when he replied, "I be hanged if I know:" then said I, "you have got into what I call a good thing; the far-famed American battery is in front at a short range, and on the left this spot is flanked at eight hundred yards by their batteries on the opposite bank of the river." At this piece of information he laughed heartily, and I told him to take off his blue pelisse coat to be like the rest of the men. "No," he said gaily, "I will never peel for any American–come, Jack, embrace me." He was a fine grown young officer of twenty years of age, and had fought in many bloody encounters in Spain and France, but this was to be his last, as well as that of many more brave men . . .

The fog was clearing slowly, though it still hung low over the Mississippi, and Captain Cooke commented on the persistent silence all around–no one in view outside their own little group, no sound of horse or footstep, only, from time to time, the words "Steady, men," which, he said were "quite unnecessary, as every soldier was, as it were, transfixed like fox-hunters."

Pakenham told Harry Smith to order the starting rocket to be fired, and the British began the advance, while the American guns roared into life. The indomitable Jackson yelled above the din: "Give it to them, boys, let's finish the business today!"

For once in his optimistic, active life a premonition of disaster seized Harry Smith, and he spoke to General Lambert.

I said, in twenty-five minutes, General, you will command the army. Sir Edward will be wounded and incapable or killed. The troops do not get on a step. He will be at the head of the first brigade he comes to.

And indeed that is what happened. With wasteful losses the British moved forward against the American fire; the leader of the center, Major General Samuel Gibbs, fell dead. Pakenham galloped up to reform the men, and he too was shot and killed. In less than half an hour the British had suffered more than two thousand casualties, including three major generals, eight colonels, six majors, eighteen captains, and fifty-four subalterns. One British lieutenant colonel had been heard saying bitterly: "My regiment has been ordered into execution. Their dead bodies are to be used as a bridge for the rest of the army to march over."

The Americans lost seventy-three wounded, and seven killed. Jackson had indeed finished the business that day; for Lambert, duly finding himself in command of the damaged army, disengaged them and withdrew into camp. The dead were buried, except for the bodies of the senior officers, which, like that of Ross, were put in casks of spirits to be shipped home for burial there. The British stayed in camp for a week. On the night of January 18 their campfires still glowed in the darkness, but these were being kept alight by the small rearguard.

The rest of the troops had drawn back. They went away to the mouth of the Mississippi, where they fired, so to speak, their final shot, surrounding Fort Bowyer on Mobile Bay and occupying it without injury to either side within three days. A week before that, the news of Jackson's victory, which made Old Hickory a national hero, reached Washington, where citizens set lighted candles in their windows as a sign of celebration, and Baltimore, where the guns of Fort McHenry boomed a salute.

On the evening of February 11, just as Fort Bowyer had been peacefully surrendered, the British sloop *Favourite,* flying a flag of truce, entered New York harbor. Anthony St. John Baker, secretary to the British peace commission, and Henry Carroll, Clay's secretary in Ghent, were on board with copies of the Treaty of Ghent. By half past eight the news was out, lamps and candles sparkled in the streets, and cheering groups were hailing the end of the war. By nine the *Commercial Advertiser* had run off a special handbill. Bells rang, cannon were shot off. In the morning, Carroll left in a postchaise for Washington. Baker was held up by landing formalities in New York. At four in the afternoon of February 14, Carroll's carriage stopped outside the house of James Monroe at I Street; Carroll sprang out, swiftly went inside, and soon emerged again with Monroe. The two men hastened to the Octagon House, where the Madisons were living for the time being, and the rest of the cabinet was quickly sent for.

The news spread, as all news does spread rapidly in the District of Columbia to this day, and congressmen and others crowded to the Octagon House. One guest realized what had happened as soon as she caught sight of Mrs. Madison's face: "No one could doubt, who beheld the radiance of joy that lighted up her countenance and diffused its beams all around, that all uncertainty was at an end."

Soon after eight o'clock Madison appeared and announced that the terms were satisfactory, whereupon Mrs. Madison's cousin Sally Coles went to the top of the servants' stairs and shouted down: "Peace! peace!"

The treaty was ratified on February 17, and again the bells rang and the cannon banged and the rockets' red glare, this time for fun, lit up the sky. The principal cities of the United States arranged lavish displays. In New York there was, among other splendors on show, "an elegant transparency" depicting a Tennessee rifleman shooting two redcoats. The smaller towns were not to be left behind in the celebrations, though from time to time unfortunate accidents occurred: for example, in Schenectady one citizen carelessly stood in front of one of the salute cannons, and was of course killed by the cannonball. Everywhere the newspapers sounded their deepest notes of patriotic rejoicing at the war's successes. *Niles' Register* was typical: "Who would not be an American? Long live the Republic! All hail! Last asylum of oppressed humanity!"

More sober observers thought that the war had increased the solidarity and reputation of the United States. James Bayard wrote: "The war has raised our reputation in Europe, and it excites astonishment that we should have been able for one campaign to have fought Great Britain single handed." He added, in a mood of confidence: "I think it will be a long time before we are disturbed again by any of the Powers of Europe." Louis Sérurier wrote to Talleyrand: "The war has given the Americans what they so essentially lacked, a national character founded on a glory common to all." A year after the war ended, Henry Clay compared the scorn and contempt that America had suffered before it started with the increased regard she was now receiving on all sides. Augustus John Foster thought that "something has been gained by it," while Albert Gallatin said that:

> The War has renewed and reinstated the national feelings which the Revolution had given and which were daily lessened. The people are more American; they feel and act more like a nation; and I hope that the permanency of the Union is thereby better secured.

The bombastic word, without which no sense of victory can completely be expressed in any country at any time, was spoken now by a Republican from Pennsylvania who declared that "victory perches on our banner and the talisman of invincibility no longer pertains to the tyrants of the Ocean—But the triumph over the Aristocrats and Monarchists is equally glorious with that over the enemy—It is the triumph of virtue over vice of republican men and republican principles over the advocates and doctrines of Tyranny." Almost he might have been writing a generation earlier, when Washington's men had wrested independence from (it was always personal) George III.

In England, several isolated voices joined the American chorus of congratulation. One was that of William Cobbett, who listed an impressive total of American achievements ("Is it nothing to have been able, with her infant navy, to have resisted with success the maritime power of England single-handed?") in fighting and in international prestige:

Is it nothing to have proved, that her Government, though free as air, is perfectly adequate to the most perilous of wars? Is it nothing to have thus entitled herself to the confidence of other nations, and made her friendship an object to be sedulously sought after by every Power of Europe?

And he paid a handsome tribute to James Madison:

Is it nothing for her Chief Magistrate; for that very Mr Madison, whom our malignant and insolent writers and others marked out to be DEPOSED; is it nothing for Americans to have seen this their plain fellow citizen, with a salary of less than six thousand pounds a year, with no heralds, guards, or gilded coaches, conducting her affairs, through this trying season, with so much ability, so much firmness, and, at the same time, with such tenderness for liberty, as to refrain from a resort even to the mild law of his country against those who have made use of that liberty for purpose of the blackest and basest treason?

Cobbett, like the Pennsylvanian, saw America's part in the war as "a dagger to the heart of tyranny" and, casting a century ahead to the era of Woodrow Wilson, prophesied the United States as a great world power, because she had "now become so conspicuous a nation":

Away now, with all their trumpery about Poland, and Saxony, and Belgium, and the Congress of Vienna! Let them do what they like with the Germans and the Cossacks, and the Dutch; let them divide them and subdivide them in a manner that they please; let them whisker them or knight them according to their fancy. We can now look to growing millions of free and enlightened citizens, descended from the same ancestors, and speaking the same language, with ourselves, inhabiting an extensive and fertile country, tendering food and freedom to the miserable and oppressed of every other clime. . .

–in which fine polemical flourish he sounds the same note, in a very similar key, to that of Emma Lazarus's verse inscribed on the base of the Statue of Liberty in the harbor of New York.

But few Englishmen felt like Cobbett in 1815. Far more would have shaken somber heads with Samuel Taylor Coleridge, who wrote in October:

The malignant witchcraft of evil passions reads good men's prayers backward . . . the hot heads in both countries made folly beget folly, both the more wrong in proportion as each is right.

The cool tone of clarity was left to the Duke, as so often happened. He had lost his brother-in-law at New Orleans and, when writing of this later, he remarked:

We have one consolation, that he fell as he lived, in the honourable discharge of his duty; and distinguished as a soldier and as a man.

I cannot but regret however that he was ever employed on such a service or with such a colleague.

The expedition to New Orleans originated with that colleague, and plunder was its object. I knew and stated in July that the transports could not approach within leagues of the landing-place, and enquired what means were provided to enable a sufficient body of troops with their artillery provisions and stores to land, and afterwards to communicate with them. Then as plunder was the object, the Admiral took care to be attended by a sufficient number of *sharks,* to carry the plunder off from a place at which he knew well that he could not remain. The secret of the expedition was thus communicated and in this manner this evil design defeated its own end. The Americans were prepared with an army in a fortified position which still would have been carried, if the duties of others, that is of the Admiral, had been as well performed as that of him whom we lament.

But Providence performed it otherwise . . .

Admiral Cochrane, having seized Fort Bowyer, was preparing for a fresh foray up the Chesapeake when the news of the Treaty of Ghent reached him, whereupon, noted Codrington, he was "most amazingly cast down." His son, Sir Thomas Cochrane, reacted quite differently: "I confess this intelligence gives me the most immense joy," he wrote in his journal, "both on my own, and my Country's account, and I devoutly hope the President will not hesitate as to whether he will approve the treaty." He went on to comment on the long period of war between Britain and "some Power or other," with its bereavements and its appallingly high cost: "the dreadful annual expense necessary to maintain the war scarcely leaves wherewithal to support life to the middling class of society." It was a voice completely different from that of his father: the nineteenth century speaking, instead of the eighteenth.

Cochrane sailed for Havana to take on supplies, leaving Malcolm in the Gulf with orders to make sure that the Indians accepted the fact of peace, in which they would "grow rich, and being free from war, will be prosperous so as to be able to defend themselves from all future encroachments of the United States." As for the Negro slaves, he said: "You will endeavour to persuade them to go back to their former masters." Cochrane then began a three-year correspondence on the vexed question of prize money, or how much was to be paid, if anything, to the crews of British ships who had succeeded in capturing or disabling enemy vessels. The irritable wrangle was not finally settled until the spring of 1818, and then, of course, to the full satisfaction of no one.

Before leaving for Havana, Cochrane had to wait for news that the Americans had ratified the peace terms. He waited at Isle Dauphine, at the entrance to Mobile Bay, where one of the biggest problems had been that of obtaining fresh food. Harry Smith and Admiral Malcolm, anxious that food should not run short, supervised the building of ovens in which the men baked bread. They hit upon the bright idea of burning oyster shells to make mortar for the brickwork. Large and small creatures had worried them: the island was alive with alligators (Harry's batman called them "navigators") and with sandflies. These were so annoying that Harry, who disliked tobacco, gave his orderly a large supply of it and told him to sit and puff away in his tent while he wrote his reports. A drink of grog at intervals completed the orderly's happiness, which he expressed by telling Harry: "Now, your honour, if you can write as long as I can smoke, you'll write the history of the world, and I'll kill all the midges."

The ratification was duly announced, and Harry sailed with Lambert in the *Brazen* to Havana. Lambert had mentioned Harry in his dispatches:

> Major Smith of the 95th Regiment, now acting as Military Secretary, is so well known for his zeal and talents, that I can with great truth say that I think he possesses every qualification to render him hereafter one of the brightest ornaments of his profession.

This comment was published in the London *Gazette* in February. News of the American acceptance of the treaty reached Prevost in Quebec on March 1, and on the next day Lieutenant General Sir George Murray arrived overland from New Brunswick with a letter from Lord Bathurst saying, disagreeably, that Prevost was to give up his post as governor in chief and come to London in order to explain his actions at Plattsburg. On March 3 Prevost wrote a letter to Bathurst expressing his embittered feelings:

> This is the first and only notice I have received from your Lordship respecting my conduct at Platsburg, and I cannot but express the surprise excited by the nature, as well as the mode of this communication. Conscious of no fault I dread not the strictest investigation, but it appears adding unnecessary poignancy to the unexpected blow, that the mortification you have judged proper to inflict should be conveyed through a third person & this an other so much my junior in the Service.

Not only was this virtual dismissal "acutely painful" to Prevost, but, he said, the world would think he had failed, and it might be years before he could serve again, "seeing myself deprived of every authority and every emolument after four years of the most arduous duties I have performed in the course of the five and thirty I have devoted to His Majesty's Service, unless," he went on mournfully, "to avoid such an interval I should prefer passing through the United States like a fugitive."

Nevertheless, he went through the correct motions, issuing orders to discharge the militia, and leaving Quebec on April 3 on foot to take the winter route to St. John. He arrived in London on May 12, and his statements were accepted by the British government. His place in Canada was taken by Lieutenant General Gordon Drummond.

On May 17 Sir James Yeo reached London and in August appeared in the Lake Champlain court-martial, which honorably acquitted the accused, saying that the defeat had been

> principally caused by the British Squadron having been urged into Battle previous to it being in a proper state to meet its Enemy by a promised Co-operation of the Land Forces, which was not carried into Effect.

This put Prevost in the scapegoat's position again, so he asked for a fresh court-martial, which was arranged for January 1816 in order to give witnesses time to travel from Canada, but Prevost, whose health had been failing for some time, died a week before it was due to take place. Spiteful letters published in the Canadian press, and a good deal of ill-informed gossip, together with the sour taste of defeat, clouded his reputation on both sides of the Atlantic for years, and indeed it is not easy even now to sort out his effect upon the war, nor to speculate what might have happened if a less cautious, prudent governor in chief had been appointed instead of him.

Meetings held in 1817 and 1818 clarified certain issues of actual or possible dispute between the two nations. They laid down, among other points, that no major warships were to be permitted on the Great Lakes; that American fishermen could come into Canadian harbors for repairs and supplies, but would not receive the same privileges as inshore fishermen; that free Canadian entry to the southern part of the western fur trading area—across today's border—was forbidden, which eventually caused the collapse of the North-West Company; and they marked out the border, drawing it straight along the forty-ninth parallel from the Lake of the Woods to the Rockies. It was left indefinite at the Oregon country, which was hopefully placed under joint British-American control.

From that time, the interests of Canada and the United States developed on separate lines for the most part. Canada clung to the British connection: the United States, concentrating on development within her own borders, pushed ever westward, finding, as the long trails wound illimitable distances toward the unattainable sunset, ever more astonishing visions of her incredible potential. The Canadian West, on the other hand, spent the next forty years under control of agents from London until again claimed for Canada in the 1860s, by which time the United States was literally fighting to see whether it would stay united.

Although when secession came it was the South that seceded, New England was the area expected to do so during the Anglo-American War of 1812, as we have seen. This was especially curious as the war increased New England's prosperity, for the British blockade did not reach up to the region until the late spring of 1814, and only intermittently then, while trade with the Maritimes, and overland from Vermont to Quebec, went on through the very smoke of battle. All permitted trade went through the New England ports, except for that which passed direct to New Orleans and, in addition, the war enlarged the manufacturing capacity of the northeastern states. Twenty thousand merino sheep from Spain were imported after 1811 to expand the woolen industry; in 1814 Francis Lowell returned to America from England and developed his new power loom at Waltham in Massachusetts, where his factory was able to put cotton through every stage of manufacturing process under one roof. His brother, John Lowell, was a prominent Federalist spokesman who advocated the New England Confederation which alarmed observers so much and affected many speeches and actions in Washington.

When the British occupied part of Maine and the Royal Navy began to make raids on the coasts, the State of Massachusetts in alarm summoned at Hartford "a New England Convention" * to discuss "public grievances and concerns," including, of course, defense, and "also to take measures, if they shall think proper, for producing a convention of delegates from all the United States, in order to revise the Constitution thereof." The rival leaders were John Lowell and Timothy Pickering for the extremists, and Harrison Gray Otis for the moderates. Otis hoped that the Convention would allow people to relieve their feelings by venting them in public; but Lowell and Pickering wished to use secession as a pistol to the head of the original thirteen states to win extra privileges for New England. Their comments were reported across the Atlantic, where the London *Times* stated simply that "New England allied with Old England would form a dignified and manly union well deserving the name of Peace."

This was going too far for the moderates, who realized that the Federalists were weak at that time in the country as a whole, and that the extreme course might lead to civil war, which they naturally wished to avoid. "To attempt upon every abuse of power to change the Constitution," they said, "would be to perpetuate the evils of revolution." For this reason, the Convention came down against secession, and the issue dropped dead. The news of New Orleans, and of the Treaty of Ghent, gave a boost to Madison's Administration, and enabled the rest of the country to accuse New England of unpatriotic conduct. At the same time, no one criticized the basic idea of States' Rights, thus leaving a loophole through which South Carolina would lead others forty-five years later.

Two points about the war afford surprise to the present-day reader: the way in which the war made so little interruption to the ordinary life of the nation; and the fact that negotiations for peace began almost as soon as the war itself. Yet the treaty itself said little except that the war was over, and that various commissions would meet to settle boundary questions. All the old thorny issues–impressment, neutral

* See Appendix X

rights, the Indians, the Newfoundland fisheries, the navigation of the Mississippi–remained unmentioned, except for the United States' agreement to restore Tecumseh's Indians to the lands they had possessed by 1811, and this was no concession at all, for most of those Indians were dead or long dispersed, and the bulk of their lands had been lost to them before that year.

Several historians have been at pains to point out that the continuing imperial dominion all over the world by nineteenth-century Britain, with its essential supremacy of the Royal Navy, helped to provide the long years of virtual world peace during which the United States could grow strong, rich, and powerful. Naturally, neither Britain nor America mentioned such a thing, even if either country thought of it. The mildly squabbling cousins remained, as it suited them, making appropriate noises of isolationism or criticism, or of critical contempt, as they saw fit. James Monroe, who created the Monroe Doctrine, said that the United States should never "come in as a cockboat in the wake of the British man-of-war"; a New York minister, Alexander McLeod, published in 1815 *A Scriptural View of the Character, Causes and Ends of the Present War,* in which he said that God had brought on the conflict in order that the young republic should chastise the British government, "a despotic usurpation–a superstitious combination of civil and ecclesiastic power–A branch of the grand antichristian apostacy–Erastian in its constitution and administration–*and* Cruel in its policy."

When English gentlemen bothered to refer to the United States they did so as they might have referred to newly discovered tropical islanders. Yet trade steadily developed between the two; from growing industry on both sides came growing interchange of goods and money and knowledge; and, as the century moved on, and the great Irish exodus took place, British men in their turn willingly became Americans.

In 1817 John Calhoun emphasized the importance of the Union's endurance, when he said:

> We are great, and rapidly–I was about to say fearfully–growing. This is our pride and our danger; our weakness and our strength. Little does he deserve to be intrusted with the liberties of this people, who does not raise his mind to these truths. We are under the most imperious obligation to counteract every tendency to disunion.

Certainly the war left the United States more united as a nation than before. Canada, too, felt an increased sense of nationhood. As long as sixty years after the war ended, a public speaker on a Memorial Day referred to it with all the old animosity, as though it were only yesterday:

> When the war was declared, our fathers knew their duty, and knew the worthlessness of the pompous proclamations and promises of President Madison's generals and agents. The blood of our United Empire Loyalist forefathers warmed again in their own bosoms, and pulsated in the hearts of their sons and grandsons, and in the hearts of hundreds of others who had adopted Canada, under the flag of British law and liberty, as their home.

This has the authentic Loyalist tone, the voice of those who had been proud of the derisive label "blue-noses," and who had taken as their slogan the words: "We bloom amid the snow."

The war left America with some unexpected and exciting victories to look back on and to commemorate for years on Memorial Days (until a deeper conflict overshadowed them in 1861), some new heroes, a national anthem (one of the bridges over the Potomac today is the Francis Scott Key Bridge), and room to expand. It left Britain with one surprising change in her outlook, not clearly recognized for a long time, but nevertheless present, the need to treat the United States as a power in her own right, not as a rather unsatisfactory client nor as an ex-rebel colony. The Treaty of Ghent left both nations free to take up again their exploration of the assets of the great North American land mass; and it marked the last time that the two nations have taken up arms against each other. Despite all the differences that persist to this day, the two are justified in calling themselves cousins, though not, to use a helpful Americanism, kissing cousins.

Three representative comments may serve to indicate the basic change of mind. In 1820, Richard Rush, then American minister to the Court of St. James's, said at the time of George III's death:

> Britain and the United States are destined to become the predominating nations of Christendom. Each an incumbrance to the other when together, their severance seems to have been the signal for unequalled progress, and boundless prospects to each; not more in material dominion than in the solid and durable glory of widening the empire of rational thought throughout the world.

Augustus Foster wrote, long after it was over:

This war was certainly productive of much ill-blood between England and America, but in the opinion of the Speaker, Mr. Clay, and his friends it was as necessary to America as a duel is to a young naval officer to prevent his being bullied and elbowed in society. Baleful as the war has been, I must confess that I think in this respect something has been gained by it.

And that redoubtable old protagonist, Henry Clay himself, said a year after the war ended:

We had become the scorn of foreign Powers, and the contempt of our own citizens. Let any man look at the degraded condition of this country before the war; the scorn of the universe, the contempt of ourselves . . . What is our present situation? Respectability and character abroad–security and confidence at home–our character and Constitutions are placed on a solid basis, never to be shaken.

For the British, the war had begun, and had continued, deep in the shadow of events in Europe. That pattern held true to the last: for on February 26, 1815, while HMS *Brazen* was still homing over the long Atlantic rollers, the brig *Inconstant* stood out of Elba on a moonlit night, and Napoleon with a party of his Old Guard went on board. They sailed shortly after midnight, and next day they passed a cruiser which hailed them in a casual, friendly fashion. The Guard, lying close behind the bulwarks without their tall bearskins, were not observed; the brig seemed innocent; and they sailed on. That night they rowed ashore near Cannes. Ten days later, Prince Metternich had gone to bed at three after a conference, saying he was not to be disturbed. But at six in the morning a servant brought in a letter; the Prince sleepily observed that it was merely from the Austrian Consul at Genoa, and did not open it for another hour and a half. When he read that Napoleon was missing from Elba, he abruptly woke up. The Duke, who was also in Vienna for the peace talks, heard at ten that morning. The Congress hurriedly reassembled, eighteen varied dignitaries declared in the name of eight governments that Napoleon had forfeited human rights; and the Anglo-American war dropped out of sight, as the gigantic shadow of Waterloo fell across the European stage.

Harry Smith, and the others sailing with him on the *Brazen,* knew nothing until they passed a merchantman in misty weather at the approaches to the Bristol Channel. The two ships passed close enough for someone on the merchantman to shout: "Ho! Bonaparte's back again!" Harry's reaction was to think with delight that he would be a lieutenant colonel yet before the year was out. Lambert refused to believe the news, and was not convinced until he reached Spithead, where the sight of the bustling activity of ships and arms and men made them all thrill at the thought of serving "under Old Hookey again."

Madison retired in 1816, and spent the remaining twenty years of his life at Montpelier, except for a short period of service in the State Constitutional Convention of 1829. His wife outlived him by thirteen years. Madison's successor at the White House was, of course, James Monroe, who died in New York in 1831. Albert Gallatin stayed in Europe as a diplomat for some time before returning to become president of the National Bank of New York. John Armstrong never came out of retirement for the remaining twenty-eight years of his life. General Dearborn seemed likely to do the same, but in 1822 he was appointed as American minister to Portugal. One of the longest active careers was that of Lewis Cass, who became a senator, and was Jackson's Secretary of War and Buchanan's Secretary of State, dying in Detroit in 1866. He was nominated as Democratic candidate for the presidency, but defeated by Zachary Taylor. William Henry Harrison became the ninth President in 1840, overwhelmingly beating his opponent and predecessor, Martin Van Buren, who was sped from office by the melancholy strains of "Farewell, dear Van–you're not our man," or, worse, "Van is a used-up man." Andrew Jackson, of course, entered the White House in 1828, and, unusual among national leaders, left it more popular than ever. Stephen Decatur gained fresh laurels later in 1815 with his expedition against the Dey of Algiers; and, as for Winfield Scott, he lived to lose a presidential nomination and to become the leading general of the United States Army, holding that office in spite of old age and ill health to the autumn of 1861, after which "Old Fuss and Feathers" survived long enough to inscribe a gift to Ulysses S. Grant in 1865 "from the oldest to the greatest general."

Perhaps, of the British protagonists, two are worth a mention for their subsequent careers. Cockburn was given the command of HMS *Northumberland,* in which he transported Napoleon to St. Helena. But

Harry Smith, who fought at Waterloo (still without a scratch), ended up as governor of Natal in South Africa, where he had a few "smart little actions" with all his old fire and dash. His Juana went everywhere with him. A little town in Natal was named after her. Harry had got his knighthood, so they called it Ladysmith.

Appendix I

The Knife-Grinder by George Canning

Friend of humanity:

Needy Knife-grinder! whither are you going?
Rough is the road—your wheel is out of order—
Bleak blows the blast; your hat has got a hole in 't,
So have your breeches!

Weary Knife-grinder! little think the proud ones,
Who in their coaches roll along the turnpike-
Road, what hard work 'tis crying all day "Knives and
Scissors to grind O!"

Tell me, Knife-grinder, how you came to grind knives?
Did some rich man tyrannically use you?
Was it the squire? or parson of the parish?
Or the attorney?

Was it the squire, for killing of his game? or
Covetous parson, for his tithes distraining?
Or roguish lawyer, made you lose your little
All in a law-suit?

(Have you not read the Rights of Man, by Tom Paine?)
Drops of compassion tremble on my eyelids,
Ready to fall, as soon as you have told your
Pitiful story.

Knife-grinder:

Story! God bless you! I have none to tell, sir,
Only last night, a-drinking at the Chequers,
This poor old hat and breeches, as you see, were
Torn in a scuffle.

Constables came up for to take me into
Custody; they took me before the justice,
Justice Oldmixon put me in the parish-
Stocks for a vagrant.

I should be glad to drink your Honour's health in
A pot of beer, if you will give me sixpence;
But for my part, I never love to meddle
With politics, sir.

Friend of humanity:

I give thee sixpence! I will see thee damn'd first–
Wretch! whom no sense of wrongs can rouse to
vengeance–
Sordid, unfeeling, reprobate, degraded,
Spiritless outcast!

(Kicks the Knife-grinder, overturns his wheel, and exits in a transport of Republican enthusiasm and universal philanthropy.)

Appendix II

THE BERLIN DECREE: NOVEMBER 21, 1806

Art. 1. The British islands are declared in a state of blockade.

Art. 2. All commerce and correspondence with the British islands are prohibited. In consequence, letters or packets, addressed either to England, to an Englishman, or in the English language, shall not pass through the postoffice and shall be seized.

Art. 3. Every subject of England, of whatever rank and condition soever, who shall be found in the countries occupied by our troops, or by those of our allies, shall be made a prisoner of war.

Art. 4. All magazines, merchandise, or property whatsoever, belonging to a subject of England, shall be declared lawful prize.

Art. 5. The trade in English merchandise is forbidden; all merchandise belonging to England, or coming from its manufactories and colonies, is declared lawful prize.

Art. 6. One half of the proceeds of the confiscation of the merchandise and property, declared good prize by the preceding articles, shall be applied to indemnify the merchants for the losses which they have suffered by the capture of merchant vessels by English cruisers.

Art. 7. No vessel coming directly from England, or from the English colonies, or having been there since the publication of the present decree, shall be received into any port.

Art. 8. Every vessel contravening the above clause, by means of a false declaration, shall be seized, and the vessel and cargo confiscated, as if they were English property.

Art. 9. Our tribunal of prizes at Paris is charged with the definitive adjudication of all the controversies, which by the French army, relative to the execution of the present decree. Our tribunal of prizes at Milan shall be charged with the definitive adjudication of the said controversies, which may arise within the extent of our kingdom of Italy.

Art. 10. The present decree shall be communicated by our minister of exterior relations, to the kings of Spain, of Naples, of Holland, and of Etruria, and to our allies, whose subjects, like ours, are the victims of the injustice and the barbarism of the English maritime laws. Our finances, our police, and our post masters general, are charged each, in what concerns him, with the execution of the present decree.

Appendix III

British Order in Council: November 11, 1807

. . . His majesty is therefore pleased, by and with the advice of his privy council, to order, and it is hereby ordered, that all the ports and places of France and her allies, or of any country at war with his majesty, and all other ports or places in Europe, from which, although not at war with his majesty, the British flag is excluded, and all ports or places in the colonies belonging to his majesty's enemies, shall, from henceforth, be subject to the same restrictions in point of trade and navigation, with the exceptions hereinafter mentioned, as if the same were actually blockaded by his majesty's naval forces, in the most strict and rigorous manner: And it is hereby further ordered and declared, that all trade in articles which are of the produce or manufacture of the said countries or colonies, shall be deemed and considered to be unlawful; and that every vessel trading from or to the said countries or colonies, together with all goods and merchandise on board, and all articles of the produce or manufacture of the said countries or colonies, shall be captured and condemned as prize to the captors. . . .

And the commanders of his majesty's ships of war and privateers, and other vessels acting under his majesty's commission, shall be, and are hereby, instructed to warn every vessel which shall have commenced her voyage prior to any notice of this order, and shall be destined to any port of France, or of her allies, or of any other country at war with his majesty, or to any port or place from which the British flag, as aforesaid, is excluded, or to any colony belonging to his majesty's enemies, and which shall not have cleared out as is hereinbefore allowed, to discontinue her voyage, and to proceed to some port or place in this kingdom, or to Gibraltar or Malta; and any vessel which, after having been so warned, or after a reasonable time shall have been afforded for the arrival of information of this his majesty's order at any port or place from which she sailed, or which, after having notice of this order, shall be found in the prosecution of any voyage contrary to the restrictions contained in this order, shall be captured, and, together with her cargo, condemned as lawful prize to the captors.

And whereas countries not engaged in the war have acquiesced in these orders of France, prohibiting all trade in any articles the produce or manufacture of his majesty's dominions; and the merchants of those countries have given countenance and effect to those prohibitions by accepting from persons, styling themselves commercial agents of the enemy, resident at neutral ports, certain documents, termed "certificates of origin," being certificates obtained at the ports of shipment, declaring that the articles of the cargo are not of the produce or manufacture of his majesty's dominions, or to that effect:

And whereas this expedient has been directed by France, and submitted to by such merchants, as part of the new system of warfare directed against the trade of this kingdom, and as the most effectual instrument of accomplishing the same, and it is therefore essentially necessary to resist it:

His majesty is therefore pleased, by and with the advice of his privy council, to order, and it is hereby ordered, that if any vessel, after reasonable time shall have been afforded for receiving notice of this his majesty's order, at the port or place from which such vessel shall have cleared out, shall be found carrying any such certificate or document as aforesaid, or any document referring to or authenticating the same, such vessel shall be adjudged lawful prize to the captor, together with the goods laden therein, belonging to the person or persons by whom, or on whose behalf, any such document was put on board.

And the right honorable the lords commissioners of his majesty's treasury, his majesty's principal secretaries of state, the lords commissioners of the admiralty, and the judges of the high court of admiralty and courts of vice admiralty, are to take the necessary measures herein as to them shall respectively appertain.

Appendix IV

The Embargo Act of December 22, 1807

Be it enacted, That an embargo be, and hereby is laid on all ships and vessels in the ports and places within the limits or jurisdiction of the United States, cleared or not cleared, bound to any foreign port or place; and that no clearance be furnished to any ship or vessel bound to such foreign port or place, except vessels under the immediate direction of the President of the United States: and that the President be authorized to give such instructions to the officers of the revenue, and of the navy and revenue cutters of the United States, as shall appear best adapted for carrying the same into full effect: *Provided,* that nothing herein contained shall be construed to prevent the departure of any foreign ship or vessel, either in ballast, or with the goods, wares and merchandise on board of such foreign ship or vessel, when notified of this act.

Sec. 2. That it shall not be lawful for any citizen or citizens of the letter vessel, having on board goods, wares and merchandise, shall be allowed to depart from one port of the United States to any other within the same, unless the master, owner, consignee or factor of such vessel shall first give bond, with one or more sureties to the collector of the district from which she is bound to depart, in a sum of double the value of the vessel and cargo, that the said goods, wares, or merchandise shall be relanded in some port of the United States, dangers of the seas excepted, which bond, and also a certificate from the collector where the same may be relanded, shall by the collector respectively be transmitted to the Secretary of the Treasury. All armed vessels possessing public commissions from any foreign power, are not to be considered as liable to the embargo laid by this act.

Appendix V

The Non-Intercourse Act of March 1, 1809

Be it enacted, That from and after the passing of this act, the entrance of the harbors and waters of the United States and of the territories thereof, be, and the same is hereby interdicted to all public ships and vessels belonging to Great Britain or France. . . .

Sec. 2. That it shall not be lawful for any citizen or citizens of the United States or the territories thereof, nor for any person or persons residing or being in the same, to have any intercourse with, or to afford any aid or supplies to any public ship or vessel as aforesaid, which shall, contrary to the provisions of this act, have entered any harbor or waters within the jurisdiction of the United States or the territories thereof; and if any person shall, contrary to the provisions of this act, have any intercourse with such ship or vessel, or shall afford any aid to such ship or vessel, either in repairing the said vessel or in furnishing her, her officers and crew with supplies of any kind or in any manner whatever, . . . every person so offending, shall forfeit and pay a sum not less than one hundred dollars, nor exceeding ten thousand dollars; and shall also be imprisoned for a term not less than one month, nor more than one year.

Sec. 3. That from and after the twentieth day of May next, the entrance of the harbors and waters of the United States and the territories thereof be, and the same is hereby interdicted to all ships or vessels sailing under the flag of Great Britain or France, or owned in whole or in part by any citizen or subject of either. . . .

Sec. 4. That from and after the twentieth day of May next, it shall not be lawful to import into the United States or the territories thereof, any goods, wares or merchandise whatever, from any port or place situated in Great Britain or Ireland, or in any of the colonies or dependencies of Great Britain, nor from any port or place situated in France, or in any of her colonies or dependencies, nor from any port or place in the actual possession of either Great Britain or France. Nor shall it be lawful to import into the United States, or the territories thereof, from any foreign port or place whatever, any goods, wares or merchandise whatever, being of the growth, produce or manufacture of France, or of any of her colonies or dependencies, or being of the growth, produce or manufacture of Great Britain or Ireland, or of any of the colonies or dependencies of Great Britain, or being of the growth, produce or manufacture of any place or country in the actual possession of either France or Great Britain. . . .

Sec. 11. That the President of the United States be, and he hereby is authorized, in case either France or Great Britain shall so revoke or modify her edicts, as that they shall cease to violate the neutral commerce of the United States, to declare the same by proclamation; after which the trade of the United States, suspended by this act, and by the [Embargo Act] and the several acts supplementary thereto, may be renewed with the nation so doing. . . .

Sec. 12. That so much of the . . . [Embargo Act] and of the several acts supplementary thereto, as forbids the departure of vessels owned by citizens of the United States, and the exportation of domestic and foreign merchandise to any foreign port or place, be and the same is hereby repealed, after the March 15, 1809, except so far as they relate to Great Britain or France, or their colonies or dependencies, or places in the actual possession of either. . . .

Sec. 19. That this act shall continue and be in force until the end of the next session of Congress, and no longer; and that the act laying an embargo on all ships and vessels in the ports and harbors of the United States, and the several acts supplementary thereto, shall be, and the same are hereby repealed from and after the end of the next session of Congress.

Appendix VI

MACON'S BILL NO. 2 OF MAY 1, 1810

Be it enacted. That from and after the passage of this act, no British or French armed vessel shall be permitted to enter the harbor or waters under the jurisdiction of the United States; . . . except when they shall be forced in by distress . . . or when charged with despatches or business from their government, or coming as a public packet for the conveyance of letters; . . .

Sec. 4. That in case either Great Britain or France shall, before the third day of March next, so revoke or modify her edicts as that they shall cease to violate the neutral commerce of the United States, which fact the President of the United States shall declare by proclamation, and if the other nation shall not within three months thereafter so revoke or modify her edicts in like manner, then the third, fourth, fifth, sixth, seventh, eighth, ninth, tenth, and eighteenth sections of the act, entitled "An act to interdict the commercial intercourse between the United States and Great Britain and France . . ." shall, from and after the expiration of three months from the date of the proclamation aforesaid, be revived and have full force and effect, so far as relates to the dominions, colonies, and dependencies, and to the articles the growth, produce or manufacture of the dominions, colonies and dependencies of the nation thus refusing or neglecting to revoke or modify her edicts in the manner aforesaid. And the restrictions imposed by this act shall, from the date of such proclamation, cease and be discontinued in relation to the nation revoking or modifying her decrees in the manner aforesaid.

Appendix VII

Prevost's Defense Statement of May 18, 1812,

Quebec, 18th May 1812

My Lord,

In obedience to the Commands signified to me in your Lordship's dispatch No. 7 of the 13th February, I now have the honor to report upon the Military position of His Majesty's North American Provinces, and the means of defending them.

Upper Canada

Commencing with Upper Canada, as the most contiguous to the Territory of the United States and frontier to it along its whole extent, which renders it, in the event of War, more liable to immediate attack.

Fort St. Joseph. Fort St. Joseph, distant about 1,500 miles from Quebec, consists of Lines of Strong Pickets enclosing a Block House.– It stands on the Island St. Joseph within the detour communicating the head of Lake Huron with Lake Superior:–It can only be considered as a Post of Assemblage for friendly Indians, and in some degree a protection for the North West Fur Trade:–The Garrison at St. Joseph's consists of a small Detachment from the Royal Artillery, and one Company of Veterans.

Fort Amherstburg. Fort Amherstburg, situated on the River Detroit at the head of Lake Erie, is of importance from its being the Dock Yard and Marine Arsenal for the Upper Lakes:–It is also a place of reunion for the Indians inhabiting that part of the Country, who assemble there in considerable numbers to receive Presents:–The Fort has been represented to me as a temporary Field Work in a ruinous State; it is now undergoing a repair to render it tenable:–The Garrison at Amherstburg consists of Subaltern's Detachment of Artillery, and about 120 men of the 41st Regiment–the whole Commanded by Lieutenant Colonel St George an Inspecting Field Officer:–The Militia in its Vicinity amounts to about 500 men.

Fort George. Fort George is a temporary Work at the head of Lake Ontario, now repairing to render it tenable, but in its most improved State, it cannot make much resistance against an Enemy in considerable force:–The Garrison at Fort George consists of a Captain's Command of Artillery, and about 400 men of the 41st Regiment, the whole Commanded by Colonel Procter:–The Militia Force in the Neighborhood of Fort George, does not exceed 2,000 Nominal men.

Fort Erie, Chippawa and Fort George form the chain of Communication between Lake Erie and Lake Ontario.

Fort Erie. At Fort Erie, there is a Captain's Command from the 41st Regiment, and at Chippawa a Subaltern's.–The American Posts directly opposed to this Line are Fort Niagara, Fort Schlosser, Black Rock, and Buffalo Creek:–In the event of Hostilities, it would be highly advantageous to gain possession of Fort Niagara to secure the Navigation of the River Niagara.

York. York is situated on the North Shore of Lake Ontario, has a good Harbour, and is the position in Upper Canada best adapted for a deposit of Military Stores, whenever it is converted into a Post of defence, and also for a Dock Yard and Marine Arsenal for this Lake. Its retired situation from the American frontier, makes it a position particularly desirable for those purposes:–The project of fortifying and strengthening this Post has been submitted for consideration:–York is the Head Quarters of Upper Canada,–its Garrison consists of three Companies of the 41st Regiment:–The Militia in its vicinity is computed at 1,500 men.

Kingston. Kingston is situated at the head of the Boat Navigation of the St. Lawrence, contiguous to a very flourishing Settlement on the American frontier, and is exposed to sudden attack, which, if successful, would cut off the communication between the Upper and Lower Province, and deprive us of our Naval resources:–The Garrison of Kingston consists of Four Companies of the 10th Royal Veteran Battalion, under the Command of Major Macpherson:–The Militia in the Neighborhood about 1,500 men.

The Americans have Posts in the vicinity of Kingston, not only opposite, but both above and below with good Harbours, which are open to the resources of a very populous Country:–In the event of

Hostilities it will be indispensably necessary for the preservation of a Communication between the Lower and the Upper Province, to establish some strong Post for the Regulars and Militia, to secure the Navigation of the St. Lawrence above the Rapids to Lake Ontario:– The total number of Militia in Upper Canada is calculated at 11,000 men, of which it might not be prudent to Arm more than 4,000.

Lower Canada

Montreal. Montreal is the principal commercial city in the Canadas, and in the event of War, would become the first object of Attack:–It is situated on an extension Island, and does not possess any means of defence:–Its security depends upon our being able to maintain an impenetrable line on the South Shore, extending from La Prairie to Chambly, with a sufficient Flotilla to command the Rivers St. Lawrence and the Richelieu.

The Garrison of Montreal at present, consists of a Brigade of Light Artillery, and the 49th Regiment:–The Militia in its neighborhood, and easily collected, would exceed 12,000 men, ill armed and without discipline, and 600 embodied, now assembled for training at La Prairie.

St. John's. St. John's is considered a frontier Post:–there ends the Navigation from Lake Champlain:–It is occupied by a Company of Royal Veterans and one of the 49th Regiment:–The Field Works formerly erected for the defence of this Post, are now in ruins, and could not be resumed to much advantage, as they are commanded by ground contiguous, and the Post can be turned by following the New Roads leading from the United States to Montreal.

Chambly. Chambly is unimportant, but as a Post of Support to St. John's, and a place of assemblage for the Militia and a Depot for their Arms and Ammunition:–It is occupied by about 300 Voltigeurs, and a Detachment of Artillery having two Field Guns.

William Henry. William Henry is 13 leagues from Chambly, and is situated at the junction of the Richelieu & St. Lawrence:–It is the most important position on the South Shore for Depots, and for a rendezvous for the Armed Vessels and Boats required for the defence of the St. Lawrence:–It is unquestionably a position which deserves being made tenable against a sudden or irregular attack:–From thence down the St. Lawrence are many excellent positions for arresting the progress of an Enemy marching on either Shore upon Quebec, particularly if he is not in possession of the Navigation of the River:–The Garrison at

William Henry consists of one Field Officer and four Companies of the 100th Regiment.

Quebec. Quebec is the only permanent Fortress in the Canadas:–It is the Key to the whole and must be maintained:–To the final defence of this position, every other Military operation ought to become subservient, and the retreat of the Troops upon Quebec must be the primary consideration:–The means of resistance afforded by the Fortifications in their present imperfect State, are not such as could justify a hope of its being able to withstand a vigorous and well conducted siege.–It requires Bomb proof Casmates for the Troops, as the Town is completely commanded from the South Shore at Point Levi, a position which it has frequently been recommended to occupy in force:–The Casmates ought to be erected on Cape Diamond, a position that points itself out for a Citadel:–It is advisable that the whole circumference of the summit of this Hill should be occupied, being the only elevation within the Walls not commanded by the height of Land on the plains of Abraham:–Such a Work would essentially defend the extension Line of Fortification, sloping from Cape Diamond to the Artillery Barrack which is old and imperfect, is commanded from the high land opposite, and is besides seen in reverse and open to an enfilade fire from positions on the bank of the St. Charles River.

The Garrison of Quebec at present consists of about 2,500 Rank and File:–The Militia of Lower Canada amounts to 60,000 men, a mere posse, ill arm'd, and without discipline, where of 2,000 are embodied for training.

In framing a general out line of Cooperation for defence with the Forces in Upper Canada, commensurate with our deficiency in strength, I have considered the preservation of Quebec as the first object, and to which all others must be subordinate:–Defective as Quebec is, it is the only Post that can be considered as tenable for a moment, the preservation of it being of the utmost consequence to the Canadas, as the door of entry for that Force The King's Government might find it expedient to send for the recovery of both, or either of these Provinces, altho' the pressure of the moment in the present extended range of Warfare, might not allow the sending of that force which would defend both, therefore considering Quebec in this view, its importance can at once be appreciated.

If the Americans are determined to attack Canada, it would be in vain the General should flatter himself with the hopes of making an effectual defence of the open Country, unless powerfully assisted from Home:–All predatory or ill concerted attacks undertaken presumptuously and without sufficient means, can be resisted and repulsed:–Still this must be done with caution, that the resources, for a future exertion, the defence of Quebec, may be unexhausted.

New Brunswick & Nova Scotia

The Province of New Brunswick and the peninsula of Nova Scotia present so many vulnerable points to an invading Army, that it is difficult to establish any precise Plan for the defence of either, and consequently much must depend upon Contingencies in the event of Invasion:–Their security very materially depends upon the Navy, and the vigilance of our Cruizers in the Bay of Fundy.

In the event of Hostilities with America, it would be an advisable measure to take possession of Moose Island, in the Bay of Passamaquoddy, improperly occupied by a small American Garrison, where we should derive great advantage from the cooperation of our Navy, and should remove the scene of Warfare to the American frontier.

Fredericton. The defence of Fredericton is out of the question, and the course of the River St. John must be defended at the discretion of the Officer Commanding that Garrison, according to the description and number of the assailing Army:–The Garrison at Fredericton at present consists of a small Detachment of Artillery, and Six Companies of the 104th Regiment.

St. John. The Town of St. John is totally indefensible on the land side, it would therefore be requisite to make provision for the removal of the Ordnance and Stores from thence:–Two or three small Vessels of War stationed in the River St. John (part of whose Crews might Man Gun Boats) would very much conduce to its security, and in case of a hasty retreat might bring away the Ordnance and Stores:–

St. John is at present Garrisoned by two Companies of the 104th Regiment, and a proportion of the Artillery:–The Militia of New Brunswick amount to about 4,000 men, much scattered, and but few of them have been trained to the use of Arms.

Halifax. In the event of an Enemy approaching Halifax by Land, Nature has done much for its protection:–At the Isthmus near Cumberland, the Militia supported by a proportion of regular Troops, may make a very protracted defence, were its Flanks secured by the

Navy:–entrance of that Bay is too wide to admit of being fortified:–If the Enemy escapes the squadron stationed in the Bay of Fundy, he may have his choice of Ground for debarkation, but must look to the destruction of his Flotilla, and no further support by water. Margaret's Bay on the Eastern Coast of Nova Scotia, offers a spacious and safe Harbour, and should any Enemy meditate the capture of Halifax, that point would probably attract his attention:–The attempt however would be very hazardous, and he must not calculate either on a Retreat, or Succour, which it is presumed would be prevented by the Squadron from Halifax:–The approach from this Bay is through a Country easily defended, and unfavorable for the Transport of Ordnance or Stores of any Kind:–The Sea defences of the Harbour of Halifax offer much to rely on, but the Land defences are so imperfect as to be undeserving of notice:–The Garrison of Halifax at present consists of about 1,500 men, including three Companies of Artillery:–The Militia of Nova Scotia amounts to upwards of 11,000 men; about 6,000 of whom have been furnished with Arms and accoutrements, and from the assistance and instruction afforded them by the Inspecting Field Officers in that District, they have made as much progress in training and discipline, as could be expected from a Class of People, who are so much scattered.

Cape Breton and Prince Edward Island

The Islands of Cape Breton & Prince Edward Island, dependencies of the British North American Provinces, are garrisoned by small Detachments of Troops stationed at the principal Town in each, but their Works of defence are so insignificant, as to be unworthy of Observation;–Nor does their Militia amount to any considerable number deserving to be noticed:

Newfoundland

The Island of Newfoundland, also a dependency of this Command, is principally defended by the Navy upon that Station during the Summer:–The Chief Town and Military depot, St. Johns, is Garrisoned by the Nova Scotia Fencible Regiment, and a Company of Artillery.

Bermudas

Of the Bermudas, their strength and resources against an attack, I cannot as yet presume to report upon, to your Lordship, as they have but recently been made a part of this Command.

I have the honour to be
My Lord,
Your Lordship's
Most Obedient and
most humble Servant
George Prevost
Quebec 1st June 1812

P.S. The following alterations have taken place since the foregoing Report was prepared–Five Companies of the Royal Newfoundland Fencibles have proceeded from Quebec, and are now on their Route to York in Upper Canada, for the Marine Service.

Four hundred Recruits belonging to the Glengary Levy are assembled at Three Rivers in Lower Canada, to be formed into a Regiment, trained and disciplined.

The Detachment of the Royal Newfoundland Fencibles from Quebec, has been replaced by an equal number of the 100th Regiment from Three Rivers.

Sgd: G.P.

Appendix VIII

Madison's War Message, June 1, 1812,

Washington, June 1, 1812

To the Senate and House of Representatives of the United States:

I communicate to Congress certain documents, being a continuation of those heretofore laid before them on the subject of our affairs with Great Britain.

Without going back beyond the renewal in 1803 of the war in which Great Britain is engaged, and omitting unrepaired wrongs of inferior magnitude, the conduct of her Government presents a series of acts hostile to the United States as an independent and neutral nation.

British cruisers have been in the continued practice of violating the American flag on the great highway of nations, and of seizing and carrying off persons sailing under it, not in the exercise of a belligerent right founded on the law of nations against an enemy, but of a municipal prerogative over British subjects. British jurisdiction is thus extended to neutral vessels in a situation where no laws can operate but the law of nations and the laws of the country to which the vessels belong, and a self-redress is assumed which, if British subjects were wrongfully detained and alone concerned, is that substitution of force for a resort to the responsible sovereign which falls within the definition of war. . . .

The practice, hence, is so far from affecting British subjects alone that, under the pretext of searching for these, thousands of American citizens, under the safeguard of public law and of their national flag, have been torn from their country and from everything dear to them; have been dragged on board ships of war of a foreign nation and exposed, under the severities of their discipline, to be exiled to the most distant and deadly climes, to risk their lives in the battles of their oppressors, and to be the melancholy instruments of taking away those of their own brethren.

Against this crying enormity, which Great Britain would be so prompt to avenge if committed against herself, the United States have in vain exhausted remonstrances and expostulations, and that no proof might be wanting of their conciliatory dispositions, and no pretext left for a continuance of the practice, the British Government was formally assured of the readiness of the United States to enter into arrangements such as could not be rejected if the recovery of British subjects were the real and the sole object. The communication passed without effect.

British cruisers have been in the practice also of violating the rights and the peace of our coasts. They hover over and harass our entering and departing commerce. To the most insulting pretensions they have added the most lawless proceedings in our very harbors, and have wantonly spilt American blood within the sanctuary of our territorial jurisdiction. . . .

Under pretended blockades, without the presence of an adequate force and sometimes without the practicability of applying one, our commerce has been plundered in every sea, the great staples of our country have been cut off from their legitimate markets, and a destructive blow aimed at our agricultural and maritime interests. In aggravation of these predatory measures they have been considered as in force from the dates of their notification, a retrospective effect being thus added, as has been done in other important cases, to the unlawfulness of the course pursued. And to render the outrage the more signal these mock blockades have been reiterated and enforced in the face of official communications from the British Government declaring as the true definition of a legal blockade "that particular ports must be actually invested and previous warning given to vessels bound to them not to enter."

Not content with these occasional expedients for laying waste our neutral trade, the cabinet of Britain resorted at length to the sweeping system of blockades, under the name of orders in council, which has been molded and managed as might best suit its political views, its commercial jealousies, or the avidity of British cruisers. . . .

Abandoning still more all respect for the neutral rights of the United States and for its own consistency, the British Government now demands as prerequisites to a repeal of its orders as they relate to the United States that a formality should be observed in the repeal of the French decrees nowise necessary to their termination nor exemplified by British usage, and that the French repeal, besides including that portion of the decrees which operates within a territorial jurisdiction, as well as that which operates on the high seas, against the commerce of the United States should not be a single and special repeal in relation to the United States, but should be extended to whatever other neutral nations unconnected with them may be affected by those decrees. . . .

It has become, indeed, sufficiently certain that the commerce of the United States is to be sacrificed, not as interfering with the belligerent rights of Great Britain; not as supplying the wants of her enemies, which she herself supplies; but as interfering with the monopoly which she covets for her own commerce and navigation. She carries on a war against the lawful commerce of a friend that she may the better carry on a commerce with an enemy—a commerce polluted by the forgeries and perjuries which are for the most part the only passports by which it can succeed. . . .

In reviewing the conduct of Great Britain toward the United States our attention is necessarily drawn to the warfare just renewed by the savages on one of our extensive frontiers—a warfare which is known to spare neither age nor sex and to be distinguished by features peculiarly shocking to humanity. It is difficult to account for the activity and combinations which have for some time been developing themselves among tribes in constant intercourse with British traders and garrisons without connecting their hostility with that influence and without recollecting the authenticated examples of such interpositions heretofore furnished by the officers and agents of that Government.

Such is the spectacle of injuries and indignities which have been heaped on our country, and such the crisis which its unexampled forbearance and conciliatory efforts have not been able to avert. . . .

Our moderation and conciliation have had no other effort than to encourage perseverance and to enlarge pretensions. We behold our seafaring citizens still the daily victims of lawless violence, committed on the great common and highway of nations, even within sight of the country which owes them protection. We behold our vessels, freighted with the products of our soil and industry, or returning with the honest proceeds of them, wrested from their lawful destinations, confiscated by prize courts no longer the organs of public law but the instruments of arbitrary edicts, and their unfortunate crews dispersed and lost, or forced or inveigled in British ports into British fleets, whilst arguments are employed in support of these aggressions which have no foundation but in a principle equally supporting a claim to regulate our external commerce in all cases whatsoever.

We behold, in fine, on the side of Great Britain a state of war against the United States, and on the side of the United States a state of peace toward Great Britain.

Whether the United States shall continue passive under these progressive usurpations and these accumulating wrongs, or, opposing force to force in defense of their national rights, shall commit a just cause into the hands of the Almighty Disposer of Events, avoiding all connections which might entangle it in the contest or views of other powers, and preserving a constant readiness to concur in an honorable reestablishment of peace and friendship, is a solemn question which the Constitution wisely confides to the legislative department of the Government. In recommending it to their early deliberations I am happy in the assurance that the decision will be worthy the enlightened and patriotic councils of a virtuous, a free, and a powerful nation. . . .

Appendix IX

The Treaty of Ghent

His Britannic Majesty and the United States of America desirous of terminating the war which has unhappily subsisted between the two Countries, and of restoring upon principles of perfect reciprocity, Peace, Friendship, and good Understanding between them, have for that purpose appointed their respective Plenipotentiaries, that is to say, His Britannic Majesty on His part has appointed the Right Honourable James Lord Gambier, late Admiral of the White now Admiral of the Red Squadron of His Majesty's Fleet; Henry Goulburn Esquire, a Member of the Imperial Parliament and Under Secretary of State; and William Adams Esquire, Doctor of Civil Laws: And the President of the United States, by and with the advice and consent of the Senate thereof, has appointed John Quincy Adams, James A. Bayard, Henry Clay, Jonathan Russell, and Albert Gallatin, Citizens of the United States; who, after a reciprocal communication of their respective Full Powers, have agreed upon the following Articles.

Article the First.

There shall be a firm and universal Peace between His Britannic Majesty and the United States, and between their respective Countries, Territories, Cities, Towns, and People of every degree without exception of places or persons. All hostilities both by sea and land shall cease as soon as this Treaty shall have been ratified by both parties as hereinafter mentioned. All territory, places, and possessions whatsoever taken by either party from the other during the war, or which may be taken after the signing of this Treaty, excepting only the Islands hereinafter mentioned, shall be restored without delay and without causing any destruction or carrying away any of the Artillery or other public property originally captured in the said forts or places, and which shall remain therein upon the Exchange of the Ratifications of this Treaty, or any Slaves or other private property; And all Archives, Records, Deeds, and Papers, either of a public nature or belonging to private persons, which in the course of the war may have fallen into the hands of the Officers of either party, shall be, as far as may be practicable, forthwith restored and delivered to the proper authorities and persons to whom they respectively belong. Such of the Islands in the Bay of Passamaquoddy as are claimed by both parties shall remain in the possession of the party in whose occupation they may be at the time of the Exchange of the Ratifications of this Treaty until the decision respecting the title to the said Islands shall have been made in conformity with the fourth Article of this Treaty. No disposition made by this Treaty as to such possession of the Islands and territories claimed by both parties shall in any manner whatever be construed to affect the right of either.

Article the Second.

Immediately after the ratifications of this Treaty by both parties as hereinafter mentioned, orders shall be sent to the Armies, Squadrons, Officers, Subjects, and Citizens of the two Powers to cease from all hostilities: and to prevent all causes of complaint which might arise on account of the prizes which may be taken at sea after the said Ratifications of this Treaty, it is reciprocally agreed that all vessels and effects which may be taken after the space of twelve days from the said Ratifications upon all parts of the Coast of North America from the Latitude of twenty three degrees North to the Latitude of fifty degrees North, and as far Eastward in the Atlantic Ocean as the thirty sixth degree of West Longitude from the Meridian of Greenwich, shall be restored on each side:–that the time shall be thirty days in all other parts of the Atlantic Ocean North of the Equinoctial Line or Equator:–and the same time for the British and Irish Channels, for the Gulf of Mexico, and all parts of the West Indies:–forty days for the North Seas for the Baltic, and for all parts of the Mediterranean:–sixty days for the Atlantic Ocean South of the Equator as far as the Latitude of the Cape of Good Hope:–ninety days for every other part of the world South of the Equator, and one hundred and twenty days for all other parts of the world without exception.

Article the Third.

All Prisoners of war taken on either side as well by land as by sea shall be restored as soon as practicable after the Ratifications of this Treaty as hereinafter mentioned on their paying the debts which they may have contracted during their captivity. The two Contracting Parties respectively engage to discharge in specie the advances which may have been made by the other for the sustenance and maintenance of such prisoners.

Article the Fourth.

Whereas it was stipulated by the second Article in the Treaty of Peace of one thousand seven hundred and eighty three between His Britannic Majesty and the United States of America that the boundary of the United States should comprehend "all Islands within twenty leagues of any part of the shores of the United States and lying between lines to be drawn due East from the points where the aforesaid boundaries between Nova Scotia on the one part and East Florida on the other shall respectively touch the Bay of Fundy and the Atlantic Ocean, excepting such Islands as now are or heretofore have been within the limits of Nova Scotia," and whereas the several Islands in the Bay of Passamaquoddy, which is part of the Bay of Fundy, and the Island of Grand Menan in the said Bay of Fundy, are claimed by the United States as being comprehended within their aforesaid boundaries, which said Islands are claimed as belonging to His Britannic Majesty as having been at the time of and previous to the aforesaid Treaty of one thousand seven hundred and eighty three within the limits of the Province of Nova Scotia: In order therefore finally to decide upon these claims it is agreed that they shall be referred to two Commissioners to be appointed in the following manner: viz: One Commissioner shall be appointed by His Britannic Majesty and one by the President of the United States, by and with the advice and consent of the Senate thereof, and the said two Commissioners so appointed shall be sworn impartially to examine and decide upon the said claims according to such evidence as shall be laid before them on the part of His Britannic Majesty and of the United States respectively. The said Commissioners shall meet at St. Andrews in the Province of New Brunswick, and shall have power to adjourn to such other place or places as they shall think fit. The said Commissioners shall by a declaration or report under their hands and seals decide to which of the two Contracting parties the several Islands aforesaid do respectively belong in conformity with the true intent of the said Treaty of Peace of one thousand seven hundred and eighty three. And if the said Commissioners shall agree in their decision both parties shall consider such decision as final and conclusive. It is further agreed that in the event of the two Commissioners differing upon all or any of the matters so referred to them, or in the event of both or either of the said Commissioners refusing or declining or wilfully omitting to act as such, they shall make jointly or separately a report or reports as well to the Government of His Britannic Majesty as to that of the United States, stating in detail the points on which they differ, and the ground upon which their respective opinions have been formed, or the grounds upon which they or either of them have so refused declined or omitted to act. And His Britannic Majesty and the Government of the United States hereby agree to refer the report or reports of the said Commissioners to some friendly Sovereign or State to be then named for that purpose, and who shall be requested to decide on the differences which may be stated in the said report or reports, or upon the report of one Commissioner together with the grounds upon which the other Commissioner shall have refused, declined or omitted to act as the case may be. And if the Commissioner so refusing, declining, or omitting to act, shall also wilfully omit to state the grounds upon which he has so done in such manner that the said statement may be referred to such friendly Sovereign or State together with the report of such other Commissioner, then such Sovereign or State shall decide ex parte upon the said report alone. And His Britannic Majesty and the Government of the United States engage to consider the decision of such friendly Sovereign or State to be final and conclusive on all the matters so referred.

ARTICLE THE FIFTH.

Whereas neither that point of the Highlands lying due North from the source of the River St. Croix, and designated in the former Treaty of Peace between the two Powers as the North West Angle of Nova Scotia, nor the North Westernmost head of Connecticut River has yet been ascertained; and whereas that part of the boundary line between the Dominions of the two Powers which extends from the source of the River St. Croix directly North to the abovementioned North West Angle of Nova Scotia, thence along the said Highlands which divide those Rivers that empty themselves into the River St. Lawrence from those which fall into the Atlantic Ocean to the North Westernmost head of Connecticut River, thence down along the middle of that River to the forty fifth degree of North Latitude, thence by a line due West on said latitude until it strikes the River Iroquois or Cataraquy, has not yet been surveyed: it is agreed that for these several purposes two Commissioners shall be appointed, sworn, and authorized to act exactly in the manner directed with respect to those mentioned in the next preceding Article unless otherwise specified in the present Article. The said Commissioners shall meet at St. Andrews in the Province of New Brunswick, and shall have power to adjourn to such other place or places as they shall think fit. The said Commissioners shall have power to ascertain and determine the points above mentioned in conformity with the provisions of the said Treaty of Peace of one thousand seven hundred and eighty three, and shall cause the boundary aforesaid from the source of the River St. Croix to the River Iroquois or Cataraquy to be surveyed and marked according to the said provisions. The said Commissioners shall make a map of the said boundary, and annex to it a declaration under their hands and seals certifying it to be the true Map of the said boundary, and particularizing the latitude and longitude of the North West Angle of Nova Scotia, of the North Westernmost head of the Connecticut River, and of such other points of the said boundary as they may deem proper. And both parties agree to consider such map and declaration as finally and conclusively fixing the said boundary. And in the event of the said two Commissioners differing, or both, or either of them refusing, declining, or wilfully omitting to act, such reports, declarations, or statements shall be made by them or either of them, and such reference to a friendly Sovereign or State shall be made in all respects as in the latter part of the fourth Article is contained, and in as full a manner as if the same was herein repeated.

Article the Sixth.

Whereas by the former Treaty of Peace that portion of the boundary of the United States from the point where the forty fifth degree of North Latitude strikes the River Iroquois or Cataraquy to the Lake Superior was declared to be "along the middle of said River into Lake Ontario, through the middle of said Lake until it strikes the communication by water between that Lake and Lake Erie, thence along the middle of said communication into Lake Erie, through the middle of said Lake until it arrives at the water communication into the Lake Huron; thence through the middle of said Lake to the water communication between that Lake and Lake Superior:" and whereas doubts have arisen what was the middle of the said River, Lakes, and water communications, and whether certain Islands lying in the same were within the Dominions of His Britannic Majesty or of the United States: In order therefore finally to decide these doubts, they shall be referred to two Commissioners to be appointed, sworn, and authorized to act exactly in the manner directed with respect to those mentioned in the next preceding Article unless otherwise specified in this present Article. The said Commissioners shall meet in the first instance at Albany in the State of New York, and shall have power to adjourn to such other place or places as they shall think fit. The said Commissioners shall by a Report or Declaration under their hands and seals, designate the boundary through the said River, Lakes, and water communications, and decide to which of the two Contracting parties the several Islands lying within the said Rivers, Lakes, and water communications, do respectively belong in conformity with the true intent of the said Treaty of one thousand seven hundred and eighty three. And both parties agree to consider such designation and decision as final and conclusive. And in the event of the said two Commissioners differing or both or either of them refusing, declining, or wilfully omitting to act, such reports, declarations, or statements shall be made by them or either of them, and such reference to a friendly Sovereign or State shall be made in all respects as in the latter part of the fourth Article is contained, and in as full a manner as if the same was herein repeated.

Article the Seventh.

It is further agreed that the said two last mentioned Commissioners after they shall have executed the duties assigned to them in the preceding Article, shall be, and they are hereby, authorized upon their oaths impartially to fix and determine according to the true intent of the said Treaty of Peace of one thousand seven hundred and eighty three, that part of the boundary between the dominions of the two Powers, which extends from the water communication between Lake Huron and Lake Superior to the most North Western point of the Lake of the Woods;–to decide to which of the two Parties the several Islands lying in the Lakes, water communications, and Rivers forming the said boundary do respectively belong in conformity with the true intent of the said Treaty of Peace of one thousand seven hundred and eighty three, and to cause such parts of the said boundary as require it to be surveyed and marked. The said Commissioners shall by a Report or declaration under their hands and seals, designate the boundary aforesaid, state their decision on the points thus referred to them, and particularize the Latitude and Longitude of the most North Western point of the Lake of the Woods, and of such other parts of the said boundary as they may deem proper. And both parties agree to consider such designation and decision as final and conclusive. And in the event of the said two Commissioners differing, or both or either of them refusing, declining, or wilfully omitting to act, such reports, declarations or statements shall be made by them or either of them, and such reference to a friendly Sovereign or State shall be made in all respects as in the latter part of the fourth Article is contained, and in as full a manner as if the same was herein repeated.

Article the Eighth.

The several Boards of two Commissioners mentioned in the four preceding Articles shall respectively have power to appoint a Secretary, and to employ such Surveyors or other persons as they shall judge necessary. Duplicates of all their respective reports, declarations, statements, and decisions, and of their accounts, and of the Journal of their proceedings shall be delivered by them to the Agents of His Britannic Majesty and to the Agents of the United States, who may be respectively appointed and authorized to manage the business on behalf of their respective Governments. The said Commissioners shall be respectively paid in such manner as shall be agreed between the two contracting parties, such agreement being to be settled at the time of the Exchange of the Ratifications of this Treaty. And all other expenses attending the said Commissions shall be defrayed equally by the two parties. And in the case of death, sickness, resignation, or necessary absence, the place of every such Commissioner respectively shall be supplied in the same manner as such Commissioner was first appointed; and the new Commissioner shall take the same oath or affirmation and do the same duties. It is further agreed between the two contracting parties that in case any of the Islands mentioned in any of the preceding Articles, which were in the possession of one of the parties prior to the commencement of the present war between the two Countries, should by the decision of any of the Boards of Commissioners aforesaid, or of the Sovereign or State so referred to, as in the four next preceding Articles contained, fall within the dominions of the other party, all grants of land made previous to the commencement of the war by the party having had such possession, shall be as valid as if such Island or Islands had by such decision or decisions been adjudged to be within the dominions of the party having had such possession.

ARTICLE THE NINTH.

The United States of America engage to put an end immediately after the Ratification of the present Treaty to hostilities with all the Tribes or Nations of Indians with whom they may be at war at the time of such Ratification, and forthwith to restore to such Tribes or Nations respectively all the possessions, rights, and privileges which they may have enjoyed or been entitled to in one thousand eight hundred and eleven previous to such hostilities. Provided always that such Tribes or Nations shall agree to desist from all hostilities against the United States of America, their Citizens, and Subjects upon the Ratification of the present Treaty being notified to such Tribes or Nations, and shall so desist accordingly. And His Britannic Majesty engages on his part to put an end immediately after the Ratification of the present Treaty to hostilities with all the Tribes or Nations of Indians with whom He may be at war at the time of such Ratification, and forthwith to restore to such Tribes or Nations respectively all the possessions, rights, and privileges, which they may have enjoyed or been entitled to in one thousand eight hundred and eleven previous to such hostilities. Provided always that such Tribes or Nations shall agree to desist from all hostilities against His Britannic Majesty and His Subjects upon the Ratification of the present Treaty being notified to such Tribes or Nations, and shall so desist accordingly.

ARTICLE THE TENTH.

Whereas the Traffic in Slaves is irreconcilable with the principles of humanity and Justice, and whereas both His Majesty and the United States are desirous of continuing their efforts to promote its entire abolition, it is hereby agreed that both the contracting parties shall use their best endeavours to accomplish so desirable an object.

Article the Eleventh.

This Treaty when the same shall have been ratified on both sides without alteration by either of the contracting parties, and the Ratifications mutually exchanged, shall be binding on both parties, and the Ratifications shall be exchanged at Washington in the space of four months from this day or sooner if practicable.

In faith whereof, We the respective Plenipotentiaries have signed this Treaty, and have thereunto affixed our Seals.

Done in triplicate at Ghent the twenty fourth day of December one thousand eight hundred and fourteen.

Gambier	[Seal]
Henry Goulburn	[Seal]
William Adams	[Seal]
John Quincy Adams	[Seal]
J. A. Bayard	[Seal]
H. Clay	[Seal]
Jon[a] Russell	[Seal]
Albert Gallatin	[Seal]

Appendix X

The Resolutions of the Hartford Convention, December 15, 1814

. . . Nothing more can be attempted in this report than a general allusion to the principal outlines of the policy which has produced this vicissitude. Among these may be enumerated–

First.–A deliberate and extensive system for effecting a combination among certain states, by exciting local jealousies and ambition, so as to secure to popular leaders in one section of the Union, the control of public affairs in perpetual succession. To which primary object most other characteristics of the system may be reconciled.

Secondly.–The political intolerance displayed and avowed in excluding from office men of unexceptionable merit, for want of adherence to the executive creed.

Thirdly.–The infraction of the judiciary authority and rights, by depriving judges of their offices in violation of the constitution.

Fourthly.–The abolition of existing taxes, requisite to prepare the country for those changes to which nations are always exposed, with a view to the acquisition of popular favour.

Fifthly.–The influence of patronage in the distribution of offices, which in these states has been almost invariably made among men the least entitled to such distinction, and who have sold themselves as ready instruments for distracting public opinion, and encouraging administration to hold in contempt the wishes and remonstrances of a people thus apparently divided.

Sixthly.–The admission of new states into the Union formed at pleasure in the western region, has destroyed the balance of power which existed among the original states, and deeply affected their interest.

Seventhly.–The easy admission of naturalized foreigners, to places of trust, honour or profit, operating as an inducement to the malcontent subjects of the old world to come to these States, in quest of executive patronage, and to repay it by an abject devotion to executive measures.

Eighthly.–Hostility to Great Britain, and partiality to the late government of France, adopted as coincident with popular prejudice, and subservient to the main object, party power. Connected with these must be ranked erroneous and distorted estimates of the power and resources of those nations, of the probable results of their controversies, and of our political relations to them respectively.

Lastly and principally.–A visionary and superficial theory in regard to commerce, accompanied by a real hatred but a feigned regard to its interests, and a ruinous perseverance in efforts to render it an instrument of coercion and war.

But it is not conceivable that the obliquity of any administration could, in so short a period, have so nearly consummated the work of national ruin, unless favoured by defects in the constitution.

To enumerate all the improvements of which that instrument is susceptible, and to propose such amendments as might render it in all respects perfect, would be a task which this convention has not thought proper to assume. They have confined their attention to such as experience has demonstrated to be essential, and even among these, some are considered entitled to a more serious attention than others. They are suggested without any intentional disrespect to other states, and are meant to be such as all shall find an interest in promoting. Their object is to strengthen, and if possible to perpetuate, the union of the states, by removing the grounds of existing jealousies, and providing for a fair and equal representation, and a limitation of powers, which have been misused. . . .

Therefore resolved,

That it be and hereby is recommended to the legislatures of the several states represented in this Convention, to adopt all such measures as may be necessary effectually to protect the citizens of said states from the operation and effects of all acts which have been or may be passed by the Congress of the United States, which shall contain provisions, subjecting the militia or other citizens to forcible drafts, conscriptions, or impressments, not authorized by the constitution of the United States.

Resolved, That it be and hereby is recommended to the said

Legislatures, to authorize an immediate and earnest application to be made to the government of the United States, requesting their consent to some arrangement, whereby the said states may, separately or in concert, be empowered to assume upon themselves the defence of their territory against the enemy; and a reasonable portion of the taxes, collected within said States, may be paid into the respective treasuries thereof, and appropriated to the payment of the balance due said states, and to the future defence of the same. The amount so paid into the said treasuries to be credited, and the disbursements made as aforesaid to be charged to the United States.

Resolved, That it be, and hereby is, recommended to the legislatures of the aforesaid states, to pass laws (where it has not already been done) authorizing the governors or commanders-in-chief of their militia to make detachments from the same, or to form voluntary corps, as shall be most convenient and conformable to their constitutions, and to cause the same to be well armed, equipped, and disciplined, and held in readiness for service; and upon the request of the governor of either of the other states to employ the whole of such detachment or corps, as well as the regular forces of the state, or such part thereof as may be required and can be spared consistently with the safety of the state, in assisting the state, making such request to repel any invasion thereof which shall be made or attempted by the public enemy.

Resolved, That the following amendments of the Constitution of the United States be recommended to the states represented as aforesaid, to be proposed by them for adoption by the state legislatures, and in such cases as may be deemed expedient by a convention chosen by the people of each state.

And it is further recommended, that the said states shall persevere in their efforts to obtain such amendments, until the same shall be effected.

First. Representatives and direct taxes shall be apportioned among the several states which may be included within this Union, according to their respective numbers of free persons, including those bound to serve for a term of years, and excluding Indians not taxed, and all other persons.

Second. No new state shall be admitted into the Union by Congress, in virtue of the power granted by the constitution, without the concurrence of two thirds of both houses.

Third. Congress shall not have power to lay any embargo on the ships or vessels of the citizens of the United States, in the ports or harbours thereof, for more than sixty days.

Fourth. Congress shall not have power, without the concurrence of two thirds of both houses, to interdict the commercial intercourse between the United States and any foreign nation, or the dependencies thereof.

Fifth. Congress shall not make or declare war, or authorize acts of hostility against any foreign nation, without the concurrence of two thirds of both houses, except such acts of hostility be in defence of the territories of the United States when actually invaded.

Sixth. No person who shall hereafter be naturalized, shall be eligible as a member of the senate or house of representatives of the United States, nor capable of holding any civil office under the authority of the United States.

Seventh. The same person shall not be elected president of the United States a second time; nor shall the president be elected from the same state two terms in succession.

Resolved, That if the application of these states to the government of the United States, recommended in a foregoing resolution, should be unsuccessful and peace should not be concluded, and the defence of these states should be neglected, as it has since the commencement of the war, it will, in the opinion of this convention, be expedient for the legislatures of the several states to appoint delegates to another convention, to meet at Boston . . . with such powers and instructions as the exigency of a crisis so momentous may require.

§

Bibliography

Airlie, Mabell, Countess of. *In Whig Society 1775-1818.* London: Hodder & Stoughton, 1921.

———. *Lady Palmerston and Her Times.* London: Hodder & Stoughton, 1922.

Beirne, Francis F. *The War of 1812.* New York: E.P. Dutton, 1949.

Billington, Ray Allen, Loewenberg, Bert James, and Brockunier, Samuel Hugh. *The Making of American Democracy, Readings and Documents.* New York: Rinehart & Co. Inc., 1950.

Brock, W.R. *The Character of American History.* Santa Fe: William Gannon, 1960.

Bryant, Arthur. *The Age of Elegance, 1812-1822.* New York: Harper & Bros., 1951.

———. *Years of Victory 1802-1812.* New York: Harper & Bros., 1945.

Carrington, C.E. *Making of the Empire. (The British Overseas: Exploits of a Nation of Shopkeepers,* Vol. I.) New York: Cambridge University Press, 1968.

Cecil, Lord Edward Christian David. *The Young Melbourne.* New York: Bobbs-Merrill Co., 1939.

Cobbett, William. *Cobbett's Political Register 1815.* London: G. Houston, 1815.

Commager, Henry Steele. *Documents of American History,* Vol. I. New York: Meredith Press, 1963.

Cooke, Captain John Henry. *A Narrative of Events in the South of France and of the Attack on New Orleans.* London: T. & W. Boone, 1935.

Creevey, Thomas. *The Creevey Papers,* ed. Maxwell. 1903-1905 and 1912.

DuMaurier, Daphne. *MaryAnne.* New York: Doubleday & Co. Inc., 1954.

Fisher, H.A.L. *Bonapartism.* Six lectures. London, 1908.

Fisher, John. *1815: An End and a Beginning.* New York: Harper & Row Publishers, Inc., 1963.

Fortescue, J.W. *A History of the British Army.* New York: Macmillan, 1930.

Foster, Vere., ed. *The Two Duchesses.* London, 1898.

Funcken, Liliane, and Funcken, Fred. *Arms and Uniforms, The Napoleonic Wars,* Vol. I. London: Ward Lock, 1973.

Guedalla, Philip. *Wellington.* New York: Harper & Bros., 1931.

———. *Palmerston.* London: Hodder & Stoughton, 1937.

Hay, Robert. *Landsman Hay: The Memoirs of Robert Hay 1789-1847,* ed. M.D. Hay. Toronto: Clark, Irwin & Co., 1953.

Heyer, Georgette. *The Spanish Bride.* New York: Doubleday, 1940.

Hibbert, Christopher. *George Fourth: Regent and King.* New York: Harper & Row Publishers, Inc., 1975.

Hill, Charles Peter. *History of the United States.* London: Edward Arnold, 1966.

Hitsman, J. Mackay. *The Incredible War of 1812.* Toronto: University of Toronto Press, 1965.

Hutchinson, J.R. *The Press-Gang Afloat and Ashore.* London: Nash, 1913.

Laffin, John. *Jack Tar: The Story of the British Sailor.* London: Cassell, 1969.

Laughton, J.K., ed. *The Naval Miscellany,* Vols. II and III. London: Navy Records Society, 1910 and 1927.

Leslie, Shane. *George the Fourth.* London: Ernest Benn, 1926.

Lewis, Charles Lee. *The Romantic Decatur.* Philadelphia: University of Pennsylvania Press, 1937.

Lewis, Michael. *A Social History of the Navy 1793-1815.* London: Allen & Unwin, 1960.

Lloyd, Christopher. *St. Vincent and Camperdown.* New York: Macmillan, 1963.

Lord, Walter. *The Dawn's Early Light.* New York: W.W. Norton, 1972.

McNaught, Kenneth. *The History of Canada.* New York: Frederick A. Praeger, Inc., 1970.

Mahan, Alfred Thayer. *The Influence of Sea-Power upon the French Revolution and Empire.* Saint Clair Shores, Mich.: Scholarly Press, 1898.

———. *Sea Power in its Relation to the War of 1812.* Boston: Little, Brown & Co., 1905.

Naval Chronicle, The, 1803-1818.

Perkins, Bradford. *Prologue to War 1805-1812: England and the United States.* Berkeley and Los Angeles: University of California Press, 1968.

Pope, Dudley. *At Twelve Mr. Byng Was Shot.* Philadelphia: J.B. Lippincott Co., 1962.

Roosevelt, Theodore. *The Naval War of 1812.* New York: G.P. Putnam's Sons, 1901.

Smith, Arthur D. *Old Fuss and Feathers: The Life and Exploits of Lieutenant-General Winfield Scott.* New York: Books for Libraries Reprint, 1937.

Smith, Lieutenant-General Sir Harry. *Autobiography.* London: John Murray, 1902.

Thistlethwaite, Frank. *The Great Experiment.* New York: Cambridge University Press, 1955.

Trevelyan, G.M. *English Social History.* London: Longmans, Green & Co. Inc., 1945. New York: Barnes & Noble, Inc., 1961 (reprint).

§

Index

THE STAR SPANGLED BANNER.
Published by John Cole, Baltimore.
CON SPIRITO.
O say can you see by the dawns ear_ly light, What so
oudly we hail'd at the twilights last gleaming, Whose stripes and bright stars thro' the
pe_ri_lous fight, O'er the ram_parts we watch'd, were so gal_lant_ly streaming, And the